The Cult of St Thomas Becket
in the Plantagenet World,
c.1170–c.1220

The Cult of St Thomas Becket
in the Plantagenet World,
c.1170–c.1220

Edited by

Paul Webster and Marie-Pierre Gelin

THE BOYDELL PRESS

First published 2016
The Boydell Press, Woodbridge
Paperback edition 2021

ISBN 978 1 78327 161 0 hardback
ISBN 978 1 78327 639 4 paperback

The Boydell Press is an imprint of Boydell & Brewer Ltd
PO Box 9, Woodbridge, Suffolk IP12 3DF, UK
and of Boydell & Brewer Inc.
668 Mt Hope Avenue, Rochester, NY 14620–2731, USA
website: www.boydellandbrewer.com

A catalogue record for this book is available
from the British Library

The publisher has no responsibility for the continued existence or accuracy of URLs for
external or third-party internet websites referred to in this book, and does not guarantee that
any content on such websites is, or will remain, accurate or appropriate

This publication is printed on acid-free paper

Typeset by BBR, Sheffield

Contents

List of Illustrations   vii
List of Contributors   ix
Preface   x
Acknowledgements   xv
List of Abbreviations   xvi

1. Introduction. The Cult of St Thomas Becket:
    An Historiographical Pilgrimage   1
    Paul Webster

2. Becket is Dead! Long Live St Thomas   25
    Anne J. Duggan

3. The Cult of St Thomas in the Liturgy and Iconography of
    Christ Church, Canterbury   53
    Marie-Pierre Gelin

4. Thomas Becket and Leprosy in Normandy   81
    Elma Brenner

5. Thomas Becket in the Chronicles   95
    Michael Staunton

6. Matilda, Duchess of Saxony (1168–89) and the Cult of
    Thomas Becket: A Legacy of Appropriation   113
    Colette Bowie

7. Leonor Plantagenet and the Cult of Thomas Becket in Castile   133
    José Manuel Cerda

8. Crown Versus Church After Becket: King John, St Thomas
    and the Interdict   147
    Paul Webster

CONTENTS

9. The St Thomas Becket Windows at Angers and Coutances:
    Devotion, Subversion and the Scottish Connection   171
    Alyce A. Jordan

Bibliography   208
Index   238

Illustrations

3.1   Thomas Becket preaching a sermon. Sens, St Etienne
       Cathedral, c.1210, Bay 23, panel 5. Courtesy of the Musées de
       Sens – J. P. Elie   69

3.2   The Martyrdom of Thomas Becket. Chartres, Notre-Dame
       Cathedral, c.1210–20, Bay 18, panels 22–23. Courtesy of
       Dr Stuart Whatling   70

3.3   Alphege killed by the Danes. Canterbury, Christ Church
       Cathedral, c.1180, Window Nt. IX, 5. © Crown Copyright. HE   73

3.4   St Dunstan frees King Eadwig's soul from the devil. Canterbury,
       Christ Church Cathedral, c.1180, Window Nt. XI, 1.
       © Crown Copyright. HE   75

3.5   Apparition of St Thomas. Canterbury, Christ Church Cathedral,
       c.1213–20, Window n. IV, 4. © Crown Copyright. HE   76

9.1   Life of St Thomas Becket, Coutances, Notre-Dame
       Cathedral, c.1230–40, Bay 217, left lancet. (Photo courtesy of
       Denis Krieger)   176

9.2   Life of St Thomas Becket, Coutances, Notre-Dame Cathedral,
       c.1230–40: detail, Thomas converses with Henry II; Thomas
       leaves France for England. (Photo courtesy of Denis Krieger)   177

9.3   Life of St Thomas Becket, Angers, Cathedral of St-Maurice,
       c.1230–35, Bay 108a, left lancet. © Centre André Chastel
       (UMR 8150), Cl. C. Gumiel   180

9.4   Life of St Thomas Becket, Angers, Cathedral of St-Maurice,
       c.1230–35: detail, the murderers of St Thomas Becket on
       horseback; the murderers of St Thomas Becket sail across the
       Channel; heraldry of the Beaumont family, viscounts of Maine.
       © Centre André Chastel (UMR 8150), Cl. C. Gumiel   181

9.5   Life of St Thomas Becket, Angers, Cathedral of St-Maurice,
        c.1230–35: detail, the coronation of Henry the Young King
        or Young King Henry refuses to meet with Thomas?; Thomas
        converses with Henry II; entombment (or translation?) of
        Thomas Becket. © Centre André Chastel (UMR 8150),
        Cl. C. Gumiel   183

9.6   St Thomas Becket ship-shaped *ampulla*, c.1250, drawing of
        obverse, Museum of London. © Museum of London   190

9.7   St Thomas Becket *ampulla*, c.1200–50, obverse, St Thomas
        flanked by knights. British Museum, #1921,0216.62.
        © Trustees of the British Museum   197

9.8   Seal of Richard de Beaumont, viscount of Maine, c.1240.
        E. Hucher, 'Monuments funéraires et sigillographiques
        des Vicomtes de Beaumont au Maine', *Revue historique et
        archéologique du Maine*, 11 (1882), 319–408, at 358   198

The editors, contributors and publishers are grateful to all the institutions and persons listed for permission to reproduce the materials in which they hold copyright. Every effort has been made to trace the copyright holders; apologies are offered for any omission, and the publishers will be pleased to add any necessary acknowledgement in subsequent editions.

Contributors

Dr Colette Bowie received her doctorate from the University of Glasgow, UK, in 2011. She is a member of the Royal Studies Network and co-founder of the Leverhulme Trust funded Angevin World Project. Colette lives and works in Glasgow.

Dr Elma Brenner is Specialist in Medieval and Early Modern Medicine at the Wellcome Library, London, UK.

Dr José Manuel Cerda is Associate Professor of History and Director of the Centre for Medieval Studies at Universidad Gabriela Mistral, Chile.

Professor Anne J. Duggan is Emeritus Professor of Medieval History at King's College London, UK.

Dr Marie-Pierre Gelin is a Teaching Fellow in the Department of History at University College London, UK.

Dr Alyce A. Jordan is Professor of Art History, Department of Comparative Cultural Studies, Northern Arizona University, USA.

Professor Michael Staunton is Associate Professor in the School of History, University College Dublin, Ireland.

Dr Paul Webster is Lecturer in Medieval History and Project Manager for the Exploring the Past adult learners' progression pathway at Cardiff University, UK, in the Cardiff School of History, Archaeology and Religion.

Preface

Thomas Becket is undoubtedly one of the best known and most written-about figures in the Middle Ages. Yet many of the political, religious and cultural repercussions of his murder, and subsequent canonisation, on the world he left behind remain to be explored in detail. Following Paul Webster's introductory exploration of existing historiography of the cult of St Thomas Becket, the main focus of this volume lies in the study of the emergence and development of the Becket phenomenon within the world from which it had been created. Anne J. Duggan's chapter highlights the way in which the creation and expansion of the cult of St Thomas are often relegated to the relative obscurity of liturgical or cultural history. In redressing the balance, Duggan examines the transformation of the murdered archbishop's status from that of victim to that of the most widely-revered medieval saint. Her article investigates the cult in the Plantagenet world and goes on to set it within the wider medieval context, considering evidence ranging from the period that followed the martyrdom down to the Reformation and beyond. In providing such broad focus, this contribution examines trends to which the other papers return in their discussion of the cult and of perceptions of St Thomas in the century following his martyrdom. Notably, these include the liturgical Becket and the efforts by the Plantagenet dynasty to build links with the religious phenomenon which Henry II had inadvertently created.

The volume then turns to aspects of the development of the cult, the reaction of religious communities to the popularity of the martyr and the impact of the conflict preceding Thomas Becket's death on the posthumous absorption of his cult into the life of monastic and hospital foundations in the Plantagenet lands. Chapters by Marie-Pierre Gelin and Elma Brenner focus on ways in which this could take place, examining different categories of religious house and the place which St Thomas occupied within them. Gelin focuses on the early development of the cult at its 'host' community at Canterbury, in terms of the integration of St Thomas into the iconography of the cathedral. Here, the monks took advantage of the opportunities presented in the aftermath of the devastating fire that swept through the cathedral in 1174, rebuilding the entire eastern end to house and celebrate the martyr's relics. The new saint took his place at the heart of the liturgy at Christ Church, but there was also a sense in which the Becket cult was integrated with those of saints who had been the focus of devotional activity at Canterbury prior to 1170, in particular the Anglo-Saxon archbishop-saints Dunstan and Alphege. The campaign drew on the portrayal of Thomas Becket in the emerging accounts of his life, death and miracles, and asserted his place as part of the spiritual genealogy of the cathedral, whilst in turn revitalising the cults of those of his predecessors numbered amongst the saints. By emphasising, indeed sometimes creating, links between the recent martyr and his archiepiscopal antecedents, the Christ Church hagiographers and liturgists inserted St Thomas within the spiritual genealogy of Canterbury Cathedral and claimed him as an integral part of the prestigious history and identity of their church.

A further aspect of the growth of the cult amongst religious communities was the increasing number dedicated to St Thomas. Here, new perspectives can be offered through consideration of the association between Becket and leper hospitals. Elma Brenner takes those of the duchy of Normandy as her focus. She considers in particular Mont-aux-Malades, outside Rouen, re-dedicated to Becket by Henry II in c.1174, but already associated with Thomas through the archbishop's friendship with the community's first prior. Here, and elsewhere in Normandy, the image of St Thomas advanced in sources such as the miracle collections can be contrasted with the development of the cult on the ground. The sources depict Becket as a healer – indeed as a saint who boasted of his ability in this field. Yet leprosy was not seen as curable. However, lepers were seen as chosen by God to suffer on earth and be saved, linking them to Christ and to martyrs, amongst whom Becket was a recent and clearly popular example. In explaining how Norman leper hospitals harnessed the cult to attract support from the rich, this article continues the theme of the integration of *Saint* Thomas into medieval society. It explores the impact on Anglo-Norman royal, aristocratic and urban benefaction in territory which, prior to 1204, lay at the heart of the Plantagenet world. Furthermore, the contribution examines the opportunities for those who had supported Henry II to use benefaction to adapt and respond to the changed religious landscape generated by the martyrdom.

Focus on the early development of the cult amongst religious communities linked to the king and archbishop highlights a number of issues which can be explored through further examination of the rapidly evolving cult. Existing studies have focused on the wide range of works – lives, collections of miracles, liturgies – composed immediately after the archbishop's death and in the ensuing decades. New perspectives can be offered through consideration of the broader range of historical writing penned in the generation following the events of December 1170, a period often seen as a golden age in the work of English chroniclers. These form the focus of the study by Michael Staunton, who examines how the legacy of the dispute and the image of the saint were applied in work written in the late twelfth and early thirteenth centuries, primarily in England. An account of the murder was central for any English chronicler, with many writers relating the archbishop's fate and legacy to their own concerns. Thus, the Becket dispute might be considered in relation to the Great Rebellion (1173–74), in debate about what the Church had obtained in relation to the issues for which Thomas had died, or in describing the regular and ongoing disputes waged by the monks of Christ Church, Canterbury. Examples from the narrative sources are used to present an alternative view of the Becket dispute and the man himself from that found in the posthumous *Lives*. The name of St Thomas could be evoked both for and against kings and ecclesiastics, perhaps resulting in the blunting of his impact as an example.

In examining the early development of the cult of St Thomas amongst religious communities and in different types of source material, the first four chapters also highlight the question of how the Plantagenet ruling family reacted to the emergence and development of the cult. The potential danger posed by St Thomas Becket, as a political saint, was not lost on the Plantagenet kings. This was true almost from the moment that Henry II knew that Becket was dead; certainly from the point when he realised that a posthumous cult was fast developing around the murdered archbishop, both nationally and internationally. Having realised that he must make a public expiation for his perceived guilt, Henry sought an association with the cult which allowed him to claim that the martyr was in effect his spiritual friend. This extended to Plantagenet involvement beyond the frontiers of the Angevin 'empire', encouraged by the daughters of Henry II and Eleanor of Aquitaine through the marriage alliances of which they were part. These themes are developed further in the second half of this volume. Chapters by Colette Bowie and José Manuel Cerda shed new light, respectively, on the role of Henry's daughters, Matilda and Eleanor (known frequently by her Castilian appellation Leonor), in the transmission of the cult of St Thomas.

Bowie considers Matilda, whose marriage to Henry the Lion, duke of Saxony and Bavaria, in 1168, was followed after 1170 by the rapid development of the Becket cult in Saxony in particular. The article asks why Matilda was involved in devotion to a figure who had caused her father so many problems whilst alive and whose death had done so much harm to Henry II's international standing. Just as Henry II quickly realised the need to establish an Angevin royal associ-ation with St Thomas, so too Matilda could promote Becket to show filial devotion and as a dynastic statement of appropriation. The depiction of the saint amongst Matilda's protectors, in an illumination showing the coronation of the duke and his wife in the Gmunden Gospels, commissioned by Henry the Lion and Matilda, suggests the latter's influence. The attachment was perhaps strengthened during the couple's exile in England and Normandy between 1182 and 1185, but also reflects the strong sense of dynastic identity which Henry II's daughter brought with her to Saxony. This is also demonstrated by Matilda's devotion to her Anglo-Saxon royal ancestors, notably St Oswald (603/604–642, king of Northumbria). The usage to which Oswald's cult had been put, indeed, suggests a model for the appropriation of devotion in which

Henry II and his daughter Matilda engaged. Bowie goes on to explore the place of the cult of St Thomas at Brunswick, where Henry II's daughter and her husband established a permanent ducal residence. At the city's cathedral, wall-paintings of the life and death of Archbishop Becket took their place alongside the community's other patron saints (John the Baptist and Blaise). Although these do not date to the lifetimes of Henry the Lion and Matilda, they were probably commissioned by their son, Henry of Brunswick, who took responsibility for commemorating the parents whose preferences he had inherited in terms of patronage of the cult of the saints. As Bowie shows, this included a prominent role for St Thomas Becket, and from its beginnings in Saxony in the late twelfth and early thirteenth centuries, the cult had spread across Germany as a whole by the fifteenth.

José Manuel Cerda's focus is on Leonor, second daughter of Henry II and Eleanor of Aquitaine, and on her role in the transmission of the cult of St Thomas to the kingdom of Castile. Leonor's arrival in the Iberian kingdom in 1170 came only weeks before Becket's murder. Cerda examines the way in which altars and churches dedicated to the martyr appeared in Iberia in the decades that followed. These provide some of the earliest testimony to the cult of Thomas Becket outside England. The article highlights that, whilst evidence relating to Leonor's role is scanty and sometimes difficult, there are sufficient indications in the period from the 1170s to the early 1200s to suggest that she and her entourage fostered the emergence of devotion to Becket at a series of locations.

Yet whilst, in Bowie's words, 'Becket was in effect becoming a patron saint of the Angevin family', tensions between the crown and the Church could easily jeopardise Plantagenet efforts to neutralise their association with the martyrdom. Returning to the English context, Paul Webster highlights how, in the early 1200s, King John emulated Henry II and Richard I in sustaining a pattern of royal religious activity linked to St Thomas. However, John's reign is as memorable as that of his father for its period of sustained dispute between king and Church. As the first prolonged example of such controversy since the martyrdom, the conflict over the election of Stephen Langton as archbishop of Canterbury provides an opportunity to understand the knock-on effects of the emergence of the cult and the legacy of the dispute that preceded it. Comparison of the sources for the two crises – in particular royal, archiepiscopal and papal letters – reveals that, like Henry II, John was not prepared to let the Church stand in the way of perceived royal rights. Yet Thomas was something of a 'ghost of Christmas past', seen as a martyr for the freedom of the Church, whose fate had influenced the portrayal of kings. Both John and Pope Innocent III invoked Becket in their arguments, and the papacy adopted a similar approach to the early thirteenth-century king as Thomas Becket had taken towards Henry II.

Where Webster's paper considers the impact of St Thomas on upheaval within the kingdom of England, the final chapter explores the legacy of the cult in France, with particular focus on the lands assembled by Henry II but lost by John in 1204. Alyce Jordan focuses on the political and genealogical statements which could be made using Becket iconography in the period following the Capetian conquest of Plantagenet Anjou and Normandy, examining the evidence of stained-glass windows, which provide some of the earliest depictions of Thomas's life in public art outside Canterbury. At Angers, the St Thomas window commissioned by Bishop Guillaume de Beaumont can be seen as a statement, indeed celebration, of his family's connections to the English and Scottish thrones: 'a subtly transgressive response to the French conquest'. The unconventional imagery contained within the stained glass points not only to religious devotion to Becket, but also to the contested political loyalties and regional identities of the 'empire' forged by Henry II. Similar trends can be seen elsewhere. Bishop Hugh de Moreville's Thomas Becket window at Coutances contains numerous features linking it with England and the Anglo-Norman Tosny family. Overall, the chapter provides evidence for lingering loyalty to the Plantagenets and suggests that the legacy of St Thomas was intertwined with the reaction to the severing of cross-channel connections in the generation forced to adapt to King John's territorial losses of 1204.

Overall, this book examines aspects of the development of the cult and the impact of the legacy of *Saint* Thomas. Its principal focus lies within the Plantagenet world – the 'empire' assembled by King Henry II, defended by his son, King Richard the Lionheart, and lost by King John. In particular, the articles explore the religious and political ramifications of the emergence of the cult of St Thomas before, during and after the changes brought about by King Philip II's takeover of large parts of the Plantagenet inheritance in the early thirteenth century. The collection integrates the use of traditional textual and archival sources, such as miracle collections, charters and royal and papal letters, with studies of the material culture inspired by the cult. Adopting a broadly chronological plan, it emphasises the wide-ranging impact of the murder and of the emergence of the cult of St Thomas on the Plantagenet orbit in the century following the martyrdom.

Acknowledgements

Our first debt of gratitude is to the organisers of the International Medieval Congress, University of Leeds, UK, for accepting and hosting the sessions from which many of the articles presented here have evolved, and for providing the forum for our discussions. We would like to extend our thanks to all who participated in those sessions or who have been involved in the project at various stages of its development, not least those whose work has since been published or is forthcoming elsewhere: Haki Antonsson, Rachel Koopmans, Sara Lutan-Hassner, Fanny Madeline, Leidulf Melve, Gesine Oppitz-Trotman, Catherine Royer-Hemet, and Sheila Sweetinburgh.

Particular thanks are also due to Anne J. Duggan and Michael Staunton, who participated in and chaired the sessions, who first suggested to the editors that they should collaborate in developing the papers as a published volume on the Becket cult, and who have since contributed a wealth of useful advice. Meanwhile, in Cardiff, Helen Nicholson has patiently enquired after progress for longer than she perhaps expected, whilst offering her thoughts on the book proposal and about how to manage the editing process at moments when doubt set in. Also in Cardiff, Dave Wyatt's support enabled time to be found for work on the introduction without detriment to the 'day job'.

Finally, we would like to thank Caroline Palmer and the team at The Boydell Press for patiently waiting for the volume to be completed, and for skilfully seeing it through to its completion. In addition, we thank our contributors, without whom this collection would not, of course, have been possible. This book has been long in the making – long enough for at least one of the editors regularly to refer to its subject as Tom. It has witnessed several hold-ups, ranging from births to jury service to the vicissitudes of the early career world of twenty-first century academia. So, to our contributors: we thank you for your patience and your willingness to collaborate in developing a book on the cult of the Angevin nemesis, St Thomas Becket.

Cardiff and Toronto, in the octave of the feast of
St Thomas the Martyr of Canterbury, December 2015.

Abbreviations

AVIII	J. González, *El Reino de Castilla durante el reinado de Alfonso VIII*, 3 vols (Madrid, 1960)
Barlow	F. Barlow, *Thomas Becket* (London, 1986; repr. London, 2000)
Bartlett, *Saints*	R. Bartlett, *Why Can the Dead Do Such Great Things? Saints and Worshippers from the Martyrs to the Reformation* (Princeton, NJ, and Oxford, 2013)
BL	British Library
Borenius, *Becket in Art*	T. Borenius, *St Thomas Becket in Art* (London, 1932; repr. Port Washington, NY, 1970)
BP *Miracula*	*Miracula S. Thomae Cantuariensis, auctore Benedicto, abbate Petriburgensi*, MTB, ii, 21–281
Cavero, *Tomás Becket*	G. Cavero Domínguez (coord), *Tomás Becket y la Península Ibérica (1170–1230)* (León, 2013)
Caviness, *Windows of Christ Church*	M. H. Caviness, *The Windows of Christ Church Cathedral, Canterbury*, Corpus Vitrearum Medii Aevi: Great Britain, 2 (Oxford, 1981)
CCM	*Cahiers de Civilisation Médiévale*
Chronicles, ed. Howlett	*Chronicles of the Reigns of Stephen, Henry II, and Richard I*, ed. R. Howlett, RS 82, 4 vols (London, 1884–89)
CTB	*The Correspondence of Thomas Becket, Archbishop of Canterbury 1162–1170*, ed. and trans. A. J. Duggan, OMT, 2 vols (Oxford, 2000)
Diceto	*Radulfi de Diceto Decani Lundoniensis Opera Historica: The Historical Works of Master Ralph de Diceto, Dean of London*, ed. W. Stubbs, RS 68, 2 vols (London, 1876)
Duggan, 'Cult'	A. J. Duggan, 'The Cult of St Thomas Becket in the Thirteenth Century', in *St Thomas Cantilupe, Bishop of Hereford: Essays in his Honour*, ed. M. Jancey (Hereford, 1982), 21–44; repr. with the same pagination in Duggan, *Friends, Networks*, no. IX

Duggan, 'Diplomacy'	A. J. Duggan, 'Diplomacy, Status, and Conscience: Henry II's Penance for Becket's Murder', in *Forschungen zur Reichs-, Papst- und Landesgeschichte: Peter Herde zum 65. Geburtstag von Freunden, Schülern und Kollegen dargebracht*, ed. K. Borchardt and E. Bünz, 2 vols (Stuttgart, 1998), vol. I, 265–90; repr. with the same pagination in Duggan, *Friends, Networks*, no. VII
Duggan, *Friends, Networks*	A. J. Duggan, *Thomas Becket: Friends, Networks, Texts, and Cult* (Aldershot, 2007)
Duggan, *Thomas Becket*	A. [J.] Duggan, *Thomas Becket* (London, 2004)
EHR	*English Historical Review*
Finucane	R. C. Finucane, *Miracles and Pilgrims: Popular Beliefs in Medieval England* (London, Melbourne and Toronto, 1977)
Gameson, 'Early Imagery'	R. Gameson, 'The Early Imagery of Thomas Becket', in *Pilgrimage: The English Experience from Becket to Bunyan*, ed. C. Morris and P. Roberts (Cambridge, 2002), 46–89
Gervase	Gervase of Canterbury, *Opera Historica*, ed. W. Stubbs, RS 73, 2 vols (London, 1879–80)
HMSO	Her/His Majesty's Stationery Office
Howden, *Chronica*	Roger of Howden, *Chronica Magistri Rogeri de Houedene*, ed. W. Stubbs, RS 51, 4 vols (London, 1868–71)
Howden, *Gesta*	[Roger of Howden], *Gesta Regis Henrici Secundi Benedicti Abbatis: The Chronicle of the Reigns of Henry II and Richard I, 1169–1192, known commonly under the name of Benedict of Peterborough*, ed. W. Stubbs, RS 49, 2 vols (London, 1867)
JEH	*Journal of Ecclesiastical History*
Jordan Fantosme, ed. Johnston	*Jordan Fantosme's Chronicle*, ed. and trans. R. C. Johnston (Oxford, 1981)
Lives of Thomas Becket	*The Lives of Thomas Becket*, ed. and trans. M. Staunton (Manchester, 2001)
MGH SS	*Monumenta Germaniae Historica: Scriptores*
MTB	*Materials for the History of Thomas Becket, Archbishop of Canterbury*, ed. J. C. Robertson and J. B. Sheppard, RS 67, 7 vols (London, 1875–85)
Nilgen	U. Nilgen, 'Thomas Becket en Normandie', in *Les saints dans la Normandie médiévale*, ed. P. Bouet and F. Neveux (Caen, 2000), 189–204

Nilson	B. Nilson, *Cathedral Shrines of Medieval England* (Woodbridge, 1998)
NMT	Nelson's Medieval Texts
ODNB	*Oxford Dictionary of National Biography*
OMT	Oxford Medieval Texts
PL	*Patrologiae cursus completus: series Latina*, ed. J.-P. Migne, 221 vols (Paris, 1841–64)
PRS	Pipe Roll Society
Recueil des historiens	*Recueil des historiens des Gaules et de la France*, ed. M. Bouquet *et al.*, new edn, directed by L. Delisle, 19 vols (Paris, 1869–80)
RS	Rolls Series
SCH	Studies in Church History
Sédières	*Thomas Becket: Actes du Colloque International de Sédières*, ed. R. Foreville (Paris, 1975)
Slocum, 'Marriage'	K. B. Slocum, 'Angevin Marriage Diplomacy and the Early Dissemination of the Cult of Thomas Becket', *Medieval Perspectives*, 14 (1999), 214–28
Slocum, *Liturgies*	K. B. Slocum, *Liturgies in Honour of Thomas Becket* (Toronto, 2004)
Vincent, 'Langton'	N. Vincent, 'Stephen Langton, Archbishop of Canterbury', in *Étienne Langton, Prédicateur, Bibliste, Théologien*, ed. L.-J. Bataillon, N. Bériou, G. Dahan and R. Quinto (Turnhout, 2010), 51–123
Vincent, 'Murderers'	N. Vincent, 'The Murderers of Thomas Becket', in *Bischofsmord im Mittelalter: Murder of Bishops*, ed. N. Fryde and D. Reitz (Göttingen, 2003), 211–72
Webb	D. Webb, *Pilgrimage in Medieval England* (London and New York, 2000)

1.

Introduction. The Cult of St Thomas Becket: An Historiographical Pilgrimage

PAUL WEBSTER

On 29 December 1170, Thomas Becket, archbishop of Canterbury, was murdered in his own cathedral by four knights who apparently believed they were acting on the wishes of King Henry II. A controversial figure in life, news of the circumstances of Becket's death sent shockwaves through England, the Plantagenet world and medieval Europe as a whole. In 1173, the London merchant's son, whose meteoric rise had taken him through the household of Archbishop Theobald to the chancellorship of England and on to the archbishopric and well-documented stand-off with the king, was officially recognised as a saint. By the end of 1174, Henry II had twice performed public penance for his part in what was popularly deemed to be martyrdom.[1] In 1220, the relics were moved to a magnificent shrine in the Trinity Chapel, where they remained until the sixteenth century. Today, a candle still marks the site once occupied by one of the foremost shrines in Western Christendom, one that rivalled Rome and Compostela as the centre of one of the most popular cults of the medieval Church.

Historians of Thomas Becket have naturally focused on the crisis in relations between crown and Church in which he was so prominent. His twentieth- and early twenty-first-century biographers tended to devote some attention to the aftermath of the murder, focusing for example on the swift occurrence of miracles and the way in which this turned his burial place into a centre of pilgrimage. 'Canterbury became almost overnight the Lourdes of its world', although the events that had taken place within the cathedral meant that the church itself was in effect closed for almost a year after Becket's death. By popular demand, however, from Easter 1171 visitors were allowed to see the tomb, at which point the monks Benedict, and later William, were delegated to record details of cures reported there. All this suggests that the emergence of the cult was a popular rather than a monk-led movement in its first days and

---

1 For an overview of Thomas Becket's life, see F. Barlow, 'Becket, Thomas (1120?–1170)', *ODNB* (Oxford, 2004) [http://www.oxforddnb.com/view/article/27201, accessed 22 July 2015].

weeks.[2] The biographies go on to outline the reaction of Henry II, the papal response, the penances imposed on the murderers, the settlement at Avranches and its confirmation at Caen in 1172, the canonisation in 1173, the Great Rebellion (1173–74) and the king's penitential pilgrimage to Canterbury in 1174. They also discuss the impact on royal policy towards the Church in England, and briefly touch upon the spread of the cult across Europe and its destruction in England by Henry VIII.[3] Anne J. Duggan offers a detailed consideration of the evolution of the image of Thomas Becket between 1171 and 1900.[4] Beyond this, modern biographers tend to say far less about the evolution of Becket's career as a saint.[5]

Outside the *genre* of biography, others have focused on the impact of Thomas's death, on the portrayal of his life and martyrdom, and the construction of the image of a saint, considering the sources written during and after his lifetime which shed light on his actions and attitude. Thus, Anne J. Duggan has conducted exhaustive research on Becket's letters, whilst Michael Staunton has written an in-depth study of the *Lives* of St Thomas, which were penned within two decades of the archbishop's death (and in seven cases within four years of the murder). As Staunton notes, the 'success of the cult is reflected in the number of Lives and the speed with which they were written'.[6] Historians have also focused on collections of Becket's miracles, developing further analysis of the 'spate of almost instant hagiographical writing' which, as Frank Barlow notes, 'was unprecedented'. The collections compiled by Benedict of Peterborough and William of Canterbury gathered more than four hundred examples of miracles.[7] Benedict's work 'had the largest circulation

---

2 For the quotation, D. Knowles, *Thomas Becket* (London, 1970), 150. See also Duggan, *Thomas Becket*, 216–17; M. Staunton, *Thomas Becket and his Biographers* (Woodbridge, 2006), 8–9; Finucane, 122–3; A. J. Duggan, 'Canterbury: The Becket Effect', in *Canterbury: A Medieval City*, ed. C. Royer-Hemet (Newcastle-upon-Tyne, 2010), 67–91, at 70–71; M.-P. Gelin, 'The Citizens of Canterbury and the Cult of St Thomas Becket', in *Canterbury: A Medieval City*, ed. C. Royer-Hemet (Newcastle-upon-Tyne, 2010), 93–118, at 100–102.

3 For example, Knowles, *Thomas Becket*, 150–55; Barlow, 251–75; Duggan, *Thomas Becket*, 214–23.

4 Duggan, *Thomas Becket*, 224–52.

5 Although Duggan offers instructive lists of further reading on the cult, on the liturgical Becket, on miracles and pilgrimage at Canterbury, on St Thomas in art and on Becket in literature: Duggan, *Thomas Becket*, 314–16. See also her article below, chapter 2.

6 A. [J.] Duggan, *Thomas Becket: A Textual History of his Letters* (Oxford, 1980); *CTB*; Staunton, *Becket and his Biographers*, *passim* and for the quotation see 11; *Lives of Thomas Becket*.

7 Barlow, 2; Duggan, *Thomas Becket*, 218; Staunton, *Becket and his Biographers*, 9, 49–55; Finucane, 125–6. See also: D. Lett, 'Deux hagiographes, un saint et un roi: conformisme et créativité dans les deux recueils de *miracula* de Thomas Becket', in *Auctor & Auctoritas: Invention et conformisme dans l'écriture médiévale. Actes du colloque de Saint-Quentin-en-Yvelines (14–16 juin 1999)*, ed. M. Zimmermann (Paris, 2001), 200–16; R. Koopmans, *Wonderful to Relate: Miracle Stories and Miracle Collecting in High Medieval England* (Philadelphia, PA, 2011), esp. 125–200, 211–24.

of any shrine collection of the age', whilst William's effort was dedicated to Henry II. Nicholas Vincent argues that the letter that prefaced the latter collection can be dated to the late 1180s, at a time when the collection, in large part written some time before this date, was being made ready for wider circulation. Vincent suggests that the letter was added because of a planned translation of the saint's relics in 1186, which ultimately did not take place. The dedicatory letter presents an interesting symbol of the process of reconciliation between Church and crown, with the question of how the miracle accounts confronted the king with the implication that he was complicit in, and in effect guilty of, the murder, addressed in the work of Gesine Oppitz-Trotman.[8] In addition to historians' focus on Benedict and William's work, further contributions have illuminated the role of other major figures in the dispute: Becket's friends and followers, partisans of Henry II, and those who sought, largely unsuccessfully, to look for the middle ground.[9]

Meanwhile, historians have also sought to explain the popular development of the cult in medieval Europe, identifying a range of important themes. As Staunton notes, 'one of the reasons for Thomas's broad appeal as a saint is that he meant different things to different people. Each could take from his memory and his image what they sought, whether it was the miracle-worker, the martyr, the champion of the Church or a combination of these.'[10] Naturally, the significance of the Becket phenomenon at Canterbury itself is a prominent feature of analysis of the cult, with the evidence that pilgrims

8 Koopmans, *Wonderful to Relate*, 114, and see also 139–58 for discussion of the dating of the two collections. For Vincent's arguments (which he acknowledges differ from those of Koopmans): N. Vincent, 'William of Canterbury and Benedict of Peterborough: The Manuscripts, Date and Context of the Becket Miracle Collections', in *Hagiographie, idéologie et politique au Moyen Âge en Occident: Actes du colloque international du Centre d'Études supérieures de Civilisation médiévale de Poitiers 11–14 septembre 2008*, ed. E. Bozóky (Turnhout, 2012), 347–87, and esp. 376–87 for the dating of William's collection and its prefatory letter. On approaches to the king's complicity: G. Oppitz-Trotman, 'Penance, Mercy and Saintly Authority in the Miracles of St Thomas Becket', in *Saints and Sanctity*, ed. P. D. Clarke and T. Claydon, SCH 47 (Woodbridge, 2011), 136–47.
9 Seen, for example, in a range of published letter collections: *The Letters of John of Salisbury, Volume I: The Early Letters 1153–1161*, ed. and trans. W. J. Millor and H. E. Butler, NMT (London, 1955), reissued OMT (Oxford, 1986); *The Letters of John of Salisbury, Volume II: The Later Letters 1163–1180*, ed. and trans. W. J. Millor and C. N. L. Brooke, OMT (Oxford, 1979); *The Letters of Peter of Celle*, ed. and trans. J. Haseldine, OMT (Oxford, 2001); A. Morey and C. N. L. Brooke, *Gilbert Foliot and his Letters* (Cambridge, 1965); *The Letters and Charters of Gilbert Foliot, Abbot of Gloucester (1139–48), Bishop of Hereford (1148–63) and London (1163–87)*, ed. A. Morey and C. N. L. Brooke (Cambridge, 1967); *The Letters of Arnulf of Lisieux*, ed. F. Barlow, Camden Third Series, 61 (London, 1939). In 2014, a conference took place at Corpus Christi College, Cambridge, entitled *Herbert of Bosham: A Medieval Polymath*.
10 Staunton, *Becket and his Biographers*, 216. See also Duggan, *Thomas Becket*, 224–69.

flocked to the shrine leading one historian to describe the cathedral as 'the English Delphi'.[11] In the late twelfth century, down to the translation master-minded by Archbishop Stephen Langton in 1220, this would have been to the tomb in the crypt of Canterbury Cathedral. Thereafter, its primary focus was the magnificent new shrine, perhaps plated with solid gold and certainly adorned with a host of precious stones and jewels, at the heart of the Trinity Chapel, constructed immediately above the site of the crypt tomb and on the site where Thomas was supposed first to have celebrated Mass.[12] In a sense, the Trinity Chapel could itself be seen as a giant architectural reliquary for the saint whose shrine it housed.[13]

As the cult developed in the first fifty years between the martyrdom and the translation of the principal relics to their new shrine, art and iconography played an increasingly important role in defining the pilgrimage experience at Canterbury.[14] A range of locations in the cathedral formed part of the pilgrim route as it developed both before and after the 1220 translation. This came to include the site of the martyrdom, the crypt tomb, the principal shrine itself, and the chapel known as the *Corona*, housing 'Becket's crown', the shrine of that part of his head removed by his murderers.[15] Ben Nilson has traced the flow of income the cathedral gained from its prize relics, arguing that the claim

---

11 For the quotation, Finucane, 164. On Canterbury, see most recently Duggan, 'Canterbury: The Becket Effect'; Gelin, 'The Citizens of Canterbury'. In terms of pilgrimage and the shrine at Canterbury, the cult of St Thomas is central to: Nilson; Webb. See also the opening to Finucane, 9–10.

12 Nilson, 37–8, 64, 71–2; J. Crook, *English Medieval Shrines* (Woodbridge, 2011), 195–7, 213–18. Various descriptions of the tomb and shrine are noted and discussed in: S. Blick, 'Reconstructing the Shrine of St Thomas Becket, Canterbury Cathedral', in *Art and Architecture of Late Medieval English Pilgrimage in Northern Europe and the British Isles*, ed. S. Blick and R. Tekippe, 2 vols (Leiden, 2005), i, 405–41, at 408–12; S. Lamia, 'The Cross and the Crown: Decoration and Accommodation for England's Premier Saints', in *Decorations for the Holy Dead: Visual Embellishments on Tombs and Shrines of Saints*, ed. S. Lamia and E. Valdez del Álamo (Turnhout, 2002), 39–56. Lamia compares sources depicting Becket's tomb and shrine with those depicting that of St Edward the Confessor. See also Gameson, 'Early Imagery', 46–7.

13 Gameson, 'Early Imagery', 83; A. F. Harris, 'Pilgrimage, Performance, and Stained Glass at Canterbury Cathedral', in *Art and Architecture of Late Medieval English Pilgrimage in Northern Europe and the British Isles*, ed. S. Blick and R. Tekippe (Leiden, 2005), 243–81, at 266; M.-P. Gelin, *Lumen ad revelationem gentium: Iconographie et liturgie à Christ Church, Canterbury 1175–1220* (Turnhout, 2006), 179–80; M. H. Caviness, 'A Lost Cycle of Canterbury Paintings of 1200', *Antiquaries Journal*, 54 (1974), 66–74.

14 Gameson, 'Early Imagery', 46–9. The process of constructing such a pilgrimage experience is charted in detail in Harris, 'Pilgrimage'.

15 Nilson, 54, and on the cathedral's pilgrim route, see also 97–8; Webb, 78–9; Crook, *English Medieval Shrines*, 218–19; Harris, 'Pilgrimage', 270–72; Gelin, *Lumen ad revelationem gentium*, 160–70. On allegory, symbolism, continental influences and the planning of the cathedral buildings linked to providing a memorial to Becket: P. Binski, *Becket's Crown: Art and Imagination in Gothic England 1170–1300* (New Haven, CT, and London, 2004), esp. 3–27; M. F. Hearn, 'Canterbury Cathedral and the Cult of Becket', *Art Bulletin*, 76 (1994), 19–54.

that Canterbury hosted more than a hundred thousand pilgrims for special events, such as the jubilees of St Thomas, is probably not a wild over-estimate. Meanwhile, sources such as the Customary of Becket's shrine, compiled in 1428, enable the historian to trace the daily pattern of activity that surrounded the shrine. The 1220 translation, and the jubilee that Archbishop Langton established alongside it, have been seen as crucial in securing the long-term continuity of the cult, whilst evidence such as Chaucer's *Canterbury Tales* reveals the enduring popularity and broad social appeal of pilgrimage to Canterbury. Although the income the monks accrued from the shrines of St Thomas fell into decline in the later Middle Ages, in the decades following the martyrdom, after the 1220 translation, and in the fourteenth century, it was at astonishingly high levels. Periods of decline were sometimes reversed in jubilee years and the period that followed, although there was a sustained dip after the jubilee of 1420.[16]

Meanwhile, the archbishops of Canterbury adopted imagery of the martyrdom on their seals, usually on the counter-seal used as an added means of strengthening the authenticity of documents. An image of Becket's death was first included on such counter-seals by Hubert Walter (archbishop of Canterbury 1193–1205). Potentially inspired by some of the earliest manuscript images to depict the martyrdom, the iconography of Hubert's seal was accompanied by the evocative words 'Martir quod stillat primatis ab ore sigillat' ('The martyr seals what issues from the mouth of the primate'). Most of his successors followed suit in including an image of the murder, drawing on various iconographic traditions, with increasingly elaborate architectural settings, and accompanied by words invoking the example provided by St Thomas. This was the case down to the reign of Henry VII, although William Courtenay (archbishop of Canterbury 1381–96) provides an exception, whilst Thomas Arundel (archbishop of Canterbury 1397–1414) set a new trend by choosing the martyrdom as the image for his great seal (or seal of dignity). The archbishops of Henry VII's reign (John Morton and Henry Deane) did not use Becket iconography on their seals, but William Warham (archbishop of Canterbury 1503–32) did, on the seal of his prerogative court. The later years of Warham's archiepiscopate played out against the backdrop of the furore surrounding Henry VIII's first divorce, in which the archbishop invoked the example of St Thomas's opposition to Henry II. Warham's successor, Thomas Cranmer (archbishop of Canterbury 1533–56), initially followed the example set by the

16 Duggan, *Thomas Becket*, 235; Nilson, 113–17, 147–54, 168–70, 180, 211–15 (table 2), 234 (graphs 1 and 2); Finucane, 193; D. H. Turner, 'The Customary of the Shrine of St Thomas of Canterbury', *Canterbury Cathedral Chronicle*, 70 (1976), 16–22; Bartlett, *Saints*, 259–61, 432; Harris, 'Pilgrimage', 254. On the jubilees, R. Foreville, *Le jubilé de saint Thomas Becket: Du XIIIe au XVe siècle (1220–1470). Étude et documents*, Bibliothèque générale de l'École pratique des hautes-études, VIe section (Paris, 1958).

bulk of his predecessors, but at the height of the Reformation (c.1538), his official seals were re-cut, discarding imagery linked to the martyrdom in favour of a depiction of the death of Christ. Even then, Becket's demise made a brief reappearance in Mary Tudor's reign, during the archiepiscopate of Cardinal Reginald Pole (archbishop of Canterbury 1555–58).[17]

The host of pilgrims flocking to the shrine took home badges or *ampullae* depicting significant moments in Thomas Becket's career as archbishop, or images of the structure they had visited in Canterbury Cathedral. This itself spawned a flourishing industry in Canterbury, one of the many ways in which the city could benefit from the economic opportunities presented by the cult.[18] In terms of the subsequent survival of pilgrim badges, particularly large numbers have been recovered in London by archaeologists and the Society of Thames Mudlarks, with further finds recorded by the Portable Antiquities Scheme ranging across the United Kingdom. The frequency of their discovery in London perhaps reflects the close association between the city and the saint, who had been born there and who was believed to be the special protector of Londoners. It is also testimony to the large number of badges sold by the vendors of pilgrimage souvenirs at Canterbury. The badges depicted a range of scenes related to Becket's life and death, including the events leading up to the martyrdom. Where these were commemorated by specific feasts – such as that marking Becket's return from exile (or *Regressio*) – badges were produced to mark the occasion. Naturally, these depictions also focused heavily on the murder itself and its perpetrators (sometimes identified in inscriptions) and their swords, or showed Thomas's soul being transported to heaven by angels. Alternatively, they adopted an image such as the saint's head, clad in his archiepiscopal mitre, or portrayed the saint standing or enthroned, clad in his robes of office.[19] In an interesting modern twist, much of this material is becoming available in new forms, including online and animation.[20]

17 K. B. Slocum, '*Martir quod Stillat Primatis ab Ore Sigillat*: Sealed with the Blood of Becket', *Journal of the British Archaeological Association*, 165 (2012), 61–88. See also Binski, *Becket's Crown*, 132–4; T. Borenius, 'The Iconography of St Thomas of Canterbury', *Archaeologia*, 79 (1929), 29–54, at 44–5 and plate xvi; Borenius, *Becket in Art*, 74–5 and plates xxvii–xxviii.
18 Duggan, 'Canterbury: The Becket Effect', 81–8. See also Gelin, 'The Citizens of Canterbury'.
19 Bartlett, *Saints*, 441–2. Various examples are discussed and illustrated in: *Age of Chivalry: Art in Plantagenet England 1200–1400*, Royal Academy of Arts Exhibition Catalogue, ed. J. Alexander and P. Binski (London, 1987), 218–22 (catalogue nos. 43–63). For a more detailed study, see: B. Spencer, *Pilgrim Souvenirs and Secular Badges*, Medieval Finds from Excavations in London, 7, new edn (Woodbridge, 2010, first published London, 1998), 37–133 (catalogue nos. 1–137). A range of similar examples to those discussed in this and the following paragraph are to be found in B. Spencer, *Salisbury and South Wiltshire Museum. Medieval Catalogue, Part 2: Pilgrim Souvenirs and Secular Badges* (Salisbury, 1990), 16–24 (catalogue nos. 8–34), 70–73 (figs 12–39); Borenius, *Becket in Art*, 28–9, 76–7.
20 In addition to the works noted above, the Museum of London's holdings can also be viewed online: [http://collections.museumoflondon.org.uk/online/search/#!/results?terms=pilgrim%20

Some took this a stage further, with the *ampullae* themselves shaped in the form of the saint as archbishop, holding his cross-staff and (or) a maniple and giving a blessing, on board a ship returning to England or on horseback. Badges are even to be found which depict Becket standing on the back of a peacock! A more straightforward feature worth noting is that a number of badges preserve images of the saint's tomb or shrine, either the principal shrine or the head shrine at Canterbury.[21] Indeed, Sarah Blick has argued that the surviving badges are the 'only picture expressly created to reproduce the shrine', and provide an impression of the shrine as it might have looked to the fourteenth-century observer. They give a more accurate impression than stained-glass images (which portray either an idealised shrine, a fanciful recon-struction perhaps based on a pilgrim's account, or a structure earlier than 1220) or documentary efforts to picture the shrine produced in the centuries following the Reformation. Whilst the badges 'cannot be viewed as untouched photographs of the past', nonetheless their creators 'were trying to convey something of the original', to be sold as mementoes for those keen to preserve the memory of their pilgrimage. By extension, this evidence suggests that by the fourteenth century, the shrine bore an effigy of the saint, with a refur-bishment in the Decorated Style having taken place in around 1300.[22]

The shrine keepers also kept up a roaring trade in 'St Thomas's water', selling *ampullae* containing what was said to be a droplet of Becket's blood.[23] This had been carefully gathered up by the monks within hours of the martyrdom and

badge%20Thomas%20Becket, accessed 3 October 2015]. A project is currently underway at the British Museum to provide online images of the pilgrim badges held in their collections, to be made accessible via: *The British Museum Collection Online* [http://www.britishmuseum.org/ research/collection_online/search.aspx, accessed 3 October 2015]. For an interactive 3-D image of a mould for a pilgrim badge, visit; https://sketchfab.com/models/707caa9c575c4c7cb981e305d ac61bdb [accessed 3 October 2015]. A search for pilgrim badges linked to Thomas Becket in the database of the Portable Antiquities Scheme also returns over thirty surviving examples: [https:// finds.org.uk/database/search/results/objecttype/PILGRIM+BADGE/description/thomas+becket, accessed 3 October 2015]. Meanwhile, work based on the pilgrim badges housed at the Museum of London is discussed in M. Jeater, 'Animating Thomas Becket', *Museum of London Blog* [http:// blog.museumoflondon.org.uk/animating-thomas-becket/, accessed 3 October 2015]. My thanks to Lloyd de Beer, Amy Jeffs and Anna Wells for correspondence which drew my attention to these resources.

21 Spencer, *Pilgrim Souvenirs*, 49–50 (catalogue no. 6c), 72–6 (catalogue nos. 26–30), 78–89 (catalogue nos. 34–54), 99–120 (catalogue nos. 73–119).

22 Blick, 'Reconstructing the Shrine of St Thomas', 405–41, with the quotations at 419, 422–3, and discussion of the possible effigy at 433–6.

23 A. A. Jordan, 'The "Water of Thomas Becket": Water as Medium, Metaphor and Relic', in *The Nature and Function of Water, Baths, Bathing and Hygiene from Antiquity through the Renaissance*, ed. C. Kosso and A. Scott (Leiden, 2009), 479–500; P. A. Sigal, 'Naissance et premier développement d'un vinage exceptionnel: l'eau de saint Thomas', CCM, 44 (2001), 35–44. The water is also noted in Duggan, *Thomas Becket*, 215, 234; Finucane, 163; Bartlett, *Saints*, 441; Webb, 49; Barlow, 265–7.

played a key part in the early miracles that did so much to stir the cult into life. One in five of the miracles recorded by Benedict of Peterborough and William of Canterbury were attributed to the use of Becket's healing water.[24] Henry II even drank some of it on his famous penitential visit to Canterbury Cathedral in 1174. Each *ampulla* could be seen, in a sense, as 'a perambulatory shrine', and some came to bear mottos alluding to the saint's prowess as a healer: 'St Thomas is the best healer of the virtuous sick'. Others depicted the healing miracles themselves. Spencer argues that 'thanks to the generosity of countless pilgrims, Canterbury water was soon deposited in practically every church throughout the land, ready for use in emergencies as a thaumaturgic remedy'.[25] Slocum adds that 'it was the vision of the saint as healer which contributed the most significant component to the development of the legend of Thomas Becket'.[26] The use of blood in this form, even that of a martyr, was arguably controversial, given the centrality of the blood of Christ to the ceremony of the Mass. In Becket's case, dilution provided the solution, and as with so much of the evidence for the depiction of the cult, writers and other sources (for instance the stained glass of the Trinity Chapel at Canterbury) embraced and celebrated the phenomenon: the Lamb of Canterbury took his place in the world of the Lamb of God.[27] Later, the blood of Becket would contribute to the cult's downfall. Suspicion of pilgrimage mementoes such as those involving the 'water of St Thomas' provided Tudor critics with the ammunition to take the first steps towards the destruction of the shrine.[28]

The accounts of Becket's miracles reveal how the cult spread from Canterbury, first into Kent, then to London, then further afield.[29] As it did so, numerous locations became associated with the saint as the sites of miracles, the homes of relics (Carlisle Cathedral came to hold a sword said to have been used to martyr Becket), or through the dedication of a church. Having been born in London, Thomas came to be seen as a protector of the city, with a vision of 1241 seeing him as the destroyer of new walls at the

24 Jordan, 'Water of Thomas Becket', 484.
25 Spencer, *Pilgrim Souvenirs*, 38, and for examples of surviving *ampullae*, see also 40–63 (catalogue nos. 1–18).
26 K. B. Slocum, 'Optimus Egrorum Medicus Fit Thoma Bonorum: Images of Saint Thomas Becket as Healer', in *Death, Sickness and Health in Medieval Society and Culture*, ed. S. J. Ridyard, Sewanee Mediaeval Studies, 10 (Sewanee, TN, 2000), 173–80, at 173. For discussion of the development of the image of Becket as a doctor, in particular in the miracle collection of William of Canterbury, see Koopmans, *Wonderful to Relate*, 193–8.
27 Slocum, 'Optimus Egrorum Medicus', 173–80; Jordan, 'Water of Thomas Becket', 482–3, 489–97; Koopmans, *Wonderful to Relate*, 34–6; Gelin, *Lumen ad revelationem gentium*, 270–77; Barlow, 264–7; S. Blick, 'Comparing Pilgrim Souvenirs and Trinity Chapel Windows at Canterbury Cathedral: An Exploration of Context, Copying and the Recovery of Lost Stained Glass', *Mirator* (September, 2001) [http://www.glossa.fi/mirator/index_en.html, accessed 16 July 2016], 1–27.
28 Slocum, 'Martir quod Stillat Primatis ab Ore Sigillat', 76.
29 Duggan, 'Canterbury: The Becket Effect', 71–4.

Tower of London, a portent proven accurate, according to the chronicler Matthew Paris, when the structure subsequently collapsed.[30] Although John Crook sounds a note of caution, citing an increased interest in local saints in the 1150s and '60s, historians have highlighted the impact of the Becket phenomenon on other churches and religious communities, both in the years after 1170, and following the translation of 1220. Those that housed the relics of other major saints were at times keen to emphasise that their relics were still an effective focus for the devotions of the faithful seeking intercession. Thus, miracles linked to the hand of St James the Great, preserved at Reading Abbey, emphasised how visions of the saint informed the sick that they would only be cured at Reading, not elsewhere.[31] At other houses, new saints were in essence created, as in the case of St Amphibalus at St Albans, a legendary priest said to have been hidden by the abbey's eponymous saint. Meanwhile, evidence relating to the cults of St Frideswide of Oxford and St Cuthbert of Durham, amongst others, shows similar traits to events at Reading, with emphasis on the local saint's effectiveness where the more popular cult at Canterbury (and various other holy sites) had failed the individual intercessor. In some cases, release from various forms of suffering was achieved by seeking the combined intercession of the saints.[32] Not all such efforts met with lasting success. If the writing of the *Historia Selebiensis Monasterii* was intended to create a direct rival – in the form of Selby's prized relic of the finger of St Germanus – for the northern saints John of Beverley and Cuthbert of Durham, or even 'a northern answer to Thomas Becket', then the returns were limited. However, the impetus provided by the developing cult at Canterbury should not be discounted.[33] In addition, events such as the translation of 1220 could provide the spur to seek recognition of a local saint, as in the case of William of York, canonised in 1226.[34]

Beyond Canterbury, the spread of the cult within medieval Europe has also been traced. News of both martyrdom and miracles spread rapidly, for instance

---

30 Webb, 51–2, 165.

31 Crook, *English Medieval Shrines*, 170–91, although see also 213, where Crook observes that in the wake of the translation of St Thomas's bones in 1220, 'a large number of other local saints were also enshrined, or re-enshrined'; Nilson, 123. The popularity of Canterbury, however, clearly caused tensions within communities, as evidence from Reading also testifies: Webb, 48–9, 57. The interrelationship between the Becket cult and devotion to the hand of St James at Reading will be considered in forthcoming work to be published by Rachel Koopmans.

32 Webb, 52–60; Crook, *English Medieval Shrines*, 187, 204–11.

33 *Historia Selebiensis Monasterii: The History of the Monastery of Selby*, ed. and trans. J. Burton with L. Lockyer, OMT (Oxford, 2013), xciii–xciv; J. Burton, 'Selby Abbey and its Twelfth-Century Historian', in *Learning and Literacy in Medieval England and Abroad*, ed. S. Rees-Jones (Turnhout, 2003), 49–68, esp. 66–8. Rachel Koopmans also argues that existing trends in miracle collecting were consolidated and accelerated by the Becket cult, in particular through the work of Benedict of Peterborough: Koopmans, *Wonderful to Relate*, 7, 114–15, 134–6.

34 Crook, *English Medieval Shrines*, 246–7.

along trade routes between the kingdom of England and the Rhineland, and on the Third Crusade, to the point where St Thomas 'was venerated with varying degrees of solemnity throughout the Latin Church', from Iceland to the eastern Mediterranean. As Anne J. Duggan notes, the saint became patron of a range of bodies: brewers in London, coopers in Venice, law students in Bologna, and of the English hospice in Rome.[35] The breadth of devotion should not be taken for granted simply because of the events of Becket's death. Other bishops and archbishops murdered in this period did not achieve much beyond local renown. Thomas the saint, however, was able to take advantage of the networks in which Thomas the man had been involved in the course of his career. The friends and contacts he had made from his student days onwards were involved, variously taking action to spread the word before Henry II could gain acceptance of his own version of events, or later helping to disseminate texts, founding houses in his honour and distributing relics to new homes overseas. The monks of Canterbury Cathedral also gave away relics, either to pilgrims coming to Canterbury, or whilst on their travels within Europe, as evidence for a visit to the abbey of St-Bénigne, Dijon, in 1190, attests. The religious orders with which Becket had been associated, in particular the Cistercians, with whom he had resided in exile at the abbey of Pontigny, played an important part in disseminating texts recounting his life and miracles.[36] Historians have also highlighted the number of French pilgrims coming to Canterbury, in particular from the northern regions.[37] One of the most prolific and important twentieth-century contributions to the study of Thomas Becket was made by Raymonde Foreville, through several works on the development of the cult, especially in France, and through organising and publishing the proceedings of the 1973 Becket conference held at Sédières (département de la Corrèze, France).[38] The development and endurance of the cult in France, in particular in Normandy, continues to inspire important

35 Duggan, *Thomas Becket*, 233–4, 236; Duggan, 'Canterbury: The Becket Effect', 76–7, 89. For an overview of the European expansion of the cult, see A. J. Duggan, 'Religious Networks in Action: The European Expansion of the Cult of St Thomas of Canterbury', in *International Religious Networks*, ed. J. Gregory and H. McLeod, SCH Subsidia, 14 (Woodbridge, 2012), 20–43.
36 Duggan, 'Religious Networks'. For relics taken abroad from Canterbury by pilgrims or by the monks themselves: Duggan, 'Canterbury: The Becket Effect', 74; Gameson, 'Early Imagery', 49; H. E. J. Cowdrey, 'An Early Record at Dijon of the Export of Becket's Relics', *Bulletin of the Institute of Historical Research*, 54 (1981), 251–3.
37 Finucane, 163.
38 R. Foreville, 'Le Culte de saint Thomas Becket en Normandie: Enquête sur les sanctuaires anciennement placés sous le vocable du martyr de Canterbury', in *Sédières*, 135–52; H. Martin, 'Le culte de saint Thomas Becket dans les diocèses de la province de Tours', in *Sédières*, 153–8; J. Becquet, 'Les sanctuaires dédiés à saint Thomas de Cantorbéry en Limousin', in *Sédières*, 159–61; R. Foreville, 'Le culte de saint Thomas Becket en France: Bilan provisoire des recherches', in *Sédières*, 163–87; R. Foreville, 'La diffusion du culte de Thomas Becket dans la France de l'Ouest avant la fin du XIIe siècle', CCM, 19 (1976), 347–69, repr. with the same

research.[39] Meanwhile, devotion to St Thomas in particular regions or countries has also been the focus of detailed individual studies.[40]

In turn, consideration of different thematic contexts in which the cult can be studied has added a rich and varied range of source materials to the portfolio available to the historian. The use of Becket as a model for medieval sermon writers has been established. The saint's feast days – in particular that of his martyrdom (29 December), and from 1220 that of his translation (7 July) – provided points in the calendar at which sermons drawing on perceptions of the cause he had espoused, and the example of his martyrdom, would have been preached. Phyllis B. Roberts has collected more than 180 surviving examples of Becket sermons, dating from the 1170s to c.1400. She argues that the early examples were an important tool in the spread of the cult, playing a significant role in the wider oral transmission of devotion to Becket. Preaching, and the related evidence of notes and outlines prepared by its practitioners in the thirteenth and fourteenth centuries, also helped to sustain interest in St Thomas, in particular amongst university and clerical audiences, with preachers spanning the religious orders across Europe. Noting the potential influence of the reform of the clergy promoted by the Fourth Lateran Council of 1215, Roberts highlights how the personal piety and devotion of Becket the archbishop were emphasised, along with the way in which his defence of the freedoms of the Church led to his martyrdom. St Thomas was constructed as a good shepherd (*bonus pastor*), prepared to give his life to protect his sheep. He was also portrayed as a model in terms of his largesse to the poor, and an example to the churchmen of the day. As Rachel Koopmans notes, surviving sermons very rarely make more than passing reference to the saint's miracles. Legend might, however, be referenced, for instance the tale that Becket's father Gilbert had married a Saracen princess (who then converted).[41] Most importantly, the sermons 'were crucial to creating

---

pagination in R. Foreville, *Thomas Becket dans la tradition historique et hagiographique* (London, 1981), no. X.

39 See the contributions in this volume by Elma Brenner (chapter 4) and Alyce A. Jordan (chapter 9). Dr Jordan is also currently working on a project entitled 'Remembering Thomas Becket in Normandy', examining sites that have both medieval and later imagery devoted to St Thomas in the same church, and exploring the ways in which nineteenth- and twentieth-century Becket imagery 'converses' with its medieval counterparts.

40 See, for example, the articles collected in part 3 of Duggan, *Friends, Networks*. A further useful list of relevant works is supplied in Duggan, *Thomas Becket*, 314. For recent work on the cult in the Iberian Peninsula, see G. Cavero Domínguez (coord), *Tomás Becket y la Península Ibérica (1170–1230)* (León, 2013); F. Galván Freile, 'Culto e Iconografía de Tomás de Canterbury en la Península Ibérica (1173–1300)', in *Hagiografia peninsular en els segles medievals*, ed. F. Español and F. Fité (Lleida, 2008), 197–216. I owe these references on the cult in Spain to the work of José Manuel Cerda (chapter 7) in this volume.

41 P. B. Roberts, 'Thomas Becket: The Construction and Deconstruction of a Saint from the Middle Ages to the Reformation', in *Models of Holiness in Medieval Sermons*, ed. B. C. M. Kienzle (Louvain-la-Neuve, 1996), 1–22 at 1–12; P. B. Roberts, *Thomas Becket in the Medieval Latin*

and sustaining' St Thomas's place as 'a vivid and compelling symbol of the Church's resistance to temporal authority'.[42]

Becket also inspired a wide range of liturgy, incorporated into the rite for daily services (more frequently than the Mass) and surviving in a variety of sources such as breviaries and antiphonals.[43] The canonisation prompted the need for a ritual for the first feast day (29 December 1173), a task which fell to Benedict of Peterborough. Further liturgical works were created to mark the anniversary of Thomas's return to England (the *Regressio*), and for the feast inaugurated by the translation of 1220.[44] As with the *Lives* and accounts of Becket's miracles, liturgical texts followed the cult in its swift spread across Europe.[45] The authors of Becket liturgy pursued a variety of approaches in constructing their image of the saint. Some focused on the apparent transformation brought about by the chancellor's elevation to the role of archbishop, with others making reference to St Thomas as a good shepherd, to the martyr's adherence to the principles he had determined to defend, or to the parallels between Becket and Christ. Others simply adopted the ritual used for offices in the name of other saints.[46] Particular attributes could be highlighted, notably Thomas's perceived posthumous abilities as a healer. The link between Becket and water was emphasised here, whether in terms of the miraculous powers of

Preaching Tradition: An Inventory of Sermons about Thomas Becket c. 1170–c. 1400 (The Hague, 1992), with an overview of the evidence and its content at 9–45; Koopmans, *Wonderful to Relate*, 132–3. See also P. B. Roberts, 'Archbishop Stephen Langton and his Preaching on Thomas Becket in 1220', in *De Ore Domini: Preacher and Word in the Middle Ages*, ed. T. L. Amos, E. A. Green, and B. M. Kienzle (Kalmazoo, MI, 1989), 75–92.

42 Roberts, *Thomas Becket in the Medieval Latin Preaching Tradition*, 43.

43 S. Reames, 'Liturgical Offices for the Cult of St Thomas Becket', in *Medieval Hagiography: An Anthology*, ed. T. [F.] Head (New York, 2000), 561–93; S. L. Reames, 'The Remaking of a Saint: Stephen Langton and the Liturgical Office for Becket's Translation', *Hagiographica*, 7 (2000), 17–34; Slocum, *Liturgies*. See also: D. Stevens, 'Music in Honour of St Thomas of Canterbury', *The Musical Quarterly*, 56 (1970), 311–48; D. Stevens, 'Thomas Becket et la musique médiévale', in *Sédières*, 277–84; A. Hughes, 'Chants in the Rhymed Office of St Thomas of Canterbury', *Early Music*, 16 (1988), 185–201.

44 Duggan, *Thomas Becket*, 230. For the office for the feast day that marked the martyrdom, 29 December: Slocum, *Liturgies*, 135–238; Reames, 'Liturgical Offices', 561–2, 565–78. For the office for the feast of the translation of St Thomas, 7 July: Slocum, *Liturgies*, 239–317; Reames, 'Liturgical Offices', 578–91. On the integration of the liturgy into the life and fabric of Canterbury Cathedral: Gelin, *Lumen ad revelationem gentium*.

45 Hughes, 'Chants', 185; K. B. Slocum, 'The Making, Remaking and Unmaking of the Cult of Thomas Becket', *Hagiographica*, 7 (2000), 3–16, at 11–12. See also, for example, A. J. Duggan, 'A Becket Office at Stavelot: London, BL, MS Addit. 16964', in *Omnia disce: Medieval Studies in Memory of Leonard Boyle, O.P.*, ed. eadem, J. Greatrex, and B. Bolton (Aldershot, 2005), 161–82; repr. with the same pagination in Duggan, *Friends, Networks*, no. XI. An instructive list of hymns, sequences, and rhymed offices in honour of the saint, including their place of origin, is offered in Stevens, 'Music in Honour of St Thomas', 346–8.

46 Slocum, *Liturgies*, 4–8. See also the contrasting examples highlighted in Bartlett, *Saints*, 114, 117.

'St Thomas's water', or in his propensity for saving the drowned or aiding those in peril at sea. The office celebrated on the anniversary of the 1220 translation referred to children and adults saved from drowning.[47]

'Having been martyred, Becket became an icon.'[48] Historians of medieval art remain indebted to the work of Tancred Borenius, in the 1920s and '30s, who collected evidence of surviving imagery of the saint from across Europe and sought to identify trends in the development of the iconography of St Thomas from the Middle Ages to the Renaissance.[49] Meanwhile, historians have noted how, in England, 'every church in the land probably had an image or picture of St Thomas' prior to the Reformation, whilst numerous churches in England and Europe carried the saint's name in their dedication.[50] More broadly, 'the visual arts made their most important contribution to the cult of Becket through quantity not quality'.[51] The appeal of the cult is shown in the glass, paintings, sculpture, monumental brasses, carved wooden panels and alabasters installed in churches across medieval Europe, including the kingdom of England but also ranging from Iceland to the Mediterranean, as well as in manuscript illuminations and later woodcuts.[52] In the case of the manuscripts, prominent examples include the Queen Mary Psalter, and the so-called 'Becket Leaves' – a surviving thirteenth-century illustrated verse life of the saint.[53]

47 Slocum, *Liturgies*, 7, 200–201, 205, 221–2, 257–62, 268–9, 276–7, 284–6, 288, 290–93, 298, 303, 309–10; Slocum, '*Optimus Egrorum Medicus*', 177–9; Reames, 'Liturgical Offices', 579, 587–8, 590–91; Jordan, 'Water of Thomas Becket', 485–7.

48 Duggan, *Thomas Becket*, 232.

49 Borenius, 'Iconography'; T. Borenius, 'Addenda to the Iconography of St Thomas of Canterbury', *Archaeologia*, 81 (1931), 19–32; Borenius, *Becket in Art*; T. Borenius, 'Some Further Aspects of the Iconography of St Thomas of Canterbury', *Archaeologia*, 83 (1933), 171–86.

50 Spencer, *Salisbury and South Wiltshire Museum. Medieval Catalogue, Part 2*, 16; Foreville, 'Le culte de saint Thomas Becket en Normandie', 135. See also: Martin, 'Le culte de saint Thomas Becket dans les diocèses de la province de Tours'; Becquet, 'Les sanctuaires dédiés à saint Thomas de Cantorbéry en Limousin'; Foreville, 'Le culte de saint Thomas Becket en France'. A map of Becket dedications in the German empire is included in *Die romanische Neumarktkirche zu Merseburg und ihr Patron Thomas Becket von Canterbury*, publ. by the Förderkreis Museum, Schloss Merseburg (Merseburg, 2014), 159, a reference I owe to Professor Anne J. Duggan.

51 Gameson, 'Early Imagery', 85.

52 In addition to the works by Borenius noted above, see: A. Larue, 'Enquête sur l'iconographie et le mobilier de Thomas Becket en Normandie', in *Sédières*, 211–19; C. Brisac, 'Thomas Becket dans le vitrail français au début du XIIIe siècle', in *Sédières*, 221–31; M.-M. Gauthier, 'Le meurtre dans la cathédrale, thème iconographique médiéval', in *Sédières*, 248–53; P. A. Newton, 'Some New Material for the Study of the Iconography of St Thomas Becket', in *Sédières*, 255–63; U. Nilgen, 'The Manipulated Memory: Thomas Becket in Legend and Art', in *Memory and Oblivion: Proceedings of the XXIXth International Congress of the History of Art held in Amsterdam, 1–7 September 1996*, ed. W. Reinink and J. Stumpel (Dordrecht, 1999), 765–72.

53 Borenius, 'Iconography', 36, 50–51, plate xii, and plate xxi; Borenius, *Becket in Art*, 40–42 and plates x–xii; J. Backhouse and C. de Hamel, *The Becket Leaves* (London, 1988); J. C. Dickinson, 'Some Medieval English Representations of St Thomas Becket in France', in *Sédières*,

Modern studies have added to the range of examples of iconography of St Thomas and to our knowledge of the types of object which presented depictions of the saint or his shrine. This covers themes such as the image of Becket in medieval stained glass. Here, attention has again focused on Canterbury and the glass of the Trinity Chapel, installed after 1182 and possibly before the translation of 1220. Caviness tentatively proposes that these windows were installed in the early years of John's reign, and in the period following the monks' return to their cathedral following their exile between 1207 and 1213. A unique series of scenes from the miracles of St Thomas now fills seven of these windows, and it is likely that these were originally accompanied by two windows, at the start of the sequence, depicting Becket's life. Where pilgrims had previously read or more probably heard accounts of the miracles, perhaps in the course of their tour of the cathedral precincts, here those miracles and their message were displayed in vivid and colourful detail, whilst (after 1220) the visitor also gazed upon the shrine. Thanks to the architectural reconfigurations begun under William the Englishman, the raised area which accommodated the shrine (from 1220 to the Reformation) was located so that the viewer could see the lower scenes of the stained glass at eye-level. Where text was used in the windows, it was not necessarily meant to be read and understood, but to lend authority to what was depicted around it, in the way that the display of holy texts might aid devotional guidance to the laity during services. Overall, the windows reinforced the value of travelling to seek intercession from Thomas and encouraged 'the worshippers to envision the saint in their own space'. They provided plentiful examples of how pilgrims should act and presented Thomas's story as 'the contemporary climax to the long story of the Church'.[54]

Elsewhere, historians have highlighted the depictions of the saint in glass surviving in a range of English and European churches, including York Minster (and other churches in York), great French cathedrals such as Angers, Chartres, Coutances, Lisieux and Sens, and a host of other churches.[55] In

265–71, at 266–8. For the Queen Mary Psalter: London, BL, Royal MS 2 B vii, fols 288v–298v [digitised at http://www.bl.uk/manuscripts/FullDisplay.aspx?ref=Royal_MS_2_b_vii, accessed 12 September 2015]. The psalter is also discussed in the essay (chapter 2) by Anne J. Duggan in this volume. Further examples are discussed in Gameson, 'Early Imagery', 50, 64, 65 (plate 8), 67; Newton, 'Some New Material', 255.

54 Caviness, *Windows of Christ Church*, esp. 157–214, 313–14 and plates 109–160, 219–20 (figs 238–366a, 592–3); Gelin, *Lumen ad revelationem gentium*; Harris, 'Pilgrimage', 243–81 (with the quotation at 255); Gameson, 'Early Imagery', 72, 74–5, 76–7 (plates 15–16), 81 (for the quotation), 82 (plate 18), 83, 86 (plate 19), 87, 88 (plate 20). See also M. H. Caviness, *The Early Stained Glass of Canterbury Cathedral circa 1175–1220* (Princeton, NJ, 1977).

55 Borenius, 'Iconography', 37–8; Borenius, *Becket in Art*, 32, 33, 44–8 and plates xiii–xiv; Borenius, 'Some Further Aspects', 183–4 and plate li (fig. 1); Newton, 'Some New Material', 257–9. Note that Caviness dismisses Borenius's identification of some of the fragments of glass from York as depicting Becket miracles: Caviness, *Windows of Christ Church*, 159 n. 4. On Becket in stained glass, see also M.-P. Gelin, 'Heroes and Traitors: The Life of Thomas Becket in French

some cases, such as Chartres, where John of Salisbury became bishop from 1176 until his death in 1180, and Sens, where Herbert of Bosham resided until 1184, this can be linked to the influence of some of Becket's closest followers.[56] In addition, Catherine Brisac identifies a brief flourishing of St Thomas as a subject for window makers in France in the 1220s and 1230s, perhaps sparked by the translation of 1220, linked to cathedrals associated with the former archbishop's struggle with Henry II or to the former Plantagenet lands. These windows also provided an opportunity to present a more complete narrative of events involving the saint than many other types of iconography, whether in terms of his life and his miracles, or in the opportunity to juxtapose him with other major saints, and with Christ himself, to set the Becket cult in the wider context of salvation history, as part of a narrative of defence of the Church or an appeal for pastoral and clerical reform.[57]

Meanwhile churches across Europe housed elaborate reliquaries, some of the most beautiful including a series of caskets manufactured by the master enamel makers of Limoges in the late twelfth and early thirteenth centuries. Some fifty-two surviving examples depict the martyrdom of St Thomas, with the number of murderers varying from two to four, and some distinctive in showing one of the murderers armed with an axe.[58] Their owners came from across Europe and, whilst the caskets are now highly-prized collector's items

Stained-Glass Windows', *Vidimus*, 14 (2008) [http://vidimus.org/issues/issue-14/feature/, accessed 17 December 2015]; Larue, 'Enquête sur l'iconographie et le mobilier de Thomas Becket en Normandie', 212, 217; Brisac, 'Thomas Becket dans la vitrail français', with descriptions of the cathedral windows at 224–31; Gameson, 'Early Imagery', 67, 69–70 (plates 11–12), 71–2, 73–4 (plates 13–14). The windows at Angers and Coutances are the subject of the article by Alyce A. Jordan in this volume (chapter 9).

56 D. Luscombe, 'Salisbury, John of (late 1110s–1180)', *ODNB* (Oxford, 2004; online edn, 2011) [http://www.oxforddnb.com/view/article/14849, accessed 17 December 2015]; Gelin, 'Heroes and Traitors'.

57 Brisac, 'Thomas Becket dans la vitrail français', 223; Gameson, 'Early Imagery', 78; Gelin, 'Heroes and Traitors'; A. A. Jordan, 'Rhetoric and Reform: The St Thomas Becket Window of Sens Cathedral', in *The Four Modes of Seeing: Approaches to Medieval Imagery in Honor of Madeline Harrison Caviness*, ed. E. Staudinger Lane, E. Carson Pastan and E. M. Shortell (Farnham, 2009), 547–64.

58 S. Caudron, 'Les châsses de Thomas Becket en émail de Limoges', in *Sédières*, 233–41; S. Caudron, 'Thomas Becket et l'Œuvre de Limoges', in *Valérie et Thomas Becket: De l'influence des princes Plantagenêt dans l'Œuvre de Limoges*, ed. V. Notin *et al.* (Limoges, 1999), 56–68; J.-F. Boyer *et al.*, 'Catalogue des œuvres exposées', in *Valérie et Thomas Becket: De l'influence des princes Plantagenêt dans l'Œuvre de Limoges*, ed. V. Notin *et al.* (Limoges, 1999), 69–131, at 100–31 (nos. 15–30); Bartlett, *Saints*, 267; Borenius, 'Iconography', 48–50, plate xix and plate xx; Borenius, 'Addenda to the Iconography of St Thomas', 28–9 and plate xxii fig. 3; Borenius, *Becket in Art*, 84–92 and plates xxxiii–xxxvi; Borenius, 'Some Further Aspects', 176–7 and plate xlvi; S. Lutan-Hassner, *Thomas Becket and the Plantagenets: Atonement Through Art* (Leiden, 2015), chapter 5. See also M. Yvernault, 'Reading History in Enamel: The Journey of Thomas Becket's Experience from Canterbury to Limoges', in *Canterbury: A Medieval City*, ed. C. Royer-Hemet (Newcastle-upon-Tyne, 2010), 137–59.

(if not housed in major churches or the leading world museums), Simone Caudron has argued that they moved very little prior to the nineteenth century, allowing us to identify the likely or possible home of just under half the surviving examples, following their manufacture in Limoges. Those that survive in England were preserved by Catholic families after the Reformation. Amongst these, one was commissioned by Benedict, the monk of Canterbury who witnessed the murder in 1170, became one of the first custodians of Becket's tomb, authored one of the earliest miracle collections and went on to become abbot of Peterborough. Others, Caudron suggests, hailed from Canterbury, Chester, Durham, Hereford and Worksop. Across Europe, survival is similarly dependent on having avoided the destruction of the Reformation, and that of the various European revolutions and religious, civil and international wars. Nevertheless, Caudron attempts attributions for reliquaries (with varying levels of conviction) to eight locations in France, five in Italy, two in Germany and one each in Spain, the Netherlands and Sweden. The surviving reliquaries from Spain, both linked to the cathedral of Palencia, could have been commissioned by King Alfonso VIII of Castile and his wife Eleanor (Leonor), daughter of Henry II and Eleanor of Aquitaine.[59]

In addition, high-status churchmen incorporated images of the saint and his martyrdom into vestments and the associated artefacts of religious services. These include the so-called 'Thomas Becket mitres', depicting the murder and in some cases associating Thomas with other martyrs, St Stephen and St Lawrence. Caroline Vogt's discussion of these mitres sees them 'as a refined medium of episcopal self-fashioning'. Surviving examples can be found from the Cistercian monastery of Seligenthal near Landshut (Bavaria, Germany), from the cathedral at Sens and the sisters of Nôtre-Dame in Namur (France), the latter thought once to have been owned by Cardinal-Bishop Jacques de Vitry. Two further mitres were found upon the excavation of the graves of Archbishop Bernat d'Olivalla in Tarragona Cathedral (Spain) and of Archbishop Dom Gonçalo Pereira in Braga Cathedral (Portugal). All five were created in the late-twelfth or earlier thirteenth century in the style known as *opus anglicanum*, perhaps originating from a workshop at Canterbury itself. A further 'Becket mitre' hails from Anagni Cathedral (Italy). Vogt highlights the significance of a bishop's head, seen especially in the ritual of his consecration,

59 S. Caudron, 'La diffusion des chasses de saint Thomas Becket dans l'Europe médiévale', in *L'Œuvre de Limoges et sa diffusion: Trésors, objets, collections*, ed. D. Gaborit-Chopin and F. Sandron (Rennes, 2011), 23–41. See also Gauthier, 'Le meurtre dans la cathédrale'. On Benedict: E. King, 'Benedict (c. 1135–1193)', *ODNB* (Oxford, 2004) [http://www.oxforddnb.com/view/article/2081, accessed 4 November 2015]. Richard Gameson notes that some reliquaries, notably those housed in the Italian locations of Lucca Cathedral, the church of San Giovanni in Laterano, Rome, and Anagni Cathedral, are still in their original homes, although he is more cautious than Caudron as to the extent to which origins can be identified for other surviving examples: Gameson, 'Early Imagery', 48–9 and n. 12, 50–51.

signifying his role as Christ's vicar on earth. The depiction of the hand of God, descending from the point of the mitres, points first to the martyr, but also, by extension, to the wearer, the bishop himself.[60] Perhaps this stood as an example to the wearer, but also as a reminder to the viewer of the bishop's duty to protect his flock and defend the Church. Becket iconography can also be found in carved ivory adornments for churches, such as liturgical combs used on the hair of churchmen celebrating masses and performing roles in other services, as well as on plaques and diptychs.[61]

Historians have also considered different aspects of the enduring popularity of the cult, not least the way in which Becket retained political significance. In 1929, Josiah Cox Russell described St Thomas as the 'first and greatest' of 'the noteworthy series of contemporary anti-royal leaders who were honoured, partially at least, as saints'. 'In the person of Becket', Russell added, 'resistance to the king had been canonised'.[62] Later churchmen, for example Thomas's successors at Canterbury, Stephen Langton, Edmund Rich and Robert Winchelsey, either cultivated the image or were seen in terms of being Becket's heirs in the struggle with the crown for the freedom of the Church.[63]

Meanwhile, such 'political sainthood' can also be seen in the posthumous cults of a number of leading laymen who died in opposition to the ruler of their day.[64] In the case of Simon de Montfort, the sources incorporated accounts

---

60   C. Vogt, 'Episcopal Self-Fashioning: The Thomas Becket Mitres', in *Iconography of Liturgical Textiles in the Middle Ages*, ed. E. Wetter (Riggisberg, 2010), 117–28; C. T. Little, 'The Road to Glory: New Early Images of Thomas Becket's Life', in *Reading Medieval Images: The Art Historian and the Object*, ed. E. Sears and T. K. Thomas (Ann Arbor, MI, 2002), 201–11 at 210. See also Borenius, 'Iconography', 47 and plate xviii fig. 5; Borenius, *Becket in Art*, 83–4; Gameson, 'Early Imagery', 57 (plate 3), 58 (plate 4).

61   Little, 'The Road to Glory', 205–10; Borenius, 'Iconography', 47 and plate xviii; Borenius, *Becket in Art*, 24–5; Gameson, 'Early Imagery', 56 (plate 2).

62   J. C. Russell, 'The Canonisation of Opposition to the King in Angevin England', in *Anniversary Essays in Medieval History by Students of Charles Homer Haskins*, ed. C. H. Taylor (Boston, MA, 1929), 279–90 at 279–81.

63   See Russell, 'Canonisation of Opposition', 282. For more recent studies of Stephen Langton and Edmund Rich: Vincent, 'Langton'; C. H. Lawrence, *St Edmund of Abingdon: A Study in Hagiography and History* (Oxford, 1960); J. Creamer, 'St Edmund of Abingdon and Henry III in the Shadow of Thomas Becket', in *Thirteenth Century England XIV: Proceedings of the Aberystwyth and Lampeter Conference 2011*, ed. J. Burton, P. Schofield, and B. Weiler (Woodbridge, 2013), 129–39; Binski, *Becket's Crown*, 129–38. On Winchelsey: J. H. Denton, 'Winchelsey, Robert (c. 1240–1313)', *ODNB* (Oxford, 2004; online edn, 2008) [http://www.oxforddnb.com/view/article/29713, accessed 11 August 2015].

64   For an overview: Bartlett, *Saints*, 180–82; Webb, 165–79. This has become a rich field of historical study in recent years, as shown by: T. J. Heffernan, '"God hathe schewed ffor him many grete miracules": Political Canonization and the *Miracula* of Simon de Montfort', in *Art and Context in Late Medieval English Narrative: Essays in Honour of Robert Worth Frank, Jr.*, ed. R. R. Edwards (Cambridge, 1994), 177–91; J. R. Maddicott, 'Follower, Leader, Pilgrim, Saint: Robert de Vere, Earl of Oxford, at the Shrine of Simon de Montfort, 1273', *EHR*, 99 (1994), 641–53; D. Piroyansky, 'Bloody Miracles of a Political Martyr: The Case of Thomas Earl of Lancaster', in

of visions of St Thomas, or comparisons with Becket, to bolster the case for sanctity for a nobleman who died in opposition to the crown.[65] Contemporary chroniclers of Thomas of Lancaster depicted the archbishop as a father figure to his namesake, the earl. Both wrought posthumous cures through their blood (though in Lancaster's case the blood flowed from the tomb, rather than having been gathered up following the 'saint's' execution). Surviving wall-paintings show the martyrdom of the two Thomases together.[66] A number of bishops associated with lay reformers such as de Montfort, or with opposition to royal encroachments on perceived freedoms of the Church, could also be seen in this category, including Robert Grosseteste, Thomas Cantilupe and Richard of Wyche.[67] In the fourteenth century, Richard Scrope, archbishop of York, attracted posthumous veneration through the dubious distinction of being the first English bishop to suffer judicial execution, having joined with Percy's rebellion, in the process creating associations that allow him to be construed as a political saint who died for his opposition to the crown. Parallels with Becket were drawn, and Scrope was portrayed as St Thomas's brother in the struggle against royal authority. Like Canterbury's martyr, he also gained a reputation for protecting followers in trouble on or in water. In the context of the turbulence of the Wars of the Roses, Scrope could be seen as a Yorkist martyr, with the cult of Henry VI as a Lancastrian counterpoint. Here, however, there is evidence that the popularity of Thomas Becket was on the wane, with Henry VI's miracles deemed more efficacious, in particular that involving the cure of a baby who had choked after swallowing a Canterbury pilgrim badge![68]

The dangers of St Thomas Becket's potential as a political saint were not

Signs, Wonders, Miracles: Representations of Divine Power in the Life of the Church, ed. K. Cooper and J. Gregory, SCH, 41 (Woodbridge, 2005), 228–38; D. Piroyansky, *Martyrs in the Making: Political Martyrdom in Late Medieval England* (Basingstoke, 2008); J. M. Theilmann, 'Political Canonization and Political Symbolism in Medieval England', *Journal of British Studies*, 29 (1990), 241–66; C. Valente, 'Simon de Montfort, Earl of Leicester, and the Utility of Sanctity in Thirteenth-Century England', *Journal of Medieval History*, 21 (1995), 27–49; S. Walker, 'Political Saints in Later Medieval England', in *The McFarlane Legacy: Studies in Later Medieval Politics and Society*, ed. R. H. Britnell and A. J. Pollard (Stroud, 1995), 77–106.

65 'The Lament of Simon de Montfort', ed. T. Wright, *The Political Songs of England, From the Reign of John to that of Edward II*, Camden Society, Old Series, 6 (London, 1839), 125–7, at 125–6; Heffernan, '"God hath schewed ffor him many grete miracules"', 180.

66 'The Office of St Thomas of Lancaster', ed. T. Wright, *The Political Songs of England, From the Reign of John to that of Edward II*, Camden Society, Old Series, 6 (London, 1839), 268–72, at 268; Piroyansky, 'Bloody Miracles of a Political Martyr', 230–31; Piroyansky, *Martyrs in the Making*, 32, 35.

67 Webb, 165–6.

68 P. McNiven, 'Scrope, Richard (c. 1350–1405)', *ODNB* (Oxford, 2004; online edn, 2008) [http://www.oxforddnb.com/view/article/24964, accessed 5 Nov 2015]; Piroyansky, *Martyrs in the Making*, 49–73 (on Scrope), and see esp. 62, 70–71, although Piroyansky notes that Scrope's followers were not necessarily trying to create 'a new, northern Becket', 74–98 (on Henry VI),

lost on the Plantagenet kings, from Henry II onwards. Royal cults such as that of Edward the Confessor have been seen as a response, alongside (from the mid-fourteenth century), the rather unlikely sounding cult of Edward II.[69] Be that as it may, the crown could also develop ties with saints such as Thomas. Henry II – having realised that he must make a public expiation for his perceived guilt – sought an association with the cult which allowed him to claim that the martyr was in effect his spiritual friend.[70] His successors followed suit.[71] Historians have also recognised the way in which this trend extended into Europe. Here, marriages played a crucial role, in particular those of the daughters of Henry II and Eleanor of Aquitaine – Matilda, Eleanor and Joanna – and that of their daughter-in-law, Margaret (wife first of Henry the Young King then of King Bela III of Hungary).[72] Kay Brainerd Slocum argues that 'the female Plantagenets had a serious and well-defined political goal; they were determined to demonstrate to the world that the archbishop had forgiven his old enemy Henry II, and they wished to proclaim that their family was now firmly under the protection of the Canterbury martyr'.[73] An important reconsideration of the evidence here has been presented by Colette Bowie, who argues that in the case of Joanna, at least, the evidence is inconclusive. More positive conclusions can, however, be reached for Henry II's other daughters, providing the evidence is approached with care, whilst in the case of Margaret of France, devotion to St Thomas shown following her marriage to King Bela III of Hungary can be seen as an act of filial devotion to her father, Louis VII of France, himself closely involved in some of the prominent events of Becket's life, and in the invocation of his saintly intercession.[74] Overall, royal involvement with the cult of Canterbury's martyr is indicative of what Robert Bartlett describes as the 'radically depoliticising effect' of martyrdom,

esp. 79; J. W. McKenna, 'Popular Canonisation as Political Propaganda: The Cult of Archbishop Scrope', *Speculum*, 45 (1970), 608–23; Webb, 176–9.

69   For discussion of the cult of Edward the Confessor as part of a royal response to the 'antipodean rivalry which existed between Crown and Cross in England', see Lamia, 'The Cross and the Crown', 49. On the cult of Edward II: Webb, 172; Piroyansky, *Martyrs in the Making*, 100–104.

70   A. J. Duggan, 'Ne in dubium: The Official Record of Henry II's Reconciliation at Avranches, 21 May 1172', *EHR*, 115 (2000), 643–58; Duggan, 'Diplomacy'; T. K. Keefe, 'Shrine Time: King Henry II's Visits to Thomas Becket's Tomb', *Haskins Society Journal*, 11 (2003), 115–22.

71   Discussed in relation to Henry II's successors as king in the contributions by Anne J. Duggan (chapter 2) and Paul Webster (chapter 8) below. Also discussed in Lutan-Hassner, *Thomas Becket*, chapter 3. For Henry III, see also Binski, *Becket's Crown*, 138–46.

72   E. Jamison, 'The Alliance of England and Sicily in the Second Half of the 12th Century', *Journal of the Warburg and Courtauld Institutes*, 6 (1943), 20–32, at 23–9; Slocum, 'Marriage'; Lutan-Hassner, *Thomas Becket*, chapter 4.

73   Slocum, 'Marriage', 217.

74   C. Bowie, *The Daughters of Henry II and Eleanor of Aquitaine* (Turnhout, 2014), 141–72.

'with the blood of murdered kings, princes and bishops offering a unifying centre, around which former enemies could muster'. Bartlett sees St Thomas as a 'spectacular example' of this phenomenon, whilst Danna Piroyansky argues that the cult succeeded 'because Becket's sanctity was extended to his former enemies as well, offering patronage and protection to all the English people; it promoted ideas of repentance, remission and reconciliation'.[75]

In the later Middle Ages, whilst there were perhaps fewer pilgrims to Canterbury than in the peak years of the late-twelfth and thirteenth centuries, and there was a decline in the income recorded at the shrine of St Thomas, this may have reflected a world in which newer cults began to seem more effective. Criticism of, or doubt about Becket seem not to have been prevalent before the sixteenth century, although the Lollards 'nursed a particular resentment' for the saint.[76] Even this was not always put forward with consistency. Surprisingly, given the apparent enthusiasm with which his followers denounced Becket, it seems that one sermon by John Wyclif, attacking clerical greed, used Thomas as a positive example to the clergy.[77] A more usual pattern of devotion is suggested, however, in the way in which fifteenth-century boatmen on the Thames doffed their caps to an image of the saint incorporated into the tower (known as the Lollards' Tower because of those said to have been imprisoned there) of the archiepiscopal residence, Lambeth Palace.[78] Veneration of the saint by late medieval kings continued a tradition begun by their Angevin predecessors, as seen by Henry VII's gift to the shrine of a silver gilt statue portraying the king at prayer.[79] The evidence of early sixteenth-century stained glass surviving at York, depicting scenes from the legend surrounding Becket's parents and from the life of the saint himself, suggests enduring devotion on the eve of the Reformation. This is reinforced by the evidence of late medieval altar-dedications, wills and surviving chantry records.[80] In this context, Rachel

---

75 Bartlett, *Saints*, 182–3; Piroyansky, *Martyrs in the Making*, 13.

76 Bartlett, *Saints*, 595; Webb, 242–3; E. Duffy, *The Stripping of the Altars: Traditional Religion in England c. 1400–c. 1580* (New Haven, CT, and London, 1992), 195–6; Finucane, 210–11; P. Roberts, 'Politics, Drama and the Cult of Thomas Becket in the Sixteenth Century', in *Pilgrimage: The English Experience from Becket to Bunyan*, ed. C. Morris and P. Roberts (Cambridge, 2002), 199–237, at 201.

77 Roberts, *Thomas Becket in the Medieval Latin Preaching Tradition*, 140 (sermon 86). For the range of views of St Thomas more usually associated with those identified as Lollards: J. F. Davis, 'Lollards, Reformers and St Thomas of Canterbury', *University of Birmingham Historical Journal*, 9 (1963), 1–15.

78 Spencer, *Pilgrim Souvenirs*, 117; P. B. Roberts, 'The Unmaking of a Saint: The Suppression of the Cult of St Thomas of Canterbury', *Hagiographica*, 7 (2000), 35–46, at 35.

79 R. E. Scully, 'The Unmaking of a Saint: Thomas Becket and the English Reformation', *Catholic Historical Review*, 84 (2000), 579–602, at 585.

80 The series of thirteen scenes is dated by Rachel Koopmans to c.1525 or possibly the 1530s. They are now housed in the church of St Michael-le-Belfrey and in the chapter house of York Minister: Newton, 'Some New Material', 258–9; R. Koopmans, 'Early Sixteenth-Century Stained

Koopmans suggests that future research might usefully focus on the evidence of church fabric as a 'route into the question of the strength and visibility of Becket's cult … in the years before the English Reformation'.[81]

Henry VIII, despite having visited the shrine in 1520 with the emperor, Charles V, eventually allowed himself to be convinced that the archbishop was no saint but a treacherous rebel. Whilst he remained a believer in the intercession of saints as a means of saving the soul until well into the 1530s, he was ultimately persuaded to order the eradication of the cult of St Thomas.[82] In the ensuing anti-Becket propaganda, Thomas Cromwell promoted the notion that the archbishop's death was his own fault, because he had fallen into dispute not with the king but with the archbishop of York. The likes of William Tyndale, John Bale and John Foxe cast Becket in the light of anti-papal rhetoric, and did so with gusto.[83] Meanwhile, the Henrician reformers oversaw the destruction of almost all that stood in Becket's name in Canterbury Cathedral, with the notable exception of the stained glass in the Trinity Chapel. Whether the bones themselves were unceremoniously thrown away (perhaps even burnt), or in some way concealed, their whereabouts are no longer known. The Reformation also witnessed a wider effort to strike Becket's image from churches and his name from the liturgy.[84] Peter Roberts observes that 'the attack … was added at the last moment', but adds that this should not be construed as evidence of reluctance on the part of Henry VIII, given the king's presence at Canterbury at the time when the shrine was demolished.[85] Historians note that the evidence of surviving manuscripts provides

Glass at St Michael-le-Belfrey and the Commemoration of Thomas Becket in Late Medieval York', *Speculum*, 80 (2014), 1040–1100, with dating discussed at 1049.

81   Koopmans, 'Early Sixteenth-Century Stained Glass', 1099.

82   On the Reformation and post-Reformation Becket, see Roberts, 'Politics, Drama and the Cult of Thomas Becket'; Scully, 'The Unmaking of a Saint'; V. Houliston, 'St Thomas Becket in the Propaganda of the English Counter-Reformation', *Renaissance Studies*, 7 (1993), 43–70; Roberts, 'The Unmaking of a Saint'. In addition to what follows, see also the discussion in Anne J. Duggan's essay below, chapter 2.

83   Roberts, 'Thomas Becket: The Construction and Deconstruction of a Saint', 13–14; Roberts, 'The Unmaking of a Saint'; Houliston, 'St Thomas Becket', 44–6; Roberts, 'Politics, Drama, and the Cult of Thomas Becket', 222–6.

84   Finucane, 201, 210–12; Bartlett, *Saints*, 87; Slocum, '*Martir quod Stillat Primatis ab Ore Sigillat*', 74; Roberts, 'Thomas Becket: The Construction and Deconstruction of a Saint', 17–19; Gelin, *Lumen ad revelationem gentium*, 154–5; Scully, 'The Unmaking of a Saint', 593–7. On the fate of Becket's bones: J. Butler, *The Quest for Becket's Bones: The Mystery of the Relics of St Thomas of Canterbury* (New Haven, CT, and London, 1995); T. F. Mayer, 'Becket's Bones Burnt! Cardinal Pole and the Invention and Dissemination of an Atrocity', in *Martyrs and Martyrdom in England, c. 1400–1700*, ed. T. S. Freeman and T. F. Mayer (Woodbridge, 2007), 126–43. On the wider eradication of the shrines of the saints in England: Nilson, 191–3; Webb, 250–61, with Becket's shrine discussed at 259–60; Crook, *English Medieval Shrines*, 289–303, with Becket's shrine discussed at 300.

85   Roberts, 'Politics, Drama, and the Cult of Thomas Becket', 215–16, 226–7 (including the quotation at 227).

dozens of examples of how such erasures actually took place. Contrasting opinions have been put forward. Paul Binski describes 'a massive level of systematic destruction which erased St Thomas's image from the domain of English visual culture with Stalinist zeal'. On the other hand, Eamon Duffy notes evidence that service books were 'reformed half-heartedly', adding that images in churches were craftily adapted so that what once had appeared to be St Thomas was now a different saint.[86] In one such image, Borenius suggests, the disguise was effected by turning Becket from holy man to holy woman.[87] Cardinal Pole promoted efforts to revive the cult under Mary and was himself buried in the saint's chapel at Canterbury Cathedral, following his death in 1558. Perhaps tellingly, however, although St Thomas was restored to the calendar of saints, the Marian regime did not attempt to resurrect the shrine, and records survive which show that not everyone was content to see images of the saint restored to churches. The Henrician efforts to expunge the cult continued as part of the Elizabethan settlement of the Church.[88] In this new religious world, Becket did not die a martyr's death, but as 'a stubborn man against his king'.[89]

Whether the Tudor efforts were entirely successful is open to question. Although writers like John Foxe 'constructed the image of Becket the character actor, which surfaces from time to time in modern historiography', equally St Thomas became a symbol for English Catholics persevering in their faith and for their European supporters. Surviving medallions depict Thomas Becket on one side and Thomas More on the other. Recusant writers in England penned works in Becket's defence. He remained a focus for the devotions of the Jesuit missionaries setting out to play their part in the maintenance of the Catholic faith in England.[90] His intercession was also anticipated in support of the Catholic king of England, James II, and his queen, Mary

86 Duffy, *Stripping of the Altars*, 418–20, and see also plates 131–2, for examples of a defaced painting and lightly crossed-through manuscripts; Binski, *Becket's Crown*, 165. See also: D. MacCulloch, *Thomas Cranmer* (New Haven, CT, and London, 1996), 227–9; Borenius, *Becket in Art*, 23, 109–10; Roberts, 'Politics, Drama, and the Cult of Thomas Becket', 204 (fig. 30, a defaced manuscript of a life of St Thomas which once belonged to Archbishop Cranmer), 228–9, 231–3; S. J. Biggs, 'Erasing Becket', *British Library Medieval Manuscripts Blog* [http://britishlibrary.typepad.co.uk/digitisedmanuscripts/2011/09/erasing-becket.html, accessed 31 December 2015]; Scully, 'The Unmaking of a Saint', 597.
87 Borenius, 'Some Further Aspects', 182 and plate L (fig. 3).
88 Slocum, '*Martir quod Stillat Primatis ab Ore Sigillat*', 81–4; Finucane, 213–14; Borenius, *Becket in Art*, 111; Roberts, 'Politics, Drama, and the Cult of Thomas Becket', 233–5; Houliston, 'St Thomas Becket', 44; Roberts, 'Thomas Becket: The Construction and Deconstruction of a Saint', 19; Scully, 'The Unmaking of a Saint', 599–600.
89 Slocum, '*Martir quod Stillat Primatis ab Ore Sigillat*', 84; Duggan, *Thomas Becket*, 239; both quoting Foxe's 'Book of Martyrs'.
90 Borenius, *Becket in Art*, 30–31; Duggan, *Thomas Becket*, 239–42 with the quotation at 240; Houliston, 'St Thomas Becket', 49–70; Roberts, 'Politics, Drama, and the Cult of Thomas

of Modena, following the revolution of 1688.[91] Thus, there was a place for St Thomas in the era of the Counter-Reformation.

In more recent centuries, debate and opinion regarded Thomas and his cult have been played out against the backdrop of the differing opinions of 'High Church' Anglicans and their opponents, laced with spirited rivalry and disagreement amongst a number of the antiquarians involved in the discovery and editing of some of the principle sources in the nineteenth century.[92] There has also been what might be described as something of a literary and theatre-based cult of Henry II's nemesis.[93] Tennyson wrote a play, *Becket*, although this failed to find a theatre that would perform it. T. S. Eliot published *Murder in the Cathedral* in 1935, and the French playwright Jean Anouilh produced his *Becket, ou l'honneur de Dieu* in 1959.[94] The events of 1170 are also recalled in the 1964 film *Becket*, an adaptation of Anouilh's work, starring Richard Burton in the role of the archbishop.[95] The actor Robert Speaight, who played Thomas in a stage version of Eliot's work, performing the role more than a thousand times in Britain and North America, was inspired to write a biography of the saint 'for the ordinary reader'.[96] Even in the twenty-first century, the events at Canterbury in December 1170 have inspired the writing of opera, with the performance *King* staged in the cathedral in 2006.[97]

From the theatre of politics and religion in the late twelfth century, through

Becket', 235–7; Scully, 'The Unmaking of a Saint', 600. See also Anne J. Duggan's essay below, chapter 2.

91 Borenius, 'Addenda to the Iconography of St Thomas', 30–31.

92 See Vincent, 'William of Canterbury and Benedict of Peterborough', 349–56, 364. Anglican attitudes to St Thomas in the 1970s and '80s are discussed in Scully, 'The Unmaking of a Saint', 601.

93 The following examples present just a few of very many. A survey of St Thomas's place in drama and literature from the Reformation to the 1960s is presented in H. Nordahl and J. W. Dietrichson, *Menneske, Myte, Motiv: Erkebiskop Thomas Becket i historie og diktning* (Oslo, 1980), 148–307, with an English summary at 313–19 (esp. 315–19). See also J.-M. Grassin, 'Le mythe littéraire de Thomas Becket a l'époque moderne', in *Sédières*, 285–97, including at 290–91 a list of literature, theatre and, from the 1920s onward, films, depicting Thomas, penned and produced between the 1530s and 1970.

94 Barlow, 'Becket, Thomas'; Duggan, *Thomas Becket*, 1. Also discussed in Nordahl and Dietrichson, *Menneske, Myte, Motiv*, 208–24, 265–92.

95 'Becket (1964)', *Internet Movie Database* [http://www.imdb.com/title/tt0057877/, accessed 24 July 2015]; Duggan,*Thomas Becket*, 1.

96 R. Speaight, *Thomas Becket*, 2nd edn (London, 1949). On Speaight: P. Johnson, 'Speaight, Robert William (1904–1976)', *ODNB* (Oxford, 2004; online edn, 2011) [http://www.oxforddnb.com/view/article/31704, accessed 24 July 2015]. My thanks to Peter Jackson Eastwood, whose dissertation research prompted questions that led me to this information.

97 The making of this opera is discussed by M. Church, 'The Shocking Death of Thomas Becket is Brought to Life in Opera', *The Independent*, Tuesday 28 February 2006 [http://www.independent.co.uk/the-shocking-death-of-thomas-becket-is-brought-to-life-in-an-opera-6108168.html, accessed 16 July 2016]. The work is also mentioned in Duggan, *Thomas Becket*, viii (preface), and see also *ibid.* 1, where Duggan notes the earlier existence of Becket-themed opera, in the form of

his substantial cultural impact in the medieval world, to his place in modern day literature, on the stage and on screen, Thomas Becket – archbishop, martyr and saint – has proved himself an enduring figure. In 1931, the art historian Tancred Borenius observed that, 'Some day, perhaps, a book will be written dealing exhaustively with the subject of the cult of St Thomas Becket from all its aspects: and there can be no doubt that it would be a most important contribution towards the study and interpretation of medieval civilization.'[98] As this chapter has shown, a wide range of important studies have illuminated numerous aspects of the cult and its presentation in the decades since Borenius wrote. It is now improbable that a single volume could adequately encompass the diverse range of material in which we discern evidence of the cult and its influence across the Middle Ages and beyond. Here, the objective is to examine the development and impact of the cult in the first half-century of its existence. As will be seen, the available sources, and the impact of the cult, are considerable, seen in evidence ranging from miracle collections and chronicles to charters and letters, and from stained-glass windows to sculpture and illuminated manuscripts. Taken together, these shed new light on the Becket phenomenon within the world from which it had been created. As we approach the eight-hundredth anniversary of the translation of the saint's relics to their dominant position within the cathedral church at Canterbury, which owes so much to the cult of St Thomas, the essays in this volume seek to contribute to the appreciation of the enduring significance of one of the most notable figures of the medieval world.

the 1958 piece *L'assassinio nella cattedrale*, composed by Ildebrando Pizzetti and based on a translation of Eliot's play.
98 Borenius, *Becket in Art*, x.

2.

Becket is Dead! Long Live St Thomas

ANNE J. DUGGAN

As Hugh of Horsea (nicknamed Mauclerc) scraped Becket's brains out on the paving stones in the north transept of Canterbury Cathedral on the fifth day of Christmas (29 December) 1170, he shouted to the barons who had just cut the archbishop of Canterbury down in his own cathedral, 'Let's get out of here, knights, this one won't get up again.'[1] At that point, he can have had no inkling of what the future was to hold for his four baronial colleagues,[2] the king in whose name they claimed to have acted and, of course, for the disparaged victim. Despite King Henry's best efforts to smother the story and assume the guise of injured innocence,[3] the raw news was carried by an unknown messenger not only to the French royal court, but also to William *aux blanchesmains*, archbishop of Sens. The intelligence reached the French archbishop in time for him to summon a council of his province for Sunday, 24 January 1171, so that an appropriate response could be made. So it was that the details of Becket's murder were proclaimed before an assembly of bishops and abbots from the heartland of the French monarchy,[4] and through them the news would have circulated rapidly through the various monastic

---

1 'Abeamus hinc, milites, iste ulterius non resurget': Edward Grim, *MTB*, ii, 438. Benedict of Peterborough, who was present in the cathedral, recorded it differently (*MTB*, ii, 13): 'Mortuus est, quantocius eamus hinc'; and so did Anonymous I ('Roger of Pontigny'), who was not present (*MTB*, iv, 77): 'Eamus, mortuus est enim proditor'. For the other descriptions, without the reported speech, see William of Canterbury, *Miracula* (*MTB*, i, 135), John of Salisbury, *Vita* (*MTB*, ii, 320), William Fitz Stephen, *Vita* (*MTB*, iii, 142), and Anonymous II ('the Lambeth Anonymous', *MTB*, iv, 142).
2 Vincent, 'Murderers', 211–72.
3 See the letters to the pope from Arnulf of Lisieux and King Henry, *Cum apud regem* and *Ob reverentiam*, *MTB*, vii, 438–9 no. 738, and 440 no. 739; cf. Duggan, 'Diplomacy', 266–71. Henry sent an impressive embassy to present his case: two bishops (Roger of Worcester and Giles of Évreux), one abbot (Richard, abbot of Le Valasse in Normandy), two archdeacons (Reginald of Salisbury and R., either Robert of Lisieux or Robert of Arden), one dean (Robert of Neufbourg, dean of Évreux), two royal clerks (Richard Barre and Master Henry of Northampton) and an unnamed Templar.
4 The province of Sens comprised seven dioceses: Auxerre, Chartres, Meaux, Nevers, Orléans, Paris and Troyes, with numerous important priories and monasteries. William's report (below, n. 6) named four abbots: St-Denis (dioc. Paris), OSB; St-Germain-des-Prés (dioc. Paris), OSA;

and episcopal networks with which they were connected. Equally importantly, William of Sens executed the mandate of October 1170, in which Pope
Alexander III ordered the imposition of an interdict on Henry II's continental
lands ('in tota terra ejus cismarina') if the king failed to make good his undertaking at Fréteval to restore the archbishop's estates as they had been before
his departure.[5] Normandy escaped the ban because, as Archbishop William
explained to the pope, his colleague, Rotrou of Rouen, refused to impose the
sentence in his own Norman province.[6]

William's report, together with a personal letter and a dossier of protests
from the French court, was then carried by two of Becket's clerks (Alexander
of Wales and Gunther of Winchester) all the way through France to the papal
court in Tusculum (Frascati), no doubt broadcasting the news to every town,
bishopric and abbey through which they passed.[7] The letters they carried
all conveyed much the same message, but Louis VII's short communication
summed up the consensus with pithy clarity. It called on Alexander III 'to
unsheathe the sword of St Peter' to avenge 'the martyr of Canterbury', whose
'blood cries out for the universal Church, wailing aloud for vengeance, not
only for itself but for the whole Church'. Louis had heard that 'God's grace
is being revealed through miracles' at the tomb,[8] and he urged the pope to
believe the account of the abominable deed related by the bearers of the
letter. The envoys reached Tusculum before King Henry's embassy, and
their testimony, supported by the protests from France and also by Becket's
last letter to the pope (c.5 December 1170), detailing the difficulties he was
encountering in England,[9] ensured that the royal envoys received a hostile
reception.[10] Sweeping aside the excuses made on Henry II's behalf, Alexander
excommunicated the murderers and, although he was dissuaded from inter-
dicting the English kingdom, he imposed a personal interdict on King Henry
himself, which denied him entry to a church until he had made satisfaction.[11]

Pontigny (dioc. Auxerre), O.Cist.; and the unidentified 'Wallacensis', possibly Le Val-Secret
(dioc. Soissons, prov. Reims), Premon.

5   MTB, vii, 376–7 no. 710 (dated Anagni, 9 October 1170), at 377, to Archbishops William of
Sens and Rotrou of Rouen. A further letter, MTB, vii, 383–4 no. 715 (Segni, 13 October 1170),
mandated the prelates in Henry's continental lands (per terram regis Anglie cismarinam) to obey
such an interdict if it were imposed.

6   MTB, vii, 440–43 no. 740, at 443; Rotrou's notification is ibid., 445–6 no. 742.

7   Vestro apostolatui and Inter scribendum haec (William of Sens): MTB, vii, 440–43, 429–33 nos.
740 and 735; Ab humanae pietatis (Louis VII) and Vestrae placuit majestati (Theobald of Blois):
MTB, vii, 428–9 and 433–5 nos. 734 and 736.

8   MTB, vii, 428–9 no. 734, at 428: 'denudetur gladius Petri in ultionem Cantuariensis
martyris, quia sanguis ejus pro universali clamat ecclesia, non tam sibi, quam universae ecclesiae
conquerens de vindicta … ad tumulum agonistae … divina in miraculis revelatur gratia'.

9   Quam iustis: CTB, ii, 1344–55 no. 326 (MTB, vii, no. 723).

10 See their reports: Noverit vestra and Qui fuerint: MTB, vii, 471–8 nos. 750–51.

11 Ibid., no. 751, at 477–8; Duggan, 'Diplomacy', 270–71.

Not very much later, but certainly after Easter 1171, John of Salisbury sent a circular letter (*Ex insperato*) to friends and contacts in France, which described the murder and the beginning of the miracles at the tomb and rhetorically asked whether Thomas should be prayed for or to.[12] This important letter was certainly circulated through Abbot Peter of Celle's extensive friendship network, which extended throughout France and into the Scandinavian kingdoms,[13] and it was also probably broadcast through Poitou and perhaps Aquitaine by Bishop John of Poitiers, another known recipient, who had been one of Becket's colleagues in Theobald's household, and had remained a friend.[14]

The impact of this letter can scarcely be overestimated. Not only did it circulate widely through France and the Nordic lands, but recipients seized upon it as an authentic account of martyrdom. Evidence of its adaptation as a *passio* survives in lectionaries from Cîteaux, Clermont-Ferrand, Marchiennes and Reims, for example, and in the ancient monasteries of Moissac and St-Martial-de-Limoges it was divided into eight lections for liturgical reading.[15] A year or so later (1171–72), John himself expanded the core of the letter into his own *passio* and it, too, circulated across the network of monastic and episcopal churches, before being incorporated into monastic lectionaries from Jumièges and Lyre (Normandy) to Paris, Clairvaux, Pontigny (France and Burgundy) and Heiligenkreuz (Austria).[16] Meanwhile, the Canterbury monks presented their own petition for Becket's canonisation and Pope Alexander commissioned the two legates who were entrusted with the task of reconciling King Henry to investigate the claims that miracles were occurring at his

---

12 *The Letters of John of Salisbury, Volume II: The Later Letters 1163–1180*, ed. and trans. W. J. Millor and C. N. L. Brooke, OMT (Oxford, 1979), 724–38 no. 305 (cf. *MTB*, vii, 462–70 no. 748). The arguments of K. Bollermann and C. J. Nederman, 'John of Salisbury and Thomas Becket', in *A Companion to John of Salisbury*, ed. C. Grellard and F. Lachaud, Brill's Companions to the Christian Tradition, 57 (Leiden, 2015), 63–104, at 84, that *Ex insperato* was written 'between October 1171 and April 1172' are not convincing.

13 *Stylum scribendi: The Letters of Peter of Celle*, ed. and trans. J. Haseldine, OMT (Oxford, 2001), 658–63 no. 171, at 662–3.

14 For a fuller discussion of the role of international networks, see A. J. Duggan, 'Religious Networks in Action: the European Expansion of the Cult of St Thomas of Canterbury', in *International Religious Networks*, ed. J. Gregory and H. McLeod, SCH Subsidia, 14 (Woodbridge, 2012), 20–43.

15 Dijon, Bibl. mun. MSS 574, fols 115v–116v and 646, fols 274r–276v (Cîteaux); Clermont-Ferrand, Bibl. mun. MS 148, fol. 255; Douai, Bibl. mun. MS 838, fol. 196 (Marchiennes); Reims, Bibl. mun. MS 502, fols 7r–10r (St-Rémi); Paris, BnF. MSS lat. 2098, fols 159v–163v (Moissac) and lat. 5347, fols 144r–145r + 162r–164r (St-Martial-de-Limoges).

16 Rouen, Bibl. mun. MS U. 24 (cat. 1402), 140r–147r (Jumièges); Évreux, Bibl. de la Ville, MS lat. 10, fols 1r–7r (Lyre); Paris, Bibl. de l'Arsenal, MS 938, fols 9r–16 (St-Victor); Paris, Bibl. Ste-Geneviève, MS cc.1 in quarto 19 (cat. 1370), fols 63r–70r (Ste-Geneviève); Montpellier, Bibliothèque inter-universitaire, section médecine (formerly École de Médecine), cod. 2, fols 1ra–5rb (Clairvaux); London, BL, MS Egerton 2818 (formerly Phillipps 10227), fols 71ra–78vb (Pontigny); Heiligenkreuz, Stiftsbibliothek, Cod. 209, fols 75vb–84vb and 213, fols 88r–99r.

tomb.[17] They submitted a favourable report, supported by a dossier of miracles (perhaps Benedict of Peterborough's Book I),[18] following which the pope declared that Thomas was a saint and martyr (Segni, 21 February 1173) and ordered the universal celebration of his feast in letters dated from 12 March onwards.[19] Allowing around six weeks for the letters to reach Canterbury, the monks had more than six months to prepare for the celebration of the martyr's feast on 29 December 1173, the third anniversary of his murder.

The Liturgical Becket

There are good reasons to argue that the principal responsibility for composing the text and music for the feast was committed to the monk Benedict, who had been recording the miracles attributed to Becket's intercession since mid-1171.[20] This monk, who was successively prior of Canterbury (1175–77)

---

17 *Decretales ineditae saeculi XII*, ed. and revised S. Chodorow and C. Duggan, Monumenta Iuris Canonici Series B: Corpus Collectionum, 4 (Vatican City, 1982), 61–2 no. 36, *Dilecti filii nostri*, to Albert, Cardinal Priest of S. Lorenzo in Lucina and Theodwin, Cardinal Priest of S. Vitale, probably autumn 1171.

18 Below, at nn. 20 and 21.

19 MTB, vii, 545–6: 'Nos autem, considerata gloria meritorum quibus in vita sua magnanimiter claruit, et de miraculis ejus non solum communi et celebri fama, sed etiam dilectorum filiorum nostrorum Alberti titulo Sancti Laurentii in Lucina, et Theodwini, titulo Sancti Vitalis, presbyterorum cardinalium, ... testimonio certitudinem plenam habentes ...' (from *Gaudendum est*, addressed to Christ Church, Canterbury, 12 March 1173); cf. *ibid.*, 547–8: 'auditis innumeris et magnis miraculis quae jugiter per sancti illius viri merita fieri universitas narrat fidelium, et super his, non sine magno gaudio, per dilectos filios nostros Albertum ... et Theoduinum ... qui eadem miracula tanto perspicacius didicerunt ...' (from *Redolet Anglia*, addressed to the clergy and people of England, 12 March 1173); and *ibid.*, 549–50: 'et sub nomine ipsius multa quotidie miraculorum signa non cessat operari ... praesertim commonitione ... Alberti ... et Theodini ... qui exinde veritatem plenius investigaverant et visu et auditu cognoverant ...' (from *Qui vice beati Petri*, addressed to various recipients in Western Europe, March 1173). For the canonisation process, see R. Foreville, 'Alexandre III et la canonisation des Saints', in *Miscellanea Rolando Bandinelli: Papa Alessandro III*, ed. F. Liotta (Siena, 1986), 217–36 at 230–32.

20 BP, *Miracula*, 21–281. For the transmission of Benedict's 'great book' to continental Europe, see A. J. Duggan, 'The Lorvão Transcription of Benedict of Peterborough's *Liber miraculorum beati Thome*: Lisbon, cod. Alcobaça CCXC/143', *Scriptorium*, 51 (1997), 51–68 and *eadem*, 'The Santa Cruz Transcription of Benedict of Peterborough's *Liber miraculorum beati Thome*: Porto, BPM, cod. Santa Cruz 143', *Mediaevalia. Textos e estudos*, 20 (Porto, 2001), 27–55; both repr. with the same pagination in Duggan, *Friends, Networks*, nos XII and XIII. See also, P. Lenz, 'Construire un recueil de miracles: les *Miracula sancti Thomae Cantuariensis* de Benoît de Peterborough' (unpublished Ph.D. thesis, University of Geneva, 2003). Benedict's 'Great Book of Miracles' was joined by another, compiled from mid-1172 by his confrère William of Canterbury, *Miracula S. Thomae Cantuariensis, auctore Willelmo, monacho Cantuariensis*, MTB, i, 137–546. The composition, dating and relationship between the collections is discussed in R. Koopmans, *Wonderful to Relate: Miracle Stories and Miracle Collecting in High Medieval England* (Philadelphia, PA, 2011), 125–200, esp. 139–58. For a summary analysis of the miracles, see *ibid.*, 205–10; cf. R. Foreville,

and abbot of Peterborough (1177–93),[21] made extensive use of John of Salisbury's *Vita* to compose the twelve lections for the great night office (Matins) which formed the core of the monastic celebration of the feast. The result was a minor rhetorical masterpiece, expressing both the horror of the sacrilege and the glorious triumph of the martyr through death. The circumstances of the 'murder in the cathedral' provided a fertile range of image and symbol: the place, before an altar in the principal church in England as monks were preparing to chant Vespers; the season, on the fifth day of Christmas, following the feasts of St Stephen and the Holy Innocents, the first martyrs of the Christian Church; the victim, primate of England; the agents, servants of one of the most powerful monarchs in Christendom; and the cause, defence of the honour and dignity of the Church. The outrage in the cathedral was all the more horrifying because it was carried out by Christian knights in the name of a Christian king: the priest slain by members of his own flock in the sacred place of sacrifice. All this, and more, was captured in Benedict's lections.

At the heart of the *passio* is the murder itself, succinctly described in graphic and memorable detail:[22]

On the fifth day of the Lord's Nativity there came to Canterbury four courtiers, men of distinguished birth, forsooth, but notorious for their misdeeds. [...] The devil's henchmen, in mail, pursued him from behind with drawn swords. [...] The ravening wolves threw themselves upon the pious pastor, degenerate sons against their own father, most pitiless executioners against the Lord's anointed:

'Les "Miracula S. Thomae Cantuariensis"', in *Actes du 97e Congrès National des Sociétés Savants, Nantes 1972, Section de Philologie et d'histoire jusqu'à 1610* (Paris, 1979), 443–68.

21 D. Knowles, C. N. L. Brooke, and V. C. M. London (eds), *The Heads of Religious Houses: England and Wales 940–1216* (Cambridge, 1972; repr. 2001), 34, 61.

22 No copy of the original Canterbury liturgy survives, having fallen victim to the Henrician decree (below, at n. 128), but the great breviary compiled for Salisbury in the early thirteenth century transmits a 'secular' variant, where Becket's murder is described in Lectio V: *Breviarium ad usum insignis ecclesiae Sarum*, ed. F. Proctor and C. Wordsworth, 3 vols (Cambridge, 1879–86), i (1882), ccxlv–cclx, at cclii–ccliii: 'Quinto uero Dominicae nativitatis die, veniunt Cantuariarm aulici quatuor, viri quidem praeclari genere, sed malefactis famosi. [...] Sequuntur a tergo gladiis extractis Sathanae satellites loricati, armatorum manu multa sequente. [...] Irruentes igitur in pastorem pium lupi rapaces, in patrem proprium degeneres filii, in hostiam Christi crudelissimi lictores: consecratam capitis coronam funestis gladiis amputaverunt, et christum Domini solotenus precipitantes, cerebrum cum sanguine (quod dictu quoque horrendum est) per pavimentum crudelissime sparserunt. Sic itaque granum frumenti oppressit palea, sic vineae custos in vinea, dux in castris, in caulis pastor, cultor in area caesus est: sic iustus ab iniustis occisus domum luteam caelesti palatio commutauit.' For the full Sarum liturgy, with the music and disappointing translations, see Slocum, *Liturgies*, 209–22; cf. S. Reames, 'Liturgical Offices for the Cult of St Thomas Becket', in *Medieval Hagiography: An Anthology*, ed. T. [F.] Head (New York, 2000), 561–93. For a splendid discussion of the transmission and significance of the Translation Office, see S. Reames, 'Reconstructing and Interpreting a Thirteenth-Century Office for the Translation of Thomas Becket', *Speculum*, 80 (2005), 118–70.

they cut off the consecrated crown of his head with their bloody swords and, casting the Lord's anointed onto the ground, they most callously scattered his brains and blood upon the pavement – a thing most terrible, even to say. Thus did the chaff overwhelm the grain of corn; thus was slain the vine-keeper in the vineyard, the leader in the camp, the shepherd in the fold, the labourer on the threshing-floor; thus the just man, murdered by the unjust, exchanged a house of clay for a heavenly palace. [trans. AJD]

These words fixed an unforgettable image in the minds of all who heard or read them. By the mid-thirteenth century, they had found their way into the Old Norse *Thómas Saga Erkibyskups*.[23] Further, the new St Thomas was set firmly in the tradition of biblical martyrs, like Zachariah (Zechariah), who was stoned to death in the court of the Temple on the orders of King Jehoash (Joas) of Judah, for condemning those, including the king, who 'had transgressed the commandment of the Lord'.[24] Thomas became 'another Abel', whose blood forever cried out to heaven:[25]

For the voice of the blood spilt, the cry of the brains scattered by the bloody swords of the devil's henchmen filled both earth and heaven with reverberating clamour. [...] The earth trembled and was shaken by the cry of this blood, and the powers of heaven, too, were so moved that as if in vengeance for the spilling of innocent blood, people rose up against people and kingdom against kingdom – rather, the realm was divided against itself, and fearful sights and great signs appeared from the sky. [trans. AJD]

These powerful images were amplified in the sequence of antiphons and responsories composed to adorn the lections and psalms in the office (*historia*).[26]

23 *Thómas Saga Erkibyskups: A Life of Archbishop Thomas Becket in Icelandic*, with English translation, notes and glossary, ed. and trans. E. Magnússon, RS 65, 2 vols (London, 1875–84), i, 544–5. Cf. A. J. Duggan, 'Eystein, Thomas Becket, and the Wider Christian World', in *Eystein Erlendsson: erkebiskop, politiker og kirkebygger*, ed. K. Bjørlykke, Øystein Ekroll, *et al.* (Trondheim, 2012) 26–43, at 32. Note, however, that the Saga compilers used *Quadrilogus II*, and did not transmit the Saracen legend.
24 2 Chronicles (Paralipomenon), 24: 20–21.
25 Genesis, 4: 8–10; *Breviarium ... Sarum*, i, cclvii–cclviii, Lections VIII and IX: 'Vox enim sanguinis effusi, vox cerebri funestorum satellitum gladiis dispersi, et mundum simul et celum celebri clamore complevit. [...] Acclamore [recte A clamore] namque sanguinis hujus commota est et contremuit terra, sed et virtutes caelorum motae sunt, adeo ut quasi in ultionem sanguinis innocentis surgeret gens contra gentem, et regnum adversum regnum, immo ut regnum in seipsum fieret divisum: terroresque de caelo et signa magna fierent.' The description echoes Christ's prophecy of the last days in Luke, 21: 10–11: 'Surget gens contra gentem, et regnum adversus regnum ... terroresque de caelo, et signa magna erunt.'
26 The monastic *cursus* of antiphons and responsories has been reconstructed from twenty-five manuscripts and early printed books in *Analecta Hymnica medii aevi*, ed. C. Blume, G. Dreves, and H. M. Bannister, 55 vols (Leipzig, 1886–1922), xiii, 238–42. For the music, see D. Stevens,

The seventh responsory in the monastic *cursus* (*Mundi florem*), for example, interwove biblical images with the notion of outrage giving way to triumph:[27]

> R. Rachel, bewailing
> the flower of the world crushed by the world,
> has now ceased to lament.
> As Thomas, cut down,
> is given up for burial,
> a new Abel succeeds the old.
>
> V. The voice of the blood, the voice of the scattered brain,
> fills heaven with resounding clamour. [trans. AJD]

The biblical Rachel, mother of the Joseph who was sold into slavery in Egypt by his brothers,[28] here personifies the English Church, whose lamentation for Becket's murder – crushed by 'the world', meaning the secular power – is cut short by the realisation that his death makes him an Abel for his own time: the symbol of justice cut down by the unjust. In writing this verse, Benedict may have had in mind Peter Abelard's hymn on the Holy Innocents, *Est in Rama vox audita* ('A voice was heard in Rama'), which in turn echoed St Matthew's poignant quotation of Jeremiah's prophecy: 'Vox in Rama audita est ploratus et ululatus multus Rachel plorans filios suos' ('A voice was heard in Rama, grievously weeping and wailing, Rachel lamenting for her sons'),[29] where Rachel personified Israel weeping for its slaughtered children. Exactly two hundred years later, Thomas Brinton, the reforming bishop of Rochester, quoted the same responsory *verbatim* in a sermon preached at Rochester on St Thomas's feast, 29 December 1373.[30] The multi-layered image of justice

'Music in Honour of St Thomas of Canterbury', *The Musical Quarterly*, 56 (1970), 311–38; *idem*, 'Thomas Becket et la musique médiévale', in *Sédières*, 277–84; A. Hughes, 'Chants in the Rhymed Office of St Thomas of Canterbury', *Early Music*, 16 (1988), 185–201; *idem*, 'Rhymed Offices', *Dictionary of the Middle Ages*, x (New York, 1989), 367, 370–71; *idem*, 'British Rhymed Offices: A Catalogue and Commentary', in *Music in the Medieval English Liturgy*, ed. S. Rankin and D. Hiley (Oxford, 1993), 239–84, at 258, 262, 275–8. The liturgical meaning of *historia* is explored by R. Jonsson, *Historia: Études sur la genèse des offices versifiés*, Studia Latina Stockholmiensis, 15 (Stockholm, 1968), esp. 1–17. One of the earliest surviving witnesses to the office, with musical notation, is Edinburgh, University Library, MS 123, fols 155v–158r, ?originally from Metz (Meticuriensis). Inexplicably, not used by Slocum.

27 *Breviarium ... Sarum*, i, ccliii, *Responsory* 5 = no. 7 in the monastic *cursus* (*Analecta Hymnica*, xiii, 239, 2nd nocturn, no. 3): *Mundi florem a mundo conteri*, | *Rachel plorans jam cessa conqueri*. | *Thomas caesus dum datur funeri*: | *novus Abel succedit veteri*. Versus. *Vox cruoris, vox sparsi cerebri*: | *caelum replet clamore celebri*.

28 Genesis 30: 22–4, 37, 39–50; 37: 1–36, etc.

29 Matthew 2: 18; cf. Jeremiah 30 [31]: 15.

30 *The Sermons of Thomas Brinton (1373–1389)*, ed. Sr M. Aquinas Devlin, 2 vols, Camden Third Series, 85–6 (London, 1954), i, 122.

betrayed and innocence destroyed was completed by St John's parable of the Good Shepherd who lays down his life for his sheep – an image amplified by the opening of St Gregory's homily on the gospel text.[31]

In his liturgy for St Thomas's feast, Benedict of Canterbury constructed a particularly potent image of the martyred archbishop; and it was this image that was carried across the whole of Europe, to Trondheim in Norway, where it was incorporated into the *Ordo Nidrosiensis* before the end of the twelfth century;[32] to the papal court, where it was imbedded in the celebration of the new martyr's day;[33] and from the papal court it was received by the Franciscans and Dominicans as they constructed their own distinctive liturgies in the early thirteenth century. Benedict's Thomas Office thus became one of the most widely-distributed rhymed offices of the Middle Ages, 'found in manuscripts from Finland to Hungary at least until the sixteenth century',[34] each region or religious order adapting the material to its own requirements. Where Nidaros adopted a remarkably faithful version of Benedict's liturgy, the cathedrals of Strängnäs and Linköping in the Swedish province of Uppsala received the rhymed chants and the readings from St John and Gregory I, but substituted a composite *passio*, based on extracts from Edward Grim's *Vita*[35] and the *Passio Anon. IV* (which they may have taken from the York liturgy),[36] for Benedict's.[37] The Cluniacs at Lewes (Sussex) used the rhymed antiphons

---

31 *Breviarium … Sarum*, i, cclv: John 10: 11–16; Gregory I, Homily XIV (*PL*, lxxvi, 1127).

32 *Ordo Nidrosiensis ecclesiae*, ed. L. Gjerløw, Libri liturgici provinciae Nidrosiensis mediae aevi, 2 (Oslo, 1968), 162–3; *Antiphonarium Nidrosiensis ecclesiae*, ed. *eadem*, Libri liturgici … aevi, 3 (Oslo, 1979), 99–100. It is probable that he was depicted among the array of saints on the west front of Trondheim Cathedral: Duggan, 'Eystein, Thomas Becket, and the Wider Christian World', 32–3.

33 *The Ordinal of the Papal Court from Innocent III to Boniface VIII and Related Documents*, ed. S. J. P. Van Dijk, completed by J. H. Walker, Spicilegium Friburgense, 22 (Fribourg, 1975), 28, 56, 84; *ibid.*, 87–483, 'Ordinal of the Roman Church compiled during the reign of Innocent III 1213–6', at 132, '[In festo sancti Thome martiris.] Ad matitudinum et alias horas omnia dicantur de uno martire, preter lectiones et oratio[nem]. Leguntur ad matitudinum lectio[nes] de passione eius, s[c]ilicet Gloriosi martiris (= Benedict's passio)'. In 1209, Innocent III recalled to the monk William from Andres (Pas-de-Calais), that he had lodged at Andres when, as a Parisian student, he had gone on pilgrimage to St Thomas (*MGH SS*, xxiv, 738). For MS evidence, see Biblioteca Apostolica Vaticana, Cod. Sancti Petri in Vaticano, C 107, fols 77va–79rb (full text, in nine lectiones); A 7, fols 38ra–vb (abbreviated, in six lections, supplemented by three readings from Leo I); Cod. Vat. lat. 1276, fols 74r–76r (full text, not divided).

34 Hughes, 'Rhymed Offices', 367, 370–71. For the copy made at the imperial monastery of Stavelot-Malmedy, see A. J. Duggan, 'A Becket Office at Stavelot: London, BL, MS Addit. 16964', in *Omnia disce: Medieval Studies in Memory of Leonard Boyle, O.P.*, ed. *eadem*, J. Greatrex, and B. Bolton (Aldershot, 2005), 161–82, at 164; repr. with the same pagination in Duggan, *Friends, Networks*, no. XI.

35 *MTB*, ii, 353–450.

36 Below, nn. 39 and 40.

37 Breviarium Strengense: London, BL, MS Addit. 40,146 (pre 1220?), fols 125ra–126rb; *Breviarium Lincopense*, ed. K. Peters, Laurentius Peti Sällskapets Urkundsserie (Lund, 1951),

and responsories, but reduced Benedict's *passio* to eight very short snippets, followed by the Good Shepherd gospel and Gregory's commentary, which together supplied the remaining four readings necessary for a monastic office.[38] The great cathedral at York[39] adopted an abbreviated version of an anonymous *passio*,[40] combined with the Canterbury chants; Hereford used a much condensed version of the Canterbury text for Lections 1–6 and retained the 'Good Shepherd' gospel and the opening of Gregory I's homily for Lection 7, as well the Canterbury antiphons and responsories, but substituted further extracts from Gregory for Lections 8 and 9;[41] the Benedictine Hyde Abbey, near Winchester, used a twelve-lection *passio* based on John of Salisbury's *Vita*, combined with the Gospel reading, 'Si quis uult post me' (Luke 9: 23–6) and chants from the Common Office for a single martyr.[42] It is a matter of some interest that the text held by the figure of the enthroned Christ in Henry the Lion's Gospels, cited below, is a variant of Luke 9. 23: *QUI VVLT VENIRE POST ME. ABNEGET SEMETIPSV[M]. ET TOLLAT CRVCEM SUAM.*

In monastic churches there were three levels of celebration: the full repertoire described above, identified in calendars as an office of twelve readings (*xii. l*); an intermediate office with only three readings (*iii. l*); and a simple *memoria*, a commemorative prayer, often the one used as the collect of the St Thomas Mass:[43]

v/2/i 235–9. Strängnäs also sent a small offering to Canterbury from 1200 to 1271: A. Lindblom, *Björsätersmålningarna: The Legends of St Thomas Becket and of the Holy Cross Painted in a Swedish Church*, Arkeologiska monografier, 38 (Stockholm, 1953), 28–55 (English summary, 77–9), at 52–3 and 78–9.

38 V. Leroquais, *Le Bréviaire-Missel du prieuré clunisien de Lewes* (Paris, 1935), 4 [Cambridge, Fitzwilliam Museum, MS 369, fols 105r–107r]; cf. Slocum *Liturgies*, 167–208, for the full texts and music (the translations, esp. that of *Fragrat virtus*, 194, are very poor).

39 *Breviarium ad usum insignis ecclesie Eboracensis*, ed. S. W. Lawley, 2 vols, Surtees Society, 71 and 75 (London, 1880–82), i, 120–27, but Slocum, *Liturgies*, 226–33, is much better (apart from serious translation errors).

40 *Biblioteca Hagiographica Latina antiquae et mediae Aetatis*, ed. Socii Bollandini, [i] A-I and [ii] K-Z (Brussels, 1898 and 1900–1901), [ii] 1189 no. 8209; *MTB*, iv, 186–95, 'Passio Anon. IV', *incipit* 'Hodie, fratres'; Oxford, Bodleian Library, MS Bodl. 509, fols 15r–20r, a twelfth-century manuscript from the Cistercian monastery of Combe in Warwickshire: see A. [J.] Duggan, *Thomas Becket: A Textual History of his Letters* (Oxford, 1980), 25–6, 34; cf. London, BL, MS Addit. 38112 (Phillips 4173), fols 1–3, s. XII, from Tongerlo (O. Premon.), nr Antwerp, dioc. Cambrai.

41 *The Hereford Breviary*, ed. W. H. Frere and L. E. G. Brown, 2 vols (London, 1904), i, 165–70; cf. Slocum, *Liturgies*, 223–5.

42 *The Monastic Breviary of Hyde Abbey, Winchester* (Oxford Bodl. Library, MSS *Rawlinson liturg. E.1 and Gough liturg. 8*), ed. J. B. L. Tolhurst, Henry Bradshaw Society, 69–71, 76, 4 vols (London, 1932–33, 1938), i, fols 27v–29r. This edition should be used in preference to Slocum, *Liturgies*, 233–8, which introduces misreadings and confusions: e.g. the utterly confused text of the well-known *oratio* 'Deus pro cuius ecclesia' (below, at n. 43), which inexplicably combines the opening words of the prayer with Hyde's Lection 1, producing complete nonsense.

43 *Breviarium … Sarum*, i, ccxlvi; *The Sarum Missal*, ed. J. Wickham Legg (Oxford, 1916), 71; cf. the Bamberg Breviary, *Breviarium Eberhardi Cantoris*, ed. E. K. Farrenkopf,

Deus pro cuius ecclesia gloriosus pontifex ac martir Thomas gladiis impiorum occubuit, presta quesumus ut omnes qui eius implorat auxilium pie petitionis sue salutarem consequantur effectum.

(O God, for whose Church the glorious bishop and martyr Thomas fell by the swords of wicked men, grant, we beseech thee, that all who implore his aid may achieve the salutary outcome of their fervent prayer.) [trans. AJD]

The non-monastic (secular) churches had a similar range, between a full office of nine readings (*ix. l*),[44] an intermediate office with three (*iii. l*), and the cursory *memoria*. The choice, made by the local bishop, archbishop, abbot or prior, indicated the significance attached to the saint in the liturgical life of the particular church.[45]

Such solemn liturgies reflected the official outlook of the church or monastery where they were celebrated, but the personal devotion of the élite laity is recorded in the Books of Hours commissioned in their thousands through the later Middle Ages.[46] Although broadly following the liturgical customs of the owner's region, such books were tailored to his or her particular devotion. The so-called Nuremberg Hours, for example, made at the end of the thirteenth century for a French princess,[47] is a striking example of the genre.[48] It contains a finely executed three-lection office of St Thomas, ultimately dependent on the Canterbury/Sarum liturgy,[49] which opens with a richly illuminated initial D[50] containing a dramatic miniature of the murder.

Liturgie-Wissenschaftliche Quellen und Forschungen, 50–51 (Münster, 1969), 114: 'De sancto Thoma archiepiscopo de Kandelberc in vesperis in matutinis et in missa dicitur tantum Oratio. Require in missale libro'; *ibid.*, 18–22, 115: 'De sancto Thoma archiepiscopo de Kandelberch in vesperis in matutinis et in missa dicitur tantum hec Or[atio], Deus pro cuius ecclesia.' The same *incipit* is added to the Second Vespers of Holy Innocents (28 December), *ibid.*, 40, with the note, 'Hec oratio etiam dicitur in matutino et in missa'.

44 See, for example, Linköping Breviary: *Breviarium Lincopense*, v/2/1, 235–9 and the breviary associated with Strängnäs (prov. Uppsala), London, BL, MS Addit. 40146, fols 125ra–126rb: nine short readings, combining elements from the Canterbury-Sarum and York liturgies, with the Canterbury chants.

45 V. Leroquais, *Les Bréviaires manuscrits des bibliothèques publiques de France*, 6 vols (Paris, 1934), *passim*; *idem*, *Les Psautiers manuscrits latins des bibliothèques publiques de France*, 3 vols (Mâcon, 1940–41), *passim*; *idem*, *Les Sacramentaires et les missels manuscrits des bibliothèques publiques de France* (Paris, 1924), *passim*.

46 J. Harthan, *Books of Hours and their Owners* (London, 1977; repr. 1982).

47 Perhaps Margaret, sister of Philip IV of France, who married Edward I at Canterbury in 1299. The history of the MS is obscure, however, and it may have been brought to England not by Margaret but by Princess Catherine (daughter of Charles VI), who married Henry V in 1420.

48 Nürnberg, Stadtbibliothek, MS Solgr 4.4°: *Les Heures de Nuremberg*, ed. E. Simmons (Paris, 1994), 117–18, for the Office of St Thomas.

49 Nürnberg, Stadtbibliothek, MS Solgr 4.4°, fols 139v–153v.

50 For 'Domine, labia mea aperies' (Psalm 50 (51): 17), which opens the Office of Matins: 'O Lord, open my lips'.

On a field of gold, Thomas, in the centre of the picture, kneels before an altar on the right, beside which stands a cleric holding a processional cross, while the foremost of the four armed men crowding in behind Becket's back slashes into the crown of the martyr's head with his sword and simultaneously cuts the arm of the cleric.[51] Books like these, precious objects in their own right, as well as Breviaries and Psalters, became major channels for the transmission of the pictorial imagery of the martyrdom.[52]

Even without receiving the Canterbury/Sarum Office, the feast of St Thomas could be celebrated by the simple device of adapting the existing Common office for a martyr or martyr bishop. All that was necessary was the insertion of the name 'Thomas' and either integrating readings from one of the shorter *passiones* into the Matins office or having them read in chapter or in the refectory.[53] This is what was done by the Cistercians, who were celebrating the feast of St Thomas from 1173.[54] A note about the office of St Thomas made in the monastery of Vauclair (a daughter of Clairvaux, founded in 1134) in the 1170s, recording General Chapter resolutions, reads simply: '*De sancto Thoma. Inuitatorium. Regem sempiternum coronauit Thomam*', with musical notation (neumes) inserted above *coronauit Thomam*.[55] This was enough to show that

51 Nürnberg, Stadtbibliothek, MS Solgr 4.4⁰, fol. 139v: *Les Heures de Nuremberg*, plate 37. The narrative source was probably Edward Grim (*MTB*, ii, 437): 'et metuens nefandus miles [Reginald Fitz Urse] ne raperetur a populo, et vivus evaderet, insiliit in eum subito et summitate corone quam sancti chrismatis unctio dicaverat Deo abrasa, agnum Deo immolandum vulneravit in capite, eodem ictu praeciso brachio hec referentis;' but cf. Anonymous I (Roger of Pontigny), *MTB*, iv, 77: 'accessit Rainaldus et percussit eum ex obliquo fortiter in capite, amputavitque summitatem corone ejus, pileumque dejecit. Lapsus est ensis supra laeuam scapulam, inciditque omnia uestimenta illius usque ad nudum. Magister uero Edwardus, qui juxta virum Dei stabat, videns ictum imminere, jecit brachium econtra quasi eum protecturus; quod fere penitus abscissum est.'

52 See for example, the bottom margin of fol. 51r of the Luttrell Psalter, 1320–40 (London, BL, MS Addit. 42130). Nine of the fifty scenes of 'gothic' altars illustrated in P. Dearmer, *Fifty Pictures of Gothic Altars* (London, 1910), depict the martyrdom: plates 8, 9, 23, 24, 30, 32 (defaced), 35, 40 and 44 (a woodcut from William Caxton's printing of Jacobus de Voragine's *Golden Legend*). For the early imagery, see Gameson, 'Early Imagery', 46–89.

53 John of Salisbury's *Ex insperato* and *Passio* were so used: see above, at nn. 15 and 16.

54 S. K. Langenbahn, '"de cerebro Thomae Cantuariensis". Zur Geschichte und Hagiologie der Himmeroder Thomas Becket-Reliquie von 1178', in *875 Jahre Findung des Klosterortes Himmerod*, ed. B. Fromme (Mainz, 2010), 55–91, at 60–61 and n. 19; cf. *Twelfth-Century Statutes from the Cistercian General Chapter: Latin Text with English Notes and Commentary*, ed. C. Waddell, Cîteaux, Studia et Documenta, 12 (Brecht, 2002), 125. This date supersedes the generally accepted date of 1185 established by J.-M. Canivez: *Statuta capitulorum generalium ordinis Cisterciensis ab anno 1116 ad annum 1786. Tomus I. Ab anno 1116 ad annum 1220*, ed, J.-M. Canivez (Louvain, 1933), 102, 144, and followed in S. R. Marosszéki, 'Les origines du Chant Cistercien: Recherches sur les réformes du plain-chant cistercien au XIIe siècle', *Analecta Sacri Ordinis Cisterciensis*, 8 (1952), 1–179, at 42–3, *et passim*.

55 J. Leclercq, 'Épitres d'Alexandre III sur les Cisterciens', *Revue Bénédictine*, 64 (1954), 68–82, at 75 n. 4, citing Laon, Bibl. mun. MS 471, fol. 93v. I am grateful to Professor Nicholas Vincent

the new feast was to be observed with a full office of twelve readings, based on the existing common office. The name of the new martyr was added to the opening verse so that it would read: 'Regem sempiternum pronis mentibus adoremus. Qui martirem suum digne pro meritis *coronauit Thomam*', and the neumes indicated how the chant was to be adjusted to accommodate the martyr's name. Simultaneously, an existing Mass was adapted to celebrate the new martyr.[56]

King Henry's Penance

Much of the power of the original Canterbury office derives from its immediacy. Composed through the summer and autumn of 1173, it took shape while Henry II's 'Angevin Empire' was being convulsed by the 1173–74 rebellion. This involved his three eldest sons (Henry, Richard and Geoffrey), supported by his wife, Queen Eleanor, in league with Louis VII of France and an array of the sundry disaffected (William the Lion, king of Scots, Counts Philip of Flanders and Baldwin of Boulogne, some of the Breton nobility and the earls of Norfolk, Leicester, Chester and Derby). It was not difficult to interpret this wholly unexpected conflagration as divine vengeance for Becket's murder, a sacrilege for which many held the king morally responsible.[57] Henry II was not helped by the way in which his penance at Avranches (May 1172) had been smothered in legal and diplomatic niceties.[58] The outcome of the rebellion was unknown when Benedict composed the liturgy and his apocalyptic imagery captured the popular mood at the end of 1173: 'people' did rise up 'against people' and 'kingdom against kingdom', and 'the realm was divided against itself'.[59]

The Great Rebellion clearly changed the king's attitude to the now-canonised saint.[60] Instead of making straight for London when he returned from Normandy to Southampton on 8 July 1174 to confront the rebellious English earls and simultaneous invasions from Scotland and Flanders, he turned aside to travel to Canterbury to make personal reparation for his involvement in

---

for giving me this reference and to Dr Herwig Weigl of Vienna for sending a scan of the article to a snow-bound London in December 2010.

56 See, for example, the MSS from Rievaulx, Morimondo (dioc. Milan), and a Cistercian house in France: London, BL, MSS Addit. 46203 (Rievaulx), fols 75v–80v; Addit. 39759 (Morimondo), fol. 61rb; and Addit. 57531 (France), fols 29va–vb; cf. D. Choisselet and P. Vernet, *Les ecclesiastica officia cisterciens du XIIème siècle*, La Documentation Cistercienne, 22 (Reiningue, 1989), 74–5.

57 Gervase, ii, 81 (*Gesta regum*).

58 Duggan, 'Diplomacy, Status, and Conscience', 272–8.

59 Above, at n. 25.

60 Argued in Duggan, 'Diplomacy', 278–85.

Becket's murder. As described by an eye-witness (William of Canterbury) soon after the event,[61] he dismounted at Harbledown,[62] two miles to the north of the city, walked to the chapel of St Dunstan, outside the walls, where he removed his shoes and outer garments, then walked barefoot through the West Gate to the tomb in the crypt. There the bishop of London (Gilbert Foliot), speaking in the king's name, acknowledged his guilt, and Henry submitted to penitential discipline, placed four marks of gold and a silk cloth on the tomb, granted £40 a year to the monastery in perpetuity,[63] promised to build a monastery in the martyr's honour and received absolution. Then he spent the night (12–13 July 1174) in prayer before the tomb, attended Mass the following morning, and carried relics (*lipsana*) with him as a token of his pilgrimage when he set out for London. There, on 17 July, he received the welcome news that the king of Scots had been captured near Alnwick (Northumberland) on the very day (13 July) on which he had completed his penance at Canterbury. Like many a lesser Canterbury pilgrim whose prayer was heard, the king had cause to be grateful to the martyr.[64]

61 William of Canterbury, *Miracula*, vi, 93, 'De adventu regis ad tumulum martyris Thomae': *MTB*, i, 487–9.
62 A leprosarium on a little hill to the north of Canterbury: D. Knowles and R. N. Hadcock, *Medieval Religious Houses in England and Wales* (London, 1971), 312, 322. His grant of an annual 20 marks (£13 6s 8d) from royal incomes in Canterbury was formalised in a charter at Westminster issued 14 x 18 July 1174. Although it was said to be an interim grant, until the king made alternative arrangements, he never did. It was paid throughout the Middle Ages, and continues to be paid by the City of Canterbury to the alms-house which replaced the leprosarium at the Reformation: Henry II, *Acta* no. 1230 (cited from the draft electronic version of N. Vincent's forthcoming edition of the Charters of Henry II, for which I warmly thank Professor Vincent); W. Dugdale, *Monasticon Anglicanum*, rev. edn by J. Caley, H. Ellis and B. Bandinel, 6 vols in 8 (London, 1817–30; repr. 1846), vi/2, 654; W. Urry, 'Two Notes on Guernes de Pont-Sainte-Maxence: Vie de St Thomas', *Archaeologia Cantiana*, 66 (1953), 92–7 at 97; *idem, Canterbury under the Angevin Kings* (London, 1967), 434.
63 Henry II, *Acta*, no. 462, issued at Westminster 14 x 18 July 1174: Canterbury Cathedral Library, Chartae Antiquae B337; endorsed: *carta noua H(enrici) ii. de xl. libr(atis) terre quas dedit ecclesie et sancto Th(ome)* (s. xii/xiii.); and numerous copies and extracts. Its key directive stated: 'Sciatis me dedisse in perpetuam elemosinam et presenti carta confirmasse Deo et beato Thome et ecclesie sancte Trinitatis Cant' quindecim libratas redditus in Berchesores [Barksore] et in Hokes [Hook], et in Aisse et in Rissendona [Rushenden] et xxv. libratas redditus in Lesdona [Leysdown], ita quod due predicte portiones xl. libratas reddituum faciant.' Aisse is East or West Ashe, Isle of Sheppey. It was probably this charter that William of Canterbury had in mind, but two separate grants were involved, the first for 25 *libratis*, and the second for 15 *libratis*: Duggan, 'Diplomacy', 280–81.
64 *Jordan Fantosme*, ed. Johnston, 148 (lines 2011–12); *Chronique de la Guerre entre les Anglois et les Ecossais en 1173 et 1174*, in *Chronicles*, ed. Howlett, iii, 370 (lines 2017–18). Also discussed in the essay by Colette Bowie in this volume (chapter 6). Cf. Ralph de Diceto (Diss): Diceto, i, 383–5; William of Newburgh, *Historia Rerum Anglicanum* in *Chronicles*, ed. Howlett, i, 187–9; Gervase, i, 248–9. For the enigmatic Jordan, who may have had Winchester connections,

'Dunc', dit li reis Henris, 'Deus en eit mercié,
E saint Thomas martyr et tuz les sainz Dé.'

('Then,' says King Henry, 'God be thanked for it,
And St Thomas the Martyr and all God's saints.')

The king's relief at hearing that news would have been augmented by the intelligence that a planned invasion led by his eldest son (against which he had warned the people of Canterbury on his departure from the city, advising that they take refuge 'beyond the Medway')[65] had failed, because bad weather had dispersed the Young King's fleet near Gravelines. The result of these two coincidental events was the virtual collapse of the English segment of the rebellion, as one after another its leaders surrendered their castles and made their peace.[66] Within the month, Henry was able to return to Normandy to mop up the remaining opposition there, safe in the knowledge that his authority was secure in England. Ralph de Diceto (Diss), the dean of St Paul's in London, summed up the situation in these words:[67]

Sic igitur in articulo temporis, per intercessionem sanctissimi Thomae martyris, rex pater, per omnia regni sui confinia potentissimus, vii° idus Augusti navem ascendit apud Porcestre, ducens secum regem Scottorum, comitem Leircestrensem, comitem Cestrensem, Hugonem de Castello, quos habebat in vinculis.

(So, just in time, the father king, most powerful within the confines of his kingdom through the intercession of St Thomas the Martyr, on 7 August 1174 boarded ship at Portchester, taking with him the king of Scots, the earl of Leicester, the earl of Chester and Hugh de Castello, [all of] whom he held in chains.) [trans. AJD]

However one interprets Henry II's reactions – and I have seen a king forced by general, not to say popular opinion, and political events to make his peace with the martyr – there is no doubt that he made substantial penitential payments: £30,000 to the Holy Land;[68] £40 per annum to Christ Church, Canterbury; and £13 6s 8d per annum to the leper-house at Harbledown.

---

see M. Strickland, 'Fantosme, Jordan (*fl.* 1170–1180)', *ODNB* (Oxford, 2004) [http://www.oxforddnb.com/view/article/48310, accessed 20 November 2010].

65   William of Canterbury, *MTB*, i, 489.
66   E.g. Earl Hugh of Norfolk, William, Earl Ferrers, and Roger de Mowbray. Even Bishop Hugh of Durham, who had not rebelled but had not attempted to prevent the Scottish invasions either, deemed discretion the better part of valour and surrendered Durham, Norham and Northallerton: Howden, *Chronica*, ii, 64–5.
67   Diceto, i, 383–5 at 385; cf. Robert of Torigni, *Chronica*, in *Chronicles*, ed. Howlett, iv, 264–5; Howden, *Gesta*, i, 72; Howden, *Chronica*, ii, 61–3; *Continuation of Sigebert of Gembloux*, MGH SS, vi, 414, 'Que res [Canterbury penance] ei, ut credimus, victoriam contulit.'
68   H. E. Mayer, 'Henry II of England and the Holy Land', *EHR*, 97 (1982), 721–39.

More significant as an index of his private sentiments is the fact that, with the single exception of 1188,[69] he repeated the Canterbury pilgrimage every time he returned to England from his overseas territories. He was thus seen to join the public veneration of the new martyr, to whom many attributed his triumph in the rebellion.[70] Warren and Barlow saw the Canterbury penance of 1174 as merely a public relations operation to deprive the rebels of their totem and align the new St Thomas firmly with the monarchy,[71] but that exclusively political interpretation ignores his recurrent visits to Canterbury and the extent of his penitential actions.[72] The ascription to King Henry of real repentance, made at the time by Jordan Fantosme, may be closer to the truth than historians like to think.[73]

> 'Seint Thomas,' dist li reis, 'guardez-mei mun reaume.
> A vus me rent culpable dunt li autre unt le blasme'.
>
> ('St Thomas', said the king, 'guard my realm for me.
> To you I declare myself guilty of that for which others have the blame'.)

The original voices of outrage had been such that King Henry had sought to repair his reputation by the intervention in Ireland (1171–72), which was justified as beneficial to the Irish Church and people,[74] before accepting the penances imposed by two papal legates at Avranches in 1172.[75] Although Henry considered that the concessions which he made as part of the settlement

---

69 When the interdict imposed by the monks had closed the cathedral to divine service: Duggan, 'Diplomacy', 280–83.

70 *Jordan Fantosme*, ed. Johnston, 140 (lines 1905–7); *Chronique*, ed. Howlett, 362 (lines 1911–13). Peter of Blois to Archbishop Walter of Palermo in late 1179–80: *MTB*, vii, 575; Herbert of Bosham, *Liber Melorum* (a supplement to the *Vita Sancti Thome*), *MTB*, iii, 544–8; Howden, *Gesta*, i, 72; Howden, *Chronica*, ii, 61–3; Diceto, i, 385; Robert of Torigni, *Chronica*, 264–5.

71 W. L. Warren, *Henry II* (London, 1973), 135; Barlow, 269–70.

72 For further expressions of his penance, see Elma Brenner's essay in this volume, chapter 4.

73 *Jordan Fantosme*, ed. Johnston, 120 (lines 1599–1600); *Chronique*, ed. Howlett, 336–8 (lines 1605–6); also discussed in the essays by Michael Staunton (chapter 5), Colette Bowie (chapter 6) and José Manuel Cerda (chapter 7) in this volume. Cf. *Jordan Fantosme*, ed. Johnston, 142 (lines 1912–14); *Chronique*, ed. Howlett, 362 (lines 1918–20): 'Li reis iert veirement al martir saint Thomas, | U il se rendit cupable, pechiere, e las, | E prist la penitence.' (The king was truly reconciled to St Thomas, | and to him he confessed his guilt, his sin, and his sorrow, | and underwent the penance imposed upon him.)

74 J. A. Watt, *The Church and the Two Nations in Medieval Ireland* (Cambridge, 1970), 36–8; M. T. Flanagan, 'Henry II, the Council of Cashel and the Irish Bishops', *Peritia: Journal of the Medieval Academy of Ireland*, 10 (1996), 184–211; A. J. Duggan, 'The Making of a Myth: Giraldus Cambrensis, *Laudabiliter*, and Henry II's Lordship of Ireland', *Studies in Medieval and Renaissance History*, Third Series, 4 (2007), 107–68, at 157–8.

75 Duggan, 'Diplomacy', 272–8; *eadem*, '*Ne in dubium*: The Official Record of Henry II's Reconciliation at Avranches (21 May, 1172)', *EHR*, 115 (2000) 643–58; repr. with the same pagination in *eadem*, *Friends, Networks*, no. VIII.

were 'few or none' ('aut paucas aut nullas'),[76] this 'compromise' of Avranches represented the first political reverse in Henry's reign and marked the beginning of negotiations which resulted in an important concession on clerical immunity, agreed with Cardinal Hugh Pierleone in 1175–76. Historians are divided in their assessment of what Henry lost by these agreements, but they were more than had been conceded in the seven years' dispute with Thomas: right of appeal to the papacy and confirmation of clerical immunity from secular judgment in criminal matters (except for treason and breaches of the forest law).[77] Both were to remain in force until the Henrician Reformation and 'benefit of clergy' survived in a much modified form until 1827.[78] Although highly critical of Becket in many ways, Frank Barlow conceded that:[79]

> things were never quite the same again, whether in the English Church or in Latin Christendom at large. ... Through his stand against Henry and his martyrdom, [Thomas] brought the archaic English customs to the notice of the Pope and cardinals and all canon lawyers and had succeeded in getting them scrutinised, debated and in part abolished or reformed.

The Plantagenet Patron

Whether for personal or for political reasons, the man whom many – perhaps most – contemporaries held morally responsible for Becket's murder joined the ranks of the devotees who flocked to the martyr's tomb in a manner not dissimilar to theirs: a penitent seeking forgiveness; a petitioner seeking divine favour. Nor was he the only member of his family to invoke the name of St Thomas.

The younger King Henry, whose coronation in flagrant defiance of Canterbury's rights in 1170 initiated the final act of the Becket drama, visited the tomb in 1172, even before the canonisation,[80] and he claimed in a letter to Alexander III that his rebellion was motivated by anger for Becket's unavenged murder – 'for that sacred blood was crying out to us' ('clamabat enim sacer ille ad nos sanguis')[81] – as well as by opposition to his father's ecclesiastical policy. 'To extend the renown of our tutor, the glorious martyr St Thomas, formerly archbishop of Canterbury',[82] he even went so far as to promise to abolish the

---

76 In a letter to Bishop Bartholomew of Exeter: *MTB*, vii, 518–19 no. 773, at 519.
77 Duggan, *Thomas Becket*, 222–3.
78 Abolished by statute: 7 and 8 George IV, c. 28, §6: *The Statutes of the United Kingdom of Great Britain and Ireland, 7 & 8 George IV, 1827*, ed. G. K. Richards (London, 1827), 166.
79 Barlow, 274.
80 Lansdowne Anonymous, third fragment, *MTB*, iv, 178–9.
81 *Recueil des historiens*, xvi, 643–8 no. 66, at 644.
82 *Recueil des historiens*, xvi, 643–8 no. 66, at 645: 'Ad amplificandam gloriam gloriosi martyris alumni nostri, sancti videlict Thomae quondam Cantuariensis antistitis'.

'leges iniquas' for which Becket had been exiled.[83] Whether the young Henry would have kept the promise or not is a matter for speculation, since the rebellion failed in 1174 and he died in 1183, six years before his father.

There is less uncertainty about his brother Richard's public devotion to St Thomas, however. On the eve of his departure on the Third Crusade in 1189, King Richard held a council at Canterbury on 27 November. There, accompanied by Queen Eleanor, he reconciled the monks of Canterbury with their archbishop, Baldwin, in a great ecclesiastical gathering, which included three archbishops (Canterbury, Rouen, Dublin), nine bishops, five named abbots, 'et alii abbates et priores multi'. He made peace with King William of Scotland, releasing him from his liege homage[84] and restoring the fortresses of Roxburgh and Berwick in return for 10,000 marks, before commending himself and his enterprise to the martyr's favour.[85] Arriving on 27 November, he departed for Dover on 5 December: and it is likely that he attended the feast of the 'return of St Thomas', which was celebrated at Canterbury on 2 December – and which later generated two pilgrim badges: Thomas on horseback; and Thomas arriving by boat at Sandwich.[86] During the crusade, he contributed to the maintenance of a chapel and cemetery founded at Acre by William, chaplain of the chronicler Ralph de Diceto (Diss), dean of St Paul's in London,[87] from which descended the military order of St Thomas of Acre (Acon) in the 1220s;[88] and on his release from imprisonment in Germany, accompanied by Queen Eleanor, he returned to give thanks at Becket's tomb on 13 March 1194.[89] Even King John visited the

83   Constitutions of Clarendon: MTB, v, 71–83, no. 45.

84   Chronicle of Melrose: Chronica de Mailros, e codice unico in bibliotheca Cottoniana servato, ed. J. Stevenson, Bannatyne Club, 49 (Edinburgh, 1835), 98.

85   Howden, Gesta, ii, 97–9, 102; Howden, Chronica, iii, 23–7; Diceto, ii, 72; Gervase, i, 474.

86   Recorded in the 'Burnt Breviary' in Canterbury Cathedral Library, Addit. MS 6. It was also celebrated at Arbroath: English Benedictine Calendars After AD 1100, ed. F. Wormald, Henry Bradshaw Society 77 (London, 1939), i, 65 n. 2; cf. ibid., 79, for Canterbury. For the badges, see B. Spencer, Pilgrim Souvenirs and Secular Badges, Medieval Finds from Excavations in London, 7 (London, 1998), 79–89 fig. 34–6, 36a (ship); fig. 37–54a (Thomas on horseback).

87   Diceto, ii, 80–81. William became the first prior of the foundation, which served not only the spiritual needs of crusaders, but cared for the poor, the wounded and the dying, and provided Christian burial in the cemetery.

88   A. J. Forey, 'The Military Order of St Thomas of Acre', EHR, 92 (1977), 481–503, esp. 481, 487, 489. A priory of St Thomas of Canterbury existed in Acre itself before Alexander III's death, last mentioned in 1212 (Papsturkunden für Kirchen im Heiligen Lande, ed. R. Hiestand, Vorarbeiten zum oriens pontificius, 3, Abhandlungen … Göttingen, phil.-hist. Klasse, 3rd Ser., 136 [Göttingen, 1985], 394 no. 199), but its later history is shrouded in mystery. For the place of the London house in the ceremonial history of the City of London, see Liber Albus: The White Book of the City of London, trans. H. T. Riley (London, 1861), 23–5 and 27; cf. Forey, 'The Military Order', 502–3 and A. J. Duggan, 'Canterbury: The Becket Effect', in Canterbury: A Medieval City, ed. C. Royer-Hemet (Newcastle-upon-Tyne, 2010), 67–91, at 76.

89   Gervase, i, 524; Diceto, ii, 80–81. Afterwards, he visited Bury St Edmunds, on his way north to Nottingham, which was holding out for Richard's brother John.

tomb at least three times, on the third of which (1202) he and his new queen, Isabella, were re-crowned on Easter Sunday (25 March) by Archbishop Hubert Walter.[90] Robertson speculated that the custom of the Wardens of the Cinque Ports sending to the tomb of St Thomas the coronation canopy, which they held over the heads of the king and queen during coronation ceremonies, may have been begun on this occasion.[91]

By the time of John's death (1216), the trend of royal veneration of the English martyr was firmly set. Henry III continued the family tradition, despite his life-long commitment to St Edward the Confessor. The translation of St Thomas's relics from their crypt tomb to the heart of the Trinity Chapel in the main cathedral at Canterbury was one of the most splendid state occasions of Henry's reign.[92] It was attended by dignitaries from across Europe,[93] in addition to the young king himself, who accompanied the precious relic,[94] and he assigned taxes due from Christ Church to maintain four great candles permanently around the shrine.[95] Thereafter, the day of the translation (7 July) was celebrated as a second feast with its own special liturgy. Moreover,

90   Howden, *Chronica*, iv, 160; Diceto, ii, 172. This was John's third, and Isabella's second coronation: Gervase, ii, 93 (*Gesta regum*); Matthew Paris, *Chronica Majora*, ed. H. R. Luard, RS 57, 7 vols (London, 1872–83), ii, 467, 475. For further discussion of John's relationship with the cult, see the essay by Paul Webster (chapter 8) in this volume.

91   W. A. Scott Robertson, *The Crypt of Canterbury Cathedral: Its Architecture, its History and its Frescoes* (London, 1880), 41.

92   On the political significance, see R. Eales, 'The Political Setting of the Becket Translation of 1220', in *Martyrs and Martyrologies*, ed. D. Wood, SCH, 30 (Oxford, 1993), 127–39.

93   Possibly three from Hungary: the bishop of Csanád (his attendance reported in a letter from Honorius III on 20 December 1220: A. Theiner, *Vetera Monumenta historica Hungariam sacram illustrantia*, i [Rome, 1859], 26 no 44: 'Ex insinuatione Venerabilis fratris … Canadiensis Episcopi nobis innotuit, quod cum ipse in reditu peregrinationis sue a translatione corporis beati Thome Martyris Cantuariensis per Papiensem transierirt civitatem'), Alexander of Várad (now Oradea), also mentioned in the papal letter, and Archbishop John of Esztergom: L. Solymosi, 'Magyar főpapok angliai zarándoklata 1220-ban (The pilgrimage of Hungarian prelates to England in 1220)', *Történelmi Szemle* (Historical Miscellany), 55, no 4 (2013), 527–40 at 527 and 536. For these references I am very grateful to Professor Martyn Rady.

94   Described by Walter of Coventry, *Memoriale*, ed. W. Stubbs, RS 58, 2 vols (London, 1872–73), ii, 245–6; *Rogeri de Wendover liber qui dicitur Flores Historiarum ab anno domini MCLIV annoque Henrici Anglorum Regis Secundi Primo*, ed. H. G. Hewlett, RS 84, 3 vols (London, 1886–89), ii, 254; Matthew Paris, *Chronica Majora*, iii, 59–60.

95   *Curia Regis Rolls of the Reign of Henry III Preserved in the Public Record Office: A.D. 1237–1242*, HMSO (London, 1979) 175, 181, 208 (24 Henry III); cf. 374–5 (26 Henry III). On royal pilgrimages, see N. Vincent, 'The Pilgrimages of the Angevin Kings 1154–1272', in *Pilgrimage: The English Experience from Becket to Bunyan*, ed. C. Morris and P. Roberts (Cambridge, 2002), 12–45. On the so-called images of Becket's shrine in the miracle windows at Canterbury, see now R. Koopmans, 'Visions, Reliquaries, and the Image of "Becket's Shrine" in the Miracle Windows of Canterbury Cathedral', *Gesta*, 54 (2015), 37–57. Koopmans argues persuasively that all the 'shrine' images are, in fact, depictions of reliquaries.

the year of the translation (1220–21) was designated as a year of jubilee,[96] which was repeated every fifty years until the abolition of the cult in 1538.[97] Visits to the shrine in jubilee years attracted special spiritual benefits in the form of indulgences for those who wished to avail themselves of them by confessing their sins, and from at least 1370, the indulgence was plenary.[98] Edward I visited the shrine six times between 1279 and 1305.[99] Particularly memorable was the year 1285: in addition to the customary monetary offerings, he gave four statuettes and models of two ships (*naves*), all fashioned in pure gold, and various brooches ornamented with precious stones, to the value of £347;[100] in July of that year, he donated the royal crown of Scotland (confiscated from John Balliol) to the shrine; and on 8 September of the same year his marriage to Margaret of France, sister of Philip IV, was celebrated at Canterbury. She may have been the recipient of the Nuremburg Hours, mentioned above.[101] Not much later, the so-called 'Queen Mary Psalter', an even more splendid devotional book made either for Margaret's niece, Isabella of France, Edward II's queen (married 1308; †1358), or possibly for Edward himself, contains in its *bas-de-page* miniatures the most complete pictorial cycle of Becket's career still surviving. It illustrates the major incidents in St Thomas's life, from birth to presentation in heaven, even including the 'Saracen legend' of Thomas's mother.[102] Edward II and Edward III were to continue the patronage through the fourteenth century.[103] Even as late as

96   Modelled on the Old Testament jubilee described in Leviticus 25: 8–9, which was a year of special celebration: Duggan, 'Cult', 38–9. The fullest treatment remains R. Foreville, *Le jubilé de saint Thomas Becket: Du XIIIe au XVe siècle (1220–1470). Étude et documents*, Bibliothèque générale de l'École pratique des hautes-études, VIe section (Paris, 1958).

97   Below, at n. 128.

98   R. Foreville, 'Mort et survie de saint Thomas Becket', CCM, 14 (1971), 21–38, at 29.

99   Foreville, *Le jubilé*, 15 n. 4; A. J. Taylor, 'Edward I and the Shrine of St Thomas of Canterbury', *Journal of the British Archaeological Association*, 132 (1979), 22–8.

100   C. E. Woodruff, 'The Financial Aspect of the Cult of St Thomas of Canterbury', *Archaeologia Cantiana*, 44 (1932), 13–32, at 29 n. 1; Nilson, 119; M. Prestwich, *Edward I* (Berkeley, CA, 1988), 112.

101   Scott Robertson, *Crypt of Canterbury Cathedral*, 44–5; see above, nn. 47 and 48.

102   London, BL, MS Royal 2 B vii, fols 236v, 237r, and 287v–299r *passim*; cf. A. R. Stanton, *The Queen Mary Psalter: A Study of Affect and Audience*, Transactions of the American Philosophical Society, 91 Pt. 6 (Philadelphia, PA, 2001), 142–6 and 231–40, 'The Case for Isabelle'. For the Latin version, see MTB, ii, 453–8; cf. Duggan, *Textual History*, 178 n. 7. For the mid/late thirteenth-century Old English version, which forms the opening of a long *Life* of St Thomas, datable to the second half of the thirteenth century, see *The Early South-English Legendary; or, Lives of Saints: 1. Ms. Laud, 108, in the Bodleian Library*, ed. C. Horstmann, Early English Text Society, Original Series, 87 (London, 1887), 106–77 at 106–12.

103   Scott Robertson, *Crypt of Canterbury Cathedral*, 50 n.; cf. A. J. Mason, *What Became of the Bones of St Thomas? A Contribution to his Fifteenth Jubilee* (Cambridge, 1920), esp. 96–107, 'Caput and Corona', and especially M. Ormrod, 'The Personal Religion of Edward III', *Speculum*, 64 (1989), 849–77.

1520, Henry VIII himself, accompanied by the emperor Charles V, visited the shrine in the course of a high-level diplomatic encounter.[104]

Once established, as it was by the end of the twelfth century, royal participation in the Becket cult might be considered as merely a formal extension of the public religious practices expected of the king and his family, although Professor Vincent warns against too rigorous a separation between the political and the sacred.[105] Edward I's rich offerings suggest a personal devotion; and something more than lip-service is evident in the behaviour of Edward the Black Prince and King Henry IV, both of whom chose to be buried close to the shrine in 1376 and 1413 respectively, and Henry V went to Canterbury in November 1415 to give thanks for the victory at Agincourt.[106]

More dispersed was the influence of Henry II's three daughters, Matilda, Eleanor and Joanna. Their marriages – to Henry the Lion of Saxony (1168), Alfonso VIII of Castile (1170) and William II of Sicily (1177) respectively – encouraged the consolidation of the cult of St Thomas across Europe. The recognition of St Thomas as a family saint in Saxony[107] is splendidly manifested in the so-called coronation page of the Helmarshausen Gospels, commissioned by Henry the Lion between 1185 and 1188 for presentation to the altar of Our Lady in the newly built basilica of Saints John the Baptist and Blaise in Brunswick. Henry is shown kneeling before a standing Matilda, both splendidly attired, flanked by their kin, with their patron saints above. Matilda's principal protectors are St Gregory the Great and St Thomas, the latter bearing his martyr's palm.[108] That tiny presence on a manuscript page merely hints at the embrace of the English martyr as a patron of the Welfs, later proclaimed in the addition of St Thomas to the patronage of the basilica in Brunswick (which housed the Welf family mausoleum) and the painting of a now much-restored depiction of the *Regressio* and martyrdom in the choir.[109] The work was carried out under the auspices of Henry and Matilda's eldest son, Henry V, count

104 Foreville, 'Mort et survie', 31.

105 Vincent, 'Pilgrimages', 43, 'I would suggest that there is a point at which royal piety and religious ritual can come close to a convergence with the sacred'.

106 R. Barber, 'Edward, Prince of Wales and of Aquitaine (1330–1376)', *ODNB* (Oxford, 2004; online edn, 2008) [http://www.oxforddnb.com/view/article/8523, accessed 24 October 2010]; W. Urry, 'The Resting Places of St Thomas', in *Sédières*, 195–209, at 207.

107 See Colette Bowie's essay in this volume, chapter 6.

108 Herzog August Bibliothek Wolfenbüttel, Cod. Guelf. 105, noviss. 2, fol. 171v. On this image, see esp. O. G. Oexle, 'Lignage et parenté, politique et religion dans la noblesse du XIIs.: l'évangéliaire de Henri le Lion', CCM, 36 (1993), 339–58 and plates 1–4. This magnificent manuscript was sold for eight million pounds sterling to a German consortium at Sotheby's, London, in December 1983 (*Country Life*, 5 January 1984); cf. *Das Evangeliar Heinrichs des Löwen: Kommentar zum Faksimile*, ed. D. Kötzsche (Frankfurt-am-Main, 1989).

109 J. Petersohn, *Der südliche Ostseeraum im kirchlich-politischen Kräftespiel des Reichs, Polens und Dänemarks vom 10. bis 13. Jahrhundert: Mission – Kirchenorganisation – Kultpolitik* (Cologne, 1979), 137.

palatine of the Rhine (†1227), whose own devotion may have been encouraged by the fact that he had been born in the year of Becket's canonisation (1173). More than thirty years ago, Jürgen Petersohn showed how Brunswick became the centre of liturgical and cultural life in North Germany. From there, the cult of the English martyr was carried to Halberstadt and Merseburg in Saxony,[110] to the cities of the Hansa (whose members traded with England), Hamburg, Lübeck and Bremen,[111] and also to Ratzeburg, to the south of Hamburg.[112]

In the Spanish peninsula, the church of San Tomás Cantuariense in Salamanca, said to have been designed by English masons, dates from Eleanor's time as queen of Castile;[113] and on Sicily the devotion of Queen Joanna is evident in the splendid sanctuary mosaic in Monreale Cathedral (c.1188), where St Thomas of Canterbury (*CANTUR*'), flanked by two Roman martyrs (Saints Silvester and Lawrence), stands in an iconic pose giving a blessing in the Greek manner. Joanna's marriage was almost certainly the occasion on which Bishop Reginald of Bath sent to her prospective mother-in-law, Queen Margaret, the little pendant reliquary, fashioned in gold and rock crystal to contain some of the earliest relics of the new saint: fragments 'of the blood and blood-stained garments of St Thomas the Martyr and of his hair shirt, cowl, shoes and shirt'. Denuded of its crystal face and of the relics which had lain beneath, this unique testament to the export of Becket's cult in the wake of a royal wedding can still be seen in the Metropolitan Museum of New York.[114] It is even possible that Henry's former daughter-in-law, Margaret of France, widow of the younger Henry, reinforced devotion to St Thomas the Martyr in Hungary when she married Béla III in 1186.[115] The Pray codex, originally from Vác, provides evidence that his cult was established in Hungary by 1192/95,

---

110   Petersohn, *Der südliche Ostseeraum*, 138–9; M. Barth, 'Zum Kult des hl. Thomas Becket in deutschen Sprachgebiet, in Skandinavien und Italien', *Freiburger Diözesan-Archiv*, 80 (1960), 97–166, at 156–7. The fine Romanesque Neumarktkirche at Merseburg, dedicated to St Thomas the Martyr, was founded sometime between 1173 and 1188. Its restoration was noted by Günter Kowe in the *Mitteldeutsche Zeitung*, 28 May 1993; cf. U. Real, 'Die Merseburger Neumarktkirche St Thomas. Überlegungen zur Funktion der Kirche und zum Patrozinium des Thomas von Canterbury', in *Pfarrkirchen in Städten des Hanseraumes: Beiträge eines Kolloquiums vom 10. bis 13. Dezember 2003 in der Hansestadt Stralsund*, ed. F. Biermann, M. Schneider and T. Terberger, *Archäologie und Geschichte im Ostseeraum*, 1 (Rahden, 2006), 275–90; for the existence of the church in 1188, see *MGH Diplomata Frederici I*, 5 vols (Hannover, 1975–1990) iv, 271 no. 985. For a splendid collection of recent studies, see *Die romanische Neumarktkirche zu Merseburg und ihr Patron Thomas Becket von Canterbury*, publ. by the Förderkreis Museum, Schloss Merseburg (Merseburg, 2014); cf. 159 for a map of Becket dedications in the German empire.

111   Barth, 'Zum Kult', 159–60.

112   Petersohn, *Der südliche Ostseeraum*, 135; Barth, 'Zum Kult', 138–9.

113   See José Manuel Cerda's essay in this volume, chapter 7.

114   P. A. Newton, 'Some New Material for the Study of the Iconography of St Thomas Becket', in *Sédières*, 255–63.

115   *MGH SS*, xxvi, 248, 42–3; Z. J. Kosztolnyik, *From Coloman the Learned to Béla III (1095–1196): Hungarian Domestic Policies and Their Impact upon Foreign Affairs* (Boulder, CO, 1987), 212.

and probably much earlier.[116] Fr Radó listed him as one of the special patrons of the Hungarian Church (with Saints Stephen and Ladislas),[117] and two ecclesiastical foundations from the late twelfth century confirm this liturgical evidence: the collegiate church of Szent Tamás outside Esztergom[118] and the church of St Thomas in Pest.[119] Whether this segment of Becket's cult should be ascribed to the influence of the French-educated Archbishop Lukács of Esztergom (1158–81)[120] or to that of Queen Margaret, or to both, is difficult to say, but the church in honour of St Thomas the Martyr in Borszörcsök in the district of Veszprém is situated in part on crown land assigned to the queen of Hungary.[121] It is also significant that her great-granddaughter, St Margaret of Hungary (1242–71), after whom the Margit Sziget (Margaret Island) in the Danube at Budapest is named, was said to have modelled her penitential habits on St Thomas, whose *Vita* she read with devotion.[122] Independently of Queen Margaret, however, the foundation of a Cistercian monastery at Egres (now Igriş in Romania) in 1179, populated by monks from Pontigny, would have augmented the cult of St Thomas in the region.[123]

Patron of the Plantagenets and Welfs he may have become, but St Thomas's favour was not exclusive. William the Lion, the king of Scots whose capture at Alnwick in 1174 was ascribed to Thomas's pardon of the repentant Henry, was equally a devotee of the new martyr, founding the Augustinian monastery of Arbroath in his honour in 1178;[124] Count Matthew of Boulogne made what

116 Budapest, Biblioteca nazionale Széchényi, MS Nyelvemlékek 1: P. Radó, OSB., revised L. Mezey, *Libri liturgici manuscripti bibliothecarum Hungariae et limitropharum regionum* (Budapest, 1973), 40–51, esp. 51.

117 Radó, *Libri liturgici manuscripti*, 15, 17, 51, and *passim*; cf. *Fragmenta codicum in bibliothecis Hungariae, i/1: Fragmenta latina codicum in bibliotheca universitatis Budapestensis, i/2: Fragmenta latina codicum in bibliotheca seminarii cleri Hungariae Centralis*, ed. L. Mesey (Budapest and Wiesbaden, 1983; repr. Budapest, 1988), i/1, 61, 195; i/2, 85, 128.

118 G. Győrffy, 'Thomas à [sic] Becket and Hungary', *Angol Filológiai Tanulmányok [Hungarian Studies in English]*, iv (1969), 45–52, at 50–51; idem, *Az Árpad-Kori Magyarorszag Történeti Földrajsa* (Budapest, 1987), 253, 259, 270, 273, 283–4. Since it was founded on Church land, Professor Peter Erdő (now Cardinal) inclines to the belief that it was an archiepiscopal foundation, despite its reception of royal patronage under Imre (1196–1206).

119 The oldest surviving parish church in Pest (and second oldest in foundation), situated near the *Erszébet hid* (Elizabeth Bridge), now the Belváros (city) church, dedicated to Our Lady. For the earlier dedication of this church to St Thomas, I am indebted to Professor Peter Erdő, now cardinal archbishop of Esztergom-Budapest.

120 Z. J. Kosztolnyik, 'The Church and Béla III of Hungary (1172–92): The Role of Archbishop Lukács of Esztergom', *Church History*, 49 (1980), 375–86. For Lukasz's dates, see *Decretales ineditae*, 161.

121 Győrffy, 'Thomas à Becket', 51. The earliest surviving reference to this church is from 1299, and the date of foundation has not yet been established.

122 Győrffy, 'Thomas à Becket', 51.

123 Győrffy 'Thomas à Becket', 49; L. Janauschek, *Origines Cisterciensium* (Vienna, 1877), i, 177.

124 C. Renardy, 'Notes concernant le culte de saint Thomas Becket dans le diocèse de Liège aux XIIe et XIIIe siècles', *Revue belge de philologie et d'histoire*, 55 (1977), 381–9, at 383; *Liber S. Thome*

may have been a penitential visit to the tomb in 1173 and granted free passage through his territories to the Canterbury monks, 'pro honore Dei et beati Thome archiepiscopi Cantuariensis et gloriosi martiris';[125] and King Louis VII of France made a sudden pilgrimage to the tomb in August 1179 to pray for the recovery of his only son,[126] giving precious gifts, including an annual donation of French wine, with which to celebrate the feast of St Thomas.[127]

The ghost of Becket hovered over the remainder of Henry's reign, and more than a ghost persisted as a discernible influence on religious attitudes for the rest of the Middle Ages, until 16 November 1538, when Henry VIII decided to exorcise the ghost forever. His peremptory edict left no room for

de Aberbrothoc. Registrum abbacie de Aberbrothoc, ed. C. Innes and P. Chalmers, Bannatyne Club, 86, 2 vols (Edinburgh, 1848–56), i, xi, 1–8; cf. ii, xxxi and frontispiece for the seal, with depiction of Becket's martyrdom; *Chronicon de Lanercost MCII–MCCCXLVI*, ed. J. Stevenson, Bannatyne Club, 65, and Maitland Club, 46 (Edinburgh, 1839), 11: 'Rex vero Willelmus Scottorum supra memoratus, ob familiarem amorem inter ipsum et Sanctum Thomam dum adhuc in curia regis Henrici esset contractum, divulgatum in mundo et approbato in coelo ejus martyrio, abbatiam de Aberbroutok in honore ipsius fundavit et redditibus ampliavit.'

125 Canterbury Cathedral Library, Chartae Antiquae F132; William of Canterbury, *Miracula S. Thomae Cantuariensis, auctore Willelmo, monacho Cantuariens*, MTB, i, 264: cf. J. O. Moon, 'The European Connection – Aspects of Canterbury Cathedral Priory's Temporalities Overseas', in *Canterbury, A Medieval City*, ed. C. Royer-Hemet (Newcastle-upon-Tyne, 2010), 177–93, at 180 and 188–9. The penance was for his scandalous marriage (1160) to Mary of Blois, a life-long nun and abbess of Romsey. Laura Napran ('Marriage and Excommunication: The Comital House of Flanders', in *Exile in the Middle Ages: Selected Proceedings from the International Medieval Congress, University of Leeds 8–11 July 2002*, ed. L. Napran and E. van Houts [Turnhout, 2004], 69–79 at 78) is mistaken when she says that Pope Alexander III 'refers to Matthew as count, showing that the Pope had recognised his succession to the county of Boulogne'. The cited letter does not. It instructs the archbishop of Reims to urge 'praedictum comitem', meaning Matthew's father, Count Thierry of Flanders, to take action against his son, who is scrupulously denied both the comital title and the normal diplomatic designation as 'dilectus filius noster' (*PL*, cc, 184–5 no. 114: Tours, 18 December 1163). Nor did the earlier letter, also to Henry of Reims (*PL*, cc, 184 no. 113: Tours, 10 December 1163), treat Matthew as count: he is simply 'M. filius comitis Flandrensis'; and the pope declares that the excommunication pronounced by the bishop of Thérouanne against Matthew and the secular canons he had intruded into two monasteries was issued lawfully (*canonice*) and ordered Henry to observe it himself. Whether he did or not is another matter.
126 Howden: *Gesta*, i, 240–42; Howden, *Chronica*, ii, 192–3; Diceto, i, 432–3; Gervase, i, 293.
127 According to J. B. Sheppard, 'A Notice on Some Manuscripts Selected from the Archives of the Dean and Chapter of Canterbury', *Archaeological Journal*, 33 (1876), 151–67, at 163, Louis' gift of 100 *muys* of wine yielded 1600 gallons *per annum*. This 'wine of St Thomas' was sent, more or less regularly, for more than 350 years: Moon, 'The European Connection', 178–9, 189, and especially, *Norman Charters from English Sources: Antiquaries, Archives and the Rediscovery of the Anglo-Norman Past*, ed. N. Vincent, PRS 97, ns 59 (London, 2013), 98–104, 203–4 no. 77, Canterbury, [23/24 August], 1179. Successive confirmations by French kings: *ibid.*, 204–10 nos. 80–83, 212–17 nos. 84–9; successive quittance from customs by English kings: *ibid.*, 217–20 nos. 91–3; and further quittances and grants by counts of Flanders and Boulogne and others: *ibid.*, 220–47 nos. 94–121.

doubt: 'his [Becket's] pictures throughout the realm are to be plucked down and his festivals shall no longer be kept, and the services in his name shall be razed out of all books'.[128] The ferocity of that attack is itself an indication of the power of Becket's name, even after 350 years. Where *Magna Carta* had come to symbolise the rights of the 'people', the *causa beati Thome* had become the symbol of the rights of the Church from the days of Stephen Langton, who had opposed King John and presided over the translation of the martyr's relics, to those of Stephen's successor William Warham (1503–32), who had been prepared to defend himself against a *praemunire* charge in 1532 with the assertion that, 'The case that I am put to trouble for is one of the articles that St Thomas of Canterbury died for,' and he arranged to be buried close to the place of Becket's martyrdom.[129] Only three years later (1535), St Thomas's name was invoked by his namesake, Thomas More, in his last letter, sent from the Tower to his daughter Margaret (Roper). In the letter, More prayed that he would 'go to God' on the following day, since it was the eve of St Thomas (6 July, the eve of the Translation on 7 July), and he concluded with an echo of the last line of *Felix locus*, one of Benedict of Canterbury's antiphons for the original main feast (29 December): 'pray for me, and I shall pray for you and all our friends, *that we may merrily meet in heaven*'.[130] It is a curious coincidence that More's severed head was later placed in the Roper vault in the very church of St Dunstan where Henry II had disrobed for his penitential procession to Becket's tomb in 1174.

It was this still potent symbol that Henry VIII attacked root and branch when he ordered the total destruction of the shrine in Canterbury and the systematic erasure of his cult from the calendars and service books of the *Ecclesia Anglicana*. Even then, however, after the removal of the shrine and

128 *Letters and Papers, Foreign and Domestic, on the Reign of Henry VIII*, ed. J. S. Brewer, J. Gairdner and R. H. Brodie (London, 1862–1910), 13/ii, 848; cf. E. Duffy, *The Stripping of the Altars: Traditional Religion in England c. 1400–c. 1580* (New Haven, CT, and London, 1992), 412 and plates 131 and 132; Duggan, *Thomas Becket*, 238.

129 J. J. Scarisbrick, 'Warham, William (1450?–1532)', *ODNB* (Oxford, 2004; online edn, 2008) [http://www.oxforddnb.com/view/article/28741, accessed 22 October 2010]. His career was in many ways similar to Becket's. He came from a modest background, had discharged numerous diplomatic missions before appointment as archbishop of Canterbury (1503–32) and Lord Chancellor (1504–15), and was confronted with the matrimonial crisis and the sustained onslaught on ecclesiastical independence; he may have been prepared to follow St Thomas to a martyr's death, had he not died in 1532; cf. F. R. H. Du Boulay, 'The Fifteenth Century', in *The English Church and the Papacy in the Middle Ages*, ed. C. H. Lawrence (London, 1965; revised 1999), 185–242, at 241–2.

130 *The Correspondence of Sir Thomas More*, ed. E. F. Rogers (Princeton, NJ, 1947), 564. Benedict's antiphon finished with the verse: 'Felix pater, succurre miseris, | Ut felices jungamur superis' (Oh blessed father, help us poor folk, | That we may happily be united in heaven): *Breviarium … Sarum*, i, cclvi. In the Sarum liturgy, it preceded the Gospel reading, 'Ego sum pastor Bonus (I am the good shepherd)': John 10: 11–16.

the scattering or concealment of his bones,[131] Becket's name was not forgotten. St Thomas the Martyr was chosen as the principal patron of the *Collegio Inglese*, established by the Jesuits in Rome in 1579 for the training of English Catholic priests, who were inspired to answer the call to martyrdom.[132] There St Thomas can still be seen, kneeling before the Trinity, in the fine altarpiece painted for the College chapel by Durante Alberti in 1581. St Thomas, in a red chasuble, kneels on the left, while an angel holds the sword of his martyrdom above his uncovered head. St Edmund, the martyred king of the East Angles (killed by Vikings in 869), in brown robes, kneels on the right, as a second angel holds three arrows, the symbol of his martyrdom, above his head.[133] It was before this image that newly ordained priests prayed before departing for what lay ahead of them in England. Between the two English martyr-saints stands a depiction of the Flaminian Gate (*Porta Flaminia*, now the Porta del Popolo), through which they would pass out of Rome on their missionary journey.[134]

Henry II may have obtained the canonisation of Edward the Confessor in 1161; Henry III may have devoted much gold and personal attention to rebuilding the abbey church at Westminster which housed his shrine;[135] but the cult of St Thomas at Canterbury easily outstripped that of St Edward at Westminster,[136] both in England and outside it, in a cult which left its imprint in liturgical and spiritual life across the whole of the Latin West. Yet, although St Thomas became a patron of the royal house, he was also very much a 'people's saint', so much so that Geoffrey Chaucer was able to use the Canterbury pilgrimage as a microcosm of contemporary English life:[137]

131   For an excellent review of the numerous theories surrounding the fate of Becket's relics, see J. Butler, *The Quest for Becket's Bones: The Mystery of the Relics of St Thomas of Canterbury* (New Haven, CT, and London, 1995); cf. T. F. Mayer, 'Becket's Bones Burnt! Cardinal Pole and the Invention and Dissemination of an Atrocity', in *Martyrs and Martyrdom in England, c. 1400–1700*, ed. T. S. Freeman and T. F. Mayer (Woodbridge, 2007), 126–43.

132   Duggan, *Thomas Becket*, 239–52. For the wider context, see P. Roberts, 'Politics, Drama, and the Cult of Thomas Becket in the Sixteenth Century', in *Pilgrimage: The English Experience from Becket to Bunyan*, ed. C. Morris and P. Roberts (Cambridge, 2002), 199–237.

133   C. M. Richardson, 'Durante Alberti, the Martyrs' Picture and the Venerable English College, Rome', *Papers of the British School at Rome*, 73 (2005), 223–63.

134   It is not without significance that it was 'From without the Flaminian Gate' that Cardinal Wiseman announced his appointment as the first archbishop of Westminster after the restoration of the Catholic hierarchy to England in 1850, for he was a former student and rector of the *Collegio Inglese*.

135   Spencer, *Pilgrim Souvenirs*, 182.

136   The contrast in popularity between St Thomas's shrine in Canterbury and St Edward's in Westminster is amply demonstrated by the great disparity in the volume of surviving pilgrim badges generated by the two cults. Where Spencer, *Pilgrim Souvenirs*, devotes 92 pages (37–128) to the Becket finds, those for St Edward occupy fewer than four (182–5), and some of them are doubtful.

137   Geoffrey Chaucer (c.1340–1400), 'Prologue' to the *Canterbury Tales*, lines 15–18: *The Riverside Chaucer*, ed. L. D. Benson (based on the edition of F. N. Robinson), 3rd edn (Oxford,

And specially, from every shires ende
Of Engelond, to Caunterbury they wende,
The hooly blisful martir for to seke,
That hem hath holpen, whan that they were seeke.

Until its destruction in 1538, his shrine drew men and women in their many thousands to pray or give thanks for favours received though his intercession.[138] For the English Church he became a heroic inspiration. The archbishops of Canterbury placed his image on their seals; so did the monks of the cathedral church[139] and Canterbury's citizens;[140] so also did the aldermen of London, who asked him to continue to protect the city that had given him birth,[141] and the mayors of London, who placed him on their seals beside St Paul.[142] Even Old London Bridge had an impressive stone chapel of St Thomas at its centre point.[143] All that, of course, was swept away by Henry VIII's edict; but

2008), 23. Chaucer's pilgrims are depicted in a sixteenth-century Flemish MS of John Lydgate's *Siege of Thebes*. Like the contemporary *Tale of Beryn*, this was a supplement to the *Canterbury Tales*, composed c.1420–22: H. Loxton, *Pilgrimage to Canterbury* (Newton Abbot, 1978), frontispiece; cf. *The Canterbury Interlude and Merchant's Tale of Beryn*, published online from *The Canterbury Tales: Fifteenth-Century Continuations and Additions*, ed. J. M. Bowers (Kalamazoo, MI, 1992), which likewise began with a prologue describing the pilgrims.

138   The most probing study is Nilson, esp. 147–54 and 211–15. Contrary to the general view (e.g. Loxton, *Pilgrimage to Canterbury*, 173), Nilson argues (148–53) that the recorded figures which show a steep decline in income in the fifteenth century are seriously misleading, since, instead of transmitting all the offerings to the prior as in the past, the shrine-keepers themselves disbursed stipends and expenses of various kinds and were also responsible for the purchase of wax. For the impact on the city, see Duggan, 'Canterbury: The Becket Effect', 67–91. For the continuing popularity through the later Middle Ages, *eadem*, '"The hooly blisful martir for to seke"', in *Chaucer in Context: A Golden Age of English Poetry*, ed. G. Morgan (Oxford, Berlin, *et alibi.*, 2012), 15–41.

139   *Age of Chivalry: Art in Plantagenet England 1200–1400*, Royal Academy of Arts Exhibition Catalogue, ed. J. Alexander and P. Binski (London, 1987), 399–400 no. 461.

140   W. Urry, *Thomas Becket: His Last Days*, ed. P. A. Rowe (Stroud, 1999), 179.

141   On the reverse of the common seal of the 'barons' (aldermen) of London, c.1219: *ME QVE TE PEPERI NE CESSES THOMA TVERI* (May thou never cease, O Thomas, to protect me who gave thee birth): described in *Age of Chivalry*, 273 no. 193, which shows the obverse (with St Paul), from London, The National Archives, E329/428.

142   For the first (before 1278) and second (1381) seal, see *Age of Chivalry*, 274 nos. 194 and 195.

143   A scale model of the bridge with the St Thomas chapel on its eastern side can be seen in the church of St Magnus the Martyr (Lower Thames Street), in whose parish it was until desecration at the Reformation, when it was put to secular uses (house, warehouse). It is also represented in a modern stained-glass window. The first chapel was built under the supervision of Peter of Colechurch (Cheapside) between 1176 and 1209, and the second, in splendid perpendicular gothic style between 1384 and 1397 by Henry Yevele (c.1320–1400), the great architect (master mason) who, among other works, refaced Westminster Hall and rebuilt the naves of Westminster Abbey and Canterbury Cathedral. It is Yevele's design which is represented in the model and window in St Magnus Church. Magnus is generally identified with Magnus Erlendsson, St Magnus of Orkney, †1118.

St Thomas can still be seen, holding his *corona* in his hands, in one of the niches on the west front of Wells Cathedral;[144] and the London hospital established in Southwark under his patronage, 'for the reception and care of the poor and sick' ('ad pauperum et infirmorum susceptionem pariter et sustentationem'), still stands on the south bank of the Thames, though on a different site, and, after four hundred years of disguise under the name of St Thomas the Apostle, it again bears his name.[145] In Canterbury Cathedral itself, whose east end was rebuilt as a *martyrium* to enshrine his relics between 1174 and 1186 to a design probably influenced by early Christian models like the basilica of S. Costanza in Rome,[146] eight of the original array of twelve stained-glass windows, designed to celebrate his life and miracles,[147] remain as a tantalising reminder of the man and the saint, despite the haunting emptiness of the place in the Trinity Chapel where the shrine once stood.[148]

144   P. Binski, *Becket's Crown: Art and Imagination in Gothic England 1170–1300* (New Haven, CT, and London, 2004), 117, fig. 96; detail, 13, fig. 12.

145   As defined in Gilbert Foliot's letter granting an indulgence to all who supported the building programme 1173 x 80: *The Letters and Charters of Gilbert Foliot, Abbot of Gloucester (1139–48), Bishop of Hereford (1148–63) and London (1163–87)*, ed. A. Morey and C. N. L. Brooke (Cambridge, 1967), 482 no. 452. After a devastating fire in 1212, St Thomas's Hospital was re-founded on a new site by Peter des Roches, bishop of Winchester, in 1215, and re-located to its present site, across the Thames from the Houses of Parliament, in 1862.

146   Binski, *Becket's Crown*, 24–5, and fig. 23–4; cf. T. Tatton-Brown, 'Canterbury and the Architecture of Pilgrimage Shrines in England', in *Pilgrimage: The English Experience from Becket to Bunyan*, ed. C. Morris and P. Roberts (Cambridge, 2002), 90–107. For the debate about the design of 'Becket's Crown', see esp. P. Draper, 'Interpretations of the Rebuilding of Canterbury Cathedral, 1174–1186: Archaeological and Historical Evidence', *Journal of the Society of Architectural Historians*, 56 (1997), 184–203, which rightly challenges the interpretations of P. Kidson, 'Gervase, Becket, and William of Sens', *Speculum*, 68 (1993), 969–91 and M. F. Hearn, 'Canterbury Cathedral and the Cult of Becket', *Art Bulletin*, 76 (1994), 19–54.

147   The array comprised Trinity Chapel windows, n.VII–n.II and s.II–s.VII, but the original glass from n.VI and s.III–s.V has been lost. For the position and content of the surviving windows, see M. H. Caviness, *The Early Stained Glass of Canterbury Cathedral circa 1175–1220* (Princeton, NJ, 1977), 164–6 (appendix, fig. 6), and plates 92–3, 115, 159, 162, 164, 167, 169, 171–5, 185–91, 194, 197 and 197a–h, 199, 205–6, 208–11; Caviness, *Windows of Christ Church*. For excellent coloured plates, see M. A. Michael, *Stained Glass of Canterbury Cathedral* (London, 2004).

148   Binski, *Becket's Crown*, fig. 1; cf. 25, fig. 16.

3.

The Cult of St Thomas in the Liturgy and Iconography of Christ Church, Canterbury

MARIE-PIERRE GELIN

On Christmas Day 1170, a few weeks after his return to England after seven years in exile in France, Archbishop Thomas Becket preached a sermon in his cathedral at Canterbury. While speaking of the men who had preceded him in the see, 'the holy men who are [buried] here ... he said that they had one martyr archbishop, St Alphege, and that it was possible that before long they would have another.'[1] A few days later, on 29 December, Thomas Becket was killed in the cathedral by four royal knights, not very far from the spot where he had preached on Christmas Day, and he indeed became the other martyr of Canterbury, as he had seemingly foreseen. The liturgy for his feast day further adds that at the point of death, he commended his soul to several saints, among them to 'sanctis hujus ecclesiae patronis', while one of his biographers specifies that he explicitly invoked St Alphege.[2] Archbishop Thomas is thus presented as belonging to the long line of archbishops of Canterbury who displayed admiration and veneration for their sainted predecessors. Alphege (1006–12), for instance, was devoted to the memory of St Dunstan (959–88); Anselm (1093–1109) defended Alphege's claim to sanctity against the doubt expressed by Lanfranc (1070–89); Lanfranc himself turned to St Dunstan for help and support on several occasions.[3] Thomas Becket himself, during

---

1 'qui ibi sunt confessores, loqueretur, ait, unum eos habere martyrem archiepiscopum, sanctum Elphegum; possibile esse, ut et alterum in brevi ibi haberent', William FitzStephen, *MTB*, iii, 130.
2 'the saint patrons of this church', *lectio* vi of the Matins office on the Day of St Thomas, *Breviarium ad usum insignis ecclesiae Sarum*, ed. F. Procter and C. Wordsworth, 3 vols (Cambridge, 1882), cclii; 'vir sanctus ... dixit, "Deo et beato Dionysio sanctoque Elphego me commendo!"' ('the holy man said ... I commend myself to God and the blessed Denis and St Alphege'), Anonymous I ('Roger of Pontigny'), *MTB*, iv, 77.
3 Alphege commissioned Adelard to write liturgical lections to celebrate the feast day of St Dunstan: *Memorials of St Dunstan*, ed. W. Stubbs, RS 63 (London, 1874), 53–68. In an episode

his pontificate, sought to have Anselm formally canonised by the pope, although the quarrel with Henry II prevented him from seeing this task through.[4]

From the point of view of the monastic community, Archbishop Thomas did not fit easily in the traditions of Christ Church. As a secular clerk, he had spent most of his career serving the Crown. Even after he became archbishop of Canterbury, his relations with the monastic community, whose nominal abbot he was, had been at best distant and at worst confrontational.[5] The monks, however, rapidly and enthusiastically supported the beginnings of the cult of the new martyr.[6] After the murderers had departed, they removed the body to the front of the main altar of the cathedral and carefully collected the blood which had been spilled.[7] While preparing the archbishop's body for burial, they discovered that he had been wearing monastic garments under his archiepiscopal vestments, as well as a hair shirt next to his skin, revealing Becket's austere habits of discipline.[8] This discovery, maybe more than the murder in the cathedral itself, allowed the monks to claim Becket as one of their own, although he had been an absentee abbot and had not always placed the interests of the monastery at the forefront of his actions. It also allowed the monks to inscribe him fully in the long line of archbishops whose

of his *Life of Anselm*, Eadmer recounted how Lanfranc had sought Anselm's advice about whether Alphege should be venerated as a saint or not: Eadmer, *Vita Sancti Anselmi*, ed. R. W. Southern, NMT (London, 1962), 50–54. Lanfranc accepted Anselm's argument that the reason for which Alphege had died was enough to count him a martyr and the liturgical calendars show continued devotion at Christ Church. According to Osbern, Lanfranc sought (and received) Dunstan's help in his struggle against Odo of Bayeux, as well as in the case of the cure of a possessed man; he also experienced a vision of St Dunstan during an illness, from which he miraculously recovered: *Memorials*, 144, 146–50 and 151–2.

4   R. Foreville, 'Regard neuf sur le culte de saint Anselme à Canterbury au XIIe siècle (à la mémoire de William G. Urry)', in *Les Mutations socio-culturelles au tournant des XIe–XIIe siècles*, *Spicilegium Beccense* II (Paris, 1984), 299–316 at 299.

5   Richard Southern pointed out that 'the relationship between a medieval archbishop or bishop of a monastic cathedral could never be entirely cordial': R. W. Southern, *The Monks of Canterbury and the Murder of Archbishop Becket* (Canterbury, 1985), 8. The relationship between Becket and the Canterbury monks seems however to have been particularly strained. In all the archbishop's voluminous correspondence, only three letters are addressed to the community, in which he generally upbraids them for their lack of support in his cause: *CTB*, ii, 911–21 (no. 209), 1092–7 (no. 254), 1238–41 (no. 292).

6   Anne J. Duggan noted that the monks' 'delay and hesitation' in accepting the cult of Thomas Becket 'lasted short of twelve hours' after the murder: Duggan, *Thomas Becket*, 214.

7   Gervase, i, 228; *MTB*, iii, 150, 519; *MTB*, iv, 78; *The Letters of John of Salisbury, Volume II: The Later Letters 1163–1180*, ed. and trans. W. J. Millor and C. N. L. Brooke, OMT (Oxford, 1979), 724–38 (no. 305) at 737.

8   As reported by several of the biographers, for instance Benedict of Peterborough, *MTB*, ii, 17; William FitzStephen, *MTB*, iii, 148; Herbert of Bosham, *MTB*, iii, 521; Anonymous I, *MTB*, iv, 78; or Gervase, i, 229.

bodies rested in the cathedral and with whose memory they saw themselves as entrusted.

In the decades following the murder of Thomas Becket, Christ Church underwent a series of major upheavals, which led the monastic community to embark on an extensive campaign of architectural, liturgical and iconographic creation. The archbishop's relics soon attracted scores of pilgrims to Canterbury, and after he was canonised in 1173 his cult became one of the most important and most popular of the Middle Ages.[9] It would hardly be surprising, therefore, to find that the cult of Thomas Becket overshadowed the cults of the other archbishops buried in the cathedral, in particular his Anglo-Saxon predecessors St Dunstan and St Alphege.[10] Indeed, the scale of the celebrations and commemorations (textual, liturgical and iconographic) dedicated to Becket at Christ Church surpassed in complexity and lavishness those which had been created for either Dunstan or Alphege. I would, however, like to argue in favour of evidence indicating that far from being consigned to oblivion, the Anglo-Saxon archbishops saw their cults revitalised and maybe even enhanced by the development of devotion to St Thomas at the end of the twelfth century.

The aim of this paper is to examine how certain liturgical and iconographic aspects of the cult of St Thomas, as it was established at Christ Church in the last decades of the twelfth century, made deliberate reference to the cults of his Anglo-Saxon predecessors who were, after him, the two more important saints of the cathedral. The reconstruction of the eastern end of the cathedral was seized by the monastic community as an opportunity to accommodate the growing popularity of the new saint on the one hand, and on the other to reinvigorate the older cults through the creation of new iconographic cycles. The way in which these older cults may have been used by the monastic community to enhance the reputation of the new Canterbury saint allowed the monks to establish his place in the traditions of the monastery and in inscribing him in the long line of archbishops.

---

9   The pope announced the canonisation of the archbishop on 21 February 1173 in three letters sent to England in March 1173: *MTB*, vii, 544–8 (nos. 783–5). Anne J. Duggan has analysed in detail the ways in which the cult of Becket spread to the whole of Europe through the manuscript tradition of the liturgies, the *Vitae* and the miracle compilations: Duggan, 'Cult'; A. J. Duggan, 'John of Salisbury and Thomas Becket', *The World of John of Salisbury*, ed. M. Wilks, SCH Subsidia, 3 (Oxford, 1984), 427–38; A. J. Duggan, 'A Becket Office at Stavelot: London, BL, MS Addit. 16964', in *Omnia disce: Medieval Studies in Memory of Leonard Boyle*, ed. A. J. Duggan, J. Greatrex and B. Bolton (Aldershot, 2005), 160–82; repr. with the same pagination in Duggan, *Friends, Networks*, no. XI. The papers published in *Sédières* provide further insights into the early development of the cult.

10   Which, for instance, is the opinion of M. Budny and T. Graham, 'Les cycles des saints Dunstan et Alphège dans les vitraux romans de la cathédrale de Canterbury', *CCM*, 38 (1995), 55–78, at 62.

Old and New Cults

In September 1174, 'by the just but obscure judgement of God', in the words of the monk Gervase, the cathedral of Christ Church, Canterbury, was partially destroyed by fire.[11] Coming only a few years after the dramatic murder of Archbishop Thomas Becket, the conflagration was another dramatic event for the monastic community of Christ Church. The subsequent reconstruction of the eastern end of the cathedral started in 1175 and was largely finished by 1220. The monk Gervase documented the stages of the planning and reconstruction in a text which offers an almost unique insight into the rebuilding process, known as the *Tractatus de combustione et reparatione ecclesiae Cantuariensis*.[12] The rebuilding was planned on a grand scale to accommodate the new devotional and liturgical needs of the monastic community and of the pilgrims who had started flocking to the tomb of St Thomas soon after his murder.[13] As described by Gervase, the entire eastern end of the new building – the Trinity Chapel and the Corona – was from the start intended by the monks to house the shrine of St Thomas.[14] As was often the case during

---

11 'justo sed occulto Dei judicio', Gervase, i, 3. The cathedral had already been damaged by fire in 1011, when the Danes sacked Canterbury, and again in 1067. The 1174 fire seems to have affected mostly the eastern end, leaving the nave intact.

12 The tract opens the first volume of William Stubbs's edition of Gervase's historical works: Gervase, i, 3–29. It was in all probability written around 1188, and possibly as late as 1199, as argued in C. Davidson Cragoe, 'Reading and Rereading Gervase of Canterbury', *Journal of the British Archaeological Association*, 154 (2001), 40–53, esp. 48–50. It was translated into English by R. Willis, *The Architectural History of Canterbury Cathedral* (London, 1845), 32–62.

13 F. Woodman, *The Architectural History of Canterbury Cathedral* (London, 1981), esp. chapter 3. The various stages of the design of the eastern end of Christ Church in relation to the political context and the development of the cult of St Thomas are analysed in a series of articles by P. Draper, 'William of Sens and the Original Design of the Choir Termination of Canterbury Cathedral 1175–1179', *Journal of the Society of Architectural Historians*, 42 (1983), 238–48; P. Draper, 'Interpretations of the Rebuilding of Canterbury Cathedral, 1174–1186: Archaeological and Historical Evidence', *Journal of the Society of Architectural Historians*, 56 (1997), 184–203. See also the differing opinions of P. Kidson, 'Gervase, Becket and William of Sens', *Speculum*, 68 (1993), 969–91; and M. F. Hearn, 'Canterbury Cathedral and the Cult of Becket', *Art Bulletin*, 76 (1994), 19–52. More recently, Paul Binski has offered a more aesthetic analysis of the eastern end of Christ Church: P. Binski, *Becket's Crown: Art and Imagination in Gothic England, 1170–1300* (New Haven, CT, and London, 2004), chapter 1.

14 After describing how the burnt remains of the old structure were pulled down and the initial stages of the rebuilding, Gervase mentions how, in the fifth year of the works, the architect 'praeterea ex parte orientali ad incrementum ecclesiae fundamentum fecit, eo quod capella Sancti Thomae ibidem ex novo fieri debuit' (laid the foundation for the enlargement of the church at the eastern part, because a chapel of St Thomas was to be built there): Gervase, i, 26; trans. in Willis, *Architectural History*, 51. The archbishop's remains were initially interred in the crypt by the monks after the murder. The canonisation of St Thomas and the influx of pilgrims made that situation quite unsatisfactory and a translation was therefore quickly intended into the upper church, although it did not happen until 1220 and the pontificate of Stephen Langton.

major rebuilding campaigns, this presented the monastic community with an opportunity to update the liturgy and rituals celebrated in their church. Gervase held the office of sacrist at Christ Church and as such he was much concerned with the treasures and relics present in the cathedral. He outlined the various stages of the building campaign in relation to the resting places of the archbishops within the sanctuary and his text, which has often been used by architectural historians to trace the history of the physical fabric of Christ Church, also provides a fascinating insight into how the members of the monastic community perceived the space of the church as a 'spiritual landscape', organised around the altars, the relics of the saints and, maybe most importantly, the remains of the archbishops.[15]

Christ Church was, from the end of the twelfth century, associated first and foremost with the cult of St Thomas and the relics of the martyr drew increasingly important crowds of pilgrims on his feast days.[16] Undoubtedly, the new martyr attracted far more devotion than any of his predecessors whose remains were at Christ Church, or even than any of the other saints whose relics Christ Church possessed.[17] The other saints who had long been venerated at Christ Church nonetheless retained their importance for the monastic community, in particular the cults of the former archbishops of Canterbury, first among whom were St Dunstan and St Alphege. The monastic community of Christ Church took great pride in its role as guardian of the tombs and remains of the archbishops of Canterbury, a role it had held since the pontificate of Archbishop Cuthbert (740–60) in the eighth century, when Christ Church had replaced the other Canterbury abbey, St Augustine's, as the burial site for the archbishops. All of them, save one, had been buried there, initially in a separate structure, the church of St John. The archbishops' remains were

15 On the architectural history of the cathedral, see n. 13 above. The uses of the space of the cathedral to map out a spiritual journey, both geographical and temporal, are analysed in E. Robertson Hamer, 'Christ Church, Canterbury: The Spiritual Landscape of Pilgrimage', *Essays in Medieval Studies*, 7 (1990), 59–69; M.-P. Gelin, 'Gervase of Canterbury, Christ Church and the Archbishops', *JEH*, 60 (2009), 449–63.

16 The records of the offerings made at the shrine show that even before the translation of Thomas Becket's relics in 1220 the offerings were considerable and remained greatly superior to that of any other English shrine until the fifteenth century: Nilson, 147–54. On the basis of these offerings, Nilson estimated that in jubilee years, Canterbury may have seen more than one hundred thousand pilgrims throng for St Thomas's feast day: Nilson, 113–15.

17 In addition to the remains of the archbishops, Christ Church possessed one of the most impressive relic collections in England, many of which had been brought back from Rome by Archbishop Plegmund (890–923): Gervase, ii, 350. An inventory compiled by Prior Henry of Eastry (1285–1331) in 1315 shows how extensive the collection was: London, BL, MS Cotton Galba E. iv, fols. 112–186v; *The Inventories of Christ Church, Canterbury*, ed. J. Wickham-Legg and W. H. St John Hope (London, 1902), 9–94.

subsequently buried near the altars and the relics they contained within the main cathedral church.[18]

Nowhere is the importance of the cults of the archbishops more apparent than in the narrative of Gervase.[19] At the time Gervase wrote his account, seven of these archbishops were considered as saints and two, St Dunstan and St Alphege, had been particularly revered by the monastic community since the Anglo-Saxon period.[20] They were buried in the monks' choir, on either side of the main altar and enjoyed a particularly elevated status in the liturgical practices of Christ Church. Lavish cycles of stained-glass windows dedicated to St Dunstan and St Alphege, around the choir, and to St Thomas, around the Trinity Chapel, were part of the rich decoration of the new church.[21] Although put in place about thirty years apart, these three cycles appear to have been intended by those who conceived them – the monks of Christ Church – to put forward a specific, unified image of the archbishops of Canterbury.[22] Associated with prominent shrines and splendid liturgical ceremonies, the cycles allowed the monks to re-assert their claim to being the guardians of the relics of the archbishops. Their lives – and death, in the case of St Alphege – provided the monastic community with types which prefigured the fate of St Thomas.

Even at the highest point of their veneration in the pre-Conquest period, Dunstan and Alphege never enjoyed the same popularity as St Thomas and, while the latter rapidly became a saint of international repute, the other cults

---

18   These altars were mostly located at the eastern end of the church, but also in the crypt and the nave: Gervase, i, 10–17 and ii, 345–8. S. Robertson, 'Burial-Places of the Archbishops of Canterbury', *Archaeologia Cantiana*, 20 (1893), 276–94; M. Sparks, 'The Liturgical Use of the Nave 1077–1540', in *Canterbury Cathedral Nave: Archaeology, History and Architecture*, ed. K. Blockley, M. Sparks and T. Tatton-Brown (Canterbury, 1997), 121–8, at 121–3, figs 46 and 53.

19   It is a theme Gervase also developed in his *Actus Pontificum*, a history of the archbishops of Canterbury: Gervase, ii, 325–414. See also Gelin, 'Gervase of Canterbury', 451–5.

20   The saintly archbishops are Cuthbert (741–60), the first archbishop to be buried at Christ Church; Bregwine (760–64); Æthelhard (790–805); Oda (942–58); Dunstan (959–88); Alphege (1006–12); and Anselm (1093–1109).

21   According to the numbering of the international Corpus Vitrearum Mediii Aevi, the windows of the life of St Alphege probably originally occupied windows Nt. III and Nt. II and those of St Dunstan windows St. II and St. III, 'possibly extending to St. XI': Caviness, *Windows of Christ Church*, 64. Those dedicated to the life of St Thomas were windows n. VII and n. VI, while the windows depicting the miracles spanned the openings n. V to n. II and s. II to s. VII: M. H. Caviness, *The Early Stained Glass of Canterbury Cathedral circa 1175–1220* (Princeton, NJ, 1977), 164–6 (appendix, fig. 6). See also *eadem*, *Windows of Christ Church*, plates 92–3, 115, 159, 162, 164, 167, 169, 171–5, 185–91, 194, 197 and 197a–h, 199, 205–6, 208–11 for the surviving panels from these windows. The hagiographic windows have all but disappeared, except maybe for a single panel which may have come from one of them originally, now in an American collection: Caviness, *Windows of Christ Church*, 177.

22   The dating of the various cycles is discussed below.

remained essentially local.[23] Veneration of St Dunstan and St Alphege was not limited to Canterbury alone in the Middle Ages, but only at Christ Church did their cults develop to such an extent. The creation of substantial picture cycles describing the life and death of the two Anglo-Saxon saints in the rebuilt cathedral, the location of altars dedicated to them in close proximity to the main altar of the church and inclusion of several important liturgical celebrations in the monastery's calendars all point to the regard in which they continued to be held by the Christ Church monks.

As the old structure was pulled down in preparation for the rebuilding, the relics contained in the altars and the remains of the archbishops interred within the cathedral were removed while waiting to be reinstalled in the new church. Gervase dedicated the bulk of his account of the rebuilding to listing exhaustively the altars near which the archbishops had been buried, not only in the choir which had just burned, but also in the structure which had preceded it and which had been destroyed in 1067.[24] The first archbishops whose bodies were removed by the monks were St Dunstan and St Alphege.[25] St Dunstan had left a particularly strong impression on the cathedral community. A monk from Glastonbury, he was bishop first of Worcester and then of London. Archbishop of Canterbury from 959 to 988, he was remembered as having been one of the principal actors in the reform of English monasticism at the end of the tenth century.[26] Furthermore, he was usually credited with having introduced Benedictine monastic practices at Christ Church, although in

---

23 For an analysis of the early cult of St Dunstan, see A. Thacker, 'Cults at Canterbury: Relics and Reform under Dunstan and his Successors', in *Saint Dunstan: His Life, Times and Cult*, ed. N. Ramsay, M. Sparks and T. Tatton-Brown (Woodbridge, 1992), 221–45. In the same volume, N. Ramsay and M. Sparks further examine the development of the cult of St Dunstan at Christ Church during the rest of the Middle Ages: N. Ramsay and M. Sparks, 'The Cult of St Dunstan at Christ Church, Canterbury', in *Saint Dunstan: His Life, Times and Cult*, ed. N. Ramsay, M. Sparks and T. Tatton-Brown (Woodbridge, 1992), 311–23.

24 Gervase included a description of no fewer than four distinct structures in his account: (i) the old Anglo-Saxon cathedral destroyed in 1067: Gervase, i, 7–9, quoting a text by the Canterbury monk Eadmer, *De reliquiis S. Audoenis et quorumdam aliorum sanctorum quae Cantuariae in aecclesia Domini Sancti Saluatoris habentur*, ed. A. Wilmart, *Revue des sciences religieuses*, 15 (1935), 184–219, 354–79; (ii) the nave built by Lanfranc in the late eleventh century: Gervase, i, 9–12; (iii) Prior Conrad's choir rebuilt while Anselm was archbishop: Gervase, i, 12–16; and finally (iv) the choir and Trinity Chapel built between 1174 and 1184: Gervase, i, 19–29. See also Gelin, 'Gervase of Canterbury', 457.

25 Gervase, i, 5–6.

26 Six *Lives* of Archbishop Dunstan were written in the Middle Ages. They have been published in *Memorials of St Dunstan*. Eadmer's *Vita et Miracula S. Dunstani* has recently been published with an English translation: *Eadmer of Canterbury: Lives and Miracles of Sts Oda, Dunstan and Oswald*, ed. and trans. A. J. Turner and B. J. Muir, OMT (Oxford, 2006). St Dunstan's career and his impact at Christ Church are examined in N. Ramsay, M. Sparks and T. Tatton-Brown (eds), *Saint Dunstan: His Life, Times and Cult* (Woodbridge, 1992).

effect this does not seem to have been the case.[27] As such, he embodied, in the Christ Church tradition, the ideal of the 'monk-archbishop', dedicated to the service of the Church of Canterbury and the welfare – both physical and spiritual – of its community. More importantly, his struggles with royal power and his exile during the reign of King Eadwig made him an ideal type of the tribulations suffered by his successor Thomas Becket.[28] From early on he was venerated at Christ Church, as attested by the commission of a *Vita* and liturgical lections by two of his successors, as well as by the high solemnity accorded to his feast day in the liturgical calendars of the monastery.[29]

Although now less well-known than Dunstan, Alphege was held in perhaps even higher regard at Christ Church. He had had a distinguished ecclesiastical career before becoming archbishop of Canterbury in 1006, but he owed his fame mostly to his martyrdom at the hands of the Vikings in 1012.[30] Having been taken prisoner by a party of Danish raiders, he angered them by refusing to pay the large ransom they were demanding; after a drunken feast, they

---

27 At Christ Church, the tradition, based on Bede's account, was that St Augustine had established monks after his arrival in England in 597, though there is no strong evidence for the presence of a monastic community before the pontificate of Ælfric (995–1005), even though Dunstan must have brought monks with him when he was elected: Bede, *The Ecclesiastical History of the English People*, ed. and trans. B. Colgrave and R. A. B. Mynors, OMT (Oxford, 1969), i, 27. For an analysis of the composition of the clergy serving the cathedral since its foundation, see J. A. Robinson, 'The Early Community at Christ Church, Canterbury', *Journal of Theological Studies*, 27 (1926), 225–40; T. Symons, 'The Introduction of Monks at Christ Church, Canterbury', *Journal of Theological Studies*, 27 (1926), 409–11; D. Knowles, 'The Early Community at Christ Church, Canterbury', *Journal of Theological Studies*, 39 (1938), 126–31; N. Brooks, 'The Anglo-Saxon Cathedral Community 597–1070', in *A History of Canterbury Cathedral*, ed. P. Collinson, N. Ramsay and M. Sparks (Oxford, 1995), 1–37.
28 Dunstan was sent into exile by Eadwig in 956 and he spent time in Ghent before returning to England in 957, M. Lapidge, 'Dunstan [St Dunstan] (*d.* 988)', *ODNB* (Oxford, 2004) [http://www.oxforddnb.com/view/article/8288, accessed 20 September 2015].
29 The *Life* was dedicated to Ælfric (995–1005) and the lections to Alphege by their author, Adelard: *Memorials of St Dunstan*, 3–52 and 53–68. The lections contained in the letter written to Archbishop Alphege remained the basis of the breviary office for St Dunstan: *Memorials of St Dunstan*, xxxi; *The Monastic Breviary of Hyde Abbey, Winchester* (Oxford Bodl. Library, MSS Rawlinson liturg. E.1 and Gough liturg. 8), ed. J. B. L. Tolhurst, Henry Bradshaw Society, 69–71, 76, 4 vols (London, 1932–33, 1938), iii, fols. 256–7. The liturgical calendar contained in London, BL, MS Addit. 37517, fols 2–3, shows that St Dunstan's feast day was celebrated with twelve lections and the entry is written in capitals: *English Kalendars Before 1100*, ed. F. Wormald, Henry Bradshaw Society, 72 (London, 1934), 62. Alan Thacker argued that although Dunstan's sanctity was recognised immediately upon his death, the development of his cult was notably slow at Christ Church. The two earliest lives of the saint were written by outsiders and the location of the tomb within the Anglo-Saxon cathedral made access difficult, thus hindering the development of a popular cult: Thacker, 'Cults at Canterbury', 223, 225–6.
30 He had, in particular, held the see of Winchester between 984 and 1006, to which he was appointed on Dunstan's recommendation: H. Leyser, 'Ælfheah (*d.* 1012)', *ODNB* (Oxford, 2004; online edn, 2006) [http://www.oxforddnb.com/view/article/181, accessed 20 December 2015].

pelted him with ox bones before killing him with an axe blow to the head. The gruesome manner of his death, as well as the circumstances, encouraged a cult to develop quite rapidly at his tomb in St Paul's Cathedral in London, where miracles started happening. Alphege's resistance against a party of Danish raiders and subsequent demise at their hands may indeed have been seen by many as a symbol of the struggles of the English population against the new Danish king, Cnut, and the high tribute he was exacting from the country.[31] His remains were solemnly translated from London to Canterbury in 1023, possibly as an attempt by Cnut to remove an embarrassing cult from London and to deprive the disgruntled inhabitants of the city of a focal point for their resentment of his rule.[32] Liturgical calendars from the eleventh century show that the day of the martyrdom of St Alphege became fairly widely celebrated in the years following his death, although Christ Church was probably the only church where it was celebrated with solemnity.[33] Like Dunstan, he had started his ecclesiastical career as a monk, distinguishing himself with his ascetic practices. His martyrdom at the hands of angry soldiers, though for reasons substantially different from those that caused the murder of Thomas Becket, made him another prefiguration of the fate of the recent martyr in the eyes of the community.

Alphege had been closely involved in the development and promotion of the cults of his predecessors while he was bishop of Winchester and it seems that he continued this process when he became archbishop.[34] As already mentioned, he promoted the cult of St Dunstan, and his translation to Canterbury also coincided with a renewed interest in the cult of his predecessor.[35] The

---

31   Cnut became king of England in 1016 after several years of renewed raiding by the Danes and of heavy tributes being exacted from the population: M. K. Lawson, *Cnut: The Danes in England in the Early Eleventh Century* (London and New York, 1993), 18.

32   The party of Danish raiders who captured and murdered Alphege were associated with Cnut's father, Swein Forkbeard, a fact which may have been inconvenient for Cnut. M. Lawson pointed out that Alphege's cult was not the only one to have political overtones in the troubled years after the conquest of England by Cnut: the cults of St Edmund of East Anglia and St Edward the Martyr also served as a focus for anti-Danish feeling: Lawson, *Cnut*, 95 and 140–43.

33   *English Kalendars Before 1100*, nos. 2, 4, 6–20. In most of these calendars, the feast day of the martyrdom of St Alphege (19 April) is not recorded with any specific grading.

34   He pursued his predecessor St Aethelwold's relentless efforts to promote the cult of the most famous Winchester saint, St Swithun. Wulfstan of Winchester, precentor of the cathedral, dedicated his *Narratio metrica de S. Swithuno* to Bishop Alphege and in the dedicatory preface (*Epistola specialis*), credited him with having completed a large tower above the high altar, a ring-crypt where the relics of the other Winchester saints could be kept and displayed and a massive organ: M. Lapidge *et al.*, *The Cult of St Swithun*, Winchester Studies 4 ii (Oxford, 2003), 67–8, 335–6. For his role in Dunstan's cult, see Thacker, 'Cults at Canterbury', 240–41.

35   In the liturgical calendar included in the Arundel Psalter (London, BL, MS Arundel 155, fols 2–10v), dated 1012–23, with many later, in particular twelfth-century additions, Dunstan and Alphege are the only two archbishops whose feasts were originally (that is to say before the twelfth century) included in addition to St Augustine: *English Kalendars Before 1100*, 169–81.

Canterbury monk Osbern wrote a *Vita* of Alphege, as well as an account of the translation of his remains from London to Canterbury, maybe at the request of Archbishop Lanfranc.[36] There is some evidence that the texts could have been used in liturgical contexts. In the 1120s and '30s, the Christ Church scriptorium embarked on the realisation of a *de luxe* passionale, containing the lives of all the saints venerated in the cathedral. Now surviving only in fragmentary form and scattered between three libraries, this huge manuscript probably comprised seven volumes originally.[37] The two texts of the *Life of St Alphege* and of the translation of his relics from London to Canterbury can be found in the surviving fragments of this manuscript.[38] Both are divided into nine *lectiones*, which could have been used for the celebrations of the feasts of the *passio* and of the *translatio*. The *Life of St Dunstan*, contained in the same passionale, was also divided into lessons which could be read at the office.[39]

By the middle of the eleventh century, Dunstan and Alphege appeared as

The dating is discussed at length in R. Pfaff, 'Lanfranc's Supposed Purge of the Anglo-Saxon Calendar', in *Warriors and Churchmen in the High Middle Ages: Essays presented to Karl Leyser*, ed. T. Reuter (London, 1992), 95–108; repr. with the same pagination in *Liturgical Calendars, Saints and Services in Medieval England* (Aldershot, 1998); T. A. Heslop, 'The Canterbury Calendars and the Norman Conquest', in *Canterbury and the Norman Conquest: Churches, Saints and Scholars*, ed. R. Eales and R. Sharpe (London, 1995), 53–85. Their feasts are distinguished by a grading of 'III', the highest employed by the compiler of the calendar. According to Wormald, this notation 'probably indicates the number of cantors used at the Divine Office on those days': *English Benedictine Calendars After A.D. 1100*, ed. F. Wormald, Henry Bradshaw Society, 77 (London, 1939), i, 48. It is reserved for the most important feasts of the monastery and is used for only a handful of celebrations, such as the Nativity, the Epiphany or the Assumption of the Virgin.

36 *Vita S. Elphegi authore Osberno*, ed. H. Wharton, *Anglia Sacra*, 2 vols (London, 1691), i, 122–48. The *Translatio* has been edited in the 'Textual Appendix' to A. R. Rumble, *The Reign of Cnut, King of England, Denmark and Norway* (London and New York, 1994), 283–315. Osbern was precentor of the community and a talented musician. It is therefore not surprising that at least some of his hagiographical compositions were chosen as the basis for the offices honouring the archbishops. He appears to have been fascinated by the relics held by Canterbury and to have made it his life's endeavour to spread their fame, even when little information was available regarding the life of the saints, as was for instance the case with Alphege. For an analysis of his role in the promotion of the older Christ Church cults, see J. Rubenstein, 'The Life and Writings of Osbern of Canterbury', in *Canterbury and the Norman Conquest: Churches, Saints and Scholars, 1066–1109*, ed. R. Eales and R. Sharpe (London, 1995), 27–40.

37 Canterbury Cathedral Library, MSS Lit. E. 42 and Lit. E. 42A (part 1); Maidstone, Kent County Archives Office (S/Rm Fae. 2); London, BL, MS Cotton Nero C vii, fols 29–78; London, BL, MS Harley 315, fols 1–39, and Harley MS 624, fols 84–143. The Canterbury fragments are discussed in N. R. Ker, *Medieval Manuscripts in British Libraries, Vol. II, Abbotsford-Keele* (Oxford, 1977), and more recently in R. Gameson, *The Earliest Books of Canterbury Cathedral: Manuscripts and Fragments to c. 1200* (London, 2008), 226–47. This was a long-term project which took many years to complete, as shown by the many hands involved in the copying and in the illuminating, as well as in the variety of formats adopted.

38 The *Life* can be found in London, BL, Cotton MS Nero C. vii, fols 45–57, while the account of the translation is in London, BL, MS Harley 624, fols 137–9.

39 London, BL, MS Harley 315, fol. 15v.

the most prominent saints of Christ Church. The few decades after the Norman Conquest seem to have been in marked contrast. No mention was made by Lanfranc in the customary he wrote for Christ Church of the celebration of St Dunstan, and Eadmer mentioned how sceptical Lanfranc was of Alphege's claims to sanctity.[40] Lanfranc had their bodies removed from the choir of the Anglo-Saxon church after the 1067 fire, first to the western end of the church and then, as reconstruction progressed, to the refectory, and from there to an unspecified location.[41] Nevertheless, their veneration seems to have endured at Christ Church in spite of the upheaval of the Norman Conquest. As recorded by Gervase, both had been returned at some point to their former, prominent resting places on either side of the main altar of the cathedral in the new choir built during Anselm's pontificate and consecrated in 1130, from which they were again carefully removed after the 1174 fire.[42] Gervase mentioned how, in Prior Conrad's choir, the images of St Dunstan and St Alphege were placed on a beam crossing the choir above the main altar, on either side of that of the Lord, a sign of the high esteem in which they were held.[43]

Dunstan was remembered with two feasts: his death was commemorated on 19 May and his ordination on 21 October. Alphege, for his part, was remembered on 19 April (*passio*), 8 June (*translatio*) and 16 November (*ordinatio*). In three Christ Church liturgical calendars which seem to have been in constant use from before the Norman Conquest to the translation

---

40   In the customary of Lanfranc (often referred to as the *Constitutions*), only Alphege appears among the main liturgical celebrations the monks need to observe, as a feast of second rank: *The Monastic Constitutions of Lanfranc*, ed. and trans. D. Knowles, 2nd edn, rev. by C. N. L. Brooke, OMT (Oxford, 2002), 55–65.

41   Eadmer, *Vita Sancti Dunstani*, in *Memorials of St Dunstan*, 232, 236. Eadmer, in his *Vita Sancti Bregwini*, mentions how the remains of the Anglo-Saxon archbishops were kept in chests located in the gallery of the north transept and it is possible that this included the relics of Dunstan and Alphege: *Anglia Sacra*, ed. H. Wharton, 2 vols (London, 1691), ii, 188.

42   Gervase, i, 5. Their translation back into the choir a few days before Easter 1180 was done secretly, at the behest of Alan, the prior of the convent, and gave rise to indignation on the part of the community who felt deprived of a splendid and solemn celebration: Gervase, i, 22–3.

43   'Ad cornua altaris orientalia erant duae columpnae ligneae auro et argento decenter ornatae, quae trabem magnam sustentabant, cujus trabis capita duorum pilariorum capitellis insidebant. Quae per transversum ecclesiae desuper altare trajecta, auro decorata, majestatem Domini, imaginem Sancti Dunstani, et Sancti Aelfegi, septem quoque scrinia auro et argento cooperta, et multorum sanctorum reliquiis referta sustentabat' (At the eastern horns of the altar were two wooden columns, gracefully ornamented with gold and silver, and sustaining a great beam, the extremities of which rested upon the capitals of two of the pillars. This beam, carried across the church above the altar, and decorated with gold, sustained the representation of the Lord, the images of St Dunstan and of St Elphege, together with seven chests, covered with gold and silver, and filled with the relics of divers saints): Gervase, i, 13; trans. in Willis, *Architectural History*, 43–4. It is not clear, however, what kind of 'imagines' were meant by Gervase. Since they are said to have been placed on a beam across the choir, it seems possible that they were three-dimensional representations of the archbishops, maybe even reliquaries.

of St Thomas in 1220, the feast days of St Dunstan and St Alphege stand out as some of the most important saints' festivals, second only to those of Thomas Becket, both in terms of numbers of celebrations dedicated to them and in terms of the solemnity with which these celebrations were observed.[44] The death of Dunstan on 19 May is distinguished with a grading of 'III' in both the earliest (BL MS Arundel 155) and latest (BL MS Cotton Tiberius B. iii) calendars, as is the *passio* of Alphege.[45] The calendars furthermore show an increase in the liturgical attention given to those celebrations through the period. An octave to the main feast of St Dunstan on 19 May is thus noted in the latest calendar and was added in the twelfth century in the earliest one. The same thing can be observed for the octave of the feast of Alphege's translation to Canterbury on 8 June. This veneration, however, may have remained essentially liturgical, limited to the celebrations mentioned in the calendars, as there seem to have been few miracles occurring at the tomb of either prelate.[46] For instance, it does not seem that any pilgrimage developed at the site of the archbishops' burial and overall popular devotion remained limited. These elements show that the older cults were not superseded by that of Thomas Becket and that they remained central to the way the monastic

44 The earliest of these calendars can be found in London, BL, MS Arundel 155 (see n. 35 above). The second calendar of interest is contained in Oxford, Bodleian Library, MS Add. C 260, and is representative of the early post-Conquest period, although it too was added to at later dates. It is edited and discussed in Heslop, 'Canterbury Calendars', 53–85. The third calendar can be found in London, BL, MS Cotton Tiberius B. iii, fols 2–7v, and is possibly the most interesting. It is edited in *English Benedictine Kalendars after A.D. 1100*, i, 68–79. Compiled around 1200–20, not only does it exhibit an unusual degree of complexity in its recording of the grading of the feasts, but it also includes many feasts of local Christ Church saints which seldom appear elsewhere, in particular feasts concerning the archbishops, for instance the feast of the *Regressio sancti Thome de exilio* (2 December), rare outside of Christ Church: *English Benedictine Kalendars after A.D. 1100*, i, 64–5. Another calendar compiled at Christ Church in this period is the famous Eadwine Psalter (Cambridge, Trinity College MS R.17.1), probably dating from around the middle of the twelfth century: *The Canterbury Psalter*, with an introduction by M. R. James (London, 1935); R. Pfaff, 'The Calendar', in *The Eadwine Psalter: Text, Image and Monastic Culture in Twelfth-Century Canterbury*, ed. M. Gibson, T. A. Heslop, and R. W. Pfaff (London and University Park, PA, 1992), 62–87. This calendar, although the closest in time to the conception of the iconographic programme of the rebuilt cathedral, unfortunately presents characteristics which make it a slightly less than reliable witness to the liturgical practices of the monastic community. In particular, it does not seem to have been kept up to date and shows several important omissions; for instance, neither of the main Becket feasts (the martyrdom and the translation) were added to it. It is therefore not included here.
45 See n. 35 above.
46 Even the inclusion of a feast in a liturgical calendar does not necessarily mean that it was still celebrated by the community and may simply reflect an earlier state of the liturgy, or even the personal devotion of the scribe compiling the document: V. Ortenberg, 'Aspects of Monastic Devotions to the Saints in England, c.950 to c.1100: The Liturgical and Iconographical Evidence' (unpublished Ph.D. thesis, University of Cambridge, 1987), 34; Pfaff, 'The Calendar', 62; Heslop, 'Canterbury Calendars', 55.

community perceived its history and traditions. As late as the last quarter of the twelfth century, Gervase could still call Dunstan and Alphege the *patroni ecclesiae*, thus underlining the high regard these two saints were still held in by the community, even after the tomb of St Thomas had become the main pilgrimage and devotion locus in the church.[47]

Types and Prefigurations

Devotion to the Anglo-Saxon saints at the cathedral gained in solemnity at the time of the rebuilding and their liturgical importance was reflected in the newly created iconographic programmes which adorned the walls of the rebuilt cathedral. Elements foregrounded in these pictorial narratives were chosen for their resonance with the dramatic events of the pontificate of Thomas Becket. In the new choir, their prominent resting places on either side of the main altar were further enhanced with extensive stained-glass narratives located in the windows of the triforium of the choir, in close proximity to their altars.[48] Madeline Caviness estimated that these *Lives* of Dunstan and Alphege could have included up to fifteen panels each, making them almost as long as the cycle dedicated to Thomas Becket's life in the Trinity Chapel. Only a few panels remain of these two cycles, now grouped in two triforium windows on the north side of the cathedral.[49] It seems likely that these cycles were planned and created as the building works progressed eastwards, and they could already have been in place when the monastic community formally re-entered the choir at Easter 1180.[50]

Three panels from a *Life* of St Alphege and six from a *Life* of St Dunstan

---

47 Gervase, i, 5. Although the exact date of the composition of the *Tractatus* is not known, C. Davidson Cragoe suggested that it could have been written as late as 1199, to provide background information to the two papal envoys who were investigating the outstanding dispute between the convent and Archbishop Baldwin: Davidson Cragoe, 'Reading and Rereading Gervase of Canterbury', 48–50.

48 Alphege's altar was located on the north side of the main altar, Dunstan's on the south. Madeline Caviness suggested that the original stained-glass cycles dedicated to the Anglo-Saxon saints could have been located in the windows directly above those altars, Nt. III and Nt. II (Alphege) and St. II and St. III, 'possibly extending to St. XI' (Dunstan), Caviness, *Windows of Christ Church*, 64.

49 Caviness, *Windows of Christ Church*, 64; Budny and Graham, 'Les cycles des saints Dunstan et Alphège', 57. Other saints were honoured in the windows: St John the Evangelist, St Stephen, St Martin and St Gregory, but only one window was dedicated to each of them: Caviness, *Windows of Christ Church*, 127–9, 138–9.

50 Caviness, *Windows of Christ Church*, 63; Budny and Graham, 'Les cycles de saints Dunstan et Alphège', 55–6. As the bodies of the saints were translated into the choir a few days before Easter 1180 (see n. 42 above), this completion date seems likely. The ceremony of the re-entry of the community into the choir is described in Gervase, i, 23–4.

can be seen today in the cathedral. Heavily restored, the narratives they illustrated are difficult to reconstruct, but the episodes that remain are nonetheless significant when looked at in the context of the growing cult of St Thomas and of the renewed interest in those of Dunstan and Alphege. The studies of the Canterbury glass cycles by Madeline Caviness and by Mildred Budny and Timothy Graham have shown that of the nine surviving panels, eight depict an episode from the *Lives* written by Osbern and Eadmer, with two episodes (the miracle at Calne and the vision of King Eadwig) being found only in Osbern.[51]

As mentioned by Gervase, the Trinity Chapel was from the start of the rebuilding intended to house the shrine of St Thomas and to become the focus of his cult.[52] The decoration of the Trinity Chapel was, therefore, likely to have been planned at an early stage, in order for it to be completed by the time St Thomas's relics were translated from the crypt.[53] The account of the rebuilding stops in the year 1184. After that date, expenses occasioned by the dispute between the convent and Archbishop Baldwin (1184–90) placed considerable strain on the monastery's finances. This may explain, in part at least, why the pace of the rebuilding slowed down.[54] Completion of the eastern end was undoubtedly further delayed by the turmoil created by the contested election of Stephen Langton to the archbishopric in 1207, which eventually led to an interdict being placed on the kingdom by the pope and to the eviction of the monks from the monastery and their exile until 1213.[55] The windows of the Trinity Chapel were in all probability not fully glazed before the community returned, although it seems likely that the work was finished by the time the translation of the remains of St Thomas took place on 7 July 1220.[56] Although they were completed at such different dates, it seems probable that those who conceived the hagiographic cycles intended, from an early stage, that the programme should function as a whole, with similar themes being illustrated in all three narratives and significant visual similarities being underlined to create unity between different parts of the programme across the space of the church.

51   The panels are Nt. X, 5 and Nt. XI, 9: Caviness, *Early Stained Glass of Canterbury Cathedral*, 145; Budny and Graham, 'Les cycles de saints Dunstan et Alphège', 63–75.
52   Cf. n. 14 above.
53   The translation eventually took place in 1220 under the pontificate of Archbishop Langton (1207–28), who made it coincide with the celebration of the first jubilee of St Thomas: R. Foreville, *Le Jubilé de saint Thomas Becket: Du XIIIe au XVe siècle (1220–1470). Études et documents*, Bibliothèque générale de l'École pratique des hautes-études, VIe section (Paris, 1958).
54   Gervase, i, 29.
55   C. Holdsworth, 'Langton, Stephen (c. 1150–1228)', *ODNB* (Oxford, 2004) [http://www.oxforddnb.com/view/article/16044, accessed 21 December 2015]. On the impact of this period on the rebuilding process, see Caviness, *Early Stained Glass of Canterbury Cathedral*, 24–5. On the impact of Becket's legacy during the period of the contested election and interdict, see the essay by Paul Webster in this volume (chapter 8).
56   Caviness, *Windows of Christ Church*, 164.

Twelve stained-glass windows located in the lower walls around the Trinity Chapel were dedicated to St Thomas and the way in which he was remembered at Christ Church. According to Madeline Caviness, two of the windows originally told the story of the life of the saint, while up to a further ten recounted many of the miracles that had already been wrought by him, mostly at the site of his tomb in the crypt.[57] These twelve windows constituted what was undoubtedly one of the most extensive iconographic programmes ever dedicated to a single saint in the Middle Ages. Like the cycles of the Anglo-Saxon archbishops, the representations in these windows were based on literary works produced at Christ Church. Two monks of the community, Benedict and William, started compiling miracle accounts soon after they started happening. The miracles depicted in the Trinity Chapel windows are taken from these compilations.[58] Both men prefaced their collection with a *Life of St Thomas*, and Benedict was besides probably responsible for the composition of the liturgy of the feast day.[59] He seems also to have composed the verse *tituli* which accompany the scenes of the biblical windows in the lower windows around the choir.[60] As was the case with the earlier hagiographic cycles, the same texts were therefore used as a basis of the liturgy and the pictorial cycles.

The creation and display of an appropriate image for the archbishop was crucial in the church that housed his remains. Even after Becket had been canonised, some still expressed doubts that his life entitled him to sanctity.[61] For the monastic community, in addition, it was of paramount importance to make sure that Thomas Becket could take his place within the 'spiritual genealogy' of the archbishops.[62] This task had partly been achieved already, by the liturgical and literary texts which, as already mentioned, develop the

57 Caviness, *Windows of Christ Church*, 175–210. See also n. 21 above.

58 Benedict of Peterborough, *Miracula S. Thomae Cantuariensis*, MTB, ii, 21–281; William of Canterbury, *Miracula S. Thomae Cantuariensis, auctore Willelmo, monacho Cantuariensis*, MTB, i, 1–136. Rachel Koopmans has recently analysed these two compilations in great detail: R. Koopmans, *Wonderful to Relate: Miracle Stories and Miracle Collecting in High Medieval England* (Philadelphia, PA, 2011), 139–200.

59 S. Reames, 'Liturgical Offices for the Cult of St Thomas Becket', in *Medieval Hagiography: An Anthology*, ed. T. [F.] Head (New York, 2000), 561–93, at 561; Duggan, 'Becket Office at Stavelot', 164. The original – monastic – Canterbury liturgy in honour of St Thomas was lost due to the decree of Henry VIII that all trace of the memory of St Thomas should be destroyed: *Letters and Papers, Foreign and Domestic, on the Reign of Henry VIII*, ed. J. S. Brewer, J. Gairdner, and R. H. Brodie (London, 1862–1910), 13/ii, 848. However, a shorter, secular version has come down to us via the Salisbury breviary: *Breviarium … Sarum*, I, ccxlv–cclx. The Sarum office, including the music, can be found in Slocum, *Liturgies*. See also the discussion of specific liturgical texts for St Thomas by Anne J. Duggan in this volume (chapter 2).

60 Caviness, *Early Stained Glass of Canterbury Cathedral*, 32. These are windows n. XV–n. XI, n. VIII, s. VIII and s. IX–s. XV.

61 Lambeth Anonymous, MTB, iv, 135–7.

62 Gelin, 'Gervase of Canterbury', 452.

theme of the relationship Becket had with his predecessors. The pictorial cycles completed it.

At Canterbury, the two obvious models for St Thomas were of course Dunstan and Alphege. By the time the Trinity Chapel windows were created, the iconography of the murder of Thomas Becket was already well established. It had been elaborated and fixed remarkably rapidly in the wake of his murder in 1170.[63] Almost immediately, and probably not very surprisingly, the moment of the mortal blows had been chosen as emblematic and representative, and a very stable iconographic formula can be found in a variety of media from the 1180s onwards [Fig. 3.2].[64] Although the iconography of the martyrdom was fixed very early on, at the time the glass cycles were being conceived no pictorial narrative of the life of St Thomas had yet been created. This afforded those who conceived the programme considerable freedom in terms of the choice of scenes represented and in terms of the models that they used.

The *Lives*, the liturgical texts and the images created at Christ Church at the time developed some key themes which shaped the image of the archbishop for the rest of the Middle Ages.[65] As analysed in particular by Michael Staunton, Kay Brainerd Slocum and Sherry Reames, the hagiography and the liturgy both presented Thomas Becket as a 'new man' transformed by his election to the archbishopric, as a good shepherd, as the defender of the church, as a martyr, as a miracle-worker and above all as a type of Christ.[66] First expressed in a letter written by John of Salisbury soon after the murder, these themes were repeated and developed by all of Becket's biographers.[67] They can also be seen illustrated in the windows of the life of St Thomas at Sens and Chartres Cathedrals, which are chronologically and stylistically close to the Trinity Chapel programme.[68] The Sens window places a strong emphasis

---

63 Borenius, *Becket in Art*. Several contributions in *Sédières* examine the development of the early iconography of St Thomas. More recent contributions include C. T. Little, 'The Road to Glory: New Early Images of Thomas Becket's Life,' in *Reading Medieval Images: The Art Historian and the Object*, ed. E. Sears and T. K. Thomas (Ann Arbor, MI, 2002), 201–11; Gameson, 'Early Imagery'; M. Poza Yagüe, 'Santo Tomás Becket', *Revista Digital de Iconografía Medieval*, 5, no. 9 (2013), 53–62.

64 Colour plates of representations in various media can be seen in Poza Yagüe, 'Santo Tomás Becket', 60–62.

65 The *Lives* of St Thomas in Latin have been published in *MTB*, vols. i–iv. Michael Staunton has published a volume in which significant passages from the *Lives* have been translated: *Lives of Thomas Becket*.

66 M. W. J. Staunton, 'Politics and Sanctity in the Lives of Anselm and Becket' (unpublished Ph.D. thesis, University of Cambridge, 1994), 162–4, 169; Reames, 'Liturgical Offices'; Slocum, *Liturgies*, 5–7.

67 *Letters of John of Salisbury, Volume II*, 724–38 (no. 305); cf. *MTB*, vii, 462–70 (no. 748).

68 The window at Sens could have been completed c.1210 and the one at Chartres can be dated to 1210–20: C. Brisac, 'Thomas Becket dans le vitrail français au début du XIIIe siècle', in *Sédières*, 221–31; Caviness, *Early Stained Glass of Canterbury Cathedral*, 84–5; Caviness, *Windows*

Figure 3.1. Thomas Becket preaching a sermon.
Sens, St Etienne Cathedral, c.1210, Bay 23, panel 5.

Figure 3.2. The Martyrdom of Thomas Becket.
Chartres, Notre-Dame Cathedral, c.1210–20, Bay 18, panels 22–23.

on the pastoral and liturgical duties of the archbishop, with such scenes as Thomas preaching from a pulpitum, celebrating mass, consecrating a church or taking part in a confirmation ceremony [Fig. 3.1]. Here, Thomas Becket is presented as the good shepherd who looks after his flock and as the type of Christ.[69] As these duties are not specific to St Thomas and do not refer to particular events in his career, this window creates an almost generic image of the archbishop, a representation of an ideal prelate depicted in the course of delivering the duties of his office. The window at Chartres follows more closely the episodes of the life of the archbishop, in particular those relative to his quarrel with Henry II.[70] The narrative starts with Thomas Becket's investiture as archbishop and includes several scenes where the archbishop meets a king (either Henry II or Louis VII).[71] The martyrdom also receives a more developed treatment, with three panels dedicated to this episode and two to the murder itself [Fig. 3.2].[72] In this window, the relationship between prelate and secular power is abundantly illustrated and Thomas Becket is depicted as defender of the Church and as martyr. There can be no doubt that the Trinity Chapel programme illustrated these themes in detail in the two windows dedicated to the life of St Thomas.[73]

The *Lives* of St Dunstan and St Alphege both included episodes which allowed them to be presented as types and prefigurations of their more famous successor. Although the *Lives* of the Anglo-Saxon archbishops were undoubtedly well known at Christ Church at the end of the twelfth century, their iconography was never fixed to the same extent as that of St Thomas. No picture cycle seems to have existed to illustrate the lives of St Dunstan and St Alphege prior to the reconstruction of the cathedral, although several images of Dunstan were produced at Christ Church in the course of

---

of Christ Church, 81, 141, and 193; M.-P. Gelin, 'Heroes and Traitors: The Life of Thomas Becket in French Stained-Glass Windows', *Vidimus*, 14 (2008) [http://vidimus.org/issues/issue-14/feature/, accessed 2 October 2015]; A. A. Jordan, 'Rhetoric and Reform: The St Thomas Becket Window of Sens Cathedral', in *The Four Modes of Seeing: Approaches to Medieval Imagery in Honor of Madeline Harrison Caviness*, ed. E. Staudinger Lane, E. Carson Pastan, and E. M. Shortell (Farnham, 2009), 547–64.

69 Sens Cathedral, Bay 23, Panels 5, 7, 9 and 10 [http://www.medievalart.org.uk/Sens/23_Pages/Sens_Bay23_key.htm, accessed 7 October 2015].

70 The Chartres window can be seen at http://www.medievalart.org.uk/Chartres/18_pages/Chartres_Bay18_key.htm [accessed 7 October 2015]. See also C. Manhes-Deremble with J.-P. Deremble, *Les Vitraux narratifs de la cathédrale de Chartres: étude iconographique* (Paris, 1993), 249–53; C. and J.-P. Deremble, *Les Vitraux de Chartres* (Paris, 2003), 128–33. On the other two surviving French windows of St Thomas (Angers and Coutances), see the contribution of Alyce A. Jordan in this volume (chapter 9).

71 Chartres Cathedral, bay 18, panels 9, 11, 14, 15.

72 Chartres Cathedral, bay 18, panels 21–3.

73 Madeline Caviness suggests that the Sens *Life* originally also spanned two windows: Caviness, *Windows of Christ Church*, 314.

Figure 3.3. Alphege killed by the Danes.
Canterbury, Christ Church Cathedral, c.1180, Window Nt. IX, 5.

the eleventh and twelfth centuries, and only one of Alphege.[74] Only one of these representations illustrated an event from the lives of the archbishops, and none of them provided those who conceived the iconographic programme with narrative models.[75] In this case again, the creators of the stained-glass windows had to rely on their own ingenuity to compose their narratives. In their lives as in the liturgical texts, the archbishops were presented as being willing to endure exile and even martyrdom in defence of what they deemed to be a just cause.[76] It is clear that the theme of the difficult relationship with secular powers is one that was foregrounded in the lives of the Anglo-Saxon archbishops, as they must have been in the windows of St Thomas.[77] They both depict examples of ill-treatment of ecclesiastics by secular rulers and their representatives and outline the dramatic consequences of such actions. Dunstan had endured exile, like Thomas Becket, following a disagreement with King Eadwig in 956.[78] As for Alphege, it is undoubtedly his martyrdom which made him a type of St Thomas: his death at the hands of armed soldiers could quite clearly evoke Becket's murder [Fig. 3.3].

Visually, it was easy to bring out similarities between the three prelates. In all the surviving panels pertaining to their time in office, the archbishops are depicted wearing full liturgical vestments, with the white pallium, symbol of their office, displayed prominently [Figs 3.3, 3.4 and 3.5].[79] The colours chosen by the glass painter for the various pieces of their outfits appear to be relatively consistent throughout the whole programme: each wears a red chasuble over a green surplice and white alb, and a mitre. Furthermore, all three archbishops are systematically represented sporting short beards, which makes the figure

74   For Dunstan, these images can be found in London, BL, MS Cotton Tiberius A iii, fol. 2v (frontispiece of the *Regularis Concordia*), around 1050; London, BL, MS Harley 315, fol. 15v (a fragment of the Christ Church *Passionale* of c.1123, see n. 37 above); London, BL, MS Cotton Claudius A iii, fol. 8 (a Christ Church benedictional of the first half of the twelfth century); and in London, BL, MS Royal 10 A. xiii, fol. 2v (the frontispiece of the *Expositio super regualam beati Benedicti*, from the twelfth–thirteenth centuries). The earliest of these representa-tions are discussed in T. A. Heslop, '"Dunstanus archiepiscopus" and painting in Kent around 1120', *Burlington Magazine*, 126 (1984), 195–204. For Alphege, I have been able to locate only one image, contained in another fragment of the Christ Church *Passionale*: London, BL, MS Cotton Nero C vii on fol. 46v. In this historiated initial, Alphege is represented as a fully vested archbishop enthroned in heaven.

75   In all the depictions Dunstan is represented in full archiepiscopal vestments, usually enthroned, except in the passionale, where he is shown dressed as a monk, pinching the devil's nose.

76   According to Anselm, dying in defence of justice was enough to justify Alphege's claim to martyrdom and sanctity: Eadmer, *Vita Sancti Anselmi*, 50–54.

77   Budny and Graham, 'Les cycles de saints Dunstan et Alphège', 66.

78   *Memorials of St Dunstan*, 100–101.

79   It is worth noting that in neither the Chartres, Angers or Coutances windows is Becket repre-sented as wearing a pallium. See, for instance, fig. 3.2 here and the plates in Alyce A. Jordan's contribution in this volume (chapter 9).

Figure 3.4. St Dunstan frees King Eadwig's soul from the devil.
Canterbury, Christ Church Cathedral, c.1180, Window Nt. XI, 1.

Figure 3.5. Apparition of St Thomas.
Canterbury, Christ Church Cathedral, c.1213–20, Window n. IV, 4.

of the archbishop readily identifiable while strengthening the visual links between the three parts of the programme.[80] While the Becket windows are inscribed with short verses which specify the type of miracle performed, there are no inscriptions in the Dunstan and Alphege cycles. This complete absence of inscriptions helping to identify the scenes from the lives of Dunstan and Alphege, coupled with the definite physical similarities between the three archbishops, must have made the association between the three prelates even easier. The result is, visually, the creation of a single, unified, a-temporal figure, 'the archbishop', whose presence and actions span not only most of the history of Christ Church, but also the entire space of the choir and Trinity Chapel.

In the panels which have survived, the two early cycles deal with the theme of the relations between Church and secular powers. The easiest parallel to draw was undoubtedly between the two Canterbury martyrs, Alphege and Thomas. The scenes where Alphege is attacked and then led away by the Danish soldiers would have taken on a particular meaning when compared to the story of Thomas Becket's murder by four knights.[81] Visually, the two situations could easily be cross-referenced [Figs 3.2 and 3.3]. Soldiers in armour manhandling an archbishop in full liturgical vestments would have immediately evoked the more recent murder to the audience, especially with the addition of the cathedral in the background.

A panel of the *Life of St Dunstan* seems to indicate that something more systematic still may have been attempted. In an episode first recounted in the *Vita S. Dunstani* by Osbern, Dunstan is said to have once experienced a vision of King Eadwig's soul being carried away by devils after his death [Fig. 3.4]. Only the saint's prayers prevailed over the demons, and the king's soul was finally released.[82] In the panel, the archbishop in full liturgical garments is standing in front of the gaping jaws of hell, out of which a group of figures emerge, led by a man wearing a crown. This episode seems to have been introduced for the first time by the Anglo-Norman hagiographers and, taken in the context of the difficult relationship between archbishop and king under Lanfranc's and Anselm's pontificates, it was no doubt intended as a warning to rulers who would mistreat churchmen. Both Osbern and Eadmer place this episode after Dunstan became bishop of Worcester in 957/58, but before he was elected to Canterbury in 959. The panel, however, shows Dunstan wearing the archiepiscopal pallium. As the figure of Dunstan is heavily restored, it is

80   The exception is the scene representing Dunstan being saved from the devil by an angel (Nt. X, 2). As this episode had taken place while he was still a monk at Glastonbury, he is represented as a young man wearing the monastic habit.

81   Nt. IX, 1 and 5.

82   Osbern, *Vita S. Dunstani*, in *Memorials of St Dunstan*, 104–5. This episode is also recounted by Eadmer in his *Vita S. Dunstani*, in *Memorials of St Dunstan*, 196. Window Nt. XI, 1.

possible that the pallium was added at a later date.[83] If it is authentic, however, this slight distortion of the chronology might have been intended to increase the relevance of such an episode in the aftermath of Thomas Becket's murder. It would certainly have been seen as an admonishment to Henry II to keep on repenting and asking for St Thomas's help in order to avoid dire consequences for his soul.

It is difficult to generalise these alterations, as the cycles dedicated to the archbishops are incomplete. However slight, such modifications do nonetheless seem to point to a desire to create links – not least visually – between the principal saints venerated in the eastern end of the cathedral. The foregrounding of specific elements in the lives of Dunstan and Alphege served two purposes: first, by drawing out parallels between the Anglo-Saxon saints and Thomas Becket, the creators of the programme sought to strengthen the claims to sanctity of the more recent martyr and to make him a worthy successor to Dunstan and Alphege. Second, the inclusion of the episodes described above, scenes which may have been consciously altered and rewritten in order to increase their relevance to Thomas Becket's story, created visual and typological links between the various parts of the hagiographical programme. The two Anglo-Saxon archbishops could thus be presented as prefiguring Thomas Becket, and St Thomas in turn could be seen as uniting in him the virtues of the two Canterbury models of sanctity, St Dunstan the confessor and St Alphege the martyr.

What emerges from an analysis of the panels dedicated to Dunstan and Alphege, therefore, is the impression that the similarities which existed between their lives and that of St Thomas were deliberately brought out – sometimes at the price of slightly distorting the original narratives – in order to model Becket on his saintly predecessors and to create a sense of continuity between the archbishops. The creation of extensive visual links thus allowed the creators of the programme to weave Thomas Becket into the Canterbury tradition, at the time when his cult was being established at Christ Church. Inscribing St Thomas in the line of saintly archbishops who had preceded him in the see may have been seen as a necessity in the context of the 1180s, when the windows were created. For the monks, after the difficult period which immediately followed the archbishop's death, those years were marked by their protracted and much-publicised quarrel with Archbishop Baldwin (1184–90). After his election, Baldwin rapidly expressed his intention to found a church dedicated to St Thomas at Hackington, near Canterbury. The community took offence at this project, which threatened both their right to elect the archbishop and their possession of St Thomas's relics.[84] In this context, it may have been felt of paramount importance to reassert the links between Thomas

83 Budny and Graham, 'Les cycles des saints Dunstan et Alphège', 57.
84 The whole dispute is summarised in C. R. Cheney, *Hubert Walter* (London, 1967), 135–50.

Becket and his remains and the cathedral and its community. The sumptuous iconographic programme no doubt had a role to play in this.

Just as Gervase's account of the rebuilding was intended to underline the role of the community as guardian of the church where the archbishops' remains had been kept and honoured since the eighth century, the miracle windows of the Trinity Chapel spelt out clearly the role the monks intended to play in the cult of St Thomas.[85] In these panels, a monastic figure is almost systematically present near the tomb, dispensing the miraculous water, accepting the thanks-giving offerings and recording the cures, which were thus validated by their insertion in the 'official' compilations produced by the monks. The essential role of the monastic community in the establishment and mediation of the cult was thus underlined, while at the same time the cathedral was presented as the locus of the saint's presence and power. Like the iconography put in place in the years following the murder, the devotion to Thomas Becket, as it was developed and encouraged at Christ Church, emphasised the links between the archbishop and his cathedral.

Conclusion

In the hagiographic narratives produced at Christ Church at the end of the twelfth century, the parallels between Thomas Becket and some of his prede-cessors in the see of Canterbury were brought forward, at the price, however, of sometimes altering the *Lives* of the earlier prelates. Nothing was left to chance by those who conceived the iconographic cycles, and numerous links between the liturgy and the images, and between the different parts of the programme, can be found, weaving a dense network of echoes and references. The result was the creation of an ideal figure of the archbishop, modelled in part on St Dunstan and St Alphege, two of the most important Canterbury saints before St Thomas, an archetype of both the martyr and the confessor, bringing together the virtues of the monk and the bishop, and a champion of the rights of the Church. Seen in the context of the threat posed to the incipient cult by Archbishop Baldwin's plans, the iconographic programme can, alongside Gervase's account of the rebuilding, be seen as a re-formulation by the community of its traditional role in the creation, preservation and propagation of the cults of the archbishops, and the degree to which these cults were insepa-rable from the physical fabric of the cathedral itself. The pattern of sanctity which emerged from these narratives helped the monastic community establish the basis for the cult of St Thomas, unquestionably one of the most successful cults of the Middle Ages, on which, in turn, other cults were modelled.

---

85   Gelin, 'Gervase of Canterbury', 461.

4.

Thomas Becket and Leprosy in Normandy

ELMA BRENNER

As Thomas Becket's cult flourished throughout Europe following his murder in December 1170 and canonisation in February 1173, numerous churches and hospitals were dedicated to the saint in Normandy. The duchy of Normandy was closely connected both to England, as part of the Anglo-Norman realm (until 1204), and to Becket himself since, according to tradition, his parents were both burgesses of Norman origin, his father Gilbert coming from Rouen and his mother Matilda from Caen.[1] Becket's cult in Normandy has been studied in detail by Raymonde Foreville, Jean Fournée and Ursula Nilgen;[2] a specific aspect of that cult, the leper houses dedicated to Becket in the duchy, is the focus here. These hospitals devoted specifically to the care of leprosy sufferers were religious institutions, a status formalised at the Third Lateran Council in 1179, which decreed that all communities of lepers should have their own church, cemetery and priest.[3] A number of other saints were popular dedicatees of leper houses in Normandy and England, above all St Mary Magdalene, St Giles, St Nicholas, St Lazarus and St Julian.[4] Thomas Becket thus joined a distinguished pantheon of celestial patrons of lepers.

Deserving particular attention in Normandy are the leper house of Mont-aux-Malades outside Rouen (originally dedicated to St James, and re-dedicated to Becket by King Henry II c.1174) and that of St-Thomas at Aizier, located halfway between Rouen and Le Havre, established in the late

---

1 R. Foreville, 'Les origines normandes de la famille Becket et le culte de saint Thomas en Normandie', in *Mélanges offerts à Pierre Andrieu-Guitrancourt*, *L'année Canonique*, 17 (1973), 433–80 at 439–41; Nilgen, 190.
2 Foreville, 'Les origines normandes'; J. Fournée, 'Les lieux de culte de Saint Thomas Becket en Normandie', *Annales de Normandie*, 45 (1995), 377–92; J. Fournée, 'Contribution à l'histoire de la lèpre en Normandie: Les maladreries et les vocables de leurs chapelles', *Lèpre et lépreux en Normandie*, *Cahiers Léopold Delisle*, 46 (1997), 49–142, at 126–9; Nilgen.
3 *Decrees of the Ecumenical Councils*, trans. and ed. N. P. Tanner, 2 vols (London, 1990), i, 222–3.
4 Fournée, 'Maladreries', 76–8, 85–7, 88–91, 93–104, 116–22; B. Tabuteau, 'Le grand saint Nicolas, patron de léproseries: une histoire d'influences', *Lèpre et lépreux en Normandie*, *Cahiers Léopold Delisle*, 46 (1997), 1–18; C. Rawcliffe, *Leprosy in Medieval England* (Woodbridge, 2006), 119–27.

twelfth century on land belonging to the abbey of Fécamp. Mont-aux-Malades was a wealthy and prestigious Augustinian priory, which was associated with Becket during his lifetime through his friendship with the first prior of the leper house, Nicholas. The community had enjoyed considerable support from Henry II and other members of the Anglo-Norman royal family prior to 1173. St-Thomas at Aizier was a much smaller and less distinguished institution, but nonetheless offered important provision to lepers, as archaeological excavations of its chapel, associated buildings and cemetery have attested.[5]

The miracle collections associated with Becket's shrine at Canterbury reveal that the saint was quickly attributed with healing a wide range of afflictions. Unusually among *miracula*, these include cases of leprosy.[6] The dedication of leper houses to specific saints, however, should not be understood in terms of the expectation of healing. Although palliative care was provided at these institutions, they were not intended to be sites of recovery from sickness, since medieval people recognised that leprosy was a chronic and ultimately fatal disease. What, then, were the reasons for the dedication of a number of Norman leper houses to Becket? A key factor could have been the need to attract charitable benefactions, since Becket's cult was highly fashionable in the late twelfth and thirteenth centuries. The numerous donation charters to Mont-aux-Malades in this period, preserved in the house's rich archive, suggest that this institution's new dedication to Becket indeed encouraged the wealthy citizens of Rouen to support it.[7] The emergence of the cult coincided with a period in which the patronage of hospitals and leper houses was itself very popular, further explaining the support received by Mont-aux-Malades. Yet powerful spiritual associations may also have motivated the dedications. Many contemporaries viewed lepers as a group specially chosen by God to suffer on earth and be saved.[8] Such ideas linked lepers to Christ and to martyrs. Indeed martyrs, such as St Laurence and St Bartholomew, were among the most

---

5 C. Niel and M.-C. Truc (with B. Penna), 'La chapelle Saint-Thomas d'Aizier (Eure): premiers résultats de six années de fouille programmée', in *Étude des lépreux et des léproseries au Moyen Âge dans le nord de la France: histoire – archéologie – patrimoine*, ed. B. Tabuteau, *Histoire Médiévale et Archéologie*, 20 (2007), 47–107; C. Niel and M.-C. Truc, 'Fouille d'une léproserie médiévale' [http://w3.unicaen.fr/ufr/histoire/craham/spip.php?article120&lang=fr, accessed 24 June 2013].
6 On miracle accounts in the collections of Benedict of Peterborough and William of Canterbury that involve leprosy, see R. Koopmans, *Wonderful to Relate: Miracle Stories and Miracle Collecting in High Medieval England* (Philadelphia, PA, 2011), 153–4, 156, 165–6, 168, 177, 179, 186–7, 196. See also the discussion in Alyce A. Jordan's essay in this volume (chapter 9).
7 Rouen, Archives départementales de Seine-Maritime (ADSM), 25HP (archive of Mont-aux-Malades). For the numerous donation charters to Mont-aux-Malades in the late twelfth and thirteenth centuries, see E. Brenner, *Leprosy and Charity in Medieval Rouen* (Woodbridge, 2015), appendix 2.
8 See F.-O. Touati, 'Les léproseries aux XIIème et XIIIème siècles, lieux de conversion?', in *Voluntate dei leprosus: les lépreux entre conversion et exclusion aux XIIème et XIIIème siècles*, ed. N. Bériou and F.-O. Touati, Testi, Studi, Strumenti, 4 (Spoleto, 1991), 1–32.

popular dedicatees of leper houses in medieval England.[9] In the late twelfth and early thirteenth centuries, Becket's martyrdom was an event in living memory, no doubt making the association of his suffering with that of lepers all the more vivid. It is thus likely that a house dedicated to Becket was perceived to be a particularly appropriate place for the spiritual and bodily care of the leprous. Unlike St Thomas's role in the healing miracles, therefore, in this particular context he was linked to the earthly care and ultimate salvation of those who would not recover from sickness.

The Becket Cult and Leper Houses in Normandy

Between 1173 and the end of the fourteenth century, fifty-nine churches or chapels were dedicated to St Thomas Becket in the ecclesiastical province of Rouen (its borders roughly corresponding to those of modern-day Normandy), the majority of these dating from 1173 to 1220. These dedications ranged from chapels within cathedrals, to parish churches, to hospital and leper house chapels, to chapels that served castles.[10] Generally speaking, these were smaller scale entities rather than major monastic, cathedral or hospital churches. Among the dedications, Fournée has traced twelve leper houses associated with St Thomas in Normandy, at Rouen (Mont-aux-Malades), Caen, Aizier, Boissy-Lamberville, Cherbourg, Canville-les-Deux-Églises, Criel, Lisieux, Harcourt, Vittefleur, Vesly and St-Pierre-des-Ifs.[11] In her earlier survey, however, Raymonde Foreville did not consider the chapels at Aizier, Boissy-Lamberville, Criel, Lisieux, Vesly and Vittefleur to be connected to communities of lepers, although she did list the leper house at Arthies, first attested in 1263, which was not included by Fournée.[12] While the foundation at Vittefleur dates from the fourteenth century (1311), and the date of origin of those at Boissy-Lamberville and St-Pierre-des-Ifs is unclear, the other houses listed by Fournée were in existence in the late twelfth or thirteenth centuries.

Several of these earlier houses were associated with members of Henry II's secular and ecclesiastical élites. The leper house at Criel is said to have been established by the count of Eu (presumably Henry, count of Eu 1170–91) in the late twelfth century. The leper house at Harcourt was founded in 1179 by Robert II, lord of Harcourt, who also established a chapel dedicated to Becket in the castle at Harcourt two years earlier.[13] Also in the 1170s, Rotrou

9 Rawcliffe, *Leprosy*, 124–5.
10 Foreville, 'Les origines normandes', 448–55.
11 Fournée, 'Maladreries', 126–9.
12 Foreville, 'Les origines normandes', 467, 468, 473, 475, 477, 478. For the leper house at Arthies, also see Niel and Truc, 'La chapelle Saint-Thomas d'Aizier', 51 n. 16.
13 Foreville, 'Les origines normandes', 473.

de Beaumont-le-Roger, archbishop of Rouen (1165–84) dedicated the altar of the chapel of the leper house at Cherbourg to St Thomas. At Lisieux, the chapel of the hospital for the sick poor was dedicated to Becket by Arnulf, bishop of Lisieux, before 1180. Fournée suggests that this institution may have initially catered for lepers as well as for the sick more generally, although such dual provision would have been very unusual.[14] Arnulf also established a chapel dedicated to Becket in Lisieux Cathedral, while Archbishop Rotrou founded churches dedicated to the saint at Barfleur and St-Maclou-de-Folleville.[15]

It would appear that, in the last quarter of the twelfth century, certain members of Henry II's aristocracy felt impelled to venerate St Thomas in the same manner as their lord. They may have focused on leper houses in order to emulate Henry II's re-foundation of the leper house of Mont-aux-Malades at Rouen in dedication to Becket, enacted soon after the canonisation. Such patronage enabled the nobility to demonstrate their loyalty to the king, and was a powerful means of ensuring the future salvation of their souls and those of their family members. The likelihood that such a 'patronage network' operated in Normandy following Becket's canonisation is increased by the fact that Henry II's nobles also supported Mont-aux-Malades, both before and after 1173. For example, the king's chamberlain, Roscelin, son of Clarembaud, founded the parish church of St-Gilles at Mont-aux-Malades between 1154 and 1165, and at least three members of the Talbot family, an important Anglo-Norman lineage, patronised the leper house in the twelfth century.[16] Most interestingly, after February 1173 but before Henry II's re-dedication of c.1174, Gilbert Foliot, bishop of London (1163–87) granted the church of Vange (Essex, diocese of London) to Mont-aux-Malades, on behalf of Lady Cecily Talbot.[17] He confirmed the charter with his own seal, that of Cecily Talbot and that of 'St Thomas, a short time previously archbishop of Canterbury'.[18]

The grant by Gilbert Foliot is significant. He had earlier been one of Thomas Becket's leading opponents but now demonstrated his subscription

---

14 Fournée, 'Maladreries', 126–9.
15 Nilgen, 196.
16 Rouen, ADSM, 25HP1 (act of Roscelin, son of Clarembaud, 1154–65); 25HP1 (grant by Richard Talbot to Mont-aux-Malades, c.1166, mentioning an earlier donation to the lepers by his father); *The Letters and Charters of Gilbert Foliot, Abbot of Gloucester (1139–48), Bishop of Hereford (1148–63) and London (1163–87)*, ed. A. Morey and C. N. L. Brooke (Cambridge, 1967), 472 (no. 436: gift of Cecily Talbot to Mont-aux-Malades, 1173–74).
17 *Letters and Charters of Gilbert Foliot*, 472 (no. 436). The charter can be dated to before the re-dedication of Mont-aux-Malades because the gift is made in favour of the church of St James of Mont-aux-Malades, rather than the church of St Thomas.
18 'sancti Thome dudum Cant(uariensis) archiepiscopi': *Letters and Charters of Gilbert Foliot*, 472 (no. 436).

to Becket's cult, symbolically attaching the saint-archbishop's seal alongside his own. Rotrou, archbishop of Rouen, and Arnulf, bishop of Lisieux, both themselves involved in the Becket cult from 1173, had also been key players in the Becket dispute. Neither man had overtly opposed Becket, but equally neither had been forthcoming in his support. Rotrou and Arnulf's reserve was due to the political difficulty of the situation but also, Nilgen argues, to the fact that the Norman secular clergy was embedded in the Anglo-Norman aristocracy, which owed natural allegiance to the king. Rotrou, as a member of the great Beaumont-le-Roger family, had very different social origins to Becket, the son of a merchant.[19] Rotrou had led the failed negotiations of 1170 between Becket and Henry II, while Arnulf had supported Henry, defending the Constitutions of Clarendon to Pope Alexander III (1159–81), but had also played an important role in mediating between the exiled archbishop and the king.[20] Both Rotrou and Arnulf were also involved in arranging for Henry II to receive papal absolution for Becket's murder at Avranches in May 1172.[21] Rotrou and Arnulf's dedications to Becket, and Gilbert Foliot's involvement in the saint's cult, can be perceived as part of the process of penance followed by the protagonists of the Becket dispute after the archbishop's murder.

The leper house chapel dedicated to Becket at Caen was built in the last quarter of the twelfth century, probably in the 1190s, in the Bourg-l'Abbesse suburb, the area where the urban possessions of the nunnery of Holy Trinity were focused. There was still a leper house functioning on this site in the second half of the fifteenth century.[22] Also in the later twelfth century (or early thirteenth century), Caen's hospital for the sick poor was dedicated to St Thomas the Martyr, and bore a dual dedication to St Thomas and St Anthony. The leper house at Caen apparently received income from (or paid money to) Holy Trinity Abbey, the abbess of which had the right of presentation to its chapel. The hospital for the sick poor similarly came under the patronage of the abbess alongside the abbot of St Stephen of Caen, suggesting that the town's great monastic houses played a role in the promotion of Becket's cult in the locality.[23] In the late twelfth century, William of Calix, 'a leper', donated a house to Holy Trinity Abbey so that he would be received in 'the leper house of St Thomas' and would benefit from the prayers of the

---

19 Nilgen, 193–5.
20 Fournée, 'Maladreries', 127, 128; T. Shahan, 'Arnulf of Lisieux', in *The Catholic Encyclopedia*, I [http://www.newadvent.org/cathen/01752a.htm, accessed 29 June 2013]; Nilgen, 194.
21 Barlow, 260–61.
22 Fournée, 'Lieux de culte', 386; C. Collet, P. Leroux and J.-Y. Marin, *Caen, cité médiévale: bilan d'archéologie et d'histoire* (Caen, 1996), 71, 72; *Charters and Custumals of the Abbey of Holy Trinity Caen. Part 2: The French Estates*, ed. J. Walmsley (Oxford, 1994), 10, 129 n. 6.
23 Foreville, 'Les origines normandes', 462–3.

community of Holy Trinity.[24] This man was very probably synonymous with the Caen money-lender William of Calix, who witnessed transactions relating to Holy Trinity between 1178 and 1183.[25] The size of his gift and his likely identity suggest that the leper house of St-Thomas at Caen, like Mont-aux-Malades at Rouen, received wealthy individuals who offered a substantial entrance gift.[26] William of Calix chose to enter a very new foundation, and may have been attracted by its dedication to Becket. The fact that Holy Trinity administered this donation suggests that the nuns were directly involved in the oversight of the leper house's affairs, further pointing towards their likely role in its foundation.

St Thomas Becket and the Care of Lepers: Mont-aux-Malades, Rouen and St-Thomas, Aizier

Henry II's re-foundation of Mont-aux-Malades at Rouen in dedication to Thomas Becket c.1174 undoubtedly increased the prestige of the leper house as a religious house, as well as leading to increased charitable patronage. However, before the re-foundation Mont-aux-Malades was already a distinguished monastery, and was already associated with Becket. The first prior of Mont-aux-Malades, Nicholas, was a personal friend of the archbishop of Canterbury. The two men probably became acquainted when Becket lay ill at the Benedictine priory of St-Gervais, not far from Mont-aux-Malades, in the late summer of 1161.[27] Becket's presence at Rouen at this time reflects his links with the city: he also stayed there for lengthy periods in 1159 and 1160.[28] St-Gervais was a dependency of the abbey of Fécamp, located beyond the walls to the north-west of Rouen.[29] It was known for the medical care of another

24 'leprosus … maladeriam beati Thome': *Charters*, ed. Walmsley, 129 (cartulary document no. 17), and see also 129 n. 6, citing the 1257 Holy Trinity survey §125, which states: 'Saint-Thomas, qui estoit une leproserie, avoit distribucions sur l'abbaye.'
25 *Ibid.*, 36–7 (original charter no. 3), 112–13 (cartulary document no. 1), 128–9 (cartulary document no. 16).
26 On entrance gifts at Mont-aux-Malades, see Brenner, *Leprosy and Charity*, chapter 1.
27 P. Langlois, *Histoire du prieuré du Mont-aux-Malades-lès-Rouen, et correspondance du prieur de ce monastère avec saint Thomas de Cantorbéry, 1120–1820* (Rouen, 1851), 20; Barlow, 62; M. Chibnall, *The Empress Matilda: Queen Consort, Queen Mother and Lady of the English* (Oxford, 1991), 169; Nilgen, 192, 193.
28 Foreville, 'Les origines normandes', 447.
29 On the priory and parish of St-Gervais, Rouen, see F. Lemoine and J. Tanguy, *Rouen aux 100 clochers: dictionnaire des églises et chapelles de Rouen (avant 1789)* (Rouen, 2004), 49–51; G. Combalbert, 'Archbishops and the City: Powers, Conflicts, and Jurisdiction in the Parishes of Rouen (Eleventh–Thirteenth Centuries)', in *Society and Culture in Medieval Rouen, 911–1300*, ed. L. V. Hicks and E. Brenner, Studies in the Early Middle Ages, 39 (Turnhout, 2013), 185–223, at 191–2.

very high status individual, since, according to Orderic Vitalis, William the Conqueror received the attentions of physicians there before he died at the priory on 9 September 1087, having been brought there after falling very sick at Mantes while on military campaign.[30] The Conqueror himself instructed that he should be taken to St-Gervais because Rouen was too noisy, suggesting that the health-giving benefits of this semi-rural location were recognised.[31] The friendship between Nicholas, an Augustinian prior, and Becket was appropriate given the latter's early education in England at the Augustinian priory of Merton.[32] Nicholas loyally supported the archbishop during his exile from England (1164–70) as part of a wider 'intelligence network', and wrote several letters to him during this period. He also corresponded with John of Salisbury, a key figure in Becket's entourage.[33] The letter of Prior Nicholas to Becket of Christmas 1164, recounting the audiences that he had recently had with Henry II's mother the Empress Matilda, reveals that he moved in courtly circles. The same letter states that the community at Mont-aux-Malades was at this time praying for the exiled archbishop's cause, thus explicitly pledging its support for him.[34]

The leper community's allegiance could have placed it in a delicate situation. Since its early twelfth-century origins it had depended on the patronage of the Anglo-Norman royal family, with the earliest donation associated with the community being a grant by Geoffrey of Anjou, issued as duke of Normandy (1144–50), reconfirming the gift by King Henry I of 40 *sous* a month to 'the lepers of Rouen'.[35] Henry II was himself a generous patron prior to 1170.[36] This suggests both that Becket had a very strong personal relationship with the community, which resulted in its loyalty, and that Prior Nicholas was adept

30 On William the Conqueror's illness and death at the priory of St-Gervais, see *The Ecclesiastical History of Orderic Vitalis*, ed. and trans. M. Chibnall, OMT, 6 vols (Oxford, 1969–80), iv, 78–81, 100–101.

31 *Ibid.*, iv, 78–81.

32 Nilgen, 190, 195. On the Augustinian movement in Normandy, of which Mont-aux-Malades formed part, see M. Arnoux (ed.), *Des clercs au service de la réforme: études et documents sur les chanoines réguliers de la province de Rouen*, Bibliotheca Victorina, 11 (Turnhout, 2000).

33 Barlow, 129–30; CTB, i, 158–69 (no. 41: Prior Nicholas to Becket, Christmas season, 1164), 382–9 (no. 94: Nicholas to Becket, before 6 July 1166), 548–53 (no. 113: Nicholas to Becket, before 18 November 1166), 622–3 (no. 132: Nicholas to Becket, August 1167). See also CTB, i, 342–7 (no. 83: Becket to Nicholas, after 12 June 1166) – however, the author of this letter was probably John of Salisbury – see *The Letters of John of Salisbury, Volume II: The Later Letters 1163–1180*, ed. and trans. W. J. Millor and C. N. L. Brooke, OMT (Oxford, 1979), 64–7 (no. 157). For other relevant John of Salisbury letters, see *Letters of John of Salisbury, Volume II*, 250–53 (no. 188), 452–7 (no. 239).

34 CTB, i, 158–69 (no. 41, at 160–61, 162–9); Chibnall, *Empress Matilda*, 169–71.

35 'leprosis Rothomagi': Paris, Archives Nationales (AN), *K23 15 22.

36 For Henry II's gifts to Mont-aux-Malades before and after 1170, see Brenner, *Leprosy and Charity*, chapter 1.

in managing his relations with the Empress Matilda and, perhaps, Henry II during this difficult period.

Henry II's patronage for Mont-aux-Malades after Becket was murdered in December 1170 should be understood in the context of both this direct link between the leper house and Becket, and the king's own penance for the murder. On 12 July 1174, the king visited the saint's tomb at Canterbury, where he did penance and apparently sought Becket's intercession in order to defeat a rebellion against his rule by the Young King Henry, Eleanor of Aquitaine and Louis VII of France.[37] On his return to Normandy, Henry successfully overwhelmed the rebellion at Rouen on 14 August, and his dedication to Becket at Mont-aux-Malades, as well as his involvement in the establishment of an Augustinian priory dedicated to Becket at Dublin and his possible re-foundation of hospitals at Argentan and Caen in dedication to the martyr, should be seen in the light of these events.[38]

Following its re-dedication, Mont-aux-Malades became an important focus for the charitable patronage of Rouen's burgess élite, revealing that the house's association with the martyr saint was perceived to bring spiritual benefit to all those connected to it, including its benefactors. Between 1206 and 1218, the Rouen burgess Ralph the Jew, a convert to Christianity or the son of converts, made a gift 'to God and St Mary and St Thomas the Martyr' of Mont-aux-Malades, for the salvation of himself, his parents, ancestors, children and successors.[39] The wording of his charter suggests that he was specifically appealing to St Thomas, as well as to the Virgin Mary, for intercessory aid.

Donors like Ralph the Jew may also have sought to benefit from the potency of the relics of Becket possessed by Mont-aux-Malades. In 1610, the leper house held a reliquary containing a bone of St Thomas Becket and fragments of his stole, goblet, rochet and hair-shirt.[40] It is not known when these relics were acquired, but it is plausible that the community obtained them soon after the re-dedication. The fragments of objects owned by Becket could have been received before 1220, when Becket's body was transferred from Canterbury Cathedral crypt into the Trinity Chapel, only after which date relics of parts

37 Barlow, 269–70; W. L. Warren, *Henry II* (London, 1973), 135–6. On the Great Rebellion, see also the discussion in Anne J. Duggan's essay in this volume (chapter 2).

38 E. M. Hallam, 'Henry II as a Founder of Monasteries', *JEH*, 28 (1977), 113–32, at 125, 127–8. The Caen foundation was the hospital for the sick poor there, the Hôtel-Dieu, dedicated to Becket and St Anthony, which should not be confused with the leper house of St-Thomas in the Bourg-l'Abbesse.

39 'deo et beate Marie et Sancto Thome martyri de monte Leprosorum': Rouen, ADSM, 25HP3. On Ralph the Jew, see E. Brenner and L. V. Hicks, 'The Jews of Rouen in the Eleventh to the Thirteenth Centuries', in *Society and Culture in Medieval Rouen, 911–1300*, ed. L. V. Hicks and E. Brenner, Studies in the Early Middle Ages, 39 (Turnhout, 2013), 369–82, at 378–9.

40 Langlois, *Histoire*, 363; Nilgen, 196.

of his body began to appear.[41] These relics were presumably venerated by the lepers and other members of the community when they worshipped, directly benefiting the health of their souls. Other leper houses possessed collections of relics, such as St Bartholomew's, Oxford, the residents of which complained in 1391 that relics including a piece of St Bartholomew's skin, a rib of St Peter and a comb owned by St Edmund had been removed by Oriel College, Oxford.[42] Relics attracted gifts, as well as serving as a focus for worship. The ownership of Becket relics marked Mont-aux-Malades out as one of the key sites for the martyr's cult in Normandy. Relics of the saint were also held at Bayeux Cathedral, the Hôtel-Dieu of Lisieux and the Augustinian priories of Sausseuse and Ste-Barbe-en-Auge.[43]

In and around Rouen, the saint's cult was also prominent at other locations that were not associated with leprosy. In Rouen Cathedral, a lateral chapel dedicated to Becket was established within the larger chapel of St-Romain in 1207, and the Portail des Libraires to the cathedral's north incorporates a late thirteenth-century carved image of the saint.[44] The priory church of St-Gervais, where Becket had recovered from his illness in 1161, evidently possessed relics of the martyr from an early date, since on 7 July 1222 some of these were transferred to the cathedral.[45] In the fourteenth century, stained-glass panels depicting scenes of Becket and Henry II, and of the murder in Canterbury Cathedral, were installed in one of the choir chapels of the abbey church of St-Ouen, Rouen's largest monastic house.[46] This later iconography at St-Ouen indicates the longevity of the Becket cult at Rouen, suggesting that a major reason for the continuing flow of donations to Mont-aux-Malades into the fourteenth century was the ongoing popularity of the saint. The fact that this institution catered for lepers was, therefore, not necessarily the primary reason for the support it received, although charity for lepers was undoubtedly a key focus of piety in the twelfth and thirteenth centuries.

The chapel of St-Thomas at Aizier had a much more rural location than Mont-aux-Malades, being situated on the edge of the forest of Brotonne on the left bank of the river Seine, on a hill. Other leper houses, such as St Nicholas, Harbledown, outside Canterbury, and indeed Mont-aux-Malades, were also located on elevated ground. This made them more visible to travellers – who might potentially donate alms – and may reflect ideas about the health-giving benefits of pure air.[47] Part of the chapel at Aizier is still standing, with the choir

---

41 Nilgen, 196.
42 Rawcliffe, *Leprosy*, 124, 340 n. 177.
43 Nilgen, 196 (and n. 28), 197.
44 Nilgen, 197; Fournée, 'Lieux de culte', 380.
45 Fournée, 'Lieux de culte', 380.
46 Nilgen, 197, 199; Fournée, 'Lieux de culte', 380.
47 E. J. Kealey, *Medieval Medicus: A Social History of Anglo-Norman Medicine* (Baltimore, MD, 1981), 85, 86–7.

exhibiting a flat chevet and two fully arched openings. It is Romanesque in style, dating from the late twelfth century, probably between 1173 and 1180.[48] Excavations have uncovered a large building to the west of the chapel, in use between the thirteenth and fifteenth centuries, and a cemetery immediately to the north.[49]

The village of Aizier, with 'whatever Trostincus held there', was granted by Duke Richard II of Normandy (996–1027) to the abbey of Fécamp on 30 May 1006. He reconfirmed the grant in August 1025, adding the village of Ste-Croix[-sur-Aizier].[50] While no documentary evidence survives regarding the establishment of a leper community at Aizier or the construction of the chapel, it is noteworthy that the abbot of Fécamp in the 1170s, when the chapel was most likely built, was Henry de Sully (abbot 1139–88). De Sully was Henry II's second cousin and also made one of the earliest gifts to Mont-aux-Malades. In 1154, Henry de Sully donated four acres of land in the fief of the priory of St-Gervais to the lepers of Rouen, at the request of Henry II, Hugh of Amiens, archbishop of Rouen (1130–64), the Empress Matilda and the burgesses of Rouen.[51] Like the foundation of many of the other Norman leper houses dedicated to St Thomas Becket, therefore, the establishment of the house at Aizier could have been influenced by the example of Henry II and could fit within wider patterns of aristocratic charitable patronage.

The earliest known documentary reference to the dedication at Aizier is a charter of July 1227 now held in the archive of the abbey of Jumièges, marking the sale of a property at Vieux-Port, a village less than two kilometres from Aizier, by Richard Andreu to Richard Loquet. The vendor obliged the recipient of the property to maintain 'a lamp burning before the altar of St Thomas once a year'.[52] Although this reference, which almost certainly refers to the chapel at Aizier, does not testify to the presence of a community of lepers at this date, it does indicate that the chapel was an important local site of worship, with attention focusing on the altar dedicated to the popular saint. Written evidence for the presence of lepers at Aizier does not appear until the mid-fifteenth century: a document of 1449 relating to fishing on the river Seine refers to the 'chemin des Malades', a path leading from the chapel of St-Thomas to the Seine. A land register of 1744 mentions a pledge made by 'the sick of St-Thomas' on 13 February 1514.[53]

---

48   Niel and Truc, 'La chapelle Saint-Thomas d'Aizier', 51.
49   *Ibid.*, 63–5; Niel and Truc, 'Fouille d'une léproserie médiévale'.
50   'quicquid ibi Trostincus tenuit': *Recueil des actes des ducs de Normandie (911–1066)*, ed. M. Fauroux (Caen, 1961), 79–81, at 80 (no. 9), 124–31 (no. 34); Niel and Truc, 'La chapelle Saint-Thomas d'Aizier', 50–51.
51   Paris, AN, S4889B, liasse 1, no. 4; Langlois, *Histoire*, 12.
52   'unam lampadam ardentem ante altare sancti Thome annuatim': Rouen, ADSM, 9H1275; Niel and Truc, 'Fouille d'une léproserie médiévale'.
53   Niel and Truc, 'La chapelle Saint-Thomas d'Aizier', 51–2.

However, archaeological excavations conducted by Cécile Niel and Marie-Cécile Truc between 1998 and 2010 confirm that St-Thomas at Aizier did cater for men and women suffering from leprosy (in terms of the symptoms associated with Hansen's disease, as leprosy is clinically defined today) in the central and later Middle Ages. Although the preliminary publication (in 2007) of Niel and Truc's findings discussed excavated skeletons prior to laboratory dating, the fact that the incidence of leprosy significantly declined in Western Europe from the sixteenth century strongly indicates that those skeletal remains showing signs of leprosy are medieval burials. Among roughly thirty burials identified or excavated by 2005, Niel and Truc found that several individuals probably suffered from leprosy, indicated above all by bone changes in the face, particularly around the nose and upper jaw.[54] The more common form of leprosy, lepromatous leprosy (as opposed to the other, tuberculoid form), results in degeneration of the facial features, particularly the nose, as well as destruction of the nerves at the extremities of the body, such as the fingers and toes, resulting in loss of sensation and thus damage to these areas.[55] One female burial at Aizier shows significant bone changes to the legs and feet.[56] The signs therefore indicate that St-Thomas at Aizier accommodated leprosy sufferers, even though Raymonde Foreville did not consider this foundation to be a leper house.[57] A community of lepers at Aizier could have come into existence when the chapel was built, or subsequently. A group of lepers could also have been living on the site prior to the chapel's construction.[58]

Although we have no evidence that the chapel at Aizier housed relics, the site may well have been associated with healing. Today there is a pond south-east of the chapel of St-Thomas. In the 1830s, the site was known for having a water source associated with the healing of fevers, a connection that could plausibly date back to the Middle Ages.[59] The presence of healing waters could originally have attracted lepers, as well as many other categories of people seeking therapeutic benefits, to this place. Bathing was an important aspect of the palliative care of lepers, and the sites of several leper houses in England, such as those at Dunwich (Suffolk), Brewood (Staffordshire) and

54   Niel and Truc, 'La chapelle Saint-Thomas d'Aizier', 97–101.
55   P. Richards, *The Medieval Leper and his Northern Heirs* (Cambridge, 1977), xv, xvi; C. Rawcliffe, 'Learning to Love the Leper: Aspects of Institutional Charity in Anglo-Norman England', *Anglo-Norman Studies*, 23 (2000), 231–50, at 232; D. Marcombe, *Leper Knights: The Order of St Lazarus of Jerusalem in England, 1150–1544* (Woodbridge, 2003), 135–6; *Black's Medical Dictionary*, ed. H. Marcovitch, 41st edn (London, 2005), 406.
56   Niel and Truc, 'La chapelle Saint-Thomas d'Aizier', 100–101, 102.
57   See p. 83 above.
58   See Niel and Truc, 'La chapelle Saint-Thomas d'Aizier', 52.
59   A. Canel, *Essai historique, archéologique et statistique sur l'arrondissement de Pont-Audemer (Eure). Tome deuxième* (Paris, 1834), 92; Fournée, 'Lieux de culte', 381; Fournée, 'Maladreries', 126.

Harbledown, were close to healing springs or wells, where the water was often sulphurous.[60] It is known today that contact with sulphurous water alleviates skin complaints; lesions on the skin are one of the main symptoms of leprosy. At Burton Lazars (Leicestershire), which was very probably the location of an important leper house run by the Order of St Lazarus, a spa was opened in the second half of the eighteenth century to enable people to benefit from the healing properties of the spring there. This spring was traditionally held to have healed leprosy in the Middle Ages. Although David Marcombe notes that the spring 'lies well outside the bounds of the hospital', he argues that its presence, and the elevated topography of the site, could well have influenced the original intention to establish a leper house there.[61]

Hot herbal baths were viewed more generally as a key measure for the maintenance of health and treatment of disease in medieval Europe, and were advocated in *regimina sanitatis*, the health manuals that became increasingly popular in the later Middle Ages. In accordance with the idea that health was derived from the internal balance of the bodily humours, it was understood that sweating would allow corrupt humoral matter to leave the body and that the beneficial scent of medicinal herbs would enter through the open pores. For the treatment of lepers specifically, baths would lessen pain and keep their sores and lesions clean. Scrubbing could also restore feeling to the bodily extremities where nerves were damaged by the disease. Bathing had strong spiritual associations, mirroring the cleansing of the soul provided by baptism. Lepers had a biblical exemplar in the form of Naaman the Syrian, whose leprosy was cured after he had bathed in the river Jordan.[62] The presence of the pond at Aizier thus supports the archaeological evidence that this was an important site for the care of lepers, and suggests that this was a holy place of some significance in the locality, where perhaps many different types of people came to seek physical and spiritual healing.

Conclusion

At the time of the emergence of the cult of St Thomas Becket in the later twelfth and early thirteenth centuries, lepers held a special religious status. It was believed that the leprous suffered on earth as a result of God's will, and that their future salvation was ensured through their suffering. In this sense, like Christ and Becket, they were martyrs. On one level, therefore, the dedication of a number of leper houses in Normandy to Becket drew attention to lepers' commonality with the saint and underlined their pious suffering. However,

---

60 Rawcliffe, *Leprosy*, 227, 228–9; Marcombe, *Leper Knights*, 137–8.
61 Marcombe, *Leper Knights*, 142–6.
62 Rawcliffe, *Leprosy*, 226–32; II Kings 5:1–27.

these foundations, like those of other churches and chapels dedicated to Becket in Normandy, also reflect the saint's connections with the duchy, especially the city of Rouen, during his life, and the participation of Henry II and his aristocracy in the Becket cult. With regard to leper houses, the popularity of the cult coincided with the status of lepers as a fashionable focus of charitable patronage. The examples of Mont-aux-Malades and St-Thomas at Aizier demonstrate the diversity of the dedications to Becket, and also show that, even though the connection to lepers was significant, the dedication of a leper house church or chapel to the saint enhanced the broader spiritual significance of that site. Mont-aux-Malades came to possess a respectable collection of relics, while the altar at Aizier was marked out for veneration in a document of the 1220s. While Thomas Becket was associated with the lepers of Mont-aux-Malades during his life, he became linked to many other communities of lepers in Normandy after his death. The saint's association with Norman leper houses was linked less to bodily healing than to the cure of souls, underlining the fact that Becket's cult had a much broader significance than the healing miracles that took place at his tomb.

5.

Thomas Becket in the Chronicles[1]

MICHAEL STAUNTON

When he came to the year of Thomas Becket's death, the Limoges chronicler Geoffrey of Vigeois decided that he would pass over it, explaining that since so many people had written about the archbishop's life and death, there was no point in his covering the same material again.[2] Geoffrey's editorial decision is understandable. Although he wrote his chronicle little more than a decade after Thomas's murder in December 1170, he was evidently aware of the recent explosion of literary interest in the subject. By 1180, lengthy *Lives* of St Thomas had been written by Edward Grim, William of Canterbury, John of Salisbury, William Fitz Stephen, Guernes de Pont-Sainte-Maxence and two anonymous authors, in addition to shorter works by John of Salisbury, Alan of Tewkesbury and Benedict of Peterborough. Benedict had composed his collection of the saint's miracles, and William of Canterbury had published most of his, while Alan of Tewkesbury had completed the great task begun by John of Salisbury of putting together Thomas's collection of correspondence.[3] One could be forgiven for thinking that all that needed to be said had been said. But then and now, people have always found more to say about Thomas's life and death, and new angles from which to view it. The half-century after Becket's murder was a very productive period of historical writing, especially in England and especially in histories of recent events, and few of those who wrote about their own times could resist touching on the subject of the martyred archbishop. Here I shall look at how Thomas Becket featured in historical writing at the end of the twelfth and the beginning of the thirteenth

---

1   The research for this article was supported by a Senior Research Fellowship from the Irish Research Council for the Humanities and Social Sciences.

2   Geoffrey of Vigeois, *Chronicle*, in P. Botineau, 'Chronique de G. de Breuil, prieur de Vigeois' (unpublished Ph.D. thesis, École des Chartes, 1964), 153.

3   The *Lives*, miracles and letters are published in *MTB*. Thomas's correspondence, which forms the majority of Alan's letter collection, is edited in *CTB*. Extracts from the *Lives* are translated in *Lives of Thomas Becket*. For a comparison of the *Lives*, letters and chronicle accounts, see S. Jansen, *Wo ist Thomas Becket? Der ermordete Heilige zwischen Erinnerung und Erzählung* (Husum, 2002). For the letters see A. Duggan, *Thomas Becket: A Textual History of his Letters* (Oxford, 1980); and for the *Lives*, M. Staunton, *Thomas Becket and his Biographers* (Woodbridge, 2006).

centuries, using the term 'chronicles' in the widest possible sense to distinguish them from the *Lives*. My concern is not so much to examine what they add to our knowledge about Thomas's life and death, but how they related his legacy to their own concerns in the decades after his murder.

The cult of Thomas Becket had a remarkable geographical reach, and his murder also won the attention of chroniclers far and wide.[4] One need look no further than the Holy Land, where William of Tyre interrupted his account of local affairs to record Thomas's death and summarise his career, concluding with a brief account of his murder and the miracles which God performed through him.[5] Well beyond England other chroniclers thought it appropriate to mention Thomas's death, if only briefly. An entry from a chronicle of Reichersberg reads, 'In the year 1171, St Thomas archbishop of Canterbury suffered in England. In our lands a cow gave birth to a calf with two heads, eight feet and two tails.'[6] Becket's murder was an essential part of any English chronicle of the period and even the shortest entry, such as Ralph of Coggeshall's, tells the basic story:[7]

> St Thomas, archbishop of Canterbury, formerly chancellor of King Henry II, for the sake of preserving the liberty of ecclesiastical dignity, after he had spent seven years in exile, was crowned with martyrdom in the cathedral church of his own see before the altar of St Benedict, on the fifth day of Christmas, at the hour of vespers.

Some writers were evidently so drawn to the subject that they chose to include it even if it altered their original literary plan. The author of the *Liber Eliensis* prefaces his account of Thomas's life and death by explaining that he was pleased to have finally reached the end of his work. 'However', he continues:[8]

> the thought came into my mind of the most holy Thomas, confessor of the Lord and beloved martyr of Christ who, recently, and now in our times, is seen to have met his death. And I have resolved to extend my work by including him, so that my labour, entered upon in a holy beginning may, by the mercy of God, be allotted a joyful ending.

4 See also the discussion in the essay by Anne J. Duggan in this volume (chapter 2).

5 Willelmus Tyrensis, *Chronicon*, ed. R. B. C. Huygens, *Corpus Christianorum Continuatio Mediaevalis*, 63A (Turnhout, 1986), 940.

6 *Chronicon Magni Presbiteri*, ed. W. Wattenbach, MGH SS, xvii, 496. Thomas died on 29 December 1170, but since his death comes after Christmas, many chroniclers date it to 1171. See Gervase, i, 91, 232.

7 *Radulphi de Coggeshall Chronicon Anglicanum*, ed. J. Stevenson, RS 66 (London, 1875), 16.

8 *Liber Eliensis*, ed. E. O. Blake, Camden Third Series, 92 (London, 1962), 391–4 at 391, 437 (appendix F); *Liber Eliensis: A History of the Isle of Ely from the Seventh Century to the Twelfth*, trans. J. Fairweather (Woodbridge, 2005), 482–3.

There is also a case where Thomas's death may have ended a historical work prematurely. Stephen of Rouen's *Draco Normannicus* contains passages hostile to Thomas, comparing him to Simon Magus and mocking him for his poor Latin. This Latin verse poem ends at 1169 with the appearance of peace between Henry and Thomas, and although it has been suggested that this is the natural end, the argument that the events of 1170 led the author to abandon the manuscript remains a strong one.[9]

The *Draco Normannicus* is one of those works that gives us some original information on Thomas's life not found in the *Lives* and letters, in particular his account of Thomas's attendance at the Council of Tours in 1163. The *Chronicle of Battle Abbey*, too, throws some light on Thomas as chancellor, where it presents him siding with the king against papal authority in a dispute over the liberty of that house.[10] Most of the later chroniclers drew on the *Lives* and letters, but occasionally provide anecdotes which cannot be found elsewhere. Roger of Howden's *Gesta Regis Henrici* begins at 1169 and includes an account of the final negotiations between king and archbishop, Thomas's last days, the murder and its immediate aftermath, largely based on the *Lives* by John of Salisbury and the Anonymous I. However, in the 1190s, Howden revised and expanded his earlier work to produce the *Chronica* and, whereas in many places he follows the earlier work very closely, the section on Becket is quite different. He again draws on other sources – John of Salisbury, an anonymous *Passio* and some letters – but he also appears to use a source as yet unidentified. Howden includes an account of Thomas's trial at Northampton not found elsewhere, a day-in-the-life of Thomas as archbishop different from that given by John of Salisbury or Herbert of Bosham, and an anecdote about Thomas turning water to wine before the pope. He also makes some curious errors, mistakenly placing Thomas's appointment as chancellor in 1157 rather than 1154 and the trial at Northampton in 1165 rather than 1164. He says that Thomas's death was miraculously revealed to the hermit Godric of Finchale, 160 miles away, despite the fact that, as Howden had earlier reported, Godric died in 1169.[11] Later, he tells the story of how St Thomas appeared to English crusaders navigating around the Iberian coast and led them safely to Silva.[12] Lambert, chaplain of Ardres, wrote in the late 1190s of the special devotion of Count Baldwin II of Guines for St Thomas. He explains that the count had been knighted by Thomas, and many years later entertained the archbishop on his return from exile to death.[13] In briefly reporting the papal

9 Stephen of Rouen, *Draco Normannicus*, in *Chronicles*, ed. Howlett, ii, 675–7, 741–2, 744, 756–7; Jansen, *Wo ist Thomas Becket?*, 107–12.

10 *The Chronicle of Battle Abbey*, ed. and trans. E. Searle, OMT (Oxford, 1980), 176–209. See also the account of Thomas's dispute with the king and murder, 272–9.

11 Howden, *Gesta*, i, 7–24, 31–3; Howden, *Chronica*, ii, 6–29, 35–9. See also *Passio Prima*, ed. J. A. Giles, *PL*, cxc, cols 317–24.

12 Howden, *Gesta*, ii, 116–17; Howden, *Chronica*, iii, 42–3.

13 *Lamberti Ardensis historia comitum Ghisensium*, ed. J. Heller, in *MGH SS*, xxiv, 596, 601–2.

canonisation of St Thomas at Anagni in 1173, the *Chronicle of Melrose* adds, 'and he who saw and heard has given testimony', suggesting that the writer was present.[14] Adam of Eynsham's *Life of St Hugh* relates how the bishop of Lincoln forbade his officials from imposing financial penalties on sinners, and when they tried to defend themselves by saying that Thomas had done the same, Hugh replied, 'Believe me, this did not make him a saint, his other conspicuous virtues showed him to be one, and he deserved the martyr's palm for another cause.'[15]

All the chroniclers agreed that Thomas was a saint, and while few present a multi-dimensional picture of the chancellor and archbishop, occasional disparity may be found in their assessments of the dispute and the man. Perhaps the most original is that of William of Newburgh. William, it seems, spent all his life in and around Yorkshire, and there is no evidence that he had any contact with those involved in the Becket dispute. Nonetheless, he was a deeply moralistic historian, and one might have expected him to praise Thomas as a champion of the Church. But William was also a thoughtful and nuanced writer and his comments on Becket are a case in point. Reviewing the course of the dispute, he writes:[16]

> Many people, driven more by affection than prudence, tend to approve everything that is done by those they love and praise. But these actions of the venerable man, although they proceeded from praiseworthy zeal, by no means do I consider praiseworthy, as they brought not profit but only incited the king to anger, from which so many evil things are later known to have derived.

He draws a parallel with St Peter's attempts to compel the Gentiles to become Jews, which, though done out of praiseworthy piety, were rebuked by St Paul. William prefaces his description of Thomas's murder by noting how, on the point of return to England, he sent ahead letters of censure against the prelates who had taken part in the coronation of the Young King Henry in July 1170. 'It is not for one as lowly as me to dare to judge the actions of so great a man', he writes, but adds that perhaps the archbishop might have acted more carefully towards the newly established peace, according to the saying of the prophet, 'He who is prudent will keep silent in such a time, for the days are evil'.[17] He goes on:[18]

---

14 *Chronica de Mailros e codice unico in bibliotheca Cottoniana servato*, ed. J. Stevenson, Bannatyne Club, 49 (Edinburgh, 1835), 85. See also John 3:32; Revelation 1:2.

15 *Magna Vita Sancti Hugonis: The Life of St Hugh of Lincoln*, ed. D. L. Douie and H. Farmer, NMT, 2 vols (London, 1961–62), ii, 38. See also Hugh's opposition to the plans to establish a house of canons at Hackington and later Lambeth, i, 121–3. The proposed house of canons is discussed further below.

16 William of Newburgh, *Historia Rerum Anglicarum*, in *Chronicles*, ed. Howlett, i, 142–3.

17 Amos 5:13.

18 William of Newburgh, *Historia*, i, 161; see also James 3:2.

I neither declare the archbishop's actions praiseworthy, nor do I presume to disparage them. But this I say, that if perhaps through the slightly excessive force of praiseworthy zeal, the holy man went a little too far, he was purged by the fire of his holy passion which we know followed. So though we ought to love and praise holy men, whom we know to be far superior to us, we should nevertheless by no means either love or praise the actions which they committed through human weakness, but only those which we ought to imitate without reservation. For who can say that they ought to be imitated in their every deed, when the apostle James says, 'For we err in many ways'? Therefore we ought not to praise them for everything they do, but wisely and cautiously so that God, Whom no one can praise enough, no matter how hard we try, should have His dignity preserved.

In contrast to William of Newburgh, Ralph of Diceto, dean of St Paul's, found himself in the midst of the Becket dispute, but carefully avoided judgement on it. More than any other writer, Ralph faced a conflict of allegiances, summed up by William Fitz Stephen's report of the dean in tears on the last day of Thomas's trial at Northampton.[19] Ralph was a loyal supporter of the king, and close to senior royal servants. Moreover, his bishop, Gilbert Foliot, was Thomas's most eloquent critic during the dispute. On the other hand, Ralph's support for clerical privilege and papal authority was as strong as that of most other senior churchmen in England, and his letter of 1166 urging Richard of Ilchester to respect Thomas's censures at Vézelay, shows his search for a middle path even in the midst of the dispute.[20] He writes about the Becket dispute at some length in the *Ymagines Historiarum*, a chronicle of recent events, and an edited summary makes up his *Series causae inter Henricum regem et Thomam archiepiscopum*.[21] Writing perhaps two decades after the events, his approach appears detached and balanced, though his omissions and obfuscations have been noted.[22]

A few peculiarities of Diceto's account may be pointed out. One is the fact that he draws parallels between the murder of Thomas Becket and the killing

---

19 *MTB*, iii, 59.
20 Diceto, i, 319–20. Ralph's name appears variously as de Diceto, Disci, Dysci, and Dici in contemporary documents, suggesting that it derives from Diss in Norfolk. See *Ancient Charters, Royal and Private, Prior to A.D. 1200*, ed. J. H. Round, PRS 10 (London, 1888), 77–8; *The Letters and Charters of Gilbert Foliot, Abbot of Gloucester (1139–48), Bishop of Hereford (1148–63) and London (1163–87)*, ed. A. Morey and C. N. L. Brooke (Cambridge, 1967), 467; J. le Neve, *Fasti Ecclesiae Anglicanae, 1066–1300: Vol. 1: St Paul's, London*, rev. edn. by D. E. Greenway (London, 1968), 5.
21 Diceto, ii, 279–85.
22 C. Duggan and A. Duggan, 'Ralph de Diceto, Henry II and Becket, with an Appendix on Decretal Letters', in *Authority and Power: Studies on Medieval Law and Government Presented to Walter Ullmann on his Seventieth Birthday*, ed. B. Tierney and P. Linehan (Cambridge, 1980), 59–81.

of others: Hugh, archbishop of Tarragona, murdered with a knife; Hamo, bishop of León, killed by his nephew; William Trincavel, killed in the church of St Mary Magdalene at Béziers.[23] Another is how, in both works, he marks out with symbols the main points of the controversy.[24] The first cause he highlights is Thomas's resignation of the chancellorship upon becoming archbishop, something to which few other twelfth-century writers pay much attention, and he notes with apparent approval how, in Germany, Rainald of Dassel had retained both offices.[25] This is a good example not only of Diceto's characteristic interest in historical precedents and parallels, but also of his favourable attitude, in strong contrast to William of Newburgh, towards churchmen who play an active role in secular government. As Duggan and Duggan remark, it was entirely natural to Diceto that secular and church leaders should work in harmony, and it is possible to read his account of the Becket affair as one which does not simply seek to avoid controversy, but rather seeks reconciliation. This reconciliation is seen most clearly in Ralph's account of the rebellion of the Young King Henry against his father Henry II in 1173–74, and his sentiment is echoed by many other writers.

Some writers never forgave Henry II for his role in the murder. Ralph Niger, a former clerk of Archbishop Thomas, whom the king banished from England, habitually refers to Henry II as 'the king under whom Thomas the blessed martyr of the English suffered', and he included a savage picture of the king in his shorter chronicle.[26] But even writers more sympathetic to the king saw the rebellion of 1173–74 as punishment for his sin. Ralph of Coggeshall, for one, explicitly states that the various rebellions were just judgment for Henry's treatment of the archbishop.[27] William of Newburgh sees the rebellions as appropriate reward for the king's marrying in defiance of the Church, and because he did not sufficiently lament his obstinacy toward St Thomas.[28] According to almost all these writers, the turning-point in the rebellion was Henry II's decision to do penance at the tomb of St Thomas in July 1174. One of the earliest reports is by Jordan Fantosme, who says that when King Henry was told of the mixed news from England in 1174, he said, 'St Thomas, guard

---

23 Diceto, i, 345–6. On the latter, see William of Newburgh, *Historia*, i, 126–30.
24 Diceto, i, 307–14; ii, 280–82. Beryl Smalley argues that such juxtaposition made synthesis and judgment unnecessary: B. Smalley, *Historians in the Middle Ages: A Study of Intellectuals in Politics* (London, 1974), 116–19. See also B. Smalley, *The Becket Conflict and the Schools* (Oxford, 1973), 230–34.
25 Diceto, i, 307–8.
26 *The Chronicles of Ralph Niger*, ed. R. Anstruther, Caxton Society (London, 1851), 93, 167–9, 176; G. B. Flahiff, 'Ralph Niger: An Introduction to his Life and Works', *Mediaeval Studies*, 2 (1940), 104–26 at 107 n. 22.
27 *Radulphi de Coggeshall*, 26.
28 William of Newburgh, *Historia*, i, 281.

my realm, I admit to you my guilt for which others bear the blame'.[29] Jordan's account is brief, but later writers presented a more elaborate explanation of the outcome of the war in which standard elements are present. The account found in the second recension of Edward Grim's *Vita Sancti Thomae* appears influential, though the same theme is found so widely that its dissemination would appear to go well beyond textual transmission. There he describes how the king humbled himself before the monks of Canterbury and spent the night in vigil at the tomb of St Thomas, whereupon he learned that his adversary, William I, king of Scots, had been captured, a clear sign of Thomas's intervention.[30] Ralph of Diceto, Roger of Howden and William of Newburgh broadly echo Edward Grim's narrative and interpretation, and make some additions.[31] For those, such as Diceto, who showed high regard for both king and archbishop and whose political tendencies were towards moderation and stability, the conclusion that the penitent king had triumphed through the intercession of St Thomas allowed them to draw a line under the dispute.[32]

An exception is Gerald of Wales, whose interest in the Becket dispute lasted throughout his long literary career. Gerald grew up during the dispute, and he says that as a child, whenever he heard of a dispute regarding the law of the land and the law of the Church, he would put himself forward as an advocate of the Church.[33] When burdened by debt as a student at Paris, he prayed to St Thomas and was released from his money troubles, and he and his companions returned to England wearing medallions with images of the saint around their necks.[34] Though his early *Expugnatio Hibernica* presents a picture, familiar from other writers, of King Henry's penance at Thomas's shrine as an act of redemption, his late work, *De Principis Instructione*, presents

29 *Jordan Fantosme*, ed. Johnston, 120–21 (lines 1599–1600) and see also 142–3 (lines 1912–14). Also noted in the articles by Anne J. Duggan (chapter 2), Colette Bowie (chapter 6) and José Manuel Cerda (chapter 7) in this volume.

30 *MTB*, ii, 444–8. See also William of Canterbury, *MTB*, i, 485–95; Herbert of Bosham, *Liber Melorum*, in *PL* cxc, cols 1316–17, 1320–21; Guernes de Pont-Sainte-Maxence, *La Vie de S. Thomas le Martyr*, ed. E. Walberg (Paris, 1922), 199–205 (lines 5906–6060), 207–8 (lines 6124–55).

31 Diceto, i, 382–5; Howden, *Gesta*, i, 72; Howden, *Chronica*, ii, 61–3; William of Newburgh, *Historia*, i, 186–8, 196.

32 Though this is the dominant picture, there are some differences of tone in the description of Henry's penance, for example: *Rogeri de Wendover liber qui dicitur Flores Historiarum ab anno domini MCLIV annoque Henrici Anglorum Regis Secundi Primo*, ed. H. G. Hewlett, RS 84, 3 vols (London, 1886–89), i, 92; Robert of Torigni, *Chronica*, in *Chronicles*, ed. Howlett, iv, 264; *Liber Gaufridi Sacristae de Coldingham de statu Ecclesiae Dunhelmensis*, ed. J. Raine, in *Historiae Dunelmensis Scriptores Tres: Gaufridus de Coldingham, Robertus de Graystanes, et Willielmus de Chambre*, Surtees Society, 9 (London and Edinburgh, 1889), 10.

33 *De rebus a se gestis*, in *Giraldi Cambrensis Opera*, ed. J. S. Brewer *et al.*, RS 21, 8 vols (London, 1861–91), i, 22.

34 *De rebus a se gestis*, 49–50, 53.

the subsequent downfall of the king as a morality tale in which three main sins are dominant: his marriage to Eleanor, his role in Becket's murder and his failure to go on crusade. The third criticism is related to the second, as it was part of Henry's penance to which he submitted at Avranches in 1172.[35]

Though those works are better known, Gerald gives his fullest attention to Thomas in the *Vita S. Remigii*, the first edition of which was written around 1198. Most of this work has nothing to do with St Remigius, and a large part of it is taken up with accounts of praiseworthy prelates of Gerald's own time, presented in paired portraits. The first pair is Thomas of Canterbury and Henry of Winchester. Gerald writes that it would be presumptuous and super-fluous to extol Thomas's glory, since he had already been commemorated in writing by great men, or to hold a light to one whose light illuminates the world. Nonetheless, he concedes to present a summary of Thomas's life, death and posthumous glory, which rehearses the same comments made by countless other writers. He then tells some stories of Thomas's prophesies during life and miracles after death which he says he has not found in other writings, most of which are in fact recorded in earlier texts.[36] Much more original are his comments in the section on Bartholomew of Exeter and Roger of Worcester. There he relates how one of Thomas's murderers, William de Traci, came to confess his crime to Bartholomew. The murderer told the bishop that when his three accomplices had already inflicted their blows on Thomas, they rebuked him for being too slow to strike, reminding him that the king had bound them by oath to carry out the murder. Although, he acknowledges, the king swore that the murder had not been carried out through his hand or desire, Gerald notes that Bartholomew remained insistent in his belief that the king had mandated it.[37] Gerald goes on to state that when Henry II, 'fleeing from the face of the cardinals', crossed from Normandy to England and thence to Wales, he met Bartholomew at Milford Haven and said of the cardinals, 'If they want to talk to me, let them come to me in Ireland'. Gerald goes on to cite biblical readings on the futility of attempting to flee from God's judgment, including 'The wicked flee when no one pursues', a clever use of the words

35 *Expugnatio Hibernica: The Conquest of Ireland*, ed. A. B. Scott and F. X. Martin (Dublin, 1978), 108–113, 120–25; *De Principis Instructione*, in *Giraldi Cambrensis Opera*, viii, 159–72, 210–11, 251–3. See also R. Bartlett, *Gerald of Wales: A Voice of the Middle Ages*, 2nd edn (Stroud, 2006), 56–86; K. Schnith, 'Betrachtungen zum Spätwerk des Giraldus Cambrensis: "De principis instructione"', in *Festiva Lanx: Studien zum mittelalterlichen Geistesleben Johannes Sporl dargebracht* (Munich, 1966), 54–63.
36 *Vita S. Remigii*, in *Giraldi Cambrensis Opera*, vii, 43–56, esp. 50–56. On this work, see the introduction to the edition, and more recently M. Mesley, 'The Construction of Episcopal Identity: The Meaning and Function of Episcopal Depictions within Latin Saints' Lives of the Long Twelfth Century' (unpublished Ph.D. thesis, University of Exeter, 2009), 178–239.
37 *Vita S. Remigii*, 60–61.

thrown at Archbishop Thomas when he fled from King Henry into France in 1164.[38]

The Becket dispute was most obviously a clash between king and archbishop, but the debate was fiercest between ecclesiastics, and the debate over his legacy continued among them long after. In the *Vita S. Remigii*, Gerald takes the opportunity to compare Thomas to his two immediate successors in the see of Canterbury, Richard of Dover and Baldwin of Ford. In his discussion of Baldwin, he quotes Thomas's former cross-bearer, Alexander Llewelyn, as saying that Thomas tended to be angered by injuries to the Church; Richard was easily moved to anger but was remiss in his works; and Baldwin was hardly ever angry at all. When Thomas came riding into a vill he immediately sought the court, Richard the grange and Baldwin the church. While his successors showed their religion by the habits of their respective orders, and by their speech, Thomas showed his by his deeds.[39]

Gerald was present at the first public festival on St Thomas's day at Canterbury on 29 December 1172, among many barons of the realm. He reports that after lunch the new archbishop, Richard of Dover, made loud complaint about injuries to the dignity of his church at the hands of royal officials and, putting his hand to his head, he swore that he would expose it to the swords rather than allow this. But Hugh de Lacy, who was present, said:[40]

> There is no need, archbishop, for you to lay down your head or even your foot. You can securely maintain your rights and exercise ecclesiastical justice. God has done so much for the holy martyr, your predecessor, that the king, even if he wanted to, would not find a single rogue in his land who would dare raise his hand against you. The war is over: you hold in your hand, if you will, what the martyr has won.

Gerald also reports a discussion from around the same time in which a certain bishop complained that the Church had obtained nothing at all regarding the issues for which the archbishop died. In response, Richard, bishop of Winchester, put the blame on Richard of Dover, arguing that, 'if his successor had a tenth of [Thomas's] goodness and probity the Church would have lost nothing on these points. But what he acquired through his extraordinary

---

38 *Vita S. Remigii*, 1–2; Proverbs 28:1; MTB, ii, 338; C. Ó Clabaigh and M. Staunton, 'Thomas Becket and Ireland', in *'Listen, O Isles, Unto Me': Studies in Medieval Word and Image in Honour of Jennifer O'Reilly*, ed. E. Mullins and D. Scully (Cork, 2011), 87–101, 340–43. See also, in this section of the *Vita S. Remigii*, the miracle involving a cross which foretold Thomas's martyrdom and the actions of the bishops of Exeter and Worcester on behalf of the archbishop during his exile, 66–7.

39 *Vita S. Remigii*, 68–9.

40 *Vita S. Remigii*, 69.

energy, the other lost entirely through his cowardice.'[41] Gerald was more favourably inclined to Richard's successor, Baldwin, but Hubert Walter, the third archbishop to succeed Thomas, faces some fierce criticism. Hubert is accused of comparing himself to the martyr, while going against his example in retaining secular and ecclesiastical offices and accepting royal control of episcopal elections. Most seriously, Gerald claims that on the archbishop's orders the abbot of St Augustine was violently dragged from the altar at Faversham, where he was celebrating Mass, which Gerald calls the most atrocious crime since the murder of St Thomas.[42]

The struggle over Thomas's legacy was fought with most intensity by the custodians of his shrine and is recorded in two substantial literary sources: the Canterbury letter collection and the *Chronicle* of Gervase of Canterbury. Gervase was a monk of Canterbury who made his profession to Thomas in the first year of his archiepiscopacy. He tells us that his brother Thomas experienced a vision of the saint after his death in which he declared that his actions in life had been for his monks and clerks.[43] Gervase says that he has passed over many things about Thomas because they are described more fully elsewhere, but also asks the reader not to be angry because he has exceeded the rule of a chronicle a little in giving such attention to the saint: 'for what memory is more worthy of relation than that of a man of flesh and blood like us, yesterday hateful to the world, today glorious to the world?'[44] It has been noted that while Gervase's account of Thomas's life and death is substantial, it reveals little intimate or original knowledge about the subject, being largely derivative of the earlier *Lives* by William of Canterbury, Edward Grim and Herbert of

41 *Vita S. Remigii*, 69–70. See also *De Invectionibus*, ed. W. S. Davies, Y Cymmrodor, 30 (1920), 197–8.

42 *De Invectionibus*, 90–91, 97–8, 116–17. For the Faversham dispute, see E. Fernie, 'The Litigation of an Exempt House, St Augustine's Canterbury, 1182–1237', *Bulletin of the John Rylands Library*, 39 (1957), 390–415; C. R. Cheney, *Hubert Walter* (London, 1967), 85–7. Gerald later regretted the bitterness of his portrayal of Hubert: *Retractiones*, in *Opera*, i, 427.

43 Gervase, i, 231. Most scholarship has concentrated on Gervase's *Tractatus de combustione*, for example C. Davidson Cragoe, 'Reading and Rereading Gervase of Canterbury', *Journal of the British Archaeological Association*, 154 (2001), 40–53; P. Draper, 'William of Sens and the Original Design of the Choir Termination of Canterbury Cathedral, 1175–9', *Journal of the Society of Architectural Historians*, 42 (1983), 238–48; P. Kidson, 'Gervase, Becket, and William of Sens', *Speculum*, 68 (1993), 969–91; M. F. Hearn, 'Canterbury Cathedral and the Cult of Becket', *Art Bulletin*, 76 (1994), 19–54. M.-P. Gelin, 'Gervase of Canterbury, Christ Church and the Archbishops', *JEH*, 60 (2009), 449–63, examines this work in the light of the *Vitae Archiepiscoporum*. For a detailed discussion of Gervase's *Chronicle*, see R. W. Huling, 'English Historical Writing under the Early Angevin Kings, 1170–1210' (unpublished Ph.D. thesis, State University of New York, Binghamton, 1981), 187–45. On the Canterbury perspective in the *Lives*, see M. Staunton, 'The Lives of Thomas Becket and the Church of Canterbury', in *Cathedrals, Communities and Conflict in the Anglo-Norman World*, ed. P. Dalton, C. Insley and L. J. Wilkinson (Woodbridge, 2011), 169–86.

44 Gervase, i, 230–31.

Bosham.[45] It does, however, show traits characteristic of his chronicle as a whole. Most obvious is the distinct perspective of the monastic community of Christ Church, Canterbury, seen in the praise of his own prior's actions in the dispute and criticism of the actions of St Augustine's, Canterbury.[46] He plays up the significance of the Becket dispute in other affairs: King Henry attacked the Welsh in 1165 to escape possible censure by the pope or archbishop; in 1167 war resumed between King Henry and King Louis of France for various reasons, but especially because of Thomas.[47] In recounting the Becket dispute he even shows his fondness for significant astronomical phenomena. After describing the reconciliation between the king and archbishop in 1170, he reports that two planets seemed conjoined as if they were the same star, then separated.[48] There are inaccuracies, too: he claims that at Vézelay in 1166 the archbishop threatened the king of England, and he confuses the Assize of Clarendon with the Constitutions of Clarendon, so central to the Becket dispute.[49]

Gervase also deals with the political fallout of the murder. He claims King Henry's envoys had to bribe the cardinals to gain access to the pope, and suggests that the main reason for the king's visit to Ireland in 1171–72 was his fear that the cardinals would impose an interdict.[50] Important to him, of course, is the reopening of the church of Canterbury in 1171 and the proliferation of miracles at Thomas's tomb.[51] He describes Henry's return from Ireland to face the cardinal envoys in 1172 and the settlement he made with them at Avranches.[52] He also devotes some attention to the protracted process to choose a new archbishop, noting that the king blocked the monks' nomination of their prior, Odo, thinking that he would be an imitator of Thomas.[53] In common with other contemporary writers, Gervase attributes the victory of Henry II over the rebellion of 1173–74 to the intervention of St Thomas, and he records the visit of the two Henrys to Canterbury in 1175, where they gave thanks to God and the martyr for the peace restored.[54] Gervase records subsequent visits by Henry II to the shrine of St Thomas, in 1177, 1183 and 1187.[55] Also noted are pilgrimages by Count Philip of Flanders and William de Mandeville in 1177, on their way to the Holy Land, the celebrated visit of

45 Gervase, i, xii–xiii.
46 Gervase, i, 197, 224.
47 Gervase, i, 197, 203.
48 Gervase, i, 220–21.
49 Gervase, i, 200, 257–8.
50 Gervase, i, 232–6.
51 Gervase, i, 236–7.
52 Gervase, i, 237, 238–9.
53 Gervase, i, 239–40.
54 Gervase, i, 248–51, 256.
55 Gervase, i, 261–2, 309, 348.

King Louis of France in 1179, when he offered an annuity of wine to Christ Church, the visit of Joscius, bishop of Acre, in the same year, and of Henry the Lion in 1183.[56]

Becket's legacy hangs heavily over Gervase's treatment of later issues. Sometimes Thomas provides a yardstick with which to measure the actions of later churchmen. Gervase claims that Cardinal-Legate Hugucio was bribed by King Henry to accept the submission of clerks to secular justice regarding the forest, disregarding the example of Thomas who suffered exile, loss of property and even his own head for the protection of clerks.[57] The record of participants in the Becket dispute, too, is recalled in later affairs. Gervase reports that at the boisterous Council of Westminster in 1176, the cry went up against Roger, archbishop of York, 'Be gone, traitor to St Thomas, your hands are still stained with blood', and in recording his death Gervase calls Roger a special enemy of St Thomas.[58] Likewise, in his obituary for Gilbert Foliot, the bishop of London is called St Thomas's persecutor.[59] In contrast, the clergy of Chartres are said to have chosen John of Salisbury as their bishop in 1176 for love of St Thomas, and Gervase recalls John's service to the archbishop even in exile.[60] In recording the death of Henry the Young King in 1183, Gervase makes the point that he died in the same month and the same week as he was crowned king by Archbishop Roger of York, thirteen years before, leaving a warning to others against usurping the crown contrary to the rights of Canterbury.[61]

Most of Gervase's chronicle is taken up with the dispute over the plans by Thomas's successors, Baldwin and Hubert Walter, to establish a college of canons, first at Hackington and later at Lambeth.[62] Baldwin claimed that his plan to build a collegiate church of canons outside the city, to be dedicated to St Stephen and St Thomas, was originally projected by his predecessors, Anselm and Thomas. The monks, on the other hand, saw it as an attempt to displace Christ Church as the mother church of England, and to circumvent

---

56 Gervase, i, 262, 293, 311. On Henry the Lion, his wife Matilda and the cult of St Thomas, see Colette Bowie's essay in this volume (chapter 6).
57 Gervase, i, 257.
58 Gervase, i, 258, 297.
59 Gervase, i, 360.
60 Gervase, i, 259–60.
61 Gervase, i, 305.
62 For the dispute, see the introduction to *Epistolae Cantuarienses, the Letters of the Prior and Convent of Christ Church, Canterbury*, ed. W. Stubbs, *Chronicles and Memorials of the Reign of Richard I*, RS 38, 2 vols (London, 1864–65), ii, xxxiii–cxx; repr. A. Hassall (ed.), *Historical Introductions to the Rolls Series: By William Stubbs, D.D., formerly Bishop of Oxford and Regius Professor of Modern History in the University* (New York, 1902), 380–438. For a shorter account with more emphasis on the literary context, see the introduction to *Nigellus Wireker. The Passion of St Lawrence: Epigrams and Marginal Poems*, ed. and trans. J. M. Ziolkowski (Leiden, 1994), 16–42. For further discussion and references, see Paul Webster's essay in this volume (chapter 8).

their rights to election and appeal.[63] In common with other advocates of the convent's cause, Gervase saw the present struggles as a continuation of the struggle, persecution and ultimate triumph of St Thomas.[64] Late in the chronicle he has a monk recalling how the whole Hackington plan had emerged from King Henry's discovery that his bishops were planning to take back lost liberties and his fear that they would rise up against him following Thomas's example.[65] In addition to describing the debates at Rome regarding Thomas's intentions or otherwise for a collegiate church,[66] Gervase reports how an accomplice of Thomas's murderers, William Fitz Nigel, helped in Baldwin's persecution of the monks by breaking through the wall of their court and occupying the offices.[67] He also describes how a nephew of St Thomas was imprisoned during the dispute and how enemies of Christ Church tried to burn down the prison in which he was held.[68]

The association of the Hackington plan with the continuing persecution of St Thomas, and the role of the martyr in the convent's redemption, is presented most vividly in the vision of the Canterbury monk, Andrew John. On the night before St Catherine's feast, 25 November 1186, there appeared to Andrew a vision of St Thomas, who identified himself as his archbishop who had suffered for and in that church. The saint led him from the dormitory into a tower beside the choir and showed him a great and terrible wheel spewing flames. This, said the saint, was the Catherine wheel which Baldwin had built and which threatened ruin to the monks. Next, Baldwin appeared and announced that he had built this wheel so as to destroy the church but he needed the assistance of the monks to push it. However, the saint presented Andrew with a magnificent sword inscribed with the words 'the sword of St Peter', signifying appeal to the pope, and told him that his prior might use it to destroy the wheel. This is followed by a shorter vision in which a monk saw Baldwin trying to transfer the martyr's body from his place of rest. The archbishop admitted that he was trying to cut off Thomas's head, but in trying to do so his mitre fell off.[69]

For Gervase, the persecutions of the monks by Baldwin and Hubert Walter were all of a piece with the earlier persecutions of Thomas and the church of Canterbury, and their struggles the same. His work is evidently meant to be a continuation of the records of those struggles. This is made most clear in

63 The arguments of both sides are made in *Epistolae Cantuarienses*, 7, 8, 17–18, 18–19, 20–21, 135, 421, 423, 532–3, 556.
64 The convent's current struggles are linked to Thomas's struggle in *Epistolae Cantuarienses*, 29, 30, 45, 55, 86, 87, 163, 219–20, 260, 358, 418, 441, 450, 490, 492, 501–502, 505.
65 Gervase, i, 538–43.
66 Gervase, i, 368–9.
67 Gervase, i, 399.
68 Gervase, i, 425. See also *Epistolae Cantuarienses*, 201, 209, 211.
69 Gervase, i, 338–42. See also *Epistolae Cantuarienses*, 56, 278–9.

a feature of Gervase's chronicle which, though central to it, does not seem to have received much notice. That is, that Gervase's approach, in providing a detailed narrative of a struggle for the rights of Christ Church, played out largely in a series of public debates, is part of a long-standing Canterbury tradition, going back at least to Eadmer's *Historia Novorum* and reaching its fullest expression in the *Lives* of St Thomas. More than just sharing the form of public debates, Gervase's work often shows linguistic echoes of the Becket *Lives*. Take, for example, the visit of King Henry, Archbishop Baldwin and his suffragans to Canterbury on Ash Wednesday, 11 February 1187, with the intention of filling vacant sees. 'The whole battle was turned against the monks of Canterbury', writes Gervase, but, unlike the sons of Ephraim, the monks were not turned in the day of the battle, but rather made constant. In the chapter house, the archbishop and his advisors stood on one side, the sub-prior with his chosen monks sat opposite them with lowered countenances but remained intrepid, as sheep for the slaughter. They were made a spectacle to God, angels and men, but they ended the day with victory. The language here echoes accounts of Becket's steadfastness in the face of persecution, and in particular his stance at the Council of Northampton in 1164.[70] This may also be seen in Gervase's description of the monks' appearance before King Richard and the bishops at Westminster on 8–9 November 1189. While Gervase's account tallies in most details with a letter written shortly after to the sub-prior of Christ Church, his is much closer in character to the writings of his Canterbury predecessors. This is particularly pronounced in the account of the second and final day, when the monks are presented as sheep prepared for sacrifice, with insults hurled at them and terrors threatened by mimed actions. Just as Thomas did at Northampton, they left the council confused and frightened, but nonetheless rejoicing in their hearts that they merited to bear insults and terrors for the liberty of the Church.[71]

Gervase's language shows the influence, in particular, of Thomas's clerk and biographer, Herbert of Bosham. Herbert was still writing his *Life of St Thomas* as the dispute over Hackington was raging and he plays a walk-on part in Gervase's account of December 1187. Herbert, 'master and clerk of the glorious archbishop and martyr Thomas, came to Canterbury as if out of special love' and spoke to the convent 'with the elegant eloquence of which he was full'. The monks' cause had suffered a series of setbacks and Herbert, so outspoken in the past about Canterbury's rights, now found it necessary to advise the monks to throw themselves on the mercy of Archbishop Baldwin. But the sub-prior cut him off, saying that even if they faced prison, mutilation

---

70 Gervase, i, 353–4. Sons of Ephraim: *MTB*, iii, 320; Psalm 78:9; spectacle for men and for angels: *MTB*, iii, 310; 1 Corinthians 4:9; sheep to the slaughter: *MTB*, iii, 363; Jeremiah 12:3. See also Staunton, *Becket and his Biographers*, 129–52.

71 Gervase, i, 463–72, esp. 471–2; *Epistolae Cantuarienses*, 315–19.

or death, they would do nothing to damage their cause or the battle of the Church, for they were bound to maintain the liberty of the Church which has been handed down by predecessors. Herbert, marvelling at the constancy of the convent, said, 'Then, if this is so, you must either give in disgracefully, or stand manfully'. Here, Gervase echoes the words that Herbert, as he records in his *Life*, spoke to St Thomas many years earlier, urging him to return from exile to Canterbury and certain death.[72]

A final example also illustrates the influence on later chronicles of the image of Thomas presented in the *Lives*. On 14 September 1191, Geoffrey, archbishop of York, landed at Dover and made his way to the priory of St Martin's nearby. Two days later he was arrested by agents of the chancellor, William Longchamp, concerned at the entrance into England of King Richard's half-brother so soon after the king's departure for crusade. The violence of his arrest in a church, and his subsequent imprisonment, made for obvious comparisons with Thomas Becket. This is an image that Geoffrey himself seems to have helped to engineer, for immediately after his release he paid a visit to Thomas's shrine at Canterbury. It is also fostered in Gerald of Wales's account of the arrest in his *De Vita Galfridi*, where he notes that Thomas had fled into exile in a small boat not far away on the same shore, and now the archbishop of York seeking his church was vexed by a similar tyranny to that which Thomas had evaded. He presents Geoffrey being arrested as he stood at the altar in white cloak and stole, holding a processional cross, an image that owes much to literary and visual elaborations of Thomas's murder.[73]

Richard of Devizes too, describes the arrest in some detail, but apparently to a very different purpose. Some soldiers, writes Richard, armed under their cloaks and girded with swords, entered the monastery to arrest the archbishop, upon which the archbishop took the cross in his hands. Stretching out his hands to his followers he said to the soldiers, 'I am the archbishop. If you are seeking me, let these men go'. The soldiers said:

> Whether you are the archbishop or not is nothing to us. One thing we do know: that you are Geoffrey, the son of King Henry whom he begot in some bed or other, who, in the presence of the king, whose brother you make yourself out to be, abjured England for three years. If you have not come into the realm as a traitor to the realm, if you have brought letters releasing you from your oath, either speak or take the consequences.

---

72 Gervase, i, 394: 'aut cedendum est turpiter, aut standum viriliter'. See also *MTB*, iii, 473: 'aut regrediendum turpiter, aut procedendum audacter et agendum viriliter'.

73 *De Vita Galfridi*, in *Giraldi Cambrensis Opera*, iv, 388, 391, 396. For an analysis of contemporary comment on Geoffrey's arrest and imprisonment, see D. Balfour, 'William Longchamp: Upward Mobility and Character Assassination in Twelfth-Century England' (unpublished Ph.D. thesis, University of Connecticut, 1996), 349–65.

The archbishop replied, 'I am not a traitor, nor will I show you any letters.' At this they dragged him violently from the church, bumping his head on the muddy ground, he unwilling and resisting but not fighting back. As soon as he was past the threshold the archbishop excommunicated those who had laid hands on him, who were present and hearing him and still holding him.[74] Richard of Devizes's tone is frequently ironic, and though it is hard to say for certain, the most convincing reading of this passage is as a satire on the attempts by Geoffrey's supporters to turn him into a new martyr. The language used is that of virtually all accounts of Thomas's arrest in the cathedral, but the contrast between the two situations makes it bathetic rather than apposite. Where Thomas's words, 'I am the archbishop' and 'let these men go', are presented as evidence of his confession of the faith and similarity to Christ,[75] Geoffrey's similar words bring a reminder of his illegitimate birth. Where Thomas suffered martyrdom, Geoffrey suffers a bumped head.

What does it say about Thomas's legacy that within little over twenty years the scene of his murder is even being recalled for satirical purposes? The frequency of references to Thomas in the historical writing of the late twelfth and early thirteenth centuries suggests, most obviously, that his death was regarded as one of the most significant events of the age, not only in England but well beyond. While some writers acknowledged that a great deal had already been said and written about Thomas, most were keen to introduce additional information and comment, particularly where his story and legacy related to their own concerns. It was possible to use Thomas in support of and against kings and ecclesiastics, and his legacy had a particular bearing on the fortunes of Canterbury. The diffusion of Thomas's image, not only in writing but also in art and devotional culture, meant that his legacy was ever present, especially for those involved in Church controversies. But at the same time, this might have meant a certain blunting of his impact as an example. Notable is how all three of Thomas's successors are mocked for attempting to associate themselves with their illustrious predecessor, as are Geoffrey of York, Hugh of Lincoln's household and even King Henry II. At the end of the 1180s, Herbert of Bosham complained that Thomas was being venerated

---

74 *The Chronicle of Richard of Devizes of the Time of King Richard I*, ed. and trans. J. T. Appleby, NMT (Oxford, 1963), 40–42. Compare *MTB*, iii, 141. This accords with Richard's generally favourable treatment of Longchamp in the chronicle, and in the Winchester Annals, often attributed to Richard of Devizes: *Annales de Wintonia*, in *Annales Monastici*, ed. H. R. Luard, RS 36, 5 vols (London, 1864–69), ii, 64. Another outrage against an ecclesiastic around the same time was compared to Thomas's murder. When Bishop Albert of Louvain was murdered by agents of Emperor Henry VI in 1192, his hagiographer claimed that the crime was greater than that against St Thomas: *Vita Alberti episcopi Leodiensis*, ed. I. Heller, MGH SS, xxv (Berlin, 1880), 167–8. See R. H. Schmandt, 'The Election and Assassination of Albert of Louvain, Bishop of Liège 1191–2', *Speculum*, 42 (1967), 653–60 at 659.
75 See *MTB*, ii, 12–13, 319–20, 435–6; iv, 131; John 18:6–9.

as a miracle-worker but his actions were not being followed.[76] Perhaps the very popularity of St Thomas's appeal made it difficult for those who came after him to take up his banner. When Thomas belonged to everyone, no one could claim exclusive right to his legacy. A final point should be made about the relationship between the chronicles and the earlier literary manifestations of the cult of St Thomas. The letters and *Lives*, and even the miracles, of St Thomas are a striking example of contemporary history being recorded and interpreted. Apart from the case of Gervase, there is no evidence that the chroniclers of the next generation were directly inspired to write by the literary productions of St Thomas's cult. However, they can be seen as part of a larger trend towards the recording and interpretation of the recent past that dominated historical writing in the fifty years after the murder of Thomas Becket.

76 *MTB*, iii, 156.

6.

Matilda, Duchess of Saxony (1168–89) and the Cult of Thomas Becket: A Legacy of Appropriation

COLETTE BOWIE

In 1168, Matilda, the eldest daughter of Henry II of England, married Henry the Lion of Saxony and Bavaria, and it is clear that Saxony in particular became a centre of Becket devotion noticeably quickly after Becket's death and canonisation. Evidence of autonomous female patronage is, however, frequently difficult to establish, with various acts, such as the foundation or endowment of religious houses, often being attributed in sources either solely to their husbands or as joint acts of patronage. This is particularly true for Matilda, duchess of Saxony, for whom no charters issued in her own name survive. She appears on just two of her husband's extant charters, both of which were issued in the early years of their marriage, and both of which concern religious donations.[1] On the first of these, issued at Hertzburg in November 1170, Matilda gives her consent to a donation to the monastery of Northeim.[2] She is only referred to on the second charter, recording the gift Henry made in 1172 of three candles which were to burn in perpetuity in the Holy Sepulchre at Jerusalem for, in Henry's words, 'the sake of the forgiveness of all my sins and those of my famed wife Matilda, daughter of the glorious king of England, and those of my heirs given to me by God as a token of His mercy, and also for [the sake] of my whole lineage'.[3]

The only other extant charter on which Matilda appears is that given by her son, Henry of Brunswick, in 1223, some thirty-four years after Matilda's death. In this charter, Henry describes his 'dearest mother of most happy memory' as the donor of the altar dedicated to the Virgin which stands in the

---

1 Henry the Lion's collected charters have been edited by K. Jordan, *Die Urkunden Heinrichs des Löwen, Herzogs von Sachsen und Bayern*, Monumenta Germaniae Historica, Diplomata, 5, Laienfürsten- und Dynastenurkunden der Kaiserzeit, 1 (Leipzig, 1941–49, repr. 1957–60).
2 Jordan, *Urkunden Heinrichs des Löwen*, 123–4 (no. 83).
3 '... pro remissione omnium peccatorum meorum et inclite uxoris mee ducisse Matildis, magnifici Anglorum regis filie': Jordan, *Urkunden Heinrichs des Löwen*, 143–5 (no. 94).

church of St Blaise at Brunswick.[4] As there is no record of Matilda as either the founder or the sole patron of any religious establishments during her lifetime – although it is almost certain that, together with her husband, she was a patron of the church at Brunswick and co-donor of the famous Gmunden Gospels – the mention of Matilda in her son's charter as the sole donor of the altar at Brunswick is of great significance for evidence of Matilda's patronage.

Further light has been thrown on the problem of ascertaining the extent of Matilda's patronage by examining the early dissemination of the cult of Thomas Becket. This article will attempt to define what role Henry II's daughter Matilda played in the promulgation of popular saints' cults, and what prompted her to do so.[5] Why would Matilda promote devotion to the man who had caused her father such trouble, whose quarrel with Henry had damaged his international reputation and whose death forced Henry to perform public acts of penance? Can her role in the promotion of Becket's cult be viewed as an act of filial disloyalty? Or is there another, more political reason, for this act of patronage? In order to understand the significance of Matilda's participation in the dissemination of Becket's cult, it will be expedient to consider the importance of dynastic saints' cults, as well as to examine Henry's own reaction to Becket's death and the role which he himself played in fostering the cult of the martyred archbishop.

Henry II and Becket: From Denial to Appropriation

Henry II was at Argentan when news of Becket's murder reached him on New Year's Day 1171. Chronicle accounts and even Becket's biographers stress Henry's initial grief, noting that he fasted and shut himself in his rooms.[6] Henry's letter to Pope Alexander III, *Ob reverentiam*, dated March 1171,

---

4 *Ibid.*, 178–9 (no. 121), although the Annals of St Blaise record the donation of the altar as a joint enterprise: *Liber Memoriam Sancti Blasii*, MGH SS, xxiv (Hannover, 1879), 824.
5 The participation of Henry's second daughter, Leonor of Castile, in Becket's cult is discussed in José Manuel Cerda's essay in this volume (chapter 7). For an overview of all three daughters' participation, as well as that of Henry's daughter-in-law, Margaret of France, see C. Bowie, *The Daughters of Henry II and Eleanor of Aquitaine* (Turnhout, 2014), 141–72; and see also Anne J. Duggan's essay in this volume (chapter 2).
6 According to Herbert of Bosham, after Becket's death Henry II 'retired for forty days of penance and fasting, refusing to leave his apartments at Argentan': N. Vincent, 'The Pilgrimages of the Angevin Kings of England, 1154–1272', in *Pilgrimage: The English Experience from Becket to Bunyan*, ed. C. Morris and P. Roberts (Cambridge, 2002) 12–45, at 23; MTB, iii, 542. The author of the *Lansdowne Anonymous* blamed Henry for the incitement, although not the authorisation, of Becket's murder, and relates that Henry grieved and fasted because Thomas had been his friend, although later 'he hardly sorrowed, or not at all, or else he hid his sorrow completely': MTB, iv, 159; trans. in *Lives of Thomas Becket*, 212.

however, presents a very different picture. The letter, which in effect blames Becket for his own death, contains no such suggestions of sorrow, shock or remorse and was clearly an exercise in damage limitation.[7] Attempts to appeal to the papal curia, however, proved unsuccessful and after Easter 1171, Henry's continental lands were placed under interdict. Moreover, as the author of the *Lansdowne Anonymous* relates, because of Becket's murder, the English were everywhere vilified, with the nation as a whole being held accountable for the actions of a few and letters from such prominent men as King Louis VII of France blaming Henry for not punishing the men who had committed the crime.[8] Nevertheless, Henry was at this point still maintaining that he had neither approved nor had foreknowledge of the murder, and was attempting to suppress the nascent cult by forbidding pilgrimages to Becket's tomb. By 1172, however, Henry was beginning to take a very different stance, as stories of miracles and suggestions of Becket's sanctity grew in scope. Henry therefore began to make arrangements for a public reconciliation with the pope.[9]

On 21 May 1172, Henry engineered a public display of repentance and reconciliation at Avranches.[10] His insistence on the public nature of this reconciliation suggests that he was aware of the general view, prevalent in much of western Europe, of his culpability in Becket's murder. The absolute eradication of all doubt that Henry was guiltless was paramount for the restoration of his international standing. Royal appropriation of the burgeoning cult was also essential. Thus, two years after Avranches, Henry undertook a further act of public display by making a penitential pilgrimage, on 12 July 1174, to Becket's tomb at Canterbury.[11]

After this first, penitential, visit to Becket's tomb in 1174, Henry made at least nine further visits – every year when he was in England – as well as

7 Anne J. Duggan calls the letter 'a masterpiece of distortion and suppression', noting that Henry was 'more concerned for his reputation than for his conscience': Duggan, 'Diplomacy', 267–8. See also Duggan's essay in this volume (chapter 2).

8 See *MTB*, iv, 159. The author suggests that Henry may have been lenient with Becket's murderers because 'he understood that these attendants had done what they had done out of love or fear of him': *MTB*, iv, 159; trans. in *Lives of Thomas Becket*, 212.

9 Several preliminary negotiations preceded Henry's public reconciliation at Avranches: Gorron on 16 May 1172, Savigny on 17 May, and Avranches on 19 May. The ceremony at Avranches on 21 May was followed by a larger one at Caen on 30 May, although the reconciliation was not formally confirmed by the pope until 2 September. See Duggan, 'Diplomacy', 274–7.

10 For accounts of the proceedings at Avranches, see *MTB*, iv, 173–4; *MTB*, vii, 516 (no. 772), 518 (no. 773), and 520 (no. 774); Howden, *Gesta*, i, 32; Howden, *Chronica*, 35–7; Diceto, i, 352. For the official record of the proceedings, see A. J. Duggan, '*Ne in dubium*: The Official Record of Henry II's Reconciliation at Avranches, 21 May 1172', *EHR*, 115 (2000), 643–58; repr. with the same pagination in Duggan, *Friends, Networks*, no. VIII.

11 William of Canterbury's *Miracula* (1174) has the fullest account and is the earliest source: *MTB*, i, 173–546. See also the account given by Edward Grim: *MTB*, ii, 445–7.

accompanying Louis VII in 1179 when the French king came to pray for the health of his young son, Philip.[12] This visit demonstrates that by the late 1170s, Henry's attitude to Becket's cult had changed drastically from (or was a different form of) his initial policy of damage limitation, which was apparent in his reaction to the news of the murder and his carefully publicised actions at Avranches in May 1172. It also suggests that Becket's cult had the potential to be a common spiritual uniting factor, a sort of extended family tradition, over and above the political differences which existed between Henry and Louis.[13]

Henry's pilgrimage to Becket's tomb was a voluntary act of penance, as it had not been mandated by the pope. It is possible that Henry's penance was a public and 'conscious acknowledgement of guilt', as Anne J. Duggan has suggested, although it is more likely that Henry was driven by political considerations.[14] Henry's standing at this time, both on a national and international level, was greatly reduced due to the conflict with, and subsequent murder of, Thomas Becket. Moreover, Henry was facing the impending invasion of his eldest son, Henry the Young King, and his allies, William I ('the Lion'), king of Scots and Count Philip of Flanders. Henry's visit to Becket's tomb was the first act he undertook on coming to England to deal with this threat and was undoubtedly made in order to align the new martyr-saint with the monarchy, and thus prevent the rebels from appropriating the cult for themselves.

Henry had accidentally created a saint of his former political opponent. To prevent this cult becoming a focus for rebellion and a rallying point for his enemies, Henry had needed to act quickly in order to neutralise the potential threat that Becket's cult represented. As examples of later medieval political saints demonstrate, in the vast majority of cases, without royal endorsement such cults ultimately tended to vanish within a few short years.[15] Sometimes, as with the case of Simon de Montfort (d. 1265), such cults disappeared as

---

12 Duggan, 'Diplomacy', 283. See also R. W. Eyton, *Court, Household, and Itinerary of King Henry II* (Dorchester, 1878), 190, 213–14, 223, 228, 241, 256, 257, 259, 268, 276. Richard I prayed at Becket's shrine before departing on crusade; John visited the shrine at least three times and was re-crowned at Canterbury in 1202 before leaving for Normandy; Duggan, 'Cult', 31, 31n. See also the essays by Anne J. Duggan (chapter 2) and by Paul Webster (chapter 8) in this volume.
13 Continued royal devotion to St Thomas must, however, be considered in the context of the plurality of saints venerated in England – and elsewhere – at this time. Richard's donations, on his return from crusade, to the shrine of St Edmund, rather than to that of Becket, perhaps reveal where his true interests in the patronage of saints' cults lay. For Richard's visit to Bury St Edmunds in 1194, see *Itinerarium Peregrinorum et Gesta Regis Ricardi*, ed. W. Stubbs, *Chronicles and Memorials of the Reign of Richard I*, RS 38, 2 vols (London, 1864–65), i, 446; *Radulphi de Coggeshall Chronicon Anglicanum*, ed. J. Stevenson, RS 66 (London, 1875), 63.
14 Duggan, 'Diplomacy', 266.
15 See S. Walker, 'Political Saints in Later Medieval England', in *The McFarlane Legacy: Studies in Late Medieval Politics and Society*, ed. R. H. Britnell and A. J. Pollard (Stroud, 1995), 77–106, at 81–2. See also M. Evans, *The Death of Kings: Royal Deaths in Medieval England* (London, 2003), 175–205.

a result of direct royal suppression.[16] Conversely, the cult of Thomas, earl of Lancaster (d. 1322), and that of Richard Scrope (d. 1405), endured precisely because of royal support.[17]

The intercessory power of saints and their perceived ability to intervene in daily life was one of their crucial attributes. St Thomas certainly seemed to have intervened to save Henry's kingdom in 1174 – or at least, that was the way Henry wished to present things, and his contemporaries seem agreed on this. As most chroniclers observed, Henry's fortunes improved dramatically after his penitential visit to the new saint's tomb, seen most notably in the capture of William the Lion of Scotland at Alnwick, which occurred at the very moment that Henry was praying at Becket's shrine.[18] Jordan Fantosme's verse, written for Henry in 1174–75 to celebrate his victories over his enemies, not only has Henry commend the protection of his realm to the saint, but also shows him appearing to admit a degree of responsibility for Becket's death:[19]

> 'Seint Thomas', dist li reis, 'guardez-mei mun reaume.
> A vus me rent cupable dunt li autre unt le blasme'.

> ('St Thomas', said the king, 'guard my realm for me.
> To you I declare myself guilty of that for which others have the blame'.)

Henry later thanks God, St Thomas and all the saints for his victory over the Scots king:[20]

---

16 For de Montfort's cult, see C. Valente, *The Theory and Practice of Revolt in Medieval England* (Aldershot, 2003), 68–105; *eadem*, 'Simon de Montfort, Earl of Leicester, and the Utility of Sanctity in Thirteenth-Century England', *Journal of Medieval History*, 21 (1995), 27–49. For comparisons between de Montfort and Becket in the early fourteenth century, see 'The Lament of Simon de Montfort', ed. T. Wright, *The Political Songs of England, From the Reign of John to that of Edward II*, Camden Society, Old Series, 6 (London, 1839), 125–7, at 125–6.

17 For Scrope's cult, see Walker, 'Political Saints', 84–5; Valente, *Theory and Practice of Revolt*, 216–21. For the cult of Thomas of Lancaster, see Walker, 'Political Saints', 83–4; Evans, *Death of Kings*, 188–92; Valente, *Theory and Practice of Revolt*, 30, 47, 123–53; and for comparisons of Lancaster with Becket, see 'The Office of St Thomas of Lancaster', ed. Wright, *Political Songs*, 268–72, at 268. The efforts to sanctify the last Lancastrian monarch, Henry VI, whose cult eventually superseded that of Becket as the most popular English saint, provides a further example both of attempts to establish a dynastic saint, and of the longevity and success of cults which enjoyed royal sponsorship. For Henry's cult and its popularity, see Evans, *Death of Kings*, 199–205.

18 See Edward Grim, who relates that 'the humbled king, through the intervention of the venerable martyr, divine favour now restored … subdued the enemy', *MTB*, ii, 447–8; trans. in *Lives of Thomas Becket*, 219. See also Howden, *Gesta*, i, 72.

19 *Chronicles*, ed. Howlett, 337–8 (lines 1605–6); *Jordan Fantosme*, ed. Johnston, 120 (lines 1599–1600). Also noted in the essays by Anne J. Duggan (chapter 2), Michael Staunton (chapter 5), and José Manuel Cerda (chapter 7) in this volume.

20 *Chronicles*, ed. Howlett, 371 (lines 2017–18); *Jordan Fantosme*, ed. Johnston, 148 (lines 2011–12). Also noted in the essay by Anne J. Duggan (chapter 2) in this volume. The connection

'Dunc,' dit li reis Henris: 'Deus en seit mercié,
E saint Thomas martyr, e tuz les sainz Dé!'

('Then,' says King Henry, 'God be thanked for it,
And St Thomas the Martyr and all God's saints.')

These lines reveal that by 1174–75, Henry was ready to admit some culpability in Becket's death – or at any rate, Fantosme was able to present such sentiments to the king in verse. Moreover, they reveal that by this date, Henry had successfully managed to neutralise the political threat that Becket's cult potentially presented. Instead, Becket was promoted as the guardian of Henry's realm and, as such, as the personal protector of the Angevin dynasty, bestowing honour on Henry and his family by way of association with the Canterbury martyr.

The capture of the Scots king, the defeat or submission of the rest of the rebels and the subsequent end of the Great Rebellion were Henry's rewards for his penance; and also provided public evidence that St Thomas, once the thorn in Henry's side, was now very much a firm supporter of the Angevin cause. Henry, it seemed, had managed not only to appease the martyr-saint, but had successfully won him over to his side. Nicholas Vincent has noted that it was only after the spring of 1172 – that is, after Avranches – that Henry began to use the title of king *Dei gratia*, 'reflecting the King's desire to broadcast a new image of himself in the aftermath of the Becket conflict'.[21] This new image, of the king ruling by the grace of God *and* with the support of a powerful saint, was promulgated not merely by Henry himself, but also by his daughter, Matilda, in Saxony.

Matilda and the Cult of Becket in Saxony

When discussing the dissemination of his cult, the many monographs of Becket's life and career focus largely on the various *Vitae* written after his death. Whilst acknowledging that this dissemination was both widespread and rapid, historians of Becket have largely disregarded the role of Henry's daughters. Yet it is clear that Becket's cult reached Sicily, Saxony and Castile noticeably quickly. José Manuel Cerda discusses the involvement of Henry's daughter, Leonor of Castile, in promoting the cult of Becket, elsewhere in this volume.[22] Here, the focus will be on Henry's eldest daughter, Matilda, and her role in fostering Becket's cult in her marital lands in Saxony.

between the capture of William the Lion and Henry's visit to Becket's tomb is also made explicit in the poem, and Fantosme is keen to stress that Henry's penance was both humble and genuine.
21 Vincent, 'Pilgrimages', 38.
22 See below, chapter 7.

Anne J. Duggan has seen some paradox in the fact that any of Henry's daughters chose to promote the cult of his old adversary.[23] But was such patronage an act of filial disobedience, or even betrayal? Or was it rather an act of filial devotion, motivated by political considerations? In promoting the cult of Becket in Saxony, was Matilda trying to atone for the sins of her father, or was she, like Henry II, following her own political agenda? In fostering devotion to St Thomas in terms of a dynastic cult, was she also promoting the prestige of her natal family, and appropriating the cult for, rather than against, the Angevins?

Matilda's patronage provides the earliest surviving example of Becket veneration in Saxony. Later medieval altar-pieces depict his life in four different cities in the north of the duchy: at St Jürgen in Wismar, at Tettens in Oldenburg, at St Nicholas in Stralsund and at Hamburg Cathedral.[24] By far the most compelling piece of evidence for Matilda's influence in promoting the cult of Becket, however, is to be found in the Gmunden Gospels, otherwise known as the Gospel Book of Henry the Lion, in which both Henry and Matilda are prominently portrayed as patrons who receive the crown of eternal life as a reward for their piety. The Gospels, known to have been commissioned by Duke Henry in the 1170s, contain scenes from the Old Testament and provide the earliest known example of St Thomas of Canterbury in the whole of Germany. The work was produced for the ducal couple at Helmarshausen monastery, a leading centre of German manuscript illumination, between the mid-1170s and late 1180s.[25]

The Gospel Book's dedicatory poem, along with the accompanying miniature, the coronation image and the image of *Majestas Domini* which immediately follows it, highlights the dynastic and political purposes of the work.[26] The dedication, which offers the book to Christ in the hope of attaining eternal life and a place amongst the righteous, identifies Henry as

23 Duggan, 'Cult', 25–6.
24 See Borenius, *Becket in Art*, 58, 62, 67–9, with images at 62–3 and 69; *idem*, 'The Iconography of St Thomas of Canterbury', *Archaeologia*, 79 (1929), 29–54, at 40–43, and plate XIV, figs 1–3, plate XV, figs 1–2; *idem*, 'Some Further Aspects of the Iconography of St Thomas of Canterbury', *Archaeologia*, 83 (1933), 171–86, at 178–80, and plate XLVII, figs 1–4; *idem*, 'Addenda to the Iconography of St Thomas of Canterbury', *Archaeologia*, 81 (1931), 19–32, at 24–5, and plate XXI, fig. 1.
25 K. Jordan (trans. P. S. Falla), *Henry the Lion: A Biography* (Oxford, 1986), 157, and 206–7 for more on the scriptorium at Helmarshausen. Richard Gameson, however, has dated the Gospels to c.1185–88: Gameson, 'Early Imagery', 52. See also O. G. Oexle, 'Lignage et parenté, politique et religion dans la noblesse du XIIe siècle: l'évangéliaire de Henri le Lion', *CCM*, 36 (1993), 339–54. Oexle argues for the later date of 1188.
26 See Oexle, 'Lignage et parenté', 340, 350. The *Majestas Domini* image, united with the coronation image, depicts the enthroned Christ holding the Book of Life, which contains the names of the just, and is an allusion to Henry the Lion's Gospel Book: Oexle, 'Lignage et parenté', 353.

the patron and highlights both his and Matilda's noble ancestry: Matilda is of *stirps regalis*, Henry is of *stirps imperialis* and, furthermore, is a descendant of Charlemagne (*nepos Karoli*).[27] Although the dedication seems to make it clear that it was Henry the Lion who was the patron of the work, the accompanying miniature shows both Henry and Matilda being recommended to the Virgin. Henry presents a gilt-bound book, presumably the Gospel Book, to St Blaise; Matilda stands beside him offering a jewelled pendant and holding the hand of St Giles, the patron saint of the Ägidienkloster in Brunswick, suggesting that the donation was indeed made jointly by the ducal couple.[28] As has been noted, it is not unusual to find joint acts of patronage being attributed to the husband alone, but it is certain that the Gospel Book was presented to the church of St Blaise by both Henry and Matilda, presumably in a symbolically charged ceremony, where it was probably destined to be placed on the newly constructed altar.[29]

Moreover, the inclusion of the newly canonised Becket in the series of illuminations can surely be attributed to Matilda's influence, strengthened perhaps by her and Henry's exile at the Angevin court in France and England. Matilda and Henry were exiled from Germany from 1182–85, during which time Becket's cult was thriving. It is likely that these years spent in the Angevin realm served to strengthen their attachment to the cult of St Thomas, and Pipe Roll evidence shows that in 1184, Duke Henry made a visit to Becket's shrine at Canterbury.[30]

St Thomas of Canterbury appears in the illumination depicting the coronation of Henry and Matilda at the hands of Christ. This coronation image shows Henry kneeling, dressed in robes decorated with crosses. Behind him stand his father, Henry the Proud; his mother Gertrude, daughter of the emperor Lothair III; and his grandparents, Lothair and his consort Richenza.[31] Opposite Henry stands Matilda, and behind her, her father Henry II; her grandmother, the Empress Matilda; and an unnamed figure of indeterminate

---

27 Oexle, 'Lignage et parenté', 349–50; Jordan, *Henry the Lion*, 157–8. It seems to have been Gisele, consort of Emperor Conrad II, who first claimed descent from Charlemagne – she is described in sources as *de stirpe Caroli Magni* – and thus formed the basis of both Salian and Staufen claims to descent from Charlemagne: Oexle, 'Lignage et parenté', 351.

28 Jordan, *Henry the Lion*, 206. See also Oexle, 'Lignage et parenté', 348–9. Oexle suggests a possible English provenance for this imagery, citing the eleventh-century *Liber memorialis*, the memorial book of Newminster Abbey, Winchester (c.1031–32). Henry and Matilda had spent the winter of 1184–85 there, their son, William, being born there at this time. Oexle believes that either Henry or one of his entourage would have seen this image at Winchester, from whence the idea was transported to Brunswick: Oexle 'Lignage et parenté', 349.

29 Jordan, *Henry the Lion*, 157; Oexle, 'Lignage et parenté', 348.

30 *The Great Roll of the Pipe for the Thirtieth Year of the Reign of King Henry the Second, A.D. 1183–1184*, PRS 33 (London, 1912), 145. See also Gervase, i, 311.

31 K. Bertau, *Deutsche Literatur im europäischen Mittelalter*, 2 vols (Munich, 1972–73), i, 459, and ii, plate 64.

sex, perhaps the Empress' first husband Henry V. The apparent exclusion of Matilda of Saxony's mother, Eleanor of Aquitaine, from the Gospel illuminations is striking. If the figure was meant to portray Eleanor, then surely she, like the other female figures in the picture, would have been named. This suggested to Elisabeth van Houts that 'something clearly went wrong between Eleanor … and her daughter'.[32] Van Houts believes that Eleanor was either deliberately excluded as an act of 'damnatio memoriae', or was 'disguised as an insignificant lay woman on the instructions of Matilda herself'.[33]

However, whilst it is plausible that Eleanor's role in the Great Rebellion of 1173–74 and her position in the late 1170s and '80s as Henry's prisoner provides a reason for her absence, the 'strong pro-mother sentiment on Duke Henry's side', which van Houts has highlighted, seems to stem more from the fact that Henry had inherited his lands from these rich heiresses.[34] Moreover, all of the (named) terrestrial figures depicted in the illumination are those who were entitled to wear royal or even imperial crowns, and the impression given is very much that it is the imperial dynastic connection which is being stressed. Karl Bertau has noted the 'extraordinary and unique' nature of a German duke being depicted in art in imperial fashion, and Otto Gerhard Oexle has pointed out that whilst coronation by the hands of God was a common image in Carolingian, Ottonian and Salian iconography, this form of image was traditionally reserved solely for kings and emperors.[35]

It has been suggested, therefore, that Henry the Lion was seeking the imperial throne for himself, and the imagery in the coronation illumination certainly appears to lend weight to this hypothesis.[36] As noted above, with the exception of Henry the Lion's parents and the unidentified figure at Matilda's extreme right, who are all shown uncrowned, the ancestors depicted in the image all wear either royal or imperial crowns. The crowns on these figures are depicted as identical to those being bestowed on the ducal couple, and although the crown of eternal life is expressly referred to at each of the corners of the miniature, these earthly crowns have been taken as an indication that Henry was attempting to assert regal power in Saxony and Bavaria.[37] No other contemporary source suggests that Henry was considering such a move, however, and his motivations are therefore unclear.[38] Nonetheless, what is

32   E. van Houts, *Memory and Gender in Medieval Europe, 900–1200* (London, 1999), 96.

33   *Ibid.*, 97.

34   *Ibid.*, 97.

35   Bertau, *Deutsche Literatur*, i, 460; Oexle, 'Lignage et parenté', 342–3.

36   See Jordan, *Henry the Lion*, 158.

37   Jordan, *Henry the Lion*, 158. Such ambitions were not without precedent. In 1158, Frederick I had granted Duke Vladislav II of Bohemia royal status at the Diet of Regensburg. See Jordan, *Henry the Lion*, 159.

38   It is difficult to agree with Jordan's assessment, based solely on the evidence of the coronation image in the Gospel Book, that the seeds of Henry's conflict with the emperor were germinating

clear is that the earthly figures in the coronation image were included expressly to emphasise the prestigious lineages of the ducal couple.

In terms of celestial figures, Christ Pantocrator sits in the upper register with various saints and angels. The saints ranged with Christ are those of special importance for Duke Henry, such as St Blaise, as well as those important to England, such as Thomas Becket. St Thomas appears directly above Matilda's namesake the Empress, indicating the special relationship the saint was deemed to share with Matilda's natal family. Becket's position immediately above Matilda's ancestors clearly indicates 'his recently renewed protection and support of the Angevin rulers'.[39] His inclusion in the coronation image could designate the saint's support of the duke's alleged ambitions. More pertinently for the argument advanced here, it demonstrates the continued appropriation of the saint by members of the Angevin family.

A Legacy of Appropriation

Matilda clearly had a strong sense of family identity: her devotion to her Anglo-Saxon ancestors included the worship of seven Anglo-Saxon royal saints.[40] These appear on a head-reliquary held at Hildesheim Cathedral, which was said to contain a fragment of the skull of the royal saint Oswald, the king of Northumbria who had died in battle in 642 against the heathen King Penda of Mercia. Both the workmanship of the artefact and the inclusion of six other saintly Anglo-Saxon kings on the panel-work suggest an English provenance, which has led some historians to conclude that Matilda and her husband Henry were responsible both for the donation of the reliquary to Hildesheim and for the reintroduction of Oswald's cult in Saxony.[41]

An extant inventory from Hildesheim, dated June 1189, provides further evidence of Matilda's association with the church there. This inventory, mentioned in Hildesheim's register of donations and income from the thirteenth century and published in Karl Jordan's edited collection of Henry the Lion's charters, lists the donations to the church at Hildesheim made

in the early 1170s, as such an argument assumes that Henry played a greater and more direct role in the production of the manuscript and its illuminations than is likely to have been the case. See Jordan, *Henry the Lion*, 159.

39 Slocum, 'Marriage', 218. For further discussion linking the cults of Becket and Blaise, see the essay by Alyce A. Jordan in this volume (chapter 9).

40 Vincent, 'Pilgrimages', 40n. See also W. A. Chaney, *The Cult of Kingship in Anglo-Saxon England* (Manchester, 1970), 78, 81–2; D. Rollason, *Saints and Relics in Anglo-Saxon England* (Oxford, 1989), 137–63.

41 D. Ó Riain-Raedel, 'Edith, Judith, Matilda: The Role of Royal Ladies in the Propagation of the Continental Cult', in *Oswald: Northumbrian King to European Saint*, ed. C. Stancliffe and E. Cambridge (Stamford, 1995), 210–29, at 223.

by Matilda, 'ducissa ecclesie nostre devotissima *una cum marito suo* Heinrico duce' [my italics].[42] The phrasing of this inventory – that Matilda donated gifts *together with her husband* – suggests that the donations were made at Matilda's, rather than at Henry's, behest, and the description of her as 'ducissa ecclesie nostre' suggests that the church of Hildesheim may have regarded her as its patron. In light of the fact that the relics of the Anglo-Saxon Saint-King Oswald were also housed at Hildesheim, Matilda's patronage of this church is interesting indeed.

Dagmar Ó Riain-Raedel has argued that there exists a connection between the growth of Welf power and that of the cult of Oswald, and believes that the arrival of the reliquary must have occurred after Henry the Lion had consolidated his power in the north-east of the duchy, and therefore after his marriage to Matilda. Despite the fact that Oswald was not of the Wessex line of Anglo-Saxon kings, the suggestion that Matilda would have counted these saintly kings amongst her ancestors seems plausible in light of the political clout that was associated with blood relationships to powerful saints. Moreover, the inclusion of so many Anglo-Saxon royal saints would have served the useful political purpose of furthering Welf claims to legitimate authority over Saxony, through Henry's dynastic marriage to Matilda.[43] Their appropriation of Becket, as evidenced in the Gmunden Gospels, would have served the same political ends.

Veneration of St Oswald in Saxony did not originate with Matilda and Henry the Lion, but the dissemination of this English saint-king's cult by women of the royal English line highlights certain parallels with Matilda's appropriation of saints' cults. Ó Riain-Raedel has studied the links between the introduction of and subsequent waves of interest in the cult of St Oswald in Germany, and the English royal women who had married into the Saxon ducal dynasty during the course of the tenth to the twelfth centuries.[44] She sees a clear link between the transmission of this cult and the marriages of the Saxon dukes with women of the English royal dynasty. Edith in particular, who married Otto the Great of Saxony in c.930, was said by one contemporary chronicler to be descended from the royal saint,[45] and she also seems

---

42 Jordan, *Urkunden Heinrichs des Löwen*, 179 (no. 122).

43 Whilst these hypotheses remain speculative, the extant inventory from Hildesheim Cathedral which names Matilda as its patron serves to support this argument, and provides further evidence both of Matilda's religious patronage and of her association with Hildesheim overall.

44 Ó Riain-Raedel, 'Edith, Judith, Matilda', 210–29. See also E. van Houts, 'Women and the Writing of History in the Early Middle Ages: The Case of Abbess Matilda of Essen and Aethelweard', in *eadem, History and Family Traditions in England and the Continent, 1000–1200* (Aldershot, 1999), 53–68.

45 This was Hrotsvita of Gandersheim, who composed the *Gesta Ottonis* in c.965 at the request of Otto's niece Gerberga, abbess of Gandersheim. For the possibility that Edith was descended from Oswald, or that claims of this affinity were already being promoted by the Anglo-Saxon

to have been promoted as a saint herself after her death. An entry for 8 July in the twelfth-century *Martyrology* of Hermann the Lame of Reichenau reads as follows: 'Apud Parthenopolim [Magdeburg] civitatem Saxonie *sancta Enid reginae*, uxoris quondam primi Ottonis' [my italics].[46] This projection of sainthood was not something out of the ordinary for Saxon royal women: Edith's mother-in-law, Matilda of Ringelheim, who married the first Ottonian ruler Henry I, was herself the subject of two *Vitae* composed at the convent of Nordhausen.[47]

Whilst reference to Edith's saintly ancestry may or may not have been accurate, it is certain that her family were responsible for the continued veneration of Oswald in England. The political expedience of this for her half-brother, Athelstan, was that promotion of the Northumbrian saint-king was of assistance in his attempts to establish authority over the newly Christianised kingdom of Northumbria.[48] This early example of royal appropriation of a saint's cult serves to demonstrate that in appropriating the cult of Becket, both Henry II and his daughter Matilda were merely following established and well-tried precedents. Matilda's marriage to Henry the Lion in 1168 saw a renewed Anglo-Welf alliance, and with regards to the presentation of the Oswald relic to Hildesheim Cathedral, discussed above, Matilda's political ambitions not only exceeded those of her tenth-century predecessor Edith, but

royal house at the time of Edith's marriage to Otto, see Ó Riain-Raedel, 'Edith, Judith, Matilda', 214–15. The value of the marriage between Otto and Edith, and of Edith's role in helping to give legitimacy to Otto's rule, is highlighted. Edith's ancestry is even more impressive than Otto's and, indeed, more impressive than that of her half-brother, Athelstan, whose mother seems to have been a concubine: Ó Riain-Raedel, 'Edith, Judith, Matilda', 213, 213n.

46 'at the city of Magdeburg in Saxony, St Enid [Edith] the queen, formerly wife of Otto I': Ó Riain-Raedel, 'Edith, Judith, Matilda', 213n. Edith was buried in Magdeburg Cathedral, her joint foundation with Otto. The cathedral was dedicated to St Maurice, and it is possible that it housed relics of the saint which had once belonged to Athelstan, and which were given as a wedding gift to Edith and Otto. Ó Riain-Raedel has suggested that Otto may have presented Athelstan with a gospel-book in return: Ó Riain-Raedel, 'Edith, Judith, Matilda', 215–16. The manuscript (London, BL, MS Cotton Tiberius A. ii) is dated to c.900, and is inscribed with the names 'Odda Rex' and 'Mihthild Mater Regis'.

47 Van Houts, 'Women and the Writing of History', 59. Otto I's daughter Matilda, abbess of Quedlinburg, was the dedicatee of Widukind of Corvey's *History of the Saxon People* and commissioned one of her nuns to compose the *Annales Quedlinburgenses*: van Houts, 'Women and the Writing of History', 58. Otto's granddaughter Matilda, abbess of Essen, was responsible for directing Aethelweard to produce the now-fragmentary Latin translation of the *Anglo-Saxon Chronicle*, which highlights the dynastic links between Matilda's family and the Anglo-Saxon royal house, and may even have introduced Aethelweard to Widukind's *History*, a copy of which was held at Essen: van Houts, 'Women and the Writing of History, 60–68.

48 As Ó Riain-Raedel has pointed out, 'As the first southern king of this region, Athelstan's efforts to impose his authority could only have benefited from a claim to a relationship with a historical king and martyr of the calibre of Oswald': Ó Riain-Raedel, 'Edith, Judith, Matilda', 216.

'may well have represented something of a political statement on Matilda's part, an act of solidarity with her earlier role model'.[49] Thus, just as Henry was following royal precedent in appropriating a saint's cult for the promotion of his own dynasty, so too his daughter, Matilda, followed queenly precedents in promoting her lineage through the worship of sainted ancestors.

Through dynastic alliances with England, the Saxon ducal house was able to utilise the cult of St Oswald and their association with it to further their own political agendas.[50] Oswald's monarchical as well as saintly status 'lent a special aura to his devotees', and his credentials 'eminently qualified him for inclusion in the category of sainted ancestors, by then so prevalent in continental royal houses'.[51] Oswald became, in effect, the patron saint of the Saxon dynasty, just as Becket was later adopted as the special protector of the Angevin family. In terms of longevity and geographical diffusion, Oswald's cult seems to have been as successful in Saxony as Becket's was later to be throughout Europe.

Matilda's Secular Patronage

The above evidence suggests that Matilda was more involved as a religious patron than has heretofore been accepted. Specifically centred around Hildesheim, which probably formed part of her dower lands, Matilda's religious patronage seems to demonstrate a strong sense of her royal lineage and dynastic connections. As well as promoting the cult of Becket, she seems to have felt an especial affinity towards Anglo-Saxon saint-kings whom she may have perceived as her ancestors, and she may also have been partly responsible for the reintroduction of the cult of St Oswald in Saxony. Some historians have asserted that it was also Matilda's presence in Saxony which brought new, specifically Angevin, literary and artistic influences to her husband's lands, thereby casting Matilda in the role of literary and artistic patron, as well as a patron of religion.[52]

---

49   *Ibid.*, 223. The reliquary is now housed at the Dom- und Diözesanmuseum in Hildesheim. Richard Bailey notes that the first reference to this particular reliquary at Hildesheim occurs in 1286: R. Bailey, 'St Oswald's Heads', in *Oswald*, ed. Stancliffe and Cambridge, 195–209, at 202. The relic at Hildesheim provides the only evidence of Oswald's cult in Saxony, although the cult had been established in Bavaria long before, possibly through the efforts of a contingent of Irish monks who took up residence at Regensburg in c.1080 and whose successors appear to have been responsible for a number of German redactions of Oswald's *Life*. See Ó Riain-Raedel, 'Edith, Judith, Matilda', 225–9.

50   Ó Riain-Raedel, 'Edith, Judith, Matilda', 229.

51   *Ibid.*, 222.

52   See, for example, Jordan, *Henry the Lion*, 147; K. Norgate, 'Matilda, Duchess of Saxony (1156–1189)', rev. by T. Reuter, *ODNB* (Oxford, 2004) [http://www.oxforddnb.com/view/article/18339, accessed 9 January 2015].

Henry the Lion was certainly a wealthy and lavish patron of literature and the arts, and, according to Karl Jordan, his connection to the Angevin dynasty through his marriage to Matilda 'gave a decisive impulse to intellectual and artistic life in the ducal entourage'.[53] As well as the Gmunden Gospels, Henry the Lion is the probable patron of two illuminated psalters which were also produced at Helmarshausen and which are now housed at the Walters Art Museum, Baltimore, and the British Library.[54] Certainly the London Psalter, of which only fragments remain, contains an illuminated miniature of the ducal couple kneeling before the crucified Christ, and the miniature may have been produced to commemorate their marriage in 1168.[55] Similarly, Jordan believes that the so-called reliquary of Emperor Henry II, which features effigies both of the emperor and of various kings with ties to the English royal dynasty, was commissioned by Henry the Lion soon after his marriage to Matilda.[56]

Matilda herself was highly involved in her husband's rebuilding programme at Brunswick, and she has also been credited with introducing a new, specifically French style of poetry to the Saxon ducal court.[57] Several German romance poems had begun to appear following the canonisation of Charlemagne in 1165, and two epics in particular, the *Rolandslied* and *Tristant und Isalde*, are thought to have been composed as a direct result of Matilda's influence.[58] The German translation of the *Chanson de Roland*, or *Rolandslied*, was produced by Conrad, a cleric at Regensburg, who apparently procured his source material from England at Matilda's behest.[59] In his epilogue, Conrad states that the work was composed at the request of the 'noble spouse' of 'Duke Henry', who was herself the daughter of a 'mighty king'.[60] Evidence from the text itself, such as the conversion of pagan peoples and references to the relics of St Blaise, suggest that the Duke Henry in question was Henry the Lion and that it was his 'noble spouse' Matilda, daughter of the 'mighty king' Henry II, who had requested

---

53 Jordan, *Henry the Lion*, 200.
54 *Ibid.*, 205. The manuscripts themselves are Baltimore: The Walters Art Museum, MS W. 10; London: BL, MS Lansdowne 381.
55 Jordan, *Henry the Lion*, 206.
56 *Ibid.*, 208. This reliquary is now held at the Louvre. For the many other gold and silver reliquaries commissioned by Henry the Lion (the so-called 'Welf Treasury'), see Jordan, *Henry the Lion*, 207–8. The stylistic similarities between the St Lawrence reliquary, now in the Cleveland Museum, and the St Oswald reliquary, now in the treasury at Hildesheim Cathedral, suggest that they were made by the same craftsman, and the probability that both were produced at Hildesheim presents a further link with the ducal court of Henry the Lion. See Jordan, *Henry the Lion*, 208.
57 Norgate, 'Matilda, Duchess of Saxony'.
58 Jordan, *Henry the Lion*, 200, and 209–12 for more on these works.
59 Ó Riain-Raedel, 'Edith, Judith, Matilda', 224. For the poem: *Das Rolandslied des Pfaffen Konrad*, ed. C. Wesle (Tübingen, 1967).
60 *Das Rolandslied*, 316–17 (lines 9017–25). My thanks to Jitske Jasperse for help with the translation.

a German translation of the *Chanson de Roland*.[61] As there is no mention of Matilda's death in the work, it must have been composed before 1189, and Karl Jordan has proposed a date of between 1168 and 1172, as Henry the Lion's journey to the Holy Land is also absent from the text.[62] The *Rolandslied* is the earliest extant German rendering of the *Chanson de Roland* and, like the images in the Gospel Book, is suffused with genealogical references.[63]

The author of *Tristant und Isalde* has been identified persuasively by Jordan as the same Eilhart of Oberg who appears as witness on several charters issued by Henry the Lion's sons, Henry of Brunswick and Otto IV.[64] He would therefore have had close ties to the ducal household, and, although the date of composition is unknown, Jordan estimates it to have been completed at some time in the 1170s, probably at around the same time as the *Rolandslied*, and therefore before Matilda's death.[65] If the tale of Tristan and Isolde was indeed brought to Saxony via Henry the Lion's marriage to Matilda, then, as with the *Rolandslied*, it is likely that they were the patrons of this work. Eilhart's later associations with Henry and Matilda's sons may have been in recognition of his earlier service to their parents, which may also suggest that this work, along with the *Rolandslied*, was well-known not just at the ducal court, but also within the more intimate household of their immediate family, perhaps forming part of the literary education of Henry and Matilda's children.

Matilda, who was almost certainly literate, was also commemorated in verse as the lady Elena, or Lana (variants of Helen), by the troubadour poet Bertran de Born, whom she met at Argentan in 1182 whilst in exile in Normandy.[66] De Born addressed two poems to Matilda, which express the notion that the dullness and vulgarity of the court at Argentan was lifted only by Matilda's beauty and 'sweet conversation'.[67] Both poems are overtly erotic, even going so far as to suggest how much more beautiful Matilda would be, were she unclothed.[68] In *Casutz sui de mal en pena*, de Born laments the fact that the 'frisky, gay Elena' will 'never keep me', will 'never be mine', and hopes only that she will 'favour me with her smile'.[69] Similar sentiments are expressed in *Ges de disnar non for'oimais maitis*, which states further that the imperial

---

61 Jordan, *Henry the Lion*, 209.

62 Ibid., 209.

63 Ibid., 209–10. See also Bertau, *Deutsche Literatur*, i, 460.

64 Jordan, *Henry the Lion*, 210–11.

65 Ibid., 211.

66 *The Poems of the Troubadour Bertran de Born*, ed. W. Paden, T. Sankovitch and P. Stäblein (Berkeley and Los Angeles, CA, and London, 1986), 117n; Norgate, 'Matilda, Duchess of Saxony'. For Matilda's education, see Bowie, *Daughters of Henry II and Eleanor*, 57–64.

67 *Poems of the Troubadour Bertran de Born*, 160–73 (nos. 8 and 9). Matilda is the only one of Henry II's daughters to be immortalised in verse by de Born.

68 Ibid., 167 (no. 8, lines 37–48).

69 Ibid., 164–7 (no. 8, lines 7–9, 17–24, 50–65).

crown would be 'honoured if it encircles your head'.[70] These are interesting sentiments indeed, considering Duke Henry's alleged imperial ambitions.

Becket at Brunswick: Continuation of a Family Tradition

Bertran de Born's image of Matilda wearing an imperial crown brings us back to the political motivations for the appropriation of saints' cults. Whether or not Henry the Lion, or indeed Matilda, viewed themselves as having the right to royal or even imperial rule in Saxony, they certainly constructed a magnificent palace there for themselves and their household. The palace at Brunswick, which lay at the heart of Henry the Lion's patrimony, and which appears to have been based on the palace complex at Goslar, certainly became the permanent ducal residence, a unique phenomenon in an itinerant world.[71] The ducal couple's attachment to Brunswick is clear, and the cathedral, where both Henry and Matilda are laid to rest, also houses a series of mid-thirteenth-century wall-paintings, on the south wall of the choir, which depict Thomas Becket's life and death, beneath scenes depicting the lives of the other patron saints of the cathedral, St John the Baptist and St Blaise. Of these images, only the first four scenes are original; the subsequent three were invented to complete the series by the restorer Heinrich Brandes in the nineteenth century.[72]

As the wall-paintings at Brunswick date to the mid-thirteenth century, they cannot have been commissioned by either Matilda or Henry the Lion. In all probability, they were commissioned by Henry and Matilda's son, Henry of Brunswick, who had also been responsible for commissioning, in c.1230–40, the magnificent joint tomb for his parents which stands beneath the choir and before the high altar of the cathedral. As the artist commissioned to undertake the work had in all probability never seen either Henry or Matilda, the effigies on the tomb do not present a true likeness of the ducal couple but rather an idealised image of ducal rule. Henry holds a sword in his left hand and a representation of Brunswick Cathedral in his right; Matilda wears a circlet around her head (not, after all, de Born's imagined imperial crown) and her hands are raised in prayer.[73]

Above the tomb, at the edge of the choir and to the side of the nave, rises

70 Ibid., 170–71 (no. 9, lines 21–4).
71 The glory of Brunswick as the principal ducal residence and as Henry's ancestral patrimony is celebrated in the dedicatory poem of the Gospel Book, which asserts that Brunswick has been further augmented by Henry and Matilda through their gifts of relics: Oexle, 'Lignage et parenté', 350.
72 The original images were repainted in the nineteenth century as part of Brandes's restoration project. See Borenius, Becket in Art, 52–4, with image at 55; idem, 'Iconography', 39–40, and plate XIII, fig. 4.
73 Jordan, Henry the Lion, 214–15.

a monumental seven-branched candelabra, which was probably commissioned by Henry the Lion.[74] It has been suggested that it was originally intended to stand by Matilda's tomb and, whilst there is no corroborating evidence for this, if true it would be indicative of some emotional bond between the ducal couple.[75] Certainly, on hearing of his wife's death in July 1189, the twice-exiled Henry returned to Saxony immediately, in direct contravention of his oath to the Holy Roman Emperor, Frederick I, not to return to his lands within three years.[76] When Duke Henry died on 6 August 1195, he was buried in the cathedral on the right hand side of his wife.[77]

Henry and Matilda's son, Henry of Brunswick, not only commemorated his parents in magnificent style by commissioning their grand tomb at Brunswick Cathedral, but he also followed their preferences in terms of the patronage of saints' cults. In particular, he was devoted to St Thomas of Canterbury: he established St Thomas as patron saint of the whole duchy and officially added him to the canon of original patron saints of Brunswick Cathedral, St Blaise and St John the Baptist. It was also Henry who oversaw completion of the reconstruction of the church of St Blaise, begun by his parents in 1173, and its consecration, which was held, significantly, on 29 December 1226 – the feast day of the martyrdom of St Thomas.[78] By the mid-thirteenth century, the feast of St Thomas was celebrated throughout Saxony and Bavaria.

By the fifteenth century, the feast was celebrated throughout Germany and the cult of Thomas Becket was well established. It is clear that the beginnings of such devotion to the martyr-saint of Canterbury originated in Saxony, under the ducal rule of Henry the Lion and Matilda Plantagenet, and that their son, Henry of Brunswick, continued the tradition of patronising and promoting a saint they may well have viewed as their personal protector. Henry the Lion had personally instituted the cult of Becket at Ratzeburg, which has been viewed as a 'direct result' of his marriage to Matilda.[79] Henry had also been, in his lifetime, an avid collector of relics, which he acquired on his pilgrimages to Jerusalem and Byzantium. He commissioned goldsmiths to fashion containers for these items, including a silver reliquary depicting the three patron saints of Brunswick Cathedral: St Blaise, St John the Baptist and St Thomas of Canterbury.[80]

74 Oexle, 'Lignage et parenté', 346.

75 Jordan, *Henry the Lion*, 202.

76 *Ibid.*, 189, and 19–99 for the years following Henry the Lion's return to Saxony in 1189 until his death in 1195.

77 Arnold of Lübeck, *Chronica Slavorum*, MGH SS, xiv (Hannover, 1868), 193; *Annales Stederburgenses*, MGH SS, xvi (Hannover, 1859), 231; Jordan, *Henry the Lion*, 198.

78 Jordan, *Henry the Lion*, 201.

79 Slocum, 'Marriage', 219.

80 Jordan, *Henry the Lion*, 154–5. Henry's relic collection, known as the Welf Treasury, is now housed in museums in Berlin and in the United States. The silver St Blaise reliquary was once housed at Brunswick and is now in the collection of the Cleveland Museum of Art in Ohio.

It is the Gmunden Gospels, however, which provide the earliest surviving example of Becket veneration in Saxony, and, whilst Matilda's influence is not noted in the dedication of the Gospel Book, she certainly acted in concert with Henry the Lion in their presentation of the book to the cathedral of St Blaise. The *Liber Memoriam Sancti Blasii*, which records Matilda's death erroneously under the year 1188, names her as *domina nostra*: patron of the church.[81] If the church of St Blaise itself viewed Matilda as its patron, her involvement not just in the symbolic presentation of the Gospel Book, but also to some degree in its content and production, seems likely. Matilda's piety and generous almsgiving, as well as her noble lineage, were noted by the chronicler Arnold of Lübeck, who described Matilda as 'a most religious woman' who performed many good and charitable works, donated alms freely and richly, prayed frequently and attended Mass devotedly.[82] Clearly, in terms of religious patronage, Matilda was adept at fulfilling her role both as duchess of Saxony and as a woman from the royal English line, and was praised as such by her contemporaries. Politically, the constant emphasis on Matilda's royal ancestry, highlighted by chroniclers and made explicit in the illuminations sequence in the Gmunden Gospels, serves to demonstrate the prestige of this marriage for Henry the Lion. More spiritually – but nevertheless with clear and overt political implications – Matilda and Henry were promoting Becket as a dynastic saint; and who better to seek spiritual protection from than the holy supporter of the great Angevin realm?

Conclusion

In light of all this, the participation of Henry's daughter, Matilda, in the dissemination of Becket's cult can hardly be considered surprising. Devotion to Becket had grown quickly, and the Angevin dynasty was clearly 'instrumental in this rapid development of organised veneration'.[83] As Henry II had successfully managed to appropriate Becket's cult for his own political ends, it is unsurprising that there is evidence of continued veneration of the saint by Henry's daughter. Far from being a paradox, as Duggan has suggested, Matilda's involvement in the dissemination of Becket's cult can be viewed positively, as both an act of filial devotion and as a celebration of her great lineage. Moreover, the patronage of saints' cults by royal women was not merely an established tradition, but a role which the daughters and wives of kings were expected to fulfil.

---

81 'Anno Domini 1188 domina nostra Mechtildis fundatrix obiit': *Liber Memoriam Sancti Blasii*, 825.
82 Arnold of Lübeck, *Chronica Slavorum*, 11.
83 Slocum, 'Marriage', 217.

As Richard Gameson has pointed out, the dissemination of images of saints 'provided a forceful reminder that the holy person in heaven was still very much a living presence on earth'.[84] Art could be a form of advertising as well as dissemination, and images such as those in the Gmunden Gospels could be both possessed and appropriated. It is clear that in venerating Thomas Becket, both Henry and his daughter Matilda were attempting to do just that.[85] It cannot be coincidental that Becket was included in Henry the Lion's Gospel Book so soon after his marriage to Matilda. The latter's motives for dissemination were likely to have been a mixture of dynastic, political and genuinely pious considerations. As has been demonstrated, Henry II, from 1174 onwards, was particularly concerned with the appropriation of Becket's cult, with perhaps varying degrees of political motivation and genuine devotion. In the immediate aftermath of Henry's penitential visit to Becket's tomb, his enemies were defeated and he was triumphant. Becket was clearly on his side and was emphatically being promoted as defender of the Angevin dynasty.

Becket was, in effect, becoming a patron saint of the Angevin family. In this light, then, it is not at all surprising that Henry's daughter Matilda should play such a prominent role in the dissemination of Becket's cult. Far from being an act of filial disobedience, it was more a stamp of authority, a continuation by the daughter of the father's appropriation of a potentially dangerous cult – one which came to symbolise far less a stand against tyranny, than the whole-hearted support of the powerful Angevin dynasty, who were made all the more powerful by having such a mighty saint on their side. That Matilda was able to transplant what was essentially a family tradition, in terms of patronage, to her marital lands in Saxony, is testament both to the power and prestige of her natal family and to her consciousness of her dynastic heritage. Similarly, Matilda's involvement in the cult of the English Saint-King Oswald, as well as her promotion and patronage of secular literature from the Angevin lands of her birth, served much the same purpose. Considerations of genuine piety aside, it is nonetheless clear that politics and religion could intertwine most usefully to further the prestige of both one's family and oneself. The Angevin/Welf family tradition of patronising Becket's cult was continued and furthered by Matilda's son, Henry of Brunswick, and the cult rapidly became entrenched not just in Saxony but throughout all of Germany as a direct consequence of such patronage. Ultimately then, in terms of dynastic connections, Matilda was perhaps the most successful of Henry II's daughters in promoting her lineage through her participation in the dissemination of royally sponsored saints' cults.

84 Gameson, 'Early Imagery', 46.
85 *Ibid.*, 48.

7.

Leonor Plantagenet and the Cult of Thomas Becket in Castile[1]

JOSÉ MANUEL CERDA

When Alfonso VIII of Castile married Leonor, the sixth child of King Henry II of England and Eleanor of Aquitaine, in September 1170, the young and small Iberian kingdom entered the most important dynastic network in twelfth-century Europe, and its affairs thereafter attracted attention in the Angevin dominions. Robert of Torigni, the Norman chronicler and the princess's godfather, noted: 'by God's favour, and by his own virtue, this Alfonso has married my dearest lady and my baptismal daughter, Leonor, the daughter of the king of England, whose advice and assistance have been productive to him of many happy results.'[2] An Angevin outpost south of the Pyrenees, as it were, Leonor was to become the first dynastic link between England and Spain in the Middle Ages.[3]

On 29 December 1170, only some three months after the marriage, Thomas Becket, archbishop of Canterbury, was murdered in his cathedral. Becket, once the king's most trusted minister, had become his most stubborn adversary, and the news of his brutal assassination sent shock waves all over Europe, where it was interpreted as martyrdom in defence of the Church's liberties and juris-diction. Pilgrims flocked to the martyr's tomb at Canterbury. Many miracles

1 This article is part of a research project funded with a two-year postdoctoral fellowship granted by CONICYT (Comisión Nacional de Investigación Científica y Tecnológica) of the Chilean Government (Project no. 3090034) for the period 2008–10. I am very grateful to Anne J. Duggan and Donald Matthew, who have generously read a draft of this paper and offered comments and suggestions, and to Jitske Jasperse and Anna Harnden for bringing my attention to some bibli-ography. I also appreciate the assistance of Alfredo Rodríguez from the Cathedral Archives of Toledo, Camino Redondo from the Museum of San Isidoro, and María Jesús Herrero Sanz from Patrimonio Nacional.
2 Robert of Torigni, *Chronique de Robert de Torigni*, ed. L. Delisle, 2 vols (Rouen, 1872–73), ii, 116.
3 I have explored some of the wider implications of this marriage on the cultural and diplomatic links between Castile and England in J. M. Cerda, 'The Marriage of Alfonso VIII of Castile and Leonor Plantagenet: The First Bond between Spain and England in the Middle Ages', in *Les Stratégies Matrimoniales (IXe–XIIIe siècles)*, ed. M. Aurell (Turnhout, 2013), 143–53.

were attributed to Becket's intercession and promptly recorded. He was, accordingly, widely venerated as a saint, and the pope canonised the martyr as early as 1173. Even if the ultimate responsibility for the archbishop's death lay with the king, Henry was personally innocent. He sent embassies to Rome and was decisively defended by Peter of Blois, who wrote to the archbishop of Palermo in 1177:[4]

> In conscience I believe in no way that the king was guilty of this thing; and the most complete confirmation of this the lord Theodinus, bishop of San Vitale, and the lord Albert, the chancellor, will make to you, who because of this matter investigated in our regions performing the office of legate; they confirmed the innocence of the man.

Henry, however, was compelled to perform public penance. As Edward Grim explained, 'even though the shedding of innocent blood had not been done by or through him, the king bore responsibility for it on account of his anger', and in 1174, he humbly travelled the pilgrim road to Canterbury and confessed his fault.[5] When Henry's own penitential visit proved to have coincided with the providential defeat of Henry II's enemy, William I, the king of Scots, Henry concluded that he had been forgiven and recognised Becket as his saintly protector.

The martyr of Canterbury, once a victim of Angevin wrath, became a focus of Angevin piety. Peter of Blois assured the Sicilian prelate that 'the lord king has made the glorious martyr his chief patron in all his needs'.[6] The cult quickly took root. Within a short time, altars, shrines and churches were dedicated to the martyr throughout western Europe.[7] In his twelfth-century

---

4 *Petri Blesensis Opera Omnia*, ed. J. A. Giles, 4 vols (Oxford, 1846–47), i, 66. See also Ralph Diceto, 'Ymagines Historiarum', in Diceto, i, 345–6, 351. Theodinus and Albert were sent to hear the king's confession after the reconciliation at Avranches in 1172.

5 Edward Grim, in *MTB*, ii, 445.

6 *Petri Blesensis Opera Omnia*, i, 66. During the war against his wife and sons in 1173, Henry II implored the assistance of the martyr, according to the vernacular (French) chronicle of Jordan Fantosme: '"St Thomas", said the king, "preserve me my kingdom; I confess myself guilty to you for what others have the blame"'; 'The king was truly at St Thomas the martyr's, where he confessed himself guilty, sinful and repentant …': *Jordan Fantosme*, ed. Johnston, 120–21 (lines 1599–1600), 142–3 (lines 1912–13). Also noted in the articles by Anne J. Duggan (chapter 2), Michael Staunton (chapter 5) and Colette Bowie (chapter 6) in this volume.

7 On the earliest manifestations of the cult in Europe, see R. Foreville, 'Le culte de saint Thomas Becket en Normandie: Enquête sur les sanctuaires anciennement placés sous le vocable du martyr de Canterbury', in *Sédières*, 135–52; H. Martin, 'Le culte de saint Thomas Becket dans les diocèses de la province de Tours', in *Sédières*, 153–8; J. Becquet, 'Les sanctuaires dédiés à saint Thomas de Cantorbéry en Limousin', in *Sédières*, 159–61; R. Foreville, 'Le culte de saint Thomas Becket en France: bilan provisoire des recherches', in *Sédières*, 163–87; and R. Foreville, 'La diffusion du culte de Thomas Becket dans la France de l'Ouest avant la fin du XIIe siècle', *CCM*, 19 (1976), 347–69. A brief but useful survey of the representations of the martyrdom in

Vie Saint Thomas Le Martyr de Cantorbire, Guernes de Pont-Sainte-Maxence declared, 'kings have sought him in pilgrimage … princes, barons, dukes with their nobles, strangers from foreign countries, speaking many languages, prelates, monks, recluses, rows of foot travellers; they take phials home with them as a sign of their journey'.[8]

Devotion to the martyr of Canterbury spread out so successfully in time and space, and became so firmly established in Spain itself, that the cult travelled to places as far removed from medieval England as Latin America in the nineteenth century. In 1856, a group of Chilean clerics established the Society of St Thomas of Canterbury in order to defend the autonomy and authority of the Catholic Church under threat from secular policies.[9] Becket was then invoked under the impression that the increasing antagonism between the Church and the state in Chile was akin to the situation that had led to the dispute between the king and the archbishop seven centuries before.

It is natural to suspect that Alfonso VIII's marriage to Leonor had some influence on the spread of the Becket cult in Spain. Leonor herself would have had reason for concern about her family and its reputation and, as Kay Brainerd Slocum has pointed out, 'diplomatic connections … provide a widespread public forum in which Henry and his progeny might atone for the act which was an egregious sin in the eyes of twelfth-century Europeans'.[10] Alfonso may have had reasons of his own to be interested in the matter of relations between a king and his archbishop, quite apart from his concern about the likely value of a Plantagenet ally on the defensive. It is natural to think that some of the protagonists of such a 'devotional export' might be the daughters of Henry II; a significant example of the religious patronage exercised by powerful women in this period. The focus of this work is to examine the role of the royal family of Castile, and especially the queen, in the growth of veneration for Becket in their dominions.[11]

---

twelfth- and thirteenth-century art is in M. Poza Yagüe, 'Santo Tomás Becket', *Revista Digital de Iconografía Medieval*, 5, no. 9 (2013), 53–62.

8   *Garnier's Becket*, trans. J. Shirley (Felinfach, 1975), 157 (lines 5893–7).

9   The society was created in 1856 in the capital, Santiago, in a context that confronted ultramontane conservatives, who defended the Church's autonomy, and regalists, who endorsed state intervention in ecclesiastical matters. More details of this controversy are given in Z. Martinic, 'Relaciones Iglesia-Estado en Chile, desde 1820 hasta la muerte del arzobispo Rafael Valentín Valdivieso en 1878', *Archivum*, 4 (2002), 21–8, at 24; F. A. Encina, *Historia de Chile desde la prehistoria hasta 1891*, 20 vols (Santiago de Chile, 1948–53), xiii (1949), 260. I thank the historian Leonor Riesco for bringing this case to my attention.

10   Slocum, 'Marriage', 215.

11   A comprehensive account of the spread of the cult in Iberia has recently been published, offering a description of the documentary and artistic evidence for the period 1170–1230 for all of the Spanish kingdoms and Portugal: Cavero, *Tomás Becket*. A brief summary of the development of the cult in Castile in this period is provided at pp. 220–23, and the volume is particularly significant for the study of the martyrdom in Spanish medieval liturgy (pp. 141–203). An

There is no datable evidence for any Spanish interest in Becket earlier than 1177, when a chapel dedicated to him was set up in Toledo Cathedral. The timing of this donation was determined by the siege and conquest of the Muslim city of Cuenca during the first half of 1177. In July, the altar to be erected to Thomas Becket was endowed by Count Nuño Pérez de Lara, the most prominent member of a highly influential noble family, who had himself formerly been King Alfonso's tutor.[12] Perhaps at the suggestion of William, his English chaplain, Count Nuño had invoked the intercession of the martyr as the saintly 'winner of battles' during the arduous enterprise of the siege, just as Henry II had prayed to Becket in 1174. What the martyr had miraculously done for an English king who had called for his aid in the face of military adversity was accomplished for his Castilian kinsmen. According to the *Anales Toledanos*, the count died in the siege and, along with his wife, Teresa Fernández, left his own house in Toledo and the rights over the nearby village of Alcabón for the maintenance of the chaplain. The charter that registered the grant was witnessed by five bishops, three counts, several knights and members of the besieging host. The following year, Alfonso VIII himself confirmed this grant 'pro remedio delictorum parentum meorum', and declared that the counts of the powerful Lara family had dedicated the chapel especially 'for the remission of [unspecified] crimes against churches and ecclesiastical persons'.[13] The Lara family was a generous patron of churches and promoter of both new cults and religious orders.

The military circumstances, alongside the influence of the Poitevin clergy

article published by Fernando Galván Freile offers an iconographic survey of the presence of the Becket cult in the Iberian Peninsula in the twelfth and thirteenth centuries: F. Galván Freile, 'Culto e Iconografía de Tomás de Canterbury en la Península Ibérica (1173–1300)', in *Hagiografia peninsular en els segles medievals*, ed. F. Español and F. Fité (Lleida, 2008), 197–216. The present paper is only concerned with the agency of Queen Leonor in the spread of such devotion in Castile during Alfonso VIII's reign.

12   The charter is registered in S. Barton, *The Aristocracy in Twelfth-Century León and Castile* (Cambridge, 1997), 328. See also Cavero, *Tomás Becket*, 49–50.

13   This phrase is contained in a royal diploma confirming the donation and issued the following year by King Alfonso, in the *regesta*: J. González, *El Reino de Castilla durante el reinado de Alfonso VIII*, 3 vols (Madrid, 1960) [hereafter AVIII], ii, 506 (no. 307): 'pro remissione criminum ecclesiis et ecclesiasticis personis iuste data sunt et concessa'. See also: *Los Cartularios de Toledo: Catálogo documental*, ed. F. J. Hernández (Madrid, 1985), i, 173–4 (no. 180); M. Shadis, *Berenguela of Castile (1180–1246) and Political Women in the High Middle Ages* (New York, 2009), 36. According to Gregoria Cavero (*et al.*), Alfonso confirmed the counts' grant in January 1181 at Toledo: AVIII, ii, 603–4 (no. 355); Cavero, *Tomás Becket*, 51, 220. Although the king did then protect the altar, he was really confirming his wife's diploma of April 1179. Alfonso had already confirmed Count Nuño's donation with a royal diploma drafted in September 1178: AVIII, ii, 506 (no. 307), which is not considered by Cavero. Although there is no mention of the altar as such, the document clearly makes reference to the donation made to the cathedral of Toledo by Nuño and his wife Teresa, and the property protected corresponds to that destined by the counts for the altar and the chaplaincy.

close to Nuño and Teresa, had turned Becket into the ideal patron saint of the moment.[14] Once launched, the cult took off. After the death of her husband at Cuenca, Countess Teresa left the court of Alfonso and married Fernando II, the king of León. Her arrival in León seems to have coincided with the endowment of a church dedicated to Becket in Salamanca, for which two English scholars, Randolph and Richard, have been held responsible. This building was probably constructed in the 1180s, being the first Becket church in the kingdom of León, and one of the earliest in Europe.[15]

Countess Teresa may also have had something to do with drawing Queen Leonor into the matter of promoting the Becket cult in Spain. One of the countess's daughters was given the name Leonor, still foreign to most Castilians at that time, which suggests a close relationship with the queen, who probably became the infant's godparent.[16] When the countess left Castile for León, the queen herself emerged as a champion of Becket, and it is likely that Leonor's daughter, and later queen of León, Berenguela, continued the promotion of the cult between 1197 and 1204.[17]

The only document issued independently by Leonor's chancery to have survived to this day, a charter granted on 30 April 1179 confirming and extending the grant made by Count Nuño in 1177, has been preserved in magnificent condition at Toledo Cathedral.[18] The opening lines clearly reveal the agency of the queen: 'ego Alienor, Dei gratia regina Castelle', who placed under her protection all that pertained to the altar of St Thomas located at a chapel within the cathedral church; who entrusted the devotional services and the protection of its rights and liberties to the chaplain, William, and

14 A considerable number of clergy from Aquitaine had occupied important ecclesiastical seats in Castile during the twelfth century. Prominent examples are Jocelin of Sigüenza and Cerebrun, archbishop of Toledo. On the other hand, the bishop of Poitiers until 1181 was John of Canterbury, a member of the Becket circle. On the contribution of Aquitanian clergy to the spread of the cult, see Cavero, *Tomás Becket*, 211–15.

15 Julio González asserts that academic and intellectual life was intensified in Castile in the second half of the twelfth century, and that school teaching seems to reveal some learning experience from abroad. Moreover, some of the names of the masters teaching at the cathedral schools also indicate the presence of foreigners: AVIII, i, 630, 634. See also T. M. Vann, 'The Theory and Practice of Medieval Castilian Queenship', in *Queens, Regents, and Potentates*, ed. T. M. Vann (Sawston, 1993), 125–48, at 134, n. 35; *Documentos de los Archivos Catedralicio y Diocesano de Salamanca (siglos XII y XIII)*, ed. J. L. Martín et al. (Salamanca, 1977), 161–2 (no. 74); Cavero, *Tomás Becket*, 55, 73–6.

16 Shadis, *Berenguela*, 36.

17 See Cavero, *Tomás Becket*, 55–60; Shadis, *Berenguela*, 75–6.

18 *Los Anales Toledanos I y II*, ed. J. Porres Martin-Cleto (Toledo, 1993), 146–7; *Los Cartularios de Toledo: Catálogo documental*, 173–8 (nos. 180, 184); AVIII, i, 923–9. It is very surprising that there is hardly any consideration or analysis of this crucial diploma in Cavero, *Tomás Becket*, 51. This survey – otherwise very useful and complete – devotes an entire chapter to the documentary evidence of the spread of the cult in the peninsula (pp. 49–66), yet the most relevant document, Leonor's grant from April 1179, is only mentioned, with no commentary on its content.

his successors; and who freed the chaplaincy from all impositions in Castile. The diploma was drafted by the queen's chancellor at Toledo, two years after Alfonso's conquest of Cuenca; it was authenticated by Leonor's *signum* drawn into the document and her wax seal, 'propria manu hanc cartam roboro et confirmo', and 'for the salvation and redemption of our souls' (those of Alfonso and Leonor).[19] The donation threatened God's wrath and eternal punishment in Hell in the company of Judas for anyone who dared violate the privileges and property granted to the altar and its chaplains. Although this was formulaic phrasing found in most royal diplomas drafted in Castile at the time, the financial penalties clearly established for transgressions demonstrate the queen's authority 'per totum regnum meum' – as the diploma states – and her determination to promote devotion to the English martyrdom as 'regina Castellae'. The village of Alcabón near Toledo, with all its property and income, was given in perpetuity to William, the first chaplain, and his successors, and they were also exempted from any kind of taxation. The queen's initiative was confirmed and witnessed by the archbishop of Toledo, five bishops, and some sixteen magnates, local authorities and royal officials. Significantly, the document was drafted by Egidio, Leonor's own chancellor. Alcabón was not among Leonor's dower property granted to her by Alfonso, 'donatio propter nuptias', in 1170, and had belonged to the late Count Nuño, but the wording of the 1179 diploma implies that the Castilian consort was in command of these resources and that she acted with some independence from the king. Theresa Vann has suggested that the royal protection of the altar was probably petitioned by the citizens of Toledo, some of whom witnessed the charter, but such family devotion was nevertheless an intimate undertaking for the daughter of the English king.[20]

Alfonso had confirmed the counts' donation in 1178, but Leonor's charter reveals, as Shadis asserts, 'a queen in control of her resources and a continued attention to her family's affairs in England', and that Leonor 'did not function simply as an adjunct in her husband's patronage activities'.[21] That she remained proud of her connections with the kings of England is borne out by some of her own handiwork. Two stoles embroidered in the 1190s, decorated with red castles over golden background, claim to have been made by her: 'Alienor

19 Toledo, Cathedral Archives of Toledo, AC Toledo, A-2-G-1-5; AVIII, ii, 542–3 (no. 324). The charter is preserved in its original form and is very similar to those produced at Alfonso's chancery (35.5 cms x 25.5 cms, a seal drawn in the document depicting the hand of the queen, and another wax seal of 9 cms x 6.5 cms with some wear and damage, attached by leather tag, depicting a full-length image of the queen). The transcription is in AVIII, ii, 542–3 (no. 324). Other references are: AVIII, i, 373, 418–19; F. V. de la Cruz, *Berenguela la Grande. Enrique I el Chico (1179–1246)* (Gijón, 2006), 8–9. Richard Gameson mistakenly indicates the year 1174 for this grant: Gameson, 'Early Imagery', 51.
20 Vann, 'Theory and Practice', 133. This is also suggested by Slocum, 'Marriage', 220.
21 Shadis, *Berenguela*, 36–7; Slocum, 'Marriage', 220.

Regina Castelle Filia Henrici Regis Anglie me fecit'.[22] She was often identified as the daughter of the king of England in scribal records and chronicles, and to this day the carvings on her sarcophagus at the monastery of Las Huelgas in Burgos bear the Plantagenet crest with the golden lions, probably made in the middle of the thirteenth century, a testimony to her ancestry set in stone.[23]

The wax seal attached to the 1179 diploma supplies us with a contemporary representation of the queen. In a diploma with almost identical wording and a similar list of witnesses, King Alfonso ratified his consort's endowment of 1179 sometime during the weeks he spent in Toledo during the winter of 1180–81.[24] The initiative had clearly been taken by Leonor, but the king's charter reveals the importance achieved by the cult within the royal agenda.

Toledo was the main ecclesiastical see in the reign – and arguably in the entire peninsula – so the queen's choice to continue the counts' devotional patronage instead of establishing a shrine or an altar at the much favoured royal city of Burgos, for example, is very significant. Moreover, it is very likely that Leonor's monetary endowment to the chaplain and the chaplaincy was taken from the dower granted to her by Alfonso in 1170, part of which came precisely from the annual rents of Toledo.[25] The cult of Thomas Becket was pushed by royal initiative, but it only took root with the support of the Castilian Church.

If her charter of confirmation clearly demonstrates Leonor's interest in the Becket cult by 1179, it also appears to strengthen the case for attributing to her the evidence for an interest in Becket at Soria. This was not among Leonor's dower towns but was her husband's birthplace, so it seems a fitting place to establish a monument of expiation for the murder in the cathedral. Frescoes depicting the infamous assassination at Canterbury were discovered some thirty years ago in near pristine condition. Wooden boards protecting the pictures were recently removed to reveal the stunning painting (albeit considerably damaged since their discovery).[26] Unlike some depictions of the murder,

---

22   The stoles are now kept at the museum of the Colegiata de San Isidoro in León. 'Inventario de Bienes Muebles de la Real Colegiata de San Isidoro (León)', no. 11C-3-089-002-0024: Embroidered in silk (277 cms x 6.5 cms) dated 1197, and with inscription: '+ Alienor Regina Castelle Filia + Henrici Regis Anglie Me Fecit + Sub Era M CC XXXV Annos +'. Object: no. 11C-3-089-002-0025: same material (156 cms x 6.5 cms), dated 1198, with inscription: '… M CC XXX VI …'. See also AVIII, i, 191.

23   R. Walker, 'Leonor of England and Eleanor of Castile: Anglo-Iberian Marriage and Cultural Exchange in the Twelfth and Thirteenth Centuries', in *England and Iberia in the Middle Ages, 12th–15th Century: Cultural, Literary and Political Exchanges*, ed. M. Bullón-Fernández (New York, 2007), 67–87, at 77–83.

24   AVIII, ii, 603–4 (no. 355); Vann, 'Theory and Practice', 134; Shadis, *Berenguela*, 36–7.

25   AVIII, i, 192–3; Shadis, *Berenguela*, 25–30.

26   L. Romera, 'Iglesia de San Nicolás en Soria: las pinturas sobre el asesinato de Tomás Becket', *Revista de Arqueología*, 329 (2008), 40–43; Cavero, *Tomás Becket*, 94–8. The paintings were restored in 1977 and measure 1.9 m. x 4 m. approximately.

where four knights face Becket, with one of them cutting his head, the Soria paintings show a bearded man thrusting his sword into the archbishop's back. Due to the deterioration of the wall, his companions have disappeared from the scene. It is difficult to determine what early model or tradition might have informed this intriguing work in the church of San Nicolás, one of the most accomplished Romanesque buildings in Castile, built in the early thirteenth century and now in ruins. Although they are undoubtedly medieval, the dating has not yet been resolved, nor can the agency of the queen be established beyond doubt. According to Fernando Galván Freile, the artistic style of these paintings corresponds to the early decades of the fourteenth century, and they seem to follow not the written traditions of the *vitae*, but rather the established visual models such as the early iconographic programme of the martyrdom painted in the walls of the church of Santa María de Terrassa in Catalonia.[27]

Likewise, it is not easy to link the agency of Leonor with some Romanesque sculpture in the church of San Miguel de Almazán (province of Soria), crafted around 1200 and discovered in 1936. The stone carvings show four knights facing Archbishop Thomas, who is kneeling down, showing his palms ready for martyrdom and defenceless before the slaughter, after which angels carry his soul to the encounter with God. The depiction is similar to the funerary sculpture of the small sarcophagi at Las Huelgas and the cathedral of Burgos, belonging to two of Leonor's children who died shortly after birth and whose souls are also shown being taken to Heaven.[28]

There seems to be more reason to relate the presence of the queen of Castile with some evidence of the cult at Sigüenza. A papal bull issued by Celestine III in 1192 refers to an altar dedicated to the English martyr in the cathedral there, and the martyrdom is solemnly commemorated in the breviary of Bishop Rodrigo of Sigüenza (1192–1221).[29] The altar was most probably erected by Jocelin, the Aquitanian bishop of Sigüenza from 1168 to 1178, who had witnessed Count Nuño's grant in Becket's honour at the siege of Cuenca. Jocelin had succeeded Cerebruno (another native of Aquitaine) at Sigüenza, when Cerebruno became archbishop of Toledo, and both had accompanied Leonor across the Pyrenees to Tarazona in 1170, a magnificent cortège that was also joined by Count Nuño.[30] All three were royal advisors and courtiers of Alfonso and Leonor, and if Jocelin was responsible for the Becket altar, it

27 Galván Freile, 'Culto e Iconografía', 207–8; Cavero, *Tomás Becket*, 82–94.
28 Galván Freile, 'Culto e Iconografía', 209–10; Cavero, *Tomás Becket*, 79–82.
29 Gameson, 'Early Imagery', 51; Duggan, 'Cult', 26; A. Herrera Casado, *Heráldica Seguntina* (Guadalajara, 1990), i, 177; F.-G. Peces Rata, *La Fortis Seguntina: La Catedral de Sigüenza* (Barcelona, 1997); F.-G. Peces Rata, *Paleografía y epigrafía en la Catedral de Sigüenza* (Sigüenza, 1988), 51; E. S. Dodgson, 'Thomas Á Becket and the Cathedral Church of Sigüenza', *Notes and Queries* (1902), s.9–IX (227), 344.
30 *Anales Toledanos*, 150; Shadis, *Berenguela*, 35–6; Cavero, *Tomás Becket*, 52.

must have been one of the earliest signs in Castile of veneration for the martyr, possibly earlier than Count Nuño's dated grant. But here there is no link with Queen Leonor, apart from Jocelin's participation in welcoming her to the kingdom in 1170.

The supposition that Leonor played a more significant role than others in promoting the Becket cult in Spain is connected with the assumption that Henry II's other daughters similarly performed a filial duty by their patronage of Becket, their father's newly canonised protector.[31] The matter of royal relations with the episcopate and papacy was of perennial interest in Germany. The wonderfully illuminated Gospel book of Henry of Saxony, who had married Matilda of England in 1168, bears witness to the family veneration adopted by Henry II's eldest daughter.[32] Furthermore, one of the king's daughters-in-law was also instrumental in promoting the Becket cult in a kingdom as far away as Hungary. The Capetian Margaret was betrothed to Henry II's eldest son, also named Henry, in 1158 and once a widow (1183) she married King Bela III of Hungary in 1186.[33] As for the commitment of Leonor's youngest sister, Joan, to the cult in Sicily, it has to be remembered that links between the English and the Sicilian kingdoms long antedate Becket's death.[34] The mosaic of Becket installed as part of the elaborate decoration of William II's most lavish religious foundation at Monreale may have been commissioned after William's marriage to Joan in 1177. However, as Evelyn Jamison pointed out, the origins of Sicilian devotion to Becket probably went back to his personal contacts with the local episcopate, well before the Plantagenet princess arrived at Palermo, and, of course, the close relations of the kings with the papacy itself.[35] Unlike Leonor, Joan was married after the Becket cult had become well ingrained and there was no need for her to pioneer a new devotion. There is no reason to suppose that Becket had any interest whatever in Castile or that the problems he faced with Henry II roused any sympathy

31 According to Anne J. Duggan, 'the marriage alliances of Henry II's three daughters (and one daughter-in-law) played some part in spreading devotion to their father's chief ecclesiastical adversary': Duggan, 'Cult', 25–6.

32 See Colette Bowie's essay in this volume (chapter 6).

33 Some work has been done on the patronage of Bela and Margaret for the veneration of Thomas Becket in Hungary: Slocum, 'Marriage', 222 and n. 48. See also the discussion of further relevant evidence in the essay by Anne J. Duggan in this volume (chapter 2) and the references cited there.

34 See D. Matthew, *Britain and the Continent 1000–1300: The Impact of the Norman Conquest* (London, 2005), 96; E. Jamison, 'The Alliance of England and Sicily in the Second Half of the 12th Century', *Journal of the Warburg and Courtauld Institutes*, 6 (1943), 20–32, at 24; M. Barth, 'Zum Kult des hl. Thomas Becket im deutschen Sprachgebiet, in Skandinavien und Italien', *Freiburger Diözesan-Archiv*, 80 (1960), 97–166.

35 D. Matthew, *The Norman Kingdom of Sicily* (Cambridge, 1992), 205; Jamison, 'Alliance of England and Sicily', 24–5. Tancred Borenius, on the other hand, credits Joan with more agency in the promotion of the cult on the island: Borenius, *Becket in Art*, 13.

in the Castilian episcopate, so Leonor seems to have been more active and independent than her sisters abroad.[36]

However, apart from her diploma for Toledo Cathedral, the evidence for Leonor's active interest in the promotion of the Becket cult is inconclusive. A wooden chasse that once contained relics of the English martyr is found amongst the medieval property of the nunnery of Las Huelgas, founded by Alfonso and Leonor, and a Limoges-style reliquary casket from Palencia was produced in the last decade of the twelfth century and has scenes depicting the martyrdom.[37] Becket became the patron saint of the village of Alcabón (Toledo), and its parish church is dedicated to the martyr. There is also a thirteenth-century church named Santo Tomás de Cantorbery in Avilés (Asturias) and a chapel enlarged into a church in the sixteenth century at Vegas de Matute (Segovia).[38] However, none of these is evidently linked to the agency of the queen. There is no evidence to suggest that Leonor had anything to do with the dedication of the Becket church in Salamanca and another twelfth-century church, named Santo Tomás Cantuariense, in Toro (León), was probably dedicated to the martyr only in the eighteenth century. Nor can Leonor have had anything to do with the mural of the martyr in the church of Terrasa (Catalonia), or a chapel dedicated at Barcelona Cathedral in 1186, the most significant evidence of the spread of the cult to the northeast of Castile. Some literary influences of the Becket story over some texts written in Castile in the late twelfth and early thirteenth centuries have also been noted and demonstrate the spread of the cult in peninsular poetry, but there is no evidence to suggest the agency of the queen here.[39]

As for an interest in Becket at Burgos Cathedral, it was Archdeacon

36 M. Shadis and C. H. Berman, 'A Taste of the Feast: Reconsidering Eleanor of Aquitaine's Female Descendants', in *Eleanor of Aquitaine: Lord and Lady*, ed. B. Wheeler and J. C. Parsons (London, 2002), 177–211, at 182–3. Kay Brainerd Slocum, writing on the role of Henry II's daughters in the spread of the cult, appears to suggest that the patronage of Leonor in Castile was more active and independent compared to that of her sisters: Slocum, 'Marriage', 219–20, 223–5.
37 D. Ocón, 'Alfonso VIII, la llegada de las corrientes artísticas de la corte inglesa y el bizantinismo de la escultura hispánica a fines del siglo XII', in *Alfonso VIII y su época* (Aguilar de Campoo, 1990), 307–20, at 314, n. 30; S. Caudron, 'Thomas Becket et l'Œuvre de Limoges', in *Valérie et Thomas Becket: De l'influence des princes Plantagenêt dans l'Œuvre de Limoges*, ed. V. Notin et al. (Limoges, 1999) 56–68. The Palencia reliquary is now in the Musée de Cluny (Musée National du Moyen Âge) in Paris.
38 F. J. Fernández Conde, *La religiosidad medieval en España: Plena Edad Media (ss. XI–XII)* (Gijón, 2005), 481; Cavero, *Tomás Becket*, 76–8. A confraternity was founded in Puente Castro (León) in 1884 to preserve the memory of its patron saint and, as in other parishes dedicated to the martyr in Spain, they commemorate 29 December every year.
39 Estrella Pérez Rodríguez has suggested that the author of the *Vita Didaci*, a poem about the founder of the Castilian abbey of Benevívere, may have been an Anglo-Norman, perhaps someone from Christ Church, Canterbury, who would have been all too aware of the details of the murder in the cathedral, as well as a contemporary of Queen Leonor: E. Pérez Rodríguez, *Vita Didaci, Poema sobre el Fundador de Benevívere* (León, 2008), 182–93.

Matthew who provided the funds to support two chaplaincies at that church and for a mass to be said for sinners and the dead: 'in altaribus que ad honorem Sancti Tome Martiris et Beati Antonii Abbatis in ecclesia Sancte Marie construximus'.[40] Although the charter is not dated, José Manuel Garrido suggests that it was issued in 1202, because the archdeacon begins to appear as witness in other documents from this year. It is not clear that the chaplaincy and the altar were established at the same time or if the altar was already there. In any case, the cathedral chapter took the initiative and there is nothing to suggest any involvement by the queen. Nor can the agency of Leonor be established for a thirteenth-century codex and a reliquary related to Becket, both to be found at Burgos Cathedral.[41]

About the same time in Burgos, the construction of the royal monastery of Las Huelgas owed something to an English master, named Richard, for which he was generously rewarded in 1203, 'pro laudabili obsequio quo in constructione Burgensis monasterii nostri Sancte Marie Regalis nobis exibuistis'.[42] Had the daughter of Henry II petitioned for English expertise for the building of one the earliest Gothic structures in Iberia?[43] The marriage between Alfonso and Leonor certainly inaugurated an unprecedented alliance between England and Castile, so that, quite apart from any devotion to the martyr, the Angevin princess was probably active in promoting exchanges between these kingdoms. An entry in the English Pipe Rolls for 1184 registers some expenses concerning the purchase of utensils by Richard and Edward for the

40 *Documentación de la Catedral de Burgos (1184–1222)*, ed. J. M. Garrido (Burgos, 1983), 155, no. 363; AVIII, i, 374, nos. 24, 25.

41 Cavero, *Tomás Becket*, 105–11.

42 AVIII, iii, 310, no. 747; T. Tolley, 'Eleanor of Castile and the "Spanish" Style in England', in *England in the Thirteenth Century: Proceedings of the 1989 Harlaxton Symposium*, ed. W. M. Ormrod (Stamford, 1991), 167–92, at 186; J. González, 'Un arquitecto de las Huelgas de Burgos', *Revista de Archivos, Bibliotecas y Museos*, 53 (1947), 47–50; J. M. Lizoaín Garrido, *El Monasterio de las Huelgas: Historia de un Señorío Cisterciense Burgalés (siglos XII–XIII)* (Burgos, 1988); A. Rucquoi, *Rex, Sapientia, Nobilitas: Estudios sobre la Península Ibérica Medieval* (Granada, 2006), 82. Tolley indicates that 'Ricardo was either an Englishman or an Angevin. The former seems more likely because the architectural style, particularly of the chapter house, is distinctly English, and the form of the vaults is not of the Angevin kind' (p. 186). The oldest surviving parts of the building, contemporary with Alfonso and Leonor, are the small Romanesque cloisters known as the *claustrillas* (c.1180–90), followed by the early Gothic church built in the first decades of the thirteenth century: M. J. Herrero Sanz, *Guide to Santa María la Real de las Huelgas, Burgos* (Madrid, 2002), 16, 46, 54; AVIII, i, 654–6.

43 Here, see E. McKiernan, 'Monastery and Monarchy: The Foundation and Patronage of Santa María la Real de Las Huelgas and Santa María la Real de Sigena' (unpublished Ph.D. thesis, University of Texas at Austin, 2005), 167–8, 176, 179–82; Herrero Sanz, *Guide to Santa María la Real de las Huelgas*, 9–10. Leonor had visited France in 1199 and 1206 for diplomatic reasons and she may have appreciated some of the features of the new architecture: McKiernan, 'Monastery and Monarchy', 59.

use of those who travelled to Spain on the king's service.[44] Were they sent to honour the alliance with Castile? Leonor kept in touch with English affairs and appears as the axis of the increasing relations between Castile and the kings of England. After Henry II was buried at the abbey of Fontevraud in 1189, Leonor revealed her concern for her father's soul when the monarchs of Castile committed themselves to an annual payment to the monastery, for the benefit of his soul, 'pro remedio anime felicissime recordationis famosissimi H. regis Anglie', and possibly to reward the education Leonor had received there in her tender years.[45] Magán, a farm near Toledo which provided the gold for the abbey's endowment, and a house for the nuns of Las Huelgas in 1209, had been one of the villages included in the queen's dowry: 'quas regina domna Alienor … tenebat'.[46]

The scanty and difficult evidence available for the early phase of the Becket cult in Castile is connected not only with the queen but particularly with those men who escorted her from Bordeaux in 1170 and besieged Cuenca seven years later. The Poitevin connections of the Castilian bishops and the Lara family were also relevant for the perception of what was happening on the other side of the Pyrenees and it is sensible to recognise that Leonor's interest in her family was not dependent on any perceived respect for Becket. It is unlikely that she had ever met the archbishop of Canterbury in person. But the impact of the murder in the cathedral was, indeed, swift, profound and widespread, and the contribution of clerical migration and aristocratic patronage in transmitting the devotion to the English martyr was significant. The phenomenon also reveals the importance of devotion as a bonding element within dynastic families and the role played by powerful women in sponsoring pious undertakings in this period. In Castile, the cult was lively, as well as being royal, aristocratic and popular; the intercession of the saint was deemed effective, and his invocation owed much to the initiative of Henry II's daughter, whose

---

44 *The Great Roll of the Pipe for the Thirtieth Year of the Reign of King Henry the Second, A.D. 1183–1184*, PRS 33 (London, 1912), 137: *Et Ricardo filio Reineri et Ædwardo Blundo .xxxvj. s. et .ix. d. ad emendas nappas et patellas et alia vtensilia ad opus eorum qui transfretaverunt in Hispanias in servitio regis per breve Rannulfi de Glanuill.*

45 AVIII, iii, 475, no. 482. See also AVIII, ii, 945–7, no. 551. Among the witnesses of his grant was García Martínez, *maiordomus regine*. On Leonor's education and her relationship with Fontevraud, see R. Favreau, 'Aliénor d'Aquitaine et Fontevraud', *303 Arts, Recherches et Créations*, 81 (2004), 41–4, at 41. See also AVIII, i, 509; Rucquoi, *Rex, Sapientia, Nobilitas*, 61; M. Shadis, 'Piety, Politics, and Power: The Patronage of Leonor of England and Her Daughters Berenguela of León and Blanche of Castile', in *The Cultural Patronage of Medieval Women*, ed. J. H. McCash (Athens, GA, and London, 1996), 202–27, at 203. For some of the benefits, grants and payments conferred by Leonor's mother on Fontevraud, see M. P. Marchegay, 'Chartes de Fontevraud concernant l'Aunis et la Rochelle', *Bibliothèque de l'École des Chartes*, 19 (1857–58), 132–70 and 321–47, at 134–6, 329–39.

46 AVIII, ii, 945–7, no. 551; AVIII, iii, no. 842. See also Shadis, *Berenguela*, 37.

agency brought 'many happy results' to Alfonso's reign, in the words of the abbot of Mont St-Michel.[47]

In 2014, the year of the eighth centenary of her death, the interesting life and work of the Castilian consort, of which the promotion of the Becket cult is but a small chapter, gained relevance. Leonor Plantagenet was an active outpost of the Angevin family in Iberia, and as a member of a dynasty beleaguered by the blame for one of medieval Europe's most stunning murder cases, she was diligent in procuring the expiation of her father's memory and soul, and promoting the cult of the English saint, 'winner of battles', in her adopted kingdom.

In 1197, however, it was the queen who persuaded an unwilling Alfonso VIII to defy canonical dispositions concerning consanguinity so as to procure peace between Castile and León with the betrothal of their daughter Berenguela to Alfonso IX, who was the king of Castile's first cousin. It appears that no dispensation was issued by Pope Celestine III and the marriage was, in fact, condemned by Innocent III the following year. The newly wedded couple were excommunicated and the kingdom threatened with interdict. Early in 1204, the marriage was finally annulled and the children produced considered illegitimate by the pope, although Fernando was still considered legitimate heir in Castile and, centuries later, he was even canonised. Leonor Plantagenet had decisively promoted in her kingdom the cult of a saint who laid down his life defending ecclesiastical independence and authority. Perhaps the means justified the ends or simply the queen had not learnt the lessons taught by fate to monarchs like her father.

47 Robert of Torigni, *Chronique*, ii, 116.

8.

Crown Versus Church After Becket: King John, St Thomas and the Interdict[1]

PAUL WEBSTER

When John, the youngest son of Henry II and Eleanor of Aquitaine, was born in December 1166 or 1167, Archbishop Becket was in exile. When Becket was murdered in 1170, John was still a toddler, probably resident at Fontevraud.[2] Almost certainly, he never met St Thomas, but as the martyr's legacy unfolded, John was growing up: part of the generation that experienced the exponential growth of the Becket cult. John's reign as king (1199–1216) witnessed renewed conflict between king and Church over claims to the exercise of authority. Like the Becket crisis, this dispute involved its protagonists in diplomatic conflict on a European stage, and would be remembered as one of the most significant clashes between king and Church in English medieval history. However, unlike the Becket dispute and the period following the martyrdom, John's obstinacy resulted in a prolonged period (1208–14) in which the kingdom of England was subject to a general interdict and in which the king was personally excommunicate (1209–13). This article will examine the extent to which the legacy of St Thomas Becket, and the memory of the Becket crisis, loomed over royal relations with the Church, in particular with the papacy, during the dispute of King John's reign.

When John was a boy, Henry II was facing the consequences of the martyrdom. From 1174 until the end of his reign in 1189 he made regular

1 My thanks are due to various scholars for help that has contributed to the writing of this article: Helen Nicholson for reading a draft version; Nicholas Vincent for sending a copy of his unpublished paper on Master Simon Langton; Sophie Ambler for supplying me with a copy of David D'Avray's article on Stephen Langton; Katherine Harvey for discussion of the dating of the Burton Annals; and Lauren Davies for drawing my attention to relevant material in the work of Orderic Vitalis.
2 On John's date of birth and early upbringing at Fontevraud, see A. W. Lewis, 'The Birth and Childhood of King John: Some Revisions', in *Eleanor of Aquitaine: Lord and Lady*, ed. B. Wheeler and J. C. Parsons (New York and Basingstoke, 2002), 159–75, at 166–8. Lewis's re-dating of John's birth to 1166 is now questioned by David Crouch, based on the evidence of Gerald of Wales: D. Crouch, *William Marshal*, 3rd edn (London and New York, 2016), 88 nn. 5–6.

pilgrimages to Canterbury.[3] After the capture of the Scottish king, William the Lion, at Alnwick, following the first of these pilgrimages, Henry was able to assert the idea that St Thomas supported the crown.[4] This was a legacy inherited and continued by Richard I. On his two brief visits to England, the Lionheart included Canterbury on his itinerary.[5] Gervase of Canterbury claimed that when Richard returned from captivity in 1194, he prioritised going to Canterbury over any other church in England.[6] John, who had been present at the time of Richard's visit of 1189, continued the example set by his father and brother.[7] Prior to the death of Archbishop Hubert Walter in 1205, John made regular visits to the martyr's shrine at Canterbury at moments of significance in the regnal or religious calendar, combining this devotion with pilgrimage to the shrines of royal saints, notably St Edmund the Martyr and St Edward the Confessor.[8]

John also provided support for religious houses established by Henry II as part of the revised version of the penance agreed at Avranches in 1172.[9] In terms of the houses traditionally assumed to have been founded or re-founded by Henry as a result of this agreement, John provided support for the Augustinian canons of Waltham Holy Cross. His grants were diverse, including the gift of a tin or pewter laver or ewer (*stagneum lavatorium*), previously given to Westminster by Henry II but then removed, forest rights and confirmation of the manor of Waltham.[10] John's itinerary also records several visits to Waltham between 1204 and 1214.[11] He was remembered at the abbey as a donor of relics.[12]

---

3 Duggan, 'Diplomacy', 278–84; T. K. Keefe, 'Shrine Time: King Henry II's Visits to Thomas Becket's Tomb', *Haskins Society Journal*, 11 (2003), 115–22.
4 Keefe, 'Shrine Time', 117–18.
5 L. Landon, *The Itinerary of King Richard I with Studies on Certain Matters of Interest Connected with his Reign*, PRS 51, ns 13 (London, 1955), 17–21, 85.
6 Gervase, i, 524.
7 For John's presence at Canterbury in 1189, see Landon, *Itinerary*, 19, 21.
8 P. Webster, 'Crown, Cathedral and Conflict: King John and Canterbury', in *Cathedrals, Communities and Conflict in the Anglo-Norman World*, ed. P. Dalton, C. Insley and L. J. Wilkinson (Woodbridge, 2011), 203–19, at 204–9.
9 On Henry's penance and resultant monastic benefaction, see Duggan, 'Diplomacy', 285–7; E. M. Hallam, 'Henry II as a Founder of Monasteries', *JEH*, 28 (1977), 113–32, at 113–14, 117–18; and the essays in this volume by Anne J. Duggan (chapter 2) and Elma Brenner (chapter 4).
10 *Rotuli Litterarum Clausarum In Turri Londinensi asservati, Vol. 1, 1204–1224*, ed. T. D. Hardy, Record Commission (London, 1833), 140b, 158a; *Rotuli Chartarum in Turri Londinensi asservati, Vol. 1, pt. 1, 1199–1216*, ed. T. D. Hardy, Record Commission (London, 1837), 65b–66a; *The Early Charters of the Augustinian Canons of Waltham Abbey, Essex 1062–1230*, ed. R. Ransford (Woodbridge, 1989), 27 (no. 38), 127 (no. 201), 197–8 (nos. 294–5), and for grants by John's father and brothers to Waltham, 14–27 (nos. 26–36).
11 John is recorded at Waltham in October 1204, August 1205, October 1207, October 1208, December 1213 and January 1214: T. D. Hardy, 'Itinerary of King John, &c.', in *Rotuli Litterarum Patentium in Turri Londinensi asservati. Vol. 1, Pt. 1, 1199–1216*, ed. T. D. Hardy, Record Commission (London, 1835), unpaginated.
12 *Early Charters of the Augustinian Canons of Waltham*, 435 (no. 637).

Meanwhile, at Amesbury, a Benedictine nunnery re-founded by Henry II as a Fontevraudine community in 1177, John again honoured his father's gifts. This can be seen in the evidence of the Pipe Rolls, and through royal confirmation charters, issued for John's salvation, that of his father, mother, ancestors and successors, and 'for the honour of religion' ('pro … religionis honestate').[13]

Further evidence suggests that John supported a range of houses where Henry II's largesse may well be explained by post-martyrdom repentance. These included Gilbertine Newstead (Lincolnshire), established by Henry by 1173, and probably in 1171. Here, the dedication of the house to the Holy Trinity (the only Gilbertine house to be so) suggests a link with the memory of Thomas Becket. The feast had been promoted by the archbishop, who had ordered its celebration as his first act as a consecrated bishop.[14] John continued the association, augmenting his father's grants to Newstead with land in Howsham (Lincolnshire), in a grant issued for the king's salvation, and that of his ancestors and heirs, in pure and perpetual alms.[15] Beyond England, John followed his father's example in taking the leper hospital of Mont-aux-Malades, Rouen, under his protection. Henry II had undertaken construction of a new church there, dedicated to St Thomas, in a re-foundation dating to c.1174.[16] The king also issued grants to Carthusian Le Liget in the Touraine, supported by his father in the second half of his reign, and favoured the Augustinian foundation of St Thomas the Martyr outside Dublin, established by Henry II in 1177, perhaps in fulfilment of a promise made during his famous Canterbury pilgrimage in 1174.[17]

---

13   On the re-foundation, see S. K. Elkins, *Holy Women of Twelfth-Century England* (Chapel Hill, NC, and London, 1988), 146–7; B. M. Kerr, *Religious Life for Women c. 1100–c. 1350: Fontevraud in England* (Oxford, 1999), 70–73, 78–9. For John's grants, see *Rotuli Chartarum*, 13b–14b. For an example of the Pipe Roll payments recorded in each regnal year (barring the fifteenth and eighteenth years of John's reign, for which rolls do not survive), see *The Great Roll of the Pipe for the First Year of the Reign of King John, Michaelmas 1199 (Pipe Roll 45)*, ed. D. M. Stenton, PRS 48, ns 10 (London, 1933), 1.

14   B. Golding, *Gilbert of Sempringham and the Gilbertine Order, c. 1130–c. 1300* (Oxford, 1995), 223–4; H. Mayr-Harting, *Religion, Politics and Society in Britain 1066–1272* (Harlow, 2011), 93.

15   *Rotuli Chartarum*, 84b.

16   *Rotuli Chartarum*, 76a; L. Grant (trans. B. Duchet-Filhol), 'Le patronage architectural de Henri II et de son entourage', CCM, 37, no. 145–6 (1994), 73–84, at 76. Royal patronage of this leper house is also considered in: E. Brenner, 'Charity in Rouen in the Twelfth and Thirteenth Centuries (with special reference to Mont-aux-Malades)' (unpublished Ph.D. thesis, University of Cambridge, 2008); E. Brenner, *Leprosy and Charity in Medieval Rouen* (Woodbridge, 2015).

17   For John's grants, see *Rotuli Chartarum*, 63a; *Rotuli Normanniae in Turri Londinensi asservati: Johanne et Henrico Quinto, Angliae Regibus. Vol. I. 1200–1205, necnon de anno 1417*, ed. T. D. Hardy, Record Commission (London, 1835), 77; *Chartae, Privilegia et Immunitates, Being Transcripts of Charters and Privileges to Cities, Towns, Abbeys, and Other Bodies Corporate: 18 Henry II to 18 Richard II (1171 to 1395)*, Irish Record Commission (Dublin, 1829–30), 4–6, 8–9, available online at the website of *Circle: A Calendar of Irish Chancery Letters, c. 1244–1509* [http://chancery.tcd.ie/images/cpi/0?page=1, accessed 28 June 2012]; *Register of the Abbey of St Thomas, Dublin*, ed. J. T. Gilbert, RS 94 (London, 1889), 6–7; *Rotuli de Liberate ac de Misis et*

Meanwhile, there was considerable continuity in the Angevin attitude towards episcopal and archiepiscopal appointments. The Constitutions of Clarendon (1164), to which Becket had objected so vehemently, set out the way in which bishops and abbots were to be elected in the king's chapel, with his approval, on the advice of those churchmen the king felt it appropriate to summon. Little changed in the decades following Becket's martyrdom. Although the Third Lateran Council (1179) forbade the involvement of clergy in secular affairs, the kings of England took no notice.[18] Richard I 'had little respect for the church's freedom and worked to preserve his royal predecessors' authority over it', taking especial care in supervising elections, and proving even better able than Henry II or John at promoting men of the court to the episcopate.[19] Jörg Peltzer has argued that in the later years of Richard's reign, and in the early phase of John's, the evidence of elections to the Norman dioceses shows that the Angevins were gradually fighting against the tide of Church attitudes to lay (and in particular royal) influence over elections.[20] Yet none of these three kings experienced great difficulty in the post-Becket era in appointing bishops with a background in royal service prepared to fulfil a dual secular and ecclesiastical function, in the way Becket had conspicuously refused to do. William de Longchamp, Hubert Walter and Peter des Roches are just some of the most conspicuous examples.[21] Indeed, the executors of the interdict of John's reign, William de Ste-Mère-Eglise, bishop of London, Eustace, bishop of Ely, and Mauger, bishop of Worcester, were classic examples of bishops nominated for the role by the king.[22]

John was not prepared to let the Church stand in the way of what he perceived to be royal rights. In the case of Canterbury, he probably had

---

Praestitis regnante Johanne, ed. T. D. Hardy, Record Commission (London, 1844), 71. On Henry, see Hallam, 'Henry II as a Founder of Monasteries', 117, 118–20; Duggan, 'Diplomacy', 287.

18 C. R. Cheney, *Pope Innocent III and England* (Stuttgart, 1976), 124; Mayr-Harting, *Religion*, 185.

19 R. V. Turner, 'Richard Lionheart and English Episcopal Elections', *Albion: A Quarterly Journal Concerned with British Studies*, 29 (1997), 1–13, at 1, 11. See also D. Walker, 'Crown and Episcopacy under the Normans and Angevins', *Anglo-Norman Studies*, 5 (1983), 220–33, at 220–21, 223–4, 227–31; N. Vincent, 'Beyond Becket: King Henry II and the Papacy (1154–1189)', in *Pope Alexander III (1150–81): The Art of Survival*, ed. P. D. Clarke and A. J. Duggan (Farnham, 2012), 257–99, at 292–3. On Richard's enraged response when the monks of Durham attempted an unauthorised election in 1195, see Cheney, *Pope Innocent III*, 126–7.

20 J. Peltzer, *Canon Law, Careers and Conquest: Episcopal Elections in Normandy and Greater Anjou, c. 1140–c. 1230* (Cambridge, 2008), 167–8, with trends in canon law explored at 31–6.

21 On William, see R. V. Turner, 'Longchamp, William de (d. 1197)', *ODNB* (Oxford, 2004; online edn, 2007) [http://www.oxforddnb.com/view/article/16980, accessed 12 June 2012]. On Hubert, see Mayr-Harting, *Religion*, 186–93; C. R. Cheney, *Hubert Walter* (London, 1967). On Peter, see N. Vincent, *Peter des Roches: An Alien in English Politics, 1205–1238* (Cambridge, 1996).

22 Turner, 'Richard Lionheart and English Episcopal Elections', 9–10. On William, see also R. V. Turner, *Men Raised from the Dust: Administrative Service and Upward Mobility in Angevin England* (Philadelphia, PA, 1988), 27. On Eustace and Mauger, see Cheney, *Pope Innocent III*, 28, 142.

experience of Richard I's efforts to compel the cathedral monks to reach a settlement of their long-running dispute over Archbishop Baldwin's proposed collegiate foundation at Hackington (just outside Canterbury), revived by Archbishop Hubert Walter as a proposed college at Lambeth. John was present at Canterbury in late November and early December 1189, when Richard intervened in the dispute.[23] During the quarrel, a steady procession of deputations from the archbishop, and from the prior and monks of Canterbury, travelled to Rome to seek papal judgement. Here, the memory of Thomas Becket was kept alive as the monks drew on supposed visions of the saint as their supporter against the archbishop, with the saint seen as defender of the monastic community rather than the see.[24]

As king, John proved determined to protect his rights in relation to episcopal appointments.[25] He was quick to visit sees which fell vacant or, if he was not present, to ensure that elections took place in the presence of his officials. In 1200, he stated that he expected his wishes to be respected and that it was his right to approve the election of a new bishop of Lisieux.[26] Elsewhere, John tried unsuccessfully to block elections made by cathedral chapters: as in the cases of Sylvester, bishop of Sées, in 1202–1203 (provoking a stern rebuke and threat of interdict on Normandy from Pope Innocent III), and of Archbishop Eugenius of Armagh in 1206.[27] The early years of the reign were marked by ongoing dispute over the election to the bishopric of St David's. Perhaps most notably, the king secured his favoured candidate, Peter des Roches, for the bishopric of Winchester in 1205, despite the election being disputed and subject to adjudication at the papal curia.[28] In elections held during the general interdict, the king made a concerted effort to secure the candidates he wanted, resulting in an unsuccessful attempt to elect the chancellor, Walter de Gray, to Coventry and Lichfield. This did not always work out as John intended. For instance,

---

23 Landon, *Itinerary*, 19, 21. The dispute is summarised in Cheney, *Pope Innocent III*, 209–20.

24 For recent discussion of the dispute, see J. Sayers, 'Peter's Throne and Augustine's Chair: Rome and Canterbury from Baldwin (1184–90) to Robert Winchelsey (1297–1313)', *JEH*, 51 (2000), 249–66, at 252–6, and see also 259–61; M.-P. Gelin, 'Gervase of Canterbury, Christ Church and the Archbishops', *JEH*, 60 (2009), 449–63; S. Sweetinburgh, 'Caught in the Cross-Fire: Patronage and Institutional Politics in Late Twelfth-Century Canterbury', in *Cathedrals, Communities and Conflict in the Anglo-Norman World*, ed. P. Dalton, C. Insley and L. J. Wilkinson (Woodbridge, 2011), 187–202. For aspects of the dispute after John's reign, see C. R. Cheney, 'Magna carta beati Thome: Another Canterbury Forgery', in *Medieval Texts and Studies*, by C. R. Cheney (Oxford, 1973), 78–110. See also the discussion in Michael Staunton's essay in this volume (chapter 5).

25 For this paragraph, unless otherwise stated see Cheney, *Pope Innocent III*, 125–31, 135–41, 145–7, 153–4, 158, and see also 281–2 for the view that John took a similar line as lord of Ireland, again attracting the attention of Pope Innocent III.

26 *Rotuli Chartarum*, 99a; Peltzer, *Canon Law, Careers and Conquest*, 213.

27 For Sées, in addition to Cheney's discussion, see also Peltzer, *Canon Law, Careers and Conquest*, 124–32.

28 In addition to Cheney's discussion, see also Vincent, *Peter des Roches*, 47–55.

Hugh of Wells, elected bishop of Lincoln in 1209, effectively defected, seeking consecration at the hands of Archbishop Langton in exile.

The Canterbury dispute could have provided the king with a lesson that he could not always secure his own way in episcopal elections. However, John's desire to secure the appointment of his own candidates was apparently undimmed, even after the resolution of the interdict. Although he was not able to secure promotion for Peter des Roches from Winchester to the archbish-opric of York, nor was Archbishop Langton's brother Simon able to obtain the see.[29] Elsewhere, curialist bishops were appointed, Archbishop Langton became politically isolated and went into exile, and the bishops supported the crown in the final months of the reign.[30] Even after issuing his charter confirming free elections in 1214, re-issued in January 1215 and summarised in Magna Carta in June 1215, the king and his successors retained influence.[31] Furthermore, in a number of instances throughout the reign, John's bishops served the king in his secular affairs without incurring papal displeasure. Hubert Walter was chancellor from 1199 almost until his death in 1205, whilst John de Gray, bishop of Norwich, and Peter des Roches, bishop of Winchester, served as justiciar in Ireland and England respectively.[32] Four out of the nine bishops named in Magna Carta had assisted John without interruption during the interdict and the period of the king's excommunication.[33]

29 On des Roches, see Vincent, *Peter des Roches*, 95–8; Cheney, *Pope Innocent III*, 77. On Simon Langton, see Cheney, *Pope Innocent III*, 162–5; F. A. Cazel Jr, 'Langton, Simon (d. 1248)', *ODNB* (Oxford, 2004) [http://www.oxforddnb.com/view/article/16043, accessed 26 June 2012]. The impact of Simon's failure to become archbishop on his later career is also discussed in N. Vincent, 'Master Simon Langton, King John and the Court of France', an unpublished article supplied to me by Professor Vincent.

30 Curialist bishops elected in this period included Henry of London (elected archbishop of Dublin in 1212 or 1213 after failing to secure confirmation as bishop of Exeter), William of Cornhill (elected to Coventry and Lichfield in 1214, following a second unsuccessful attempt to secure the bishopric for Walter de Gray), Walter de Gray (elected first to Worcester in 1214, then to York in 1215), Richard Marsh (put forward for the sees of Winchester and Ely, but then elected at Durham in 1215): Cheney, *Pope Innocent III*, 131–3, 162–7. On the contrast between Langton and his episcopal colleagues in the last months of the reign, see Vincent, 'Langton', 99.

31 Cheney, *Pope Innocent III*, 168–70. For the 1214 charter, see *Select Charters and Other Illustrations of English Constitutional History*, ed. W. Stubbs, 9th edn, rev. by H. W. C. Davis (Oxford, 1921), 282–4, available online on the website of the Early English Laws project [http://www.earlyenglishlaws.ac.uk/laws/manuscripts/stubbs/?tp=ob&nb=lib-elec, accessed 3 February 2015]. For its inclusion in Magna Carta, see J. C. Holt, *Magna Carta*, 2nd edn (Cambridge, 1992), 448–51. See also K. Harvey, *Episcopal Appointments in England, c. 1214–1344: From Episcopal Election to Papal Provision* (Farnham, 2014), 19–26.

32 Cheney, *Pope Innocent III*, 19–20. Innocent had, however, requested Hubert's dismissal as justiciar during Richard's reign, prompting the archbishop's resignation from the role.

33 Cheney, *Pope Innocent III*, 378. These were Archbishop Henry of Dublin, Peter des Roches, bishop of Winchester, Walter de Gray, bishop of Worcester, and William of Cornhill, bishop of Coventry and Lichfield, all named in the preamble to the charter: Holt, *Magna Carta*, 448–9.

However, the Angevin association with the murder of an archbishop in his own cathedral created a problem for any king wishing to assert his authority over the Church: a 'ghost of Christmas past' which could not be ignored. It seems likely that this explains why Henry II failed to inspire the writing of panegyric biography, after the manner of that compiled for the Anglo-Norman rulers or the Capetian kings of France.[34] It may also explain why Hugh of Lincoln was able to stand up to the Angevins with what his biographer portrays as impunity.[35] Even John's half-brother, Geoffrey, bishop-elect of Lincoln and royal chancellor under Henry II, and archbishop of York from 1189–1212, could invoke the memory of the murdered archbishop of Canterbury when dragged from sanctuary on his attempted return to England from the Continent in 1191. On his release, Geoffrey made sure to visit Becket's tomb at Canterbury on his way to London.[36]

In this context, we can now turn to the major dispute between king and Church in the reign of King John. To summarise the main events: Hubert Walter, King Richard I's choice as archbishop of Canterbury in 1193, who served as justiciar (1193–98) under the Lionheart and Chancellor (1199–1205) under John, died in July 1205.[37] The election of Hubert's archiepiscopal successor was beset by attempted deception by the monks of Canterbury Cathedral and by 'bully-boy' tactics employed by King John. The monks sought to elect their sub-prior, Reginald, hoping to avoid a candidate imposed by the king, but conducted their election in secret. This was unknown to John for several months. In turn, he sought to promote the bishop of Norwich, John de Gray. Following appeals and counter-appeals at the papal curia, Innocent III annulled both elections and summoned the Canterbury monks to choose their archbishop in his presence. The result was the choice of the English cardinal and Master of the Paris schools, Stephen Langton. The pope consecrated the new archbishop at Viterbo in June 1207. However, King John believed that the traditional royal right of involvement and, in particular, of giving consent

---

34 N. Vincent, 'The Strange Case of the Missing Biographies: The Lives of the Plantagenet Kings of England 1154–1272', in *Writing Medieval Biography, 750–1250: Essays in Honour of Professor Frank Barlow*, ed. D. Bates, J. Crick and S. Hamilton (Woodbridge, 2006), 237–57.

35 On religion and politics in the career of Hugh of Lincoln, see Mayr-Harting, *Religion*, 193–200, 203–4. For the medieval biography of Hugh, see *Magna Vita Sancti Hugonis: The Life of St Hugh of Lincoln*, ed. D. L. Douie and H. Farmer, NMT, 2 vols (London, 1961–62).

36 For the visit to Canterbury, see M. Lovatt, 'Geoffrey (1151?–1212)', *ODNB* (Oxford, 2004; online edn, 2007) [http://www.oxforddnb.com/view/article/10535, accessed 29 June 2012]. For Geoffrey invoking the memory of the saint, see Michael Staunton's essay in this volume (chapter 5), noting that where Gerald of Wales evoked parallels of Becket, Richard of Devizes' account probably sought to provide a satire on this 'new martyr'.

37 For this paragraph, see the following unless otherwise stated. On the Canterbury election: M. D. Knowles, 'The Canterbury Election of 1205–6', *EHR*, 53 (1938), 211–20; Cheney, *Pope Innocent III*, 147–54. On the king's belief that he had been deceived, and its influence on his behaviour: Webster, 'Crown, Cathedral and Conflict', 211–16.

to an election, had been disregarded. He therefore refused to allow Archbishop Langton to enter England, allegedly threatening that he would be hanged if he attempted to do so.[38] In addition, he drove the Canterbury monks into exile, believing them to have deceived him, to the extent of committing treason. As a result of the king's ongoing intransigence, Pope Innocent III threatened, and then imposed, sentences of interdict on England (which lasted from 1208 to 1214) and personal excommunication on the king (which lasted from 1209 to 1213).

To what extent was the memory of St Thomas and the Becket dispute deployed during the Canterbury crisis of John's reign?[39] Here, there are two important elements of long-term context. A clear image of Becket had developed: as a defender of, and martyr for, the freedoms of the Church. This was prevalent by the early thirteenth century and was essentially a posthumous creation. In part this was the work of Becket's biographers.[40] It was also heavily influenced by the schoolmen of Paris, through their biblical commentaries and glosses, focused on the interrelationship of Church, king and people, coupled with a tradition dating to the Gregorian reformers and longer-term conflict between anointed rulers and the Church. The result was that kingship could be seen both positively and negatively, but in this period the behaviour of earthly monarchs was often portrayed not only unfavourably, but as an evil which it fell to the Church to combat.[41] This was the case not least because, according to the highly influential theologian Peter the Chanter, a king's subjects were tainted with their ruler's sins, since it fell to the subjects to prevent those sins, if and when they were able.[42] 'Much of that power, in turn, rested with a ruler's clerical subjects.'[43] In this context, the impact of being

38   *Annales de Burton (A.D. 1004–1263)* in *Annales Monastici*, ed. H. R. Luard, RS 36, 5 vols (London, 1864–69), i, 209–11.
39   On factors that distinguish the two disputes, see Vincent, 'Langton', 80–81.
40   On whom see M. Staunton, *Thomas Becket and his Biographers* (Woodbridge, 2006).
41   On the schoolmen, see B. Smalley, *The Becket Conflict and the Schools: A Study of Intellectuals in Politics* (Oxford, 1973); J. W. Baldwin, *Masters, Princes and Merchants: The Social Views of Peter the Chanter and his Circle*, 2 vols (Princeton, NJ, 1970); P. Buc, '*Principes Gentium Dominantur Eorum*: Princely Power Between Legitimacy and Illegitimacy in Twelfth-Century Exegesis', in *Cultures of Power: Lordship, Status and Process in Twelfth-Century Europe*, ed. T. N. Bisson (Philadelphia, PA, 1995) 310–28. The latter summarises fuller discussion in: P. Buc, *L'ambiguïté du livre: Prince, pouvoir et peuple dans les commentaires de la bible au moyen âge* (Paris, 1995). See also P. Buc, 'Pouvoir royal et commentaires de la bible (1150–1350)', *Annales: Économies, Sociétés, Civilisations*, 44 (1989), 691–713. Here, Buc notes a gradual trend to write favourably of kings and kingship, emerging in tentative form in the twelfth century, but much more pronounced by the fourteenth.
42   P. D. Clarke, *The Interdict in the Thirteenth Century: A Question of Collective Guilt* (Oxford, 2007), 39–40.
43   B. Weiler, 'Bishops and Kings in England c. 1066–c. 1215', in *Religion and Politics in the Middle Ages: Germany and England by Comparison*, ed. L. Körntgen and D. Wassenhoven (Berlin and Boston, MA, 2013), 87–134, at 129–30.

perceived to have ordered the murder of an archbishop in his own cathedral was magnified. As a result, the language deployed in the disputed election of John's reign reflects a legacy of thought about kings and their relationship with the Church influenced by interpretation of Becket and his fate. Men at the forefront of the two crises – John of Salisbury and Stephen Langton – led the way in developing the view that the kingship of their own time was flawed in the manner of that of the biblical tyrants.[44] Although there were contexts (such as sermons) where Langton accepted monarchy, he nonetheless used his biblical exegesis to argue that God was angered by the Israelites' request to have a king, with the prophet Samuel warning of the potential for tyranny that would ensue.[45]

A comparison may be drawn between the attitude of Henry II and John towards the threat of interdict and excommunication. In the late 1160s, the prospect of sanctions was enough to bring Henry II to the negotiating table. The peace of Fréteval (July 1170) arose out of threatened interdict of Henry's lands.[46] Becket observed afterwards that Henry II immediately made peace when he learned that it was proposed to interdict his lands, to excommunicate the bishops who opposed Archbishop Thomas, and perhaps even to sentence the king himself – much as Pope Alexander had acted against the Emperor Frederick I a decade earlier.[47] After the murder, in the early 1170s, Henry II's continental lands were placed under a general interdict and the pope forbade him from entering churches. This was the prelude to the agreement of penance in the Compromise of Avranches in 1172.[48] Like his father, John was keen to

---

44 See Vincent, 'Langton', 74–5, and the references collected there.

45 D. L. D'Avray, '"Magna Carta": Its Background in Stephen Langton's Academic Biblical Exegesis and its Episcopal Reception', *Studi Medievali*, 38 (1997), 423–38, at 426–7, 429.

46 Duggan, *Thomas Becket*, 183–6. For Henry II's letter announcing his climb down, see *CTB*, ii, 1258–61 (no. 299).

47 *CTB*, ii, 1260–79 (no. 300 at 1260–61), 1279–81 (no. 301 at 1280–81). See also *CTB*, ii, 1054–67 (no. 244 at 1062–3), written in 1169, when Becket told his clerks to impress upon the pope the need to 'frighten the king by fear of an interdict'; and *CTB*, ii, 1314–17 (no. 315), dated October 1170, where Pope Alexander III expressly excluded the king from those on whom Becket could impose sanctions. The excommunication of Frederick I in 1160 was not conspicuously successful. It was repeated in 1162, effectively repeated in 1163, and enhanced with a sentence of deposition in 1167. The schism did not end until 1177. T. Reuter, 'John of Salisbury and the Germans', in *The World of John of Salisbury*, ed. M. Wilks, SCH, Subsidia 3 (Oxford, 1984), 415–25 at 417–18; J. Johrendt, 'The Empire and the Schism', in *Pope Alexander III (1159–81): The Art of Survival*, ed. P. D. Clarke and A. J. Duggan (Farnham, 2012), 99–126 at 112–13. Becket was soon of the opinion Henry had gone back on his word once the threat had passed: *CTB*, ii, 1320–29 (no. 318, at 1320–21).

48 Duggan, 'Diplomacy', 265, 271–8. See also A. J. Duggan, '*Ne in dubium*: The Official Record of Henry II's Reconciliation at Avranches, 21 May 1172', *EHR*, 115 (2000), 643–58, repr. with the same pagination in Duggan, *Friends, Networks*, no. VIII. For a parallel with the events of 1105, when Henry I was on the point of being excommunicated by Archbishop Anselm of Canterbury for his failure to restore archiepiscopal lands and revenues, see J. R. Maddicott, 'The

avoid ecclesiastical sanctions, with diplomatic avenues kept open as long as possible. As late as August 1209, when the threat of the king being excommunicated was clear, the bishop-executors of Innocent III's sentences (William of London, Eustace of Ely and Mauger of Worcester) negotiated with the king in the hope of brokering a settlement. Stephen Langton himself travelled to Dover from the Continent in October 1209, in response to royal letters probably inspired by the impending excommunication.[49] The anonymous *Deeds of Pope Innocent III* closed at this point, in the opinion that the dispute had been resolved.[50]

However, there was a mutual intransigence that might not have been unfamiliar to those charged with persuading Henry II and Becket to make peace. John wanted agreement on his terms or not at all. This may reflect the extent to which times had changed since the pontificate of Alexander III. Innocent III's papacy has been described as 'the golden age of the interdict ... not indeed because it then proved most effective but because it was most frequently employed'.[51] In this period, kings were apparently used to sentences of interdict or excommunication being threatened and imposed, with examples ranging from the Iberian kingdoms, to countries at the edge of Europe such as Norway and Armenia, or to realms at the heart of western European politics such as the Empire, France and England.[52] It was a trend that was set to continue across the thirteenth century, especially in the handling of papal territorial interests in Italy.[53] However, highlighting the fact that such sentences were used more often than they worked is to overlook the fact that Innocent III's papacy was in a position to use them at all. Alexander III's struggle to assert his legitimacy as pope meant that he needed all the support he could get from European monarchs, a fact he was well aware of, as the evidence for his gratitude for Henry II's backing bears witness.[54]

In response to papal sanctions, if John was prepared to ride out a sentence of interdict, he seemed much more concerned with the threat of excommunication. His response was not entirely dissimilar to that of Henry II in 1169. Henry had ordered that everyone over the age of fifteen should swear an oath

Oath of Marlborough, 1209: Fear, Government and Popular Allegiance in the Reign of King John', *EHR*, 126 (2011), 281–318, at 291–2. Henry, however, gave in, unlike John.

49   Maddicott, 'Oath of Marlborough', 286–7.

50   *The Deeds of Pope Innocent III, by an Anonymous Author*, trans. J. M. Powell (Washington D.C., 2004), xliv–xlv, 240–41.

51   H. G. Richardson and G. O. Sayles, *The Governance of Medieval England from the Conquest to Magna Carta* (Edinburgh, 1963), 344–5, citing the remarks of L. Godefroy.

52   J. Sayers, *Innocent III: Leader of Europe* (London and New York, 1994), 79–80, 82, 84, 116; J. C. Moore, *Pope Innocent III (1160/61–1216): To Root Up and to Plant* (Leiden and Boston, MA, 2003), 70–73, 195–7, 201.

53   Clarke, *The Interdict*, 117–18.

54   Vincent, 'Beyond Becket', 271.

not to obey sentences of interdict or excommunication issued by the pope or archbishop (on pain of exile and forfeiture of possessions). Further instructions sought to prevent letters of interdict entering the country. Ironically, this was entirely counter-productive, provoking Alexander III to authorise the very sanctions Henry had sought to avoid.[55] In 1209, John ordered assemblies to be held across the land, in which 'all the men of England' performed oaths. However, these went much further than those demanded by his father (or indeed any of his predecessors), requiring freemen to swear fealty and perform homage to the king and his infant son Henry.[56] In neither case did this create lasting loyalty. Henry II found himself facing the most serious and sustained rebellion of his reign in 1173–74, leading to demands for further oaths of fealty as part of the Assize of Northampton in 1176.[57] John was faced with the uprising that led to Magna Carta and civil war. His death meant that he could not emulate his father by demanding oaths of fealty within a few years of the restoration of peace. However, such oaths were required by the minority government of Henry III, in 1218–19.[58]

During the exchanges between John and Innocent III or his representatives, the ghost of St Thomas reared its head on a number of occasions, for instance in a papal letter of 1206 to the prior and monks of Canterbury, recounting the course of Langton's election.[59] In writing to John in May 1207, Innocent impressed upon the king that 'to fight against God and the Church in this cause for which St Thomas, that glorious martyr and archbishop, recently shed his blood, would be dangerous for you'.[60] This sentiment seems to reflect a mood current in papal circles. The *Deeds of Pope Innocent* observed that St Thomas had been martyred for no purpose, because the Angevin kings, 'by the insolence of princes', kept the English Church 'in the handmaidenship of servitude'.[61] In addition, Becket was remembered in a papal letter to Langton and various English bishops, issued in 1213 as the dispute neared resolution.

55 Maddicott, 'Oath of Marlborough', 295; A. J. Duggan, 'Henry II, the English Church and the Papacy, 1154–76', in *Henry II: New Interpretations*, ed. C. Harper-Bill and N. Vincent (Woodbridge, 2007), 154–83 at 174–5; M. D. Knowles, A. J. Duggan and C. N. L. Brooke, 'Henry II's Supplement to the Constitutions of Clarendon', *EHR*, 87 (1972), 757–71; Clarke, *The Interdict*, 175–6.
56 Maddicott, 'Oath of Marlborough', 281 (quoting Gervase of Canterbury), and see also 299–307.
57 On the Great Rebellion, see W. L. Warren, *Henry II* (London, 1973), 116–43. For the oaths of 1176, see Maddicott, 'Oath of Marlborough', 295–6. Maddicott notes that similar measures were taken after Richard I's capture travelling home from the Third Crusade, again in the wake of a crime wave in 1195, and by John in 1205 when faced with the threat of French invasion.
58 Maddicott, 'Oath of Marlborough', 313.
59 Gervase, ii, lxviii–lxxii; Vincent, 'Langton', 68.
60 *Selected Letters of Pope Innocent III Concerning England (1198–1216)*, ed. and trans. C. R. Cheney and W. H. Semple, NMT (London, 1953), 89 (no. 29).
61 *Deeds of Pope Innocent*, 238; Cheney, *Pope Innocent III*, 16–17.

Here, John's opposition was seen as a characteristic inherited from Henry II: 'sometimes the perversity of the wicked passes down by succession of blood from father to son'. A direct comparison was drawn between the fate of St Thomas and John's persecution of the English bishops and the Canterbury monks.[62]

Intriguingly, King John may have invoked the memory of St Thomas in building his case before papal representatives. The annals of Burton, written during the reign of Henry III, provide a detailed account of the interdict dispute.[63] The annals describe an encounter between King John and the papal envoys Pandulf and Durand, at the royal court at Northampton in 1211. John observed that, even in the case of Becket, the archbishopric of Canterbury had been conferred by the king. In seeking to deprive him of this role when choosing the successor to Hubert Walter, John argued, Innocent III sought to deprive him of rights traditionally exercised by his predecessors.[64] Such an argument was consistent with the king's outlook on the dispute as a whole. He is said also to have cited the example of St Wulfstan of Worcester, collated to his see by Edward the Confessor, but whom William the Conqueror had allegedly attempted to depose. Wulfstan responded by plunging his staff into the tomb of the Confessor and, miraculously, proved to be the only person capable of removing it. Thus he was allowed to retain his see.[65] The story was invented in the 1130s, but had found acceptance. For John, it resonated with his view of the extent of royal authority over episcopal appointments.

However, such a viewpoint was unlikely to find favour with the papal envoys, who are said to have denounced John's interpretation in no uncertain terms. Pandulf argued that the king was wrong. St Edward had been the protector of the Church; John was its destroyer. Thus, the latter's refusal to accept Langton's appointment to Canterbury was akin to William the Conqueror's refusal to accept Wulfstan's status. Likewise, although Henry II had engineered the election of Becket, the latter had resigned his see to Pope Alexander III. Following the martyrdom, Pandulf added, Henry had conceded to the monks of Canterbury, for the remission of all his sins, that forevermore the archbishop should be elected according to the will of God, without input from the bishops, and with the assent of the king, earls and barons in attendance.[66] If so, it was

---

62 *Selected Letters of Pope Innocent III*, 142 (no. 49).
63 A. Gransden, *Historical Writing in England, c. 500 to c. 1307* (Ithaca, NY, New York and London, 1974), 408–9; *Annales de Burton*, 209–23.
64 *Annales de Burton*, 211–12.
65 *Annales de Burton*, 211. For the legend, see 'La Vie de S. Edouard le Confesseur par Osbert de Clare', ed. M. Bloch, *Analecta Bollandiana*, 41 (1923), 5–131 at 116–20; P. Draper, 'King John and St Wulfstan', *Journal of Medieval History*, 10 (1984), 41–50, at 46–7; E. Mason, 'St Wulfstan's Staff: A Legend and its Uses', *Medium Aevum*, 53 (1984), 158–79, at 157–71.
66 *Annales de Burton*, 214–15.

not a commitment that Henry II's successors had felt bound to observe, but discussion on this point is not recorded.

John may also have followed in the footsteps of the murderers of St Thomas. In 1210, the king spent Easter at Knaresborough. The occasion is remembered as the first known commemoration of Maundy Thursday by an English king, in turn suggesting that John went on to mark the other holy days of the Easter festival.[67] However, this was two years into the general interdict and the first Easter since John's excommunication. The location was significant. Knaresborough was the castle to which Becket's murderers had fled from the scene of their crime in 1170. Maundy Thursday (1171) was the day on which Pope Alexander III had excommunicated Becket's killers and all who had lodged or advised them.[68] Did King John make this link, and could this have been a conscious statement of defiance of what Becket, and latterly Innocent III and Stephen Langton, were seen to stand for? The evidence is not sufficient to sustain such a conclusion, but the coincidences of timing are at least noteworthy.

In addition, it is important to question whether John's opponents sought to portray themselves as Thomas Becket's heirs. Nicholas Vincent has observed that 'a sense of identification with Becket is crucial to any understanding of Langton's archiepiscopal career'.[69] This can be seen in Stephen's Bible commentaries, in his letters after he became archbishop and in the portrayal of his exile (the period when John refused him permission to enter England). Such allusions reflected the image of Becket constructed in the minds of the schoolmen of Paris in the decades since the martyrdom.[70] Langton followed the example of his predecessor, Hubert Walter, in choosing an image of the martyrdom for his counter seal. His successors would follow suit.[71]

Stephen Langton further sought to achieve coincidences of timing between the events of his archiepiscopate and seminal dates in the career of Archbishop Thomas.[72] Langton's consecration took place on Trinity Sunday (17 June) 1207; Becket's had taken place on Trinity Sunday (3 June) 1162. Further similarities were invoked when Langton sought to travel to England. In 1209, he questioned the adequacy of royal safe-conducts, a conscious evocation of

67 A. Kellett, 'King John in Knaresborough: The First Known Royal Maundy', *Yorkshire Archaeological Journal*, 62 (1990), 69–90.

68 Vincent, 'Murderers', 251–2 and n. 172.

69 Vincent, 'Langton', 67, and for the material in this paragraph, unless otherwise stated see also 67–73 (Langton: The New Becket?) and 81–2. As this issue has been covered by Professor Vincent, only brief coverage is given here.

70 In addition to Vincent's discussion, see Smalley, *Becket Conflict*.

71 Duggan, 'Cult', 30. See also K. B. Slocum, '*Martir quod Stillat Primatis ab Ore Sigillat*: Sealed with the Blood of Becket', *Journal of the British Archaeological Association*, 165 (2012), 61–88, esp. 63–6.

72 For this paragraph, unless otherwise stated see Vincent, 'Langton', 82, 90.

the threats which had faced Thomas Becket. In 1213, Langton crossed the channel on a Tuesday, in emulation of his predecessor in December 1170, although Stephen was not on a path that would lead to martyrdom.

Meanwhile, echoes of what St Thomas had said to Henry II can be found in the arguments made by Stephen Langton. Just as Becket referred to the excommunication of Emperor Frederick I, Langton referred to Barbarossa's demise in the waters of the river Saleph (1190) as a fitting punishment for the latter's sins.[73] When peace was proposed in 1209, Langton was to swear to uphold the rights of the king, but said that he would do this 'saving the honour of the Church': very much a phrase that would have been used by his martyred predecessor, and which had caused deadlock in the 1160s.[74] It is also noteworthy that Langton, along with at least one of the executors of the interdict, Bishop Mauger of Worcester, spent part of his exile at the Cistercian abbey of Pontigny. Mauger died there in 1212. As the former refuge of Thomas Becket in France, the choice can only be seen as a conscious association with recent conflict between crown and Church.[75]

Direct invocation of St Thomas was not the only way in which the Church tried to keep King John under control. Analysis of papal letters issued during the Canterbury dispute suggests that Innocent III went to great lengths to stress his desire to avoid imposing sanctions and that he wished the king to remain (or return to being) part of the congregation of the faithful. In assessing the pope's words, there is much to be gained from considering the language he used, in particular in the lengthy preambles to his letters. Instances in which the letters make direct reference to Thomas Becket have already been discussed. In this context it is noteworthy that Innocent III, prior to becoming pope, might have been present when Alexander III canonised Becket and is thought to have made a pilgrimage to the tomb in the crypt of Canterbury Cathedral. He also made gifts in honour of the saint to the cathedral at Anagni in 1200.[76] Furthermore, there was much in Innocent III's approach to dealing with John that we can compare with the dispute of Henry II's reign.

In an attempt to persuade the king to fall into line, Innocent presented the major players in the dispute – King John, Stephen Langton, the English

---

73 Vincent, 'Langton', 69–70. For Langton's letter drawing the comparison, which, as Vincent notes, 'leaves us in no doubt as to Langton's self-identification with Becket', see *Acta Stephani Langton Cantuariensis Archiepiscopi A.D. 1207–1228*, ed. K. Major, Canterbury and York Society, 50 (Oxford, 1950), 2–7 (no. 2).

74 *English Episcopal Acta 26: London 1189–1228*, ed. D. P. Johnson (Oxford, 2003), 97 (no. 99). For a similar parallel, see Duggan, 'Cult', 37.

75 On Langton, see *Acta Stephani Langton*, 73–4 (no. 55); Vincent, 'Langton', 82; F. M. Powicke, *Stephen Langton* (Oxford, 1928), 75–6. On Mauger: *English Episcopal Acta 34: Worcester 1186–1218*, ed. M. Cheney, D. Smith, C. Brooke, and P. M. Hoskin (Oxford, 2008), xxxvii.

76 Moore, *Pope Innocent III*, 7–8; Sayers, 'Peter's Throne and Augustine's Chair', 265; Smalley, *Becket Conflict*, 139.

bishops or the English magnates – with a series of examples drawing on biblical parallels.[77] A common theme emerges: a warning to John of the dangers to which he was exposed, both during his lifetime and after his death. The openings to papal letters could be seen as formulaic expressions of the pope's claims to authority over the issue at hand: 'doctrine and logic required the pope to write as though all Christians would rush to obey or submit at once when censured. ... Christians did not always carry compliance so far, and the pope knew it.'[78] Nonetheless, at each stage of the dispute, the examples deployed in the preambles to papal letters were tailored to suit the circumstances confronting the pope.

In the period before he imposed sanctions on John and his kingdom, Innocent III emphasised to the king the consequences of going against God's will. In particular, the pope drew a parallel between John's behaviour and that of the Old Testament kings.[79] The comparison was probably familiar to the Plantagenet kings.[80] The pope argued that the fate that befell the Old Testament rulers would be similarly reserved for John. 'We invoke the testimony of Him who is a faithful witness in Heaven', wrote Innocent, alluding to a lamentation that God turned against the line of King David.[81] Elsewhere, the pope noted how David's servant, Uzza, 'was smitten by the Lord' for acting 'piously indeed but unworthily' in daring to touch the Ark of the Covenant. Innocent drew the parallel that John had reached out to take over ecclesiastical rights such as the election of an archbishop, a role he was not worthy to fulfil.[82]

Meanwhile, the English magnates were encouraged to provide John with wise guidance so that he did not 'walk in the path of Rehoboam nor forsake the counsel of the older men'. Rehoboam, the son of King Solomon, rejected the advice of his father's ministers to lighten the yoke of the Children of Israel. Instead, he favoured the young men he had grown up with, who proposed that the burden be increased. The ensuing revolt forced Rehoboam to flee

---

77 Innocent was not the only figure involved who possessed the intellectual skills to write such letters. For Stephen Langton's use of biblical metaphors in his first letter to the English bishops, in 1207, see Vincent, 'Langton', 83–7.

78 Cheney, *Pope Innocent III*, 271–2.

79 This was not the only context in which Pope Innocent used such parallels in writing to John. For instance, in 1198, he wrote to John protesting at his treatment, as lord of Ireland, of the Irish Church. Innocent recalled the fate of King Uzziah, smitten with leprosy for daring to assume priestly duties in the Temple: Cheney, *Pope Innocent III*, 281–2; cf. 2 Chronicles 26:19. All biblical references are to the Vulgate, unless otherwise stated.

80 See Vincent, 'Strange Case of the Missing Biographies', 245–7.

81 *Selected Letters of Pope Innocent III*, 91 (no. 30); Psalm 88:38–53. For discussion of King David as a model for the behaviour of medieval rulers, in particular for their penitential activity, set in the context of eleventh-century France, see S. Hamilton, 'A New Model for Royal Penance? Helgaud of Fleury's *Life of Robert the Pious*', Early Medieval Europe, 6 (1997), 189–200.

82 *Selected Letters of Pope Innocent III*, 98 (no. 32); 1 Chronicles 13:10.

Jerusalem.[83] Here, the parallel Innocent drew is striking. Rehoboam has been described as the archetype of the puerile king in the minds of the biblical exegetes – the schoolmen with whom Innocent III had been trained.[84] In addition, there is a clear implied threat to John's throne. On the other hand, contemporary writers portrayed John as favouring the company and advice of younger men in his entourage, rather than experienced figures such as William Marshal, who had served the king's father and brothers.[85] It is tempting to think that an English envoy at the curia had told the pope about this royal character trait. However, this was clearly an analogy familiar to medieval writers. Orderic Vitalis, in an implicit condemnation of William Rufus, observed that when Henry I came to the throne in 1100, he 'did not follow the advice of rash young men as Rehoboam did, but prudently took to heart the experience and advice of wise and older men'. The comparison was also made in writing on the fourteenth-century kings of England.[86]

The emphasis was sometimes more forthright. If John continued to oppose the Church he would die. Innocent reminded John of 'the judgement of the hand that wrote: "Mene, Tekel, Peres"': the writing on the wall recorded in the Book of Daniel, which pre-figured the seizure of Belshazzar's kingdom by the Medes and Persians, the fall of the kingdom of Babylon and the death of Belshazzar. John's attempt to 'humiliate' the Church would anger God in a similar way.[87] When these threats failed, and interdict was imposed, Innocent sought further examples from the lives of the Old Testament kings. King John had 'stretched forth his sacrilegious hands wickedly to seize the property of churches'. Here, the allusion was to King Herod, who 'stretched forth his hand to vex certain of the Church', a decision which resulted in the biblical tyrant being smitten by an avenging angel.[88] This parallel bears comparison

83 *Selected Letters of Pope Innocent III*, 98 (no. 32); 1 Kings 12:8–20; see also 2 Chronicles 10:8–19.
84 Buc, 'Pouvoir royal', 693.
85 See, for example, *Magna Vita Sancti Hugonis*, ii, 144; *History of William Marshal*, ed. A Holden, trans. S. Gregory, with historical notes by D. Crouch, Anglo-Norman Text Society, Occasional Publications Series, 4–6, 3 vols (London, 2002–2004), ii, 161 (lines 13188–90); W. L. Warren, *King John* (London, 1974), 114–15.
86 *The Ecclesiastical History of Orderic Vitalis*, ed. and trans. M. Chibnall, OMT, 6 vols (Oxford, 1969–80), v, 298–9; C. Given-Wilson, *Chronicles: The Writing of History in Medieval England* (London and New York, 2004), 166, 170; C. Fletcher, *Richard II: Manhood, Youth and Politics, 1377–99* (Oxford, 2008), 19, 75, 159–60.
87 *Selected Letters of Pope Innocent III*, 98–9 (no. 32); Daniel 5:25–31. A similar allusion was made in the contemporary satire known as the 'Song on the Bishops': *Thomas Wright's Political Songs of England: From the Reign of John to that of Edward II*, ed. P. Coss (Cambridge, 1996), 6–13, at 8.
88 *Selected Letters of Pope Innocent III*, 103 (no. 34); Acts 12:1. Nicholas Vincent also concludes that John was 'addressed as a latter-day Herod' in this period: Vincent 'Master Simon Langton'. John was also compared to Herod in papal letters about the king's treatment of the archbishopric

with the portrayal of Henry II, both by Becket in describing the treatment of his followers, and after the murder in depictions of the martyrdom.[89] Further parallels are suggested by the idea that 'the bow is at the stretch' and that John should 'avoid an arrow which turns not back'. Here, the allusion was to the fall of the mighty King Saul and his son Jonathan.[90]

Pope Innocent's allusion to the writing on the wall chimes with other ideas apparently in circulation at the time of the Canterbury dispute and ensuing period of interdict and royal excommunication: the idea of prophecy of the death of kings. According to a vision said to have been experienced by Archbishop Langton's brother, Simon, in 1207, a Cistercian monk celebrating mass saw a 'mystic hand writing prophecies'. These included the demise of a king.[91] In 1213, Peter of Wakefield (or Pontefract), 'that most unwise, because most specific, of prophets' came to King John's attention, and was ultimately executed, after forecasting the end of the reign.[92] Coupled with the rumour that the pope would declare (or had declared) John deposed, there is a sense of a current of opinion predicting that the king's intransigence would cost him his throne.[93]

Innocent III also referred to the actual or impending fall of past sinners and current wrongdoers. Before he excommunicated John he drew on the Bible to allude to God's decision to destroy all men apart from Noah and his family,

of York, when his half-brother Geoffrey refused to contribute to the thirteenth levied in 1207: Cheney, *Pope Innocent III*, 296–7.

89   *CTB*, ii, 938–51 (no. 216, at 938–41). On iconographic parallels in portrayals of Henry II and Herod, see S. Lutan-Hassner, *Thomas Becket and the Plantagenets: Atonement Through Art* (Leiden, 2015).

90   *Selected Letters of Pope Innocent III*, 113 (no. 37); 2 Samuel 1:22.

91   Vincent, 'Langton', 87–8. See also Vincent 'Master Simon Langton'. For the account of the vision: *Chronicon de Lanercost. MCCI–MCCCXLVI*, ed. J. Stevenson, Bannatyne Club, 65, and Maitland Club, 46 (Edinburgh, 1839), 3.

92   For the description quoted, see Vincent, 'Strange Case of the Missing Biographies', 240. For narrative accounts, see *Annals of Stanley*, in *Chronicles of the Reigns of Stephen, Henry II and Richard I*, ed. R. Howlett, RS 82, 4 vols (London, 1884–89), ii, 514–15; Walter of Coventry, *Memoriale*, ed. W. Stubbs, RS 58, 2 vols (London, 1872–73), ii, 208–12; *Annales Prioratus de Dunstaplia (A.D. 1–1297)*, in *Annales Monastici*, ed. H. R. Luard, RS 36, 5 vols (London, 1864–69), iii, 34; *The Chronicle of Bury St Edmunds*, ed. and trans. A. Gransden, NMT (London, 1964), 1; *Annales Monasterii de Waverleia (A.D. 1–1291)*, in *Annales Monastici*, ed. H. R. Luard, RS 36, 5 vols (London, 1864–69), ii, 278; *Liber Gaufridi Sacristae de Coldingham de statu Ecclesiae Dunhelmensis*, ed. J. Raine, *Historiae Dunelmensis Scriptores Tres, Gaufridus de Coldingham, Robertus de Graystanes, et Willelmus de Chambre*, Surtees Society, 9 (London, 1839), 3–31, at 27–8. For further discussion, see J. C. Russell, 'The Development of the Legend of Peter of Pontefract', *Medievalia et Humanistica*, 13 (1960), 21–31. For links between Peter of Wakefield, the *Invectivum contra regem Johannem* and the career of Simon Langton, see Vincent, 'Master Simon Langton'.

93   Cheney, *Pope Innocent III*, 326–8; C. R. Cheney, 'The Alleged Deposition of King John', in *Studies in Medieval History Presented to Frederick Maurice Powicke*, ed. R. W. Hunt, W. A. Pantin, and R. W. Southern (Oxford, 1948), 100–16.

to divine warnings that Babylon would be attacked and to New Testament warnings that the end of all things was at hand.[94] The message to John was clear: remember the fate of biblical tyrants and sinners and submit before it becomes too late. However, the king was not to be swayed. Neither interdict nor excommunication proved effective. It was not until the later months of 1212 that John returned to the negotiating table, as he found that he was faced with the threat of domestic revolt, a possible papal sentence of deposition and with it the prospect of French invasion.[95] Innocent's response was initially suspicious. He was prepared to negotiate but unsure whether the king was serious. Here, papal letters invoked the example of God's dealings with Moses and the Children of Israel, in no uncertain terms:[96]

> behold! We set before you a blessing and a curse after the example of Him who by his servant Moses set before the Children of Israel blessings and curses, that you may choose which you prefer, either a blessing leading to salvation if you make reparation, or a curse leading to ruin, if you show contempt.

The emphasis was now on John's soul: he faced a choice between salvation and damnation. Four barons were to swear oaths, on peril of the king's soul, that John would obey the proposed terms. Here, the pope returned to parallels with biblical tyrants. If the king did not comply, he would be treated like the pharaoh who ignored the seven plagues of Egypt: 'by the example of Him who with a strong arm freed His people from the bondage of Pharaoh, we intend with a mighty arm to free the English Church from your bondage'. To reinforce the point that he was actively considering deposing John, Innocent added that 'repentance will be useless after your downfall'.[97]

Between 1207 and early 1213, therefore, the papal letters regarding the Canterbury crisis put forward a clear and consistent viewpoint: the king's actions would lead to severe temporal and eternal consequences. However, even Pope Innocent III could be persuaded to change his mind. There was a marked change in tone once the pope was convinced that the king was

---

94 *Selected Letters of Pope Innocent III*, 110, 112 (no. 37); Genesis 6:6; Isaiah 14:27; 1 Peter 4:5.

95 For the events that persuaded John that he needed the pope as an ally: Warren, *King John*, 199–205. See also Cheney, 'The Alleged Deposition'. Roger of Wendover even suggested that the pope authorised a crusade against England: *Rogeri de Wendover liber qui dicitur Flores Historiarum ab anno domini MCLIV annoque Henrici Anglorum Regis Secundi Primo*, ed. H. G. Hewlett, RS 84, 3 vols (London, 1886–89), ii, 63–4.

96 *Selected Letters of Pope Innocent III*, 130 (no. 45); Deuteronomy 11:26–8. That such parallels were also in the minds of English chroniclers is shown in the work of the Durham writer Geoffrey of Coldingham: *Liber Gaufridi Sacristae de Coldingham*, 25–9.

97 *Selected Letters of Pope Innocent III*, 132 (no. 45). The freeing of the Children of Israel is found variously in the Bible: Exodus 6:1; Deuteronomy 6:21, 7:8; Psalm 135:10–15. If Innocent considered deposing John, he never pronounced sentence: Cheney, 'Alleged Deposition', 100–16.

serious in seeking settlement. John demonstrated this through his complete climb down. He surrendered his kingdom of England and lordship of Ireland to Innocent, so that he and his heirs would continue to hold them as fiefs of the papacy.[98] The papal letters now used biblical metaphor to emphasise redemption, rebirth, turning away from evil and the new bond between kingdom and Church. Innocent referred to Joseph's response to his brothers when they sought forgiveness after the death of Jacob and the example of Christ awaking to calm a storm that had terrified his disciples.[99] The parable of the Good Samaritan was invoked, as the pope emphasised his own role, acting 'by the example of Him who poured wine and oil into the wounds of the injured traveller' in restoring the king to his senses.[100] Innocent also described John as having 'so far progressed by your good beginning as to give promise of an excellent ending'. Here, there were two possible parallels: the first with Job, whose sufferings resulted in his 'latter end' being blessed 'more than his beginning'; the second with Solomon's proverb, 'Better is the end of a prayer than the beginning'.[101] In either case, the emphasis was on the temporal rewards of following the word of God.

If the language used in the arguments put forward by Pope Innocent III did not always directly invoke the memory of St Thomas, it is nonetheless worth noting that it bears strong similarities with the sentiments raised during the Becket crisis, in particular the arguments put forward by Thomas himself. Like Innocent III when writing to John, Becket warned Henry II of the danger he was creating for his soul's prospects of salvation:[102]

---

98 Cheney, *Pope Innocent III*, 332–7; *The Letters of Pope Innocent III (1198–1216) Concerning England and Wales: A Calendar with an Appendix of Texts*, ed. C. R. Cheney and M. G. Cheney (Oxford, 1967), 156 (no. 941), 160 (no. 962); *Rotuli Chartarum*, 195a–b; *Rotuli Litterarum Clausarum*, 153b–154a; W. E. Lunt, *Papal Revenues in the Middle Ages*, 2 vols (New York, 1965), ii, 45–8; *Selected Letters of Pope Innocent III*, 177–83 (no. 67).

99 *Selected Letters of Pope Innocent III*, 149 (no. 53), 198 (no. 76); Genesis 50:20; Psalm 106:29–30; Matthew 8:26.

100 *Selected Letters of Pope Innocent III*, 168 (no. 63); Luke 10:34. Medical analogies (a regular feature of Pope Innocent's letters on all themes – an observation I owe to Dr Herwig Weigl) were frequently deployed by the pope in his letters during the dispute: *Selected Letters of Pope Innocent III*, 94 (no. 30), 98 (no. 32), 111–12 (no. 37), 118 (no. 39), 168 (no. 63). The analogy of the Good Samaritan had previously been used by Innocent in describing the interdict imposed on France in 1200 on account of King Phillip II's repudiation of Ingeborg of Denmark. Here, the pope argued that the interdict acted as the oil and the wine used to sooth the injured man's wounds: G. Conklin, 'Ingeborg of Denmark, Queen of France, 1193–1223', in *Queens and Queenship in Medieval Europe*, ed. A. J. Duggan (Woodbridge, 1997), 37–52, at 46.

101 *Selected Letters of Pope Innocent III*, 151 (no. 53); Job 8:7, 42:12; Ecclesiastes 7:9.

102 *CTB*, i, 328–43 (no. 82, at 340–43). For a similar reference, see *CTB*, ii, 1032–43 (no. 241a–b at 1034–41).

We are not saying these things to put you to shame, or to provoke you to greater indignation and rage … but to make you more cautious in making provision for the care of your soul, and to avoid the danger which is already on the doorstep, and because it is our special concern to look after your soul.

Becket made the same point in writing to those he hoped would influence Henry, for instance the Empress Matilda, emphasising that he was concerned for Henry's soul, and that the king's mother should help in 'calling him back to the right path'.[103]

Becket's warnings to Henry also prefigured those of Innocent III to John in recalling the fate of the Old Testament kings. A letter of July 1166, from Archbishop Thomas to the bishops of the province of Canterbury, exhorted them to: 'Read the scriptures, and you shall find how perished the kings who were seen to usurp the priestly office for themselves and how many they were'. The bishops should consider King Henry II's best interests, 'lest, which God forbid, he and his entire house should perish as did those who were found guilty of a similar offence'.[104] Similar ideas were later highlighted by Innocent III in writing to John. By 1169, however, Becket had taken the idea further, suggesting that Henry II surpassed the rulers of history in the scale of his oppression:[105]

turn over pages of the histories of olden times, consider again the deeds of the ancient tyrants, re-read the records of the newly born Church: you will not readily find among all its persecutors one who so pursued one man that he strove to perpetrate so great slaughter of innocents by so many skilful tricks.

Sometimes, the resemblance between ideas used by Becket and Innocent is particularly close. Both drew parallels with Moses dealing with straying members of the Children of Israel.[106] Both used the example of Uzza and, whilst acknowledging that he was not a king, both Thomas and Innocent saw the example of laying hands on the Ark of the Covenant, which 'belonged not to him but to the servants of the temple', as one that applied to a king who interfered with Church affairs or property.[107] Similarly, King Saul, whose fate was alluded to by Innocent III in writing to John, was named during the Becket crisis by John of Salisbury as a description of Henry II.[108] However,

---

103   *CTB*, i, 154–9 (no. 40).
104   *CTB*, i, 388–425 (no. 95, at 401). For further examples, see also *CTB*, i, 266–71 (no. 68), 292–9 (no. 74).
105   *CTB*, ii, 938–51 (no. 216, at 940–41). See also *CTB*, ii, 1108–16 (no. 258, at 1112–13).
106   For Becket, see *CTB*, i, 108–17 (no. 32, at 112–13). Here, Thomas's sufferings are also compared to those of Joseph when betrayed by his brothers.
107   For Becket, see *CTB*, i, 328–43 (no. 82, at 337).
108   *CTB*, i, 468–83 (no. 101, at 479). Saul's son Jonathan is also mentioned in this earlier parallel – perhaps an allusion to Henry the Young King.

here there is a striking difference of approach. Innocent used the example in the build-up to excommunicating King John. John of Salisbury made it clear that he would never advise Becket to impose excommunication on Henry II or interdict on his kingdom.[109]

This highlights that the sentiments expressed during the two disputes could be used in very different ways – unsurprisingly, given the range of biblical material at the disposal of the letter writers and the myriad ways it could be interpreted. Further examples reinforce this point. As a metaphor for dispute resolution, Innocent III referred to the calming of the storm after the terrified disciples had awakened Christ. Becket used this imagery to portray himself as a frightened disciple with no course left but to awaken Christ.[110] Likewise, Innocent wrote of John's reconciliation as a good beginning that promised a better conclusion. John of Salisbury, by contrast, had adapted the Solomonic proverb in the summer of 1166 to suggest that 'the end of this' would be 'worse than the beginning'.[111]

Finally, a comparison can be drawn between Pope Innocent III and Pope Alexander III. Innocent was keen to avoid recourse to sanctions, and after the Canterbury crisis he engaged in diplomacy on King John's side. In some ways, Alexander's care in his diplomatic engagement with kings and princes was similar, in terms of his unwillingness to resort to sanctions. However, the latter's methods were not those of the intransigent stand-off that developed between Henry and Thomas, or at times between John and Innocent. Peter Clarke has written of Alexander's 'concern to foster a modus vivendi' that characterised his policy towards lay rulers, pursuing a delicate balancing act in an effort also to safeguard the liberties of the Church.[112] Thus, Alexander urged Archbishop Thomas to make every effort to regain Henry II's goodwill, but not at the expense of caving in. The pope was equally clear that the freedoms of the Church should be preserved, making small concessions to the king but seeking to bolster the archbishop's authority.[113] His was 'an extended and subtle exercise in extremely delicate diplomacy', balancing the threat (of which Alexander admitted he was terrified) that Henry II would switch his support to the imperial anti-pope.[114] Such a threat was not an issue for Innocent III.

---

109   *CTB*, i, 468–83 (no. 101, at 481).
110   *CTB*, i, 30–33 (no. 12, at 31), 592–5 (no. 124, at 595).
111   *CTB*, i, 456–69 (no. 100, at 457).
112   P. D. Clarke, 'Introduction', in *Pope Alexander III (1150–81): The Art of Survival*, ed. P. D. Clarke and A. J. Duggan (Farnham, 2012), 1–12, at 11.
113   A. J. Duggan, '*Alexander ille meus*: The Papacy of Alexander III', in *Pope Alexander III (1150–81): The Art of Survival*, ed. P. D. Clarke and A. J. Duggan (Farnham, 2012), 13–49, at 25–32. Duggan concludes that 'the strategy worked'. See also Nicholas Vincent's quotation of Alexander's observation to Becket that '"the desire of princes should be respected and their will accommodated as far as possible"': Vincent, 'Beyond Becket', 263–4.
114   Duggan, '*Alexander ille meus*', 29, 48.

Even without the schism, Alexander was aware that precipitate action would jeopardise the delicate balance that characterised royal-papal relations. This awareness was also seen in the years after the murder. For Alexander, repeated dispute between the English crown and the papacy was not an agenda he seemed prepared to entertain.[115] His legates even acknowledged that the election of bishops needed to take into account the needs of the kingdom, much as Innocent III would later instruct his legate, Nicholas of Tusculum, that if John made 'proper petitions', candidates 'loyal to the king and useful to the state' could be appointed.[116] The tools of Alexander's diplomacy were 'the prestige of the papal office, the honeyed words of his envoys and the persuasive rhetoric of his letters'.[117] This was also true for Innocent III, but in the case of John (and others) Innocent attempted to turn that rhetoric into applied authority.

In considering Alexander III's relationship with Henry II, we are not blessed with the abundance of surviving papal letters found for Innocent III's dealings with England. Much of what does survive was preserved in sources favourable to Archbishop Thomas.[118] In terms of their language, Alexander frequently reminded Henry of the instructions of St Paul on the duties owed to Caesar and to God.[119] Such exhortation was also used by Innocent III, for instance in instructing the executors of the interdict that the sentence was to be imposed if John continued to refuse to accept Langton.[120] Similarly, Alexander frequently deployed Old Testament metaphor to reinforce exhortation that the impious mend their ways.[121] Nicholas Vincent highlights a further possible parallel between Alexander's dealings with Henry and Innocent's relations with John: 'in 1172, Henry II entered into a new phase of relations with the papacy, marked by his recognition of some form of homage or subjection for his English realm'.[122] The idea that John's decision in 1213, to turn England and Ireland into fiefs of the papacy, in some way emulated his father's actions as part of the Compromise of Avranches, requires further research, but remains an intriguing possibility.

The Canterbury dispute, the interdict and John's excommunication created the most dramatic rift between crown and Church since the Becket conflict, and it has been shown that there are many comparisons and contrasts that can be drawn, and which were drawn at the time, between the interaction between

---

115 Duggan, 'Alexander ille meus', 31–7.
116 Cheney, Pope Innocent III, 160–61.
117 Duggan, 'Alexander ille meus', 37.
118 On Alexander, see Vincent, 'Beyond Becket', 258–60. Contrast for Innocent: Selected Letters of Pope Innocent III; Letters of Pope Innocent III.
119 Vincent, 'Beyond Becket', 263–5.
120 Selected Letters of Pope Innocent III, 92 (no. 30).
121 Vincent, 'Beyond Becket', 263–5.
122 For fuller discussion, see Vincent, 'Beyond Becket', 277–81.

Church and king during these disputes. As with the secular political turbulence of John's reign, reconciliation largely took place during the minority of King Henry III. Archbishop Langton played a crucial role, particularly in 1220. First, he performed the second coronation of Henry III at Westminster Abbey on Whitsunday (17 May) 1220, at some expense to the royal coffers. Here, the king laid the foundation stone for a new Lady Chapel. A few weeks later, with Henry III in attendance, Langton presided at the first jubilee of St Thomas, 7 July 1220, when the saint's relics were translated to their new tomb in the Trinity Chapel at Canterbury Cathedral. The celebrations, at the archbishop's expense, included feasting akin to that of a royal coronation. The date of the translation also coincided with the anniversary of the burial of Henry II.[123] The two ceremonies perhaps impressed upon the king the compatibility of the cults of St Edward the Confessor and St Thomas, whilst reminding Henry III, still a boy, of examples to keep in mind in the quest to rule well. The reign would mark a return to royal association both with royal saints and canonised figures central to the English Church. Henry is famously linked to promotion of the cult of St Edward, and his devotions to the cult and shrine of St Thomas are often overlooked. However, he regularly came to Canterbury and made offerings there. His marriage to Eleanor of Provence was celebrated in Canterbury Cathedral in 1236.[124] Even in a period in which the martyr's successors, Stephen Langton and Edmund Rich, were seen by contemporaries as saints (and in Edmund's case, canonised), Becket again held a prominent place alongside royal saints in the king's devotions.[125]

---

123   R. Eales, 'The Political Setting of the Becket Translation of 1220', in *Martyrs and Martyrologies*, ed. D. Wood, SCH, 30 (Oxford, 1993), 127–39; Duggan, 'Cult', 38–9; Vincent, 'Langton', 100, 103–4, 107; 'Matthaei Parisiensis, Vita sancti Stephani archiepiscopi Cantuariensis', in *Ungedruckte Anglo-Normannische Geschichtsquellen*, ed. F. Liebermann (Strasbourg, 1879), 328–9. The 1220 translation is also discussed in the article by Anne J. Duggan (chapter 2) in this volume.

124   Duggan, 'Cult', 31; P. Binski, *Westminster Abbey and the Plantagenets: Kingship and the Representation of Power 1200–1400* (New Haven, CT, and London, 1995), 4. For some of Henry's gifts in honour of Becket, see *Calendar of the Liberate Rolls Preserved in the Public Record Office: Henry III. Vol. I. A.D. 1226–1240*, ed. W. H. Stevenson, HMSO (London, 1916), 356, 404, 488; *Calendar of the Liberate Rolls Preserved in the Public Record Office: Henry III. Vol. II. A.D. 1240–1245*, ed. J. B. W. Chapman, HMSO (London, 1930), 17; *Close Rolls of the Reign of Henry III Preserved in the Public Record Office: A.D. 1237–1242*, HMSO (London, 1911), 175–81, 208, 227.

125   On Langton: 'Matthaei Parisiensis, Vita sancti Stephani', 318–29. On Edmund: C. H. Lawrence, *St Edmund of Abingdon: A Study of Hagiography and History* (Oxford, 1960). For the argument that Becket, Stephen and Edmund were venerated as 'anti-royal' saints, see J. C. Russell, 'The Canonisation of Opposition to the King in Angevin England', in *Anniversary Essays in Medieval History by Students of Charles Homer Haskins*, ed. C. H. Taylor (Boston, MA, 1929), 279–90. For a critique of this view, see Eales, 'Political Setting', esp. 138–9; Webster, 'Crown, Cathedral and Conflict', 208.

9.

The St Thomas Becket Windows at Angers and Coutances: Devotion, Subversion and the Scottish Connection[1]

ALYCE A. JORDAN

The dramatic life and spectacular demise of Thomas Becket engendered an expansive discourse in both text and image. Depictions of the archbishop's murder appeared in manuscripts soon after his death and were widely disseminated on enamelled reliquaries produced in Limoges.[2] While this first generation of Becket imagery focused almost exclusively on the saint's murder, a shift to more elaborate renderings occurred at Canterbury Cathedral, where twelve aisle windows depicting Thomas's life and miracles encircled the magnificent shrine to which his relics were translated in 1220.[3] Four windows appeared before and soon after the Canterbury glass installation, in the French cathedrals of Sens, Chartres, Coutances and Angers. They are among the earliest surviving works of public, narrative art devoted to Becket outside of Canterbury. All four expand the visual biography of Becket's life beyond his murder and vary dramatically in form

1 I am grateful to Madeline Caviness and Michael Cothren for their careful readings and invaluable critiques of this essay, and to Lindy Grant for sharing with me her expertise in Anglo-Norman history, genealogy and architecture. I am also indebted to Catherine E. Karkov, Eva Frojmovic, Marie-Pierre Gelin and Michael Staunton, who chaired conference sessions (College Art Association, 2010, and the International Medieval Congress, Leeds, 2008, respectively) in which I presented preliminary versions of this study. This essay is dedicated to Meredith Parsons Lillich, who introduced me to the miracle of medieval stained glass.
2 Borenius, *Becket in Art*; *Enamels of Limoges 1100–1350*, ed. J. P. O'Neill *et al.*, The Metropolitan Museum of Art (New York, 1996), 14, 162–4. Fifty-two reliquaries, produced between 1180 and 1220, are known to exist. *Sédières* contains numerous articles supplementing Borenius' compilation of Becket iconography. See also C. T. Little, 'The Road to Glory: New Early Images of Thomas Becket's Life,' in *Reading Medieval Images: The Art Historian and the Object*, ed. E. Sears and T. K. Thomas (Ann Arbor, MI, 2002), 201–11.
3 M. H. Caviness, *The Early Stained Glass of Canterbury Cathedral circa 1175–1220* (Princeton, NJ, 1977), 83–97, 146–50; Caviness, *The Windows of Christ Church*, 157–214, for the Becket windows.

and content from one to the other.[4] Finally, all were produced in a short period of time surrounding the translation of the saint's relics in 1220. The windows thus compose intriguing case studies of the ways in which stories of Thomas Becket were re-presented and re-told at a seminal moment in the expansion of his cult.

This essay explores the diverse, even oppositional, stories crafted around the archbishop's life and death in the Coutances and Angers Becket narratives. The windows of Coutances and Angers differ from those of Sens and Chartres in significant ways. With its emphasis on quotidian episcopal duties, such as preaching, confirming children and celebrating Mass, the Sens window inscribes the final weeks of Becket's life within a paradigm of exemplary eccle-siastical activities.[5] At Chartres, the ideological conflicts between Church and State which drove the archbishop into exile, and for which he ultimately died, are foregrounded through a series of recurrent encounters between prelates, pontiffs and monarchs.[6] While the windows of Sens and Chartres offer distinct versions of Becket's life, both fall within the framework of the saint's venerable and venerated legacy.[7] The windows of Coutances and Angers, by contrast, proffer more ambiguous biographies, accounts I seek here to illuminate through recourse both to historical contextualisation and theoretical interpretation.

My approach to this project draws on a method of 'triangulation' pioneered by Madeline Caviness, who has demonstrated that the addition of contem-porary theories to the traditional art historical toolbox of formal analysis, iconography and historical context can assist in the process of 'pressuring' and 'prying open' works of medieval art. The complex, ambivalent readings this triangulatory approach enables offer more nuanced understandings of how images functioned – and continue to function – on multiple hermeneutic planes. Caviness's work has focused on investigations of images by, of and for medieval women, engaging contextual history in concert with contemporary feminist theories.[8] In this study, I triangulate the rich nexus of historical

4   C. Brisac, 'Thomas Becket dans le vitrail français au début du XIIIe siècle', in *Sédières*, 221–31; M.-P. Gelin, 'Heroes and Traitors: The Life of Thomas Becket in French Stained-Glass Windows', *Vidimus*, 14 (2008) [http://vidimus.org/issues/issue-14/feature/, accessed 13 January 2015].
5   A. A. Jordan, 'Rhetoric and Reform: The St Thomas Becket Window of Sens Cathedral', in *The Four Modes of Seeing: Approaches to Medieval Imagery in Honor of Madeline Harrison Caviness*, ed. E. Staudinger Lane, E. Carson Pastan, and E. M. Shortell (Farnham, 2009), 547–64.
6   For the Sens and Chartres windows, see http://www.medievalart.org.uk/Chartres/18_pages/ Chartres_Bay18_key.htm, accessed 13 January 2015, and http://www.medievalart.org.uk/ Sens/23_Pages/Sens_Bay23_key.htm, accessed 14 January 2015. On the Chartres Becket window, see C. and J.-P. Deremble, *Les Vitraux de Chartres* (Paris, 2003), 128–33.
7   Natalie A. Hansen has argued that both the Sens and Chartres windows are grounded in the liturgies devoted to St Thomas. N. A. Hansen, 'Making the Martyr: The Liturgical Persona of Saint Thomas Becket in Visual Imagery' (unpublished M.A. thesis, University of Illinois at Urbana-Champaign, 2011).
8   Caviness first articulated her method of triangulation in M. H. Caviness, 'The Feminist Project: Pressuring the Medieval Object', *Frauen Kunst Wissenschaft*, 24 (1997), 13–21. She

connections I have found linking the life and legacy of Thomas Becket with the respective patrons of the Coutances and Angers Becket windows, and with the discourses of frontier studies and postcolonial theory.[9]

I begin with discussions of the historical, religious and, in the case of Angers, genealogical landscapes which underpin these Becket narratives, thereby establishing a contextual field for their inclusion in these cathedral ensembles. Adding critical theory to this project, I then seek to articulate more subtle understandings of the particular iterations of Becket's life each window proffers. This method yields analyses that are dense and textured. They speak at once to the power of images to articulate heterogeneous ideas, and to give form to oppositional – even contradictory – motivations and identities.[10] More significant, perhaps, in the context of the present anthology, these windows reveal the particular significance of Thomas Becket as both subject and object – a character of contemporary history and a *lieu de mémoire* – and a vehicle by which a constellation of historical, cultural, even familial, associations might be channelled, conjured and reified.

Thomas Becket at Coutances and Angers

Three windows devoted respectively to St Thomas, St George and St Blaise appear in the north transept of Coutances Cathedral in Normandy.[11] The

developed her approach further in her book: M. H. Caviness, *Visualizing Women in the Middle Ages: Sight, Spectacle and Scopic Economy* (Philadelphia, PA, 2001); and in her e-book: M. H. Caviness, *Reframing Medieval Art: Difference, Margins, and Boundaries* (Tufts University, MA, 2001), 16–20 [http://dca.lib.tufts.edu/caviness/abstract.html, accessed 14 January 2015], in which she also provides a diagrammatic depiction, placing the medieval object at the apex of a triangle of unequal sides, historical analysis on the shorter side, theory on the longer side, and the modern viewer/scholar along the bottom. For additional discussion and application of Caviness's methodological model, see C. Schleif, 'Introduction/Conclusion: Are We Still Being Historical? Exposing the Ehenheim Epitaph Using History and Theory', *Different Visions: A Journal of New Perspectives on Medieval Art*, 1 (2008), 1–46 [http://differentvisions.org/issue-one/, accessed 14 January 2015]. Schleif guest-edited this inaugural edition of *Different Visions*, which was dedicated to Caviness's approach and contains articles employing her method. These papers were the result of a series of sessions also devoted to Caviness's triangulatory model, co-organised by Dr Schleif and myself for the forty-first International Congress on Medieval Studies in Kalamazoo, MI, in 2006.

9 Pertinent bibliography for medieval applications of frontier studies and postcolonial theory appears below at nn. 59–60.

10 Caviness and others have cited the particular utility of postmodern theories to expose tensions and contradictions in works of cultural production without the pressure to harmonise them into a unified 'master narrative': Caviness, *Reframing Medieval Art*, 16–18; Schleif, 'Introduction/Conclusion', 7.

11 On the Coutances windows, see K. Boulanger, 'Les Vitraux du XIIIe siècle', in *La Cathédrale de Coutances: art et histoire. Actes du colloque organisé au Centre culturel international de Cerisy du 8 au 11 octobre 2009*, ed. F. Laty, P. Bouet, and G. Désiré dit Gosset, with photographs by

St Thomas window now contains six scenes, disposed in circular medallions interspersed with demi-medallions housing single standing figures who turn inward and gesture toward the narrative panels. Becket converses with Henry II in the bottom-most medallion before departing for Canterbury by boat in the scene above. The third panel, which must have originally occupied one of the window's lower registers, presents Thomas kneeling before Pope Alexander III. Archbishop and pope met in France, where both lived in exile under the protection of King Louis VII. The narrative moves directly to the archbishop's murder, entombment and the transport of his soul to heaven [Figs 9.1–9.2].[12]

Several contextual elements could have contributed to Thomas's appearance in the Coutances transept. Becket's parents were both Norman by birth, and his cult was exceptionally strong in Normandy.[13] All three of the saints featured in the north transept windows were associated with healing miracles, and all three windows have been attributed to the patronage of Coutances's bishop (1208–38), Hugh de Morville, who took a particular interest in the health of his congregation, founding a hospital not far from the cathedral.[14] The cathedral itself boasted a well in the south transept, directly opposite the three windows, which dispensed healing waters. St Thomas, St George and, to a lesser extent, St Blaise, were all associated with miracles involving water. Blaise is perhaps best known for having saved a child from asphyxiation by placing two lit candles in a cruciform position against the

A. Poirier (Bayeux, 2012), 99–105; M. Callias Bey and V. David, *Les Vitraux de Basse-Normandie*, Corpus Vitrearum: France-Recensement VIII (Rennes, 2006), 129–30, 136–7; Nilgen, 198–9; V. Chaussé, *Les Verrières de la cathédrale Notre-Dame de Coutances*, Itinéraires du patrimoine, 210 (Caen, 1999), 16–19; J. Fournée, 'Les Vitraux de la cathédrale', in *Coutances, ville d'art et d'histoire*, Art de Basse Normandie, 95 (1987), 93–6; J. Lafond, 'Les Vitraux', in *La Cathédrale de Coutances*, ed. P. Colmet-Daage (Paris, 1967), 44–7; Abbé E.-A. Pigeon, *Histoire de la cathédrale de Coutances* (Coutances, 1876), 207–12.

12   Details of the Coutances windows can be found at http://cathedralecoutances.free.fr/vitraux1.htm, accessed 14 January 2015. A fourteenth-century renovation of the chapter house located above the sacristy, which abuts the north transept façade, resulted in a reduction in the height of the three lancets and the loss and rearrangement of panels from each: Boulanger, 'Les vitraux du XIIIe siècle', 99–100.

13   The cult of St Thomas Becket in Normandy has been extensively studied: R. Foreville, 'Le culte de saint Thomas Becket en Normandie: Enquête sur les sanctuaires anciennement placés sous le vocable du martyr de Canterbury', in *Sédières*, 135–52; R. Foreville, *Thomas Becket dans la tradition historique et hagiographique* (London, 1981). See also Duggan, 'Cult'; and the essay by Elma Brenner in this volume (chapter 4).

14   F. Neveux, 'Hugues de Morville et l'épiscopat normand des XIIe–XIIIe siècles', in *La Cathédrale de Coutances: art et histoire. Actes du colloque organisé au Centre culturel international de Cerisy du 8 au 11 octobre 2009*, ed. F. Laty, P. Bouet and G. Désiré dit Gosset, with photographs by A. Poirier (Bayeux, 2012), 47–56, at 52–3; M. Lelégard, 'L'Hôtel-Dieu de Coutances', in *Coutances, ville d'art et d'histoire*, Art de Basse Normandie, 95 (1987), 42–9.

boy's throat, miraculously dislodging the fishbone stuck therein.[15] *The Golden Legend* recounts that after George slew the dragon, the king whose subjects the dragon had terrorised built a church in the saint's honour, within which 'flowed a spring whose waters cure all diseases'.[16] Becket's healing powers were manifest through 'St Thomas's water', a tincture of water mixed with a drop of the saint's blood.[17] The Coutances window may thus visualise Becket's popularity as both healing saint and native Norman son.

The encounter between Henry II and the archbishop prior to the latter's departure for Canterbury constitutes a standard element in Becket iconography, appearing in all four French Becket windows. The windows of Sens and Chartres, however, depict this conversation in the context of a visual opposition between Henry, the evil king who drove Thomas into exile, and the good king, Louis VII, who gave the archbishop refuge on French soil.[18] Henry's inclusion at Coutances is more ambiguous. Though holding a sword, the king exhibits no overt signs of evil intent, while Thomas, for his part, inclines his head toward the king, and seems to raise his hand in a gesture of benediction [Figs 9.1–9.2].[19]

In 1171, Henry II had been universally condemned for his tacit, if not active, role in the archbishop's murder. Pope Alexander III had placed his continental lands under interdict and Henry was forbidden from entering a church. By 1172, however, Henry had made peace with the pope and had

15   Other water-themed events in the life of St Blaise include an account of seven women who threw idols into a lake, where they immediately sank, and sixty-five pagans who walked into the lake and immediately drowned. By contrast, St Blaise, when thrown into the same lake, was able to stand upon the water: Jacobus de Voragine, *The Golden Legend*, trans. W. G. Ryan, 2 vols (Princeton, NJ, 1993), i, 152–3. For further discussion linking the cults of Becket and Blaise, see the essay by Colette Bowie in this volume (chapter 6).

16   Jacobus de Voragine, *The Golden Legend*, i, 240.

17   P. A. Sigal, 'Naissance et premier développement d'un vinage exceptionnel: l'eau de saint Thomas', CCM, 44 (2001), 35–44; A. A. Jordan, 'The "Water of Thomas Becket": Water as Medium, Metaphor and Relic', in *The Nature and Function of Water, Baths, Bathing and Hygiene from Antiquity through the Renaissance*, ed. C. Kosso and A. Scott (Leiden, 2009), 479–500. These collect much of the bibliography on the archbishop's prolific healing abilities and explore some of the textual and visual articulations of his miraculous tincture.

18   The Chartres Becket window makes this dynamic especially clear through the inclusion of a grimacing devil perched on Henry II's shoulder during the king's conversation with his archbishop. See http://www.medievalart.org.uk/Chartres/18_pages/Chartres_Bay18_key.htm, accessed 14 January 2015. For the Sens window, which begins with a scene in which Louis VII negotiates peace between Thomas and Henry, see http://www.medievalart.org.uk/Sens/23_Pages/Sens_Bay23_key.htm, accessed 14 January 2015. Details of the Coutances windows can be found at http://cathedralecoutances.free.fr/vitraux1.htm, accessed 14 January 2015.

19   The left half of this conversation panel is a modern restoration, and I do not assume Henry II's stance here reproduces the medieval original. St Thomas's relatively benign pose, and the fact that Henry II is the only king appearing in the window, nonetheless distinguishes this Becket narrative from those of Sens and Chartres.

Figure 9.1. Life of
St Thomas Becket,
Coutances, Notre-Dame
Cathedral, c.1230–40,
Bay 217, left lancet.

Opposite:
Figure 9.2. Life of
St Thomas Becket,
Coutances, Notre-Dame
Cathedral, c.1230–40:
detail, Thomas converses
with Henry II; Thomas
leaves France for England.

agreed to numerous acts of atonement. The final settlement between king and pontiff transpired in Avranches, not far from Coutances, and several of Henry's major penitential foundations were located in Normandy, then part of his continental territories. In 1174, Henry made a high-profile pilgrimage to Becket's tomb to do penance for his role in the saint's murder and to invoke his aid in suppressing a widespread rebellion spearheaded by his son, the Young King Henry.[20] The elder Henry credited his decisive victory later that year to Thomas's intervention. David Knowles observed that Henry II affected 'a remarkably successful recovery' in the decade following Becket's death,[21] and it is perhaps this gentler assessment of the English king that the Coutances window depicts. That Henry might have received more generous scrutiny, pictorial or otherwise, in a Norman church, is not surprising. Philip II's conquest of Normandy in 1204 had made the region part of a rapidly expanding French realm. Frequent uprisings against French domination, however, remained a visible sign of the conflicted loyalties of its inhabitants. Henry's ambiguous depiction in the Coutances Becket window offers a counterpoint to the divergent political allegiances of Normandy itself. The inclusion of this lancet within a larger glass ensemble devoted to saints prominently associated with both England and the former Angevin empire amplifies its iconographic and contextual ambivalence.[22]

The Becket window at Angers resembles that of Coutances in its simplified arrangement of quadrilobe medallions disposed in a single column [Fig. 9.3].[23] While retaining only five of its original eight medieval panels, the Angers window offers yet another distinct interpretation of Becket's life. Two panels mirror those of other windows: the archbishop conversing with Henry II, and his entombment. The three other scenes, to my knowledge, appear nowhere else in surviving monumental Becket cycles. The first may reference either the

20 D. Knowles, *Thomas Becket* (London, 1970; repr. London, 1971), 152–4; Barlow, 260–62, 269–70; *Lives of Thomas Becket*, 215–19; Duggan, *Thomas Becket*, 221–2, 254. Henry II had his son, Henry, crowned king in 1170 by Roger of Pont l'Évêque, Archbishop of York. Following his coronation, Henry II's namesake son is identified as 'the Young King' to distinguish him from his father.

21 Knowles, *Thomas Becket*, 153.

22 While firm evidence for the import of St George in England appears only in the late thirteenth century, documentation of relics and miracles attributed to George are found in Normandy and Maine as early as 585. Blaise's cult was widespread, but he enjoyed particular veneration in England as the patron saint of wool-makers. See below at nn. 91–93.

23 On the thirteenth-century windows of Angers, see L. Grodecki, *Les Vitraux du centre et des pays de la Loire*, Corpus Vitrearum: France, Recensement II (Paris, 1981), 287–91; J. Hayward and L. Grodecki, 'Les Vitraux de la cathédrale d'Angers', *Bulletin Monumental*, 124 (1966), 29–53; K. Boulanger, 'Les Vitraux du chœur de la cathédrale d'Angers: commanditaires et iconographie', in *Anjou: Medieval Art, Architecture, and Archaeology*, ed. J. McNeill and D. Prigent, British Archaeological Association Conference Transactions, 26 (2003), 196–209; K. Boulanger, *Les Vitraux de la cathédrale d'Angers*, Corpus Vitrearum: France, Recensement III (Paris, 2010).

coronation of Henry the Young King in June 1170, or the Young King's refusal to meet with Becket following his return to England later that year.[24] Two additional panels are devoted exclusively to Becket's murderers, who appear on horseback and traversing the English Channel by boat. This window also contains the heraldic blazon (*or six chevrons gules*) of the Beaumont family, repeated four times in the lancet's borders [Figs 9.3–9.5].

I have been drawn to explore connections between these unusual scenes and the Beaumont family, not only because the very presence of their heraldry inscribes the Beaumonts into the window's narrative, but because other evidence for the veneration of Thomas Becket at Angers is conspicuous in its absence. Thomas wisely avoided the region during his exile, since it lay in the heart of Henry's continental holdings, and Raymonde Foreville determined that, with the exception of Normandy, the archbishop was not particularly honoured within the hereditary domains of the Plantagenet empire, even after the regions came under French control.[25] Angers possessed no relic of the saint, a point of some import, since the Becket lancet is one of only two windows in the twelfth- and thirteenth-century glass programmes lacking complementary representation amongst the altars and relics housed in the cathedral treasury.[26] And while Guillaume de Beaumont (bishop of Angers 1202–40) is credited with overseeing the entire choir glazing campaign, the family's heraldry appears only here and in one other window dedicated to St Julien of Le Mans, the patron saint of Le Mans Cathedral, where Guillaume had once served as a canon.[27]

---

24   Knowles, *Thomas Becket*, 127–8, 136–7; Barlow, 206–7, 228–9; *Lives of Thomas Becket*, 172–4, 185–6; Duggan, *Thomas Becket*, 181–3, 202–3. A scene of Henry's coronation, in which the youthful prince sits frontally disposed, flanked by the archbishop of York, Roger of Pont l'Évêque, Gilbert, bishop of London, and other attending bishops, appears in *The Becket Leaves*, dated c.1220–40: J. Backhouse and C. de Hamel, *The Becket Leaves* (London, 1988), 31 and fol. 3r.

25   R. Foreville, 'Le Culte de saint Thomas Becket en France: bilan provisoire des recherches', in *Sédières*, 163–87, at 168. A planned conference between Henry II and his estranged archbishop at Angers in 1166 did not occur, although Henry did meet with three of Thomas's clerks who had followed him into exile, including John of Salisbury: Barlow, 140–42; *Lives of Thomas Becket*, 142–4. Henry II financed projects in Angers and Le Mans as part of his atonement for his role in Becket's murder. He did so, however, through intermediaries, such as his seneschal, Etienne de Marsay, and these penitential foundations, most notably the *Hôpital Saint-Jean-l'Evangeliste* in Angers and the *Hôpital-Dieu de Coëffort* in Le Mans, were not named in honour of St Thomas.

26   Three thirteenth-century lists of relics survive for the cathedral. See L. de Farcy, *Monographie de la cathédrale d'Angers*, 4 vols (Angers, 1901–26), i, 159–63; Boulanger, 'Les Vitraux du chœur', 202. In 1211, Bishop Guillaume de Beaumont gifted a large golden chasse filled with relics to his cathedral. *L'obituaire de la cathédrale d'Angers*, ed. C. Urseau, Mémoires de la Société nationale d'agriculture, sciences, et arts d'Angers, 7 (1930), 10–11, reprints the inventory of Guillaume's bequest.

27   The lowest register of the St Julien of Le Mans window depicts a bishop, identified by inscription as Guillaume, kneeling opposite a shield bearing the Beaumont arms charged with two croziers – a likely reference to Guillaume and his uncle, Raoul de Beaumont, who held the

Figure 9.3. Life of St Thomas Becket, Angers, Cathedral of St-Maurice, c.1230–35, Bay 108a, left lancet.

Figure 9.4. Life of St Thomas Becket, Angers, Cathedral of St-Maurice, c.1230–35: detail, the murderers of St Thomas Becket on horseback; the murderers of St Thomas Becket sail across the Channel; heraldry of the Beaumont family, viscounts of Maine.

Bishop Guillaume's family history offers compelling links to the Angers Becket window. Guillaume's ancestors were the hereditary viscounts of Maine and vassals of the Plantagenet kings until the territories of Maine, Touraine and Anjou were conquered by France. The Beaumonts were blood relations of Henry II by virtue of their common descent from the king's grandfather, Henry I. Henry II's son John had helped secure Guillaume's elevation to the bishopric of Angers, even while embroiled in hostilities with the king of France.[28] These ancestral and political bonds were fractured, however, when Guillaume's brother, Raoul, viscount of Maine, switched allegiance to Philip Augustus in 1203, just months after Guillaume's episcopal election. Philip's conquest of the western territories soon followed, and the Beaumonts became subjects of the French Crown.[29] My analysis investigates the Angers Becket window through this web of political and genealogical ties.

Indeed, each panel proffers a connection between Archbishop Thomas, Henry II and the Beaumont family. Even a scene as generic as Thomas conversing with Henry assumes a particular resonance within the context of Beaumont history. Like the panel at Coutances, the Angers scene depicts Henry seated on the left and Thomas standing before him on the right [Figs 9.2 and 9.5]. Here, Thomas raises his right hand in a gesture of address, with his cross-bearer, Edward Grim, standing behind him. As cousins of Henry II and one of the most prominent families in the Normandy-Maine marches, members of the Beaumont clan could well have met Thomas Becket during his tenure as Henry's chancellor.[30] Thomas travelled with Henry II through

bishopric of Angers before him (1177–97). Hayward and Grodecki, 'Les Vitraux de la cathédrale d'Angers', 9–10; Boulanger, 'Les Vitraux du chœur', 199. Boulanger, *Les Vitraux de la cathédrale d'Angers*, 36, has identified two bishops depicted at the foot of the Virgin and Child window now in the nave, but originally part of the choir programme, as another likely depiction of the two Beaumont bishops.

28 Seminal works for the history of the Beaumonts of Maine include: E. Hucher, 'Monuments funéraires et sigillographiques des Vicomtes de Beaumont au Maine', *Revue historique et archéologique du Maine*, 11 (1882), 319–408; Abbé A. Angot, *Généalogies féodales mayennaises du XIe au XIIIe siècle* (Laval, 1942).

29 The best recent scholarship on the Beaumonts of Maine appears in Daniel Power's numerous studies of the frontiers of Angevin Normandy. See especially: D. Power, 'What did the Frontier of Angevin Normandy Comprise?', *Anglo-Norman Studies*, 17 (1995), 181–201; D. Power, 'King John and the Norman Aristocracy', in *King John: New Interpretations*, ed. S. D. Church (Woodbridge, 1999), 117–36; D. Power, 'The End of Angevin Normandy: The Revolt at Alençon (1203)', *Historical Research*, 74 (2001), 444–64; D. Power, '"Terra regis Anglie et terra Normannorum sibi invicem adversantur": les héritages anglo-normands entre 1204 et 1244', in *La Normandie et l'Angleterre au Moyen Âge*, ed. P. Bouet and V. Gazeau (Caen, 2003), 189–209; and D. Power, *The Norman Frontier in the Twelfth and Early Thirteenth Centuries* (Cambridge, 2004).

30 On Roscelin de Beaumont, viscount of Maine c.1145–75, who married Henry I's illegitimate daughter Constance c.1130, see Angot, *Généalogies féodales mayennaises*, 29–31, 80–81. Documentation of Roscelin's activities is minimal. More evidence of Henry II's regard for, and interactions with, Roscelin's son Richard, exist. Between 1181 and 1183, Viscount Richard

Figure 9.5. Life of St Thomas Becket, Angers, Cathedral of St-Maurice, c.1230–35: detail, the coronation of Henry the Young King or Young King Henry refuses to meet with Thomas?; Thomas converses with Henry II; entombment (or translation?) of Thomas Becket.

the Angevin territories in 1156–57, and from Normandy on to Toulouse in 1159–62.[31] Richard, viscount of Maine 1175–1200/1201, numbered among Henry II's closest allies, his loyalty evinced by Henry's gift to Richard of Bourg-le-Roi, a strategically-situated castle Henry built overlooking the primary route between Normandy and Maine.[32] Henry II's largesse included the arrangement of profitable marriages for the viscount's daughters, Constance and Ermengarde.[33] The more high-profile of these transpired in 1186 between Ermengarde de Beaumont and William I, the Lion, king of Scots. The Beaumont family's most intimate connections to Henry II and Thomas Becket may well have derived from the addition of William of Scotland to the family circle.

The Scottish Connection

William I, king of Scots (reigned 1165–1214), and his ancestors boasted their own dense network of historical ties with the kings of England. In 1100, Henry I of England wed Matilda (also known as Maud, or Edith), sister to a succession of three Scottish kings, Edgar (reigned 1097–1107), Alexander I (reigned 1107–24) and David I (reigned 1124–53); the second of these, Alexander, married one of Henry I's illegitimate daughters, Sybilla. King David I knighted the future Henry II, and he, in turn, knighted the future king of Scots, Malcolm IV (reigned 1153–65), and, in 1158/59, his younger brother, William the Lion. Malcolm and William attended Henry II's court at Woodstock in 1163, an event at which the recently consecrated archbishop of Canterbury, Thomas Becket, was also present, and King Malcolm IV intervened the following year in an attempt to facilitate a reconciliation between Henry and his estranged prelate.[34] Upon his accession to the Scottish throne in 1165, William was often in Henry II's company. He purportedly took part in Henry's

witnessed Henry II's charter for the *Hôpital d'Angers*. Richard's brother Raoul was elected bishop of Angers in 1177: Angot, *Généalogies féodales mayennaises*, 81–2.

31 Duggan, *Thomas Becket*, 18; Nilgen, 191–3.
32 Power, *Norman Frontier*, 341, 397, 402. King Richard I later renewed this gift.
33 Viscount Richard's daughter Constance married Roger IV, lord of Tosny and Conches as well as extensive holdings in England, an old Norman family with ties dating back to William the Conqueror (from whom its English holdings derived). This marital alliance thus brought together two families situated at strategic points of Normandy's southern and eastern borders. See Power, *Norman Frontier*, 487. An intriguing manifestation of this familial alliance appears in the John the Baptist window adjacent to that of Thomas Becket. See below at nn. 101–104.
34 On the life of William the Lion, see A. A. M. Duncan, *The Kingship of the Scots, 842–1292* (Edinburgh, 2002), 98–126; D. D. R. Owen, *William the Lion, 1143–1214: Kingship and Culture* (East Linton, 1997). On Malcolm's efforts to negotiate between Henry II and Thomas Becket, see Duncan, *Kingship of the Scots*, 74; *Regesta Regum Scottorum I: The Acts of Malcolm IV King of Scots, 1153–1165*, ed. G. W. S. Barrow (Edinburgh, 1960), 21, 287 (no. 313).

1166 suppression of a rebellion in Maine and may have accompanied Henry and Eleanor of Aquitaine to Angers, where the king and queen spent Easter, during which Henry met with some of Thomas Becket's clerks. William Marshal's thirteenth-century biographer noted that King William distinguished himself at a tourney held at Valennes, near Le Mans, the same year.[35] William the Lion and his younger brother David, later earl of Huntingdon, appeared at a council convened by Henry II in April 1170 at Windsor, and in May of that year, David, like his brothers before him, was knighted by Henry. The following month Henry II had his son, Henry, crowned king by the archbishop of York, in direct defiance of the prerogative of Canterbury. William of Scotland and his brother attended young King Henry's coronation, and both pledged their allegiance to the Young King the following day.[36] The singular inclusion at Angers of a panel depicting Henry's coronation may reference the attendance of King William at that significant event and (or) his subsequent act of homage to the Young King [Fig. 9.5].[37]

William's hitherto loyal service to Henry II faltered grievously in 1174 when he joined the Young King's rebellion against his father, enticed by the junior Plantagenet's promise to restore to him the lands of Northumberland, once held by the kings of Scots but long under Henry II's control. In response to this broad-based rebellion, Henry II called upon his murdered – now canonised – archbishop, doing penance at Becket's tomb and beseeching the saint to preserve his reign.[38] According to the chronicler Jordan Fantosme, Henry II's forces defeated William's army and took the Scottish king prisoner on the same day as the Angevin king's penitential performance at Canterbury. William was transported across the Channel and imprisoned first at Caen, then at Falaise. There, in December 1174, he submitted to the humiliating terms of the Treaty of Falaise, which stipulated that he pay homage to Henry for Scotland and that, henceforth, the Scottish Church be subject to that of England. Additionally, Henry took possession of five of William's most prominent castles, among them Edinburgh and Stirling, and twenty-one hostages, including his brother David and his constable, Richard of Moreville.[39]

---

35 Owen, *William the Lion*, 35.

36 Owen, *William the Lion*, 42.

37 *Regesta Regum Scottorum II: The Acts of William I King of Scots 1165–1214*, ed. G. W. S. Barrow (Edinburgh, 1971), 4.

38 Knowles, *Thomas Becket*, 153; Barlow, 269–70; *Lives of Thomas Becket*, 217–19; Duggan, *Thomas Becket*, 220–21. Also discussed in the essays by Anne J. Duggan (chapter 2), Michael Staunton (chapter 5), Colette Bowie (chapter 6) and José Manuel Cerda (chapter 7) in this volume.

39 Duncan, *Kingship of the Scots*, 99–102; Owen, *William the Lion*, 44–56. William's constable, Richard de Moreville, was brother to one of Thomas Becket's murderers, Hugh de Moreville. The position of Scottish constable was a hereditary one and had been held by the Moreville family since at least 1150. Discussion of the genealogy of the Morevilles and their connections to the

Thus humbled, William of Scotland thereafter remained Henry II's loyal ally and, by the time Henry II arranged his marriage to Ermengarde de Beaumont, had demonstrated himself sufficiently trustworthy to warrant Henry's return of Edinburgh Castle as part of Ermengarde's dowry. A lavish state affair financed by Henry, held at the royal chapel at Woodstock and attended by English and Scottish upper nobility, the marriage of William and Ermengarde was performed by Archbishop Baldwin of Canterbury on 5 September 1186. In addition to Edinburgh Castle, Ermengarde's dowry comprised land valued at a hundred marks and forty knights' fees.[40] Scholars have suggested that William might well have expected Henry to provide him with a wife of higher station than the daughter of the viscount of Maine.[41] Viewed from another perspective, Henry's choice of Ermengarde might instead speak to the high esteem in which the Plantagenet king held his *Manceau* cousin and ally.

By 1186, King William might himself have attributed Ermengarde's generous dowry and Henry's easing of the onerous terms of the Treaty of Falaise to the benevolent intervention of Thomas Becket. For William had taken seriously the widely-held belief that Henry's appeal to St Thomas at the height of his son's rebellion and his penitential acts before Becket's tomb at Canterbury were responsible for the Plantagenet king's victory in 1174. In 1178, William founded Arbroath Abbey in Thomas Becket's honour, with munificent endowments that he amplified throughout his reign. The first foundation devoted to Becket in Scotland, Arbroath became the country's second richest monastery and a pilgrimage site of major significance, a distinction it held until the Reformation. William's foundation charter states that he established Arbroath 'in honour of God and St Thomas archbishop and martyr' for 'the salvation of my soul and those of my ancestors and successors'.[42] In addition to founding Arbroath Abbey, William made a pilgrimage to Canterbury in the company of Henry II. The Scottish king journeyed to Becket's shrine once again in 1189, where he surely gave thanks to the sainted archbishop for King Richard I's annulment of the Treaty of Falaise in what came to be called the Quitclaim of Canterbury.[43] William appears early on to

Scottish Crown appear in G. W. S. Barrow, *The Anglo-Norman Era in Scottish History* (Oxford, 1980), 70–79. For further discussion of Hugh de Moreville see below at n. 45.

40 K. J. Stringer, *Earl David of Huntingdon, 1152–1219* (Edinburgh, 1985), 36; Owen, *William the Lion*, 72; *Acts of William I King of Scots*, 14.

41 Duncan, *Kingship of the Scots*, 102; Owen, *William the Lion*, 72.

42 *Acts of William I King of Scots*, 250–51 (no. 197); Owen, *William the Lion*, 60.

43 Owen, *William the Lion*, 63. William and Henry travelled to Canterbury together in the summer of 1181, on their return to Britain from Normandy. On the 1189 quitclaim charter, which rescinded all of the punitive terms of the Treaty of Falaise, see Owen, *William the Lion*, 78–9; Duncan, *Kingship of the Scots*, 105 n. 28; M. Penman, 'The Bruce Dynasty, Becket and Scottish Pilgrimage to Canterbury, c. 1178–c. 1404', *Journal of Medieval History*, 32 (2006), 346–70, at 348–50. Penman notes that William's most lavish patronage of Arbroath occurred

have selected Arbroath for his final resting place, where he was duly interred upon his death in 1214.[44]

Devotion and Subversion

The Angers Becket window places particular emphasis on events surrounding the archbishop's death. Although a scene depicting the saint's murder has not survived, it comprised a requisite component of the story and its prior existence is supported by a medieval panel depicting the saint's entombment, or possibly his 1220 *translatio*, since the ritual is overseen by a bishop rather than a monk [Figs 9.3 and 9.5]. The two images devoted to Thomas's murderers would thus have brought the total number of death-related scenes to four out of eight. This narrative elaboration can again be linked with Bishop Guillaume's family history. The devotion to Thomas Becket evinced by Guillaume's brother-in-law, William the Lion, may have derived not only from the king's hope of expiation for his ill-fated rebellion against Henry II, but also from a certain guilt-through-association stemming from the intimate connection between the Scottish monarchy and the family of one of Becket's assassins, Hugh de Moreville. The Morevilles held lands in both England and Scotland, as well as territories in Normandy, from whence the family originally hailed. William's father, David, had bestowed upon Hugh de Moreville (Hugh the assassin's father) the hereditary position of constable, whose primary responsibility involved assembling the king's military forces when the king required them. Richard de Moreville (Hugh the assassin's brother) succeeded to the post of constable in 1162, following the death of their father, and served King William in this capacity until his own death in 1189.[45] Beyond offering another

---

after 1189. The Quitclaim of Canterbury is also discussed in the essay by Anne J. Duggan in this volume (chapter 2).

44 R. L. Mackie *et al.*, *Arbroath Abbey* (Edinburgh, 1982); D. Perry, 'A New Look at Old Arbroath', *Tayside and Fife Archaeological Journal*, 4 (1998), 260–78; R. Fawcett, 'Arbroath Abbey: A Note on its Architecture and Early Conservation History', in *The Declaration of Arbroath: History, Significance, Setting*, ed. G. Barrow (Edinburgh, 2003), 50–85; R. Fawcett, *The Architecture of the Scottish Medieval Church* (New Haven, CT, and London, 2011), 72–9. On the sustained popularity of Arbroath as a pilgrimage site, and the traffic of Scottish pilgrims to Canterbury, see Penman, 'Bruce Dynasty, Becket and Scottish Pilgrimage to Canterbury', 346–70. For exploration of Arbroath's centrality in the political history of Scotland and as a vehicle for the construction of William's monarchy, see K. Stringer, 'Arbroath Abbey in Context, 1178–1320', in *The Declaration of Arbroath: History, Significance, Setting*, ed. G. Barrow (Edinburgh, 2003), 116–41.

45 Vincent, 'Murderers', 223–8. On the longstanding connections between William and the Morevilles, see Barrow, *Anglo-Norman Era*, 70–84. Another of Becket's murderers, Reginald Fitz Urse, witnessed an act of William the Lion early in the latter's reign: Barrow, *Anglo-Norman Era*, 78–9.

contextual rationale for the inclusion of a lancet devoted to Thomas Becket in the Angers choir glazing, King William's intimate connection with one of the archbishop's assailants could account for the window's general emphasis on Thomas's death and the men responsible for his murder. It does little, however, to elucidate the specific depictions those assailants assume, depictions which, by virtue of their compositional parallels to Becket iconography had, by the 1230s, become visual tropes central to the saint's own cult.

From the moment of his death in 1170, Thomas Becket distinguished himself as a prolific healer. His miraculous cures were frequently affected by the consumption or application of water mixed with a drop of the archbishop's blood, which the Canterbury monks had assiduously collected following his murder. Long before his canonisation, the curative powers of 'St Thomas's water' drew hundreds of pilgrims to Canterbury, whose monks quickly wrote up accounts of the archbishop's miraculous healings, the copiousness of which surely facilitated his speedy canonisation.[46] By the time of the translation of Becket's relics to their new shrine in 1220, an expansive verbal and visual discourse had developed around the saint's miraculous water, which accounted for approximately one in five of his preternatural healings. In addition to curing people with water, a substantial number of reports reveal that St Thomas maintained a certain sub-specialty in saving people *from* water. Seafarers delivered from tempests and children rescued from accidental falls into rivers, streams and wells comprise the majority of such miracles.[47] The Canterbury windows showcased the efficacy of the archbishop's wondrous tincture as well as his ability to save victims from drowning.[48] His liturgies shimmered with watery metaphors.[49] Thomas's skill at effecting water rescues was connected not only to his miraculous elixir but also to salient details of his own life. Two key

46 Benedict of Peterborough was the first custodian of Becket's tomb and, in 1171, commenced an account of the miracles that occurred there, as well as miracles attributed to Thomas's water that occurred elsewhere and were reported to Canterbury in letters. Benedict was joined in this task by another Canterbury monk, William, who began his own compilation of miracles in 1172. After Benedict left Canterbury to become abbot of Peterborough, William continued recording miracles on his own. Both authors added to their collections in 1178–79. Benedict's accounts appear in *MTB*, ii, 21–279. William's compilation appears in *MTB*, i, 155–545.
47 *MTB*, i, 354–7; *MTB*, ii, 50–53, 134–5, 188–92.
48 Caviness, *Early Stained Glass of Canterbury Cathedral*, 146–50; Caviness, *Windows of Christ Church*, 195–6, 206.
49 On the liturgies devoted to St Thomas: S. Reames, 'Liturgical Offices for the Cult of St Thomas Becket', in *Medieval Hagiography: An Anthology*, ed. T. [F.] Head (New York, 2000), 561–93; S. Reames, 'Reconstructing and Interpreting a Thirteenth-Century Office for the Translation of Thomas Becket', *Speculum*, 80 (2005), 118–70; K. B. Slocum, '*Optimus Egrorum Medicus Fit Thomas Bonorum*: Images of Saint Thomas as Healer', in *Death, Sickness and Health in Medieval Society and Culture*, ed. S. Ridyard, Sewanee Mediaeval Studies, 10 (Sewanee, TN, 2000), 173–80; Slocum, *Liturgies*; Jordan, 'Water of Thomas Becket', 485–8. See also the discussion of 'The Liturgical Becket' in the essay by Anne J. Duggan in this volume (chapter 2).

events in Becket's biography involved his own crossing of the English Channel. While chancellor, Thomas made this voyage many times. As archbishop, however, Thomas crossed the Channel on only four occasions, once in 1163 to attend Pope Alexander's council at Tours, again in 1164 when he fled England for France, and in returning to Canterbury in 1170 to resume his post as archbishop, an office he held barely a month before his death.[50] These latter voyages assumed prominent positions in the saint's posthumous legacy. They numbered as two of the five events in Becket's life known as 'Thomas Tuesdays' because, together with his birth, flight from Northampton and death, they transpired on the third day of the week.[51] Canterbury Cathedral and Arbroath Abbey commemorated the archbishop's fateful return from exile with a special liturgical office known as the *Regressio* of St Thomas.[52]

Whether because of their significance as *exempla* of the voyage undertaken by many Canterbury pilgrims, as links to Thomas's special skills in protecting people from drowning, shipwrecks and stormy seas, or as a material connection to 'St Thomas's water', these particular Thomas Tuesdays also became canonical elements in Becket iconography. The windows at Sens, Chartres and Coutances [Figs 9.1 and 9.2] all contain scenes of the archbishop crossing the Channel, and Thomas travelling by ship comprised one of the standard types of *ampullae* in which his miraculous water was dispensed [Fig. 9.6]. Thomas appeared also on horseback, for instance at Chartres and in manuscript illumination, a reference both to the overland portion of his flight from England and his return to Canterbury.[53] At Angers, however, these voyaging scenes showcase not the Canterbury saint but rather his aristocratic assassins, who cross the Channel by boat and journey overland on horseback, just as they did in December 1170 [Fig. 9.4].[54] The Angers panels invert this prevalent Becket imagery, proffering scenes that appropriate totemic iconographies of Thomas's life in ambiguous, destabilising, even subversive ways.

The Angers window thus posits an ambivalent account of St Thomas's life and death, one which invokes the martyred archbishop primarily as a vehicle to memorialise – even valorise – the Beaumont family's Scottish and Angevin

---

50 Knowles, *Thomas Becket*, 30–49, 79, 104; Barlow, 84–7, 115–16; Duggan, *Thomas Becket*, 16–32.

51 Duggan, 'Cult', 23 n. 8, 40 n. 105; Slocum, *Liturgies*, 247–53.

52 Duggan, 'Cult', 23 n. 7. Keith Stringer observes that the *Regressio* constituted a rare festival which was celebrated only at Canterbury and Arbroath: Stringer, 'Arbroath Abbey in Context', 116.

53 See above, n. 18, for details of the Sens and Chartres windows. St Thomas appears on horseback in the *The Becket Leaves*: Backhouse and de Hamel, *The Becket Leaves*, fol. 2v. On Becket *ampullae*, see B. Spencer, *Pilgrim Souvenirs and Secular Badges*, Medieval Finds from Excavations in London, 7 (London, 1998), 37–133; B. Spencer, *Salisbury and South Wiltshire Museum. Medieval Catalogue, Part 2: Pilgrim Souvenirs and Secular Badges* (Salisbury, 1990), 16–24.

54 Knowles, *Thomas Becket*, 139–41; Barlow, 235–8; Duggan, *Thomas Becket*, 208–9.

Figure 9.6. St Thomas Becket ship-shaped ampulla, c.1250,
drawing of obverse, Museum of London.

connections. While Bishop Guillaume's elder brother, Raoul, viscount of Maine, ultimately joined forces with Philip Augustus in the French king's quest for control of the Angevin territories, ample evidence exists that Guillaume himself sought to preserve the Beaumont family's venerable connections to its Plantagenet relatives and ancestry long after John's loss of Anjou, Maine and, in 1204, Normandy.[55]

Abbé Angot describes Guillaume as 'toujours sous l'influence anglaise', citing as evidence the bishop's entreaty of his brother not to contest a grant made by Richard I to the abbey of Mélinais lest he disgrace the honour of the Beaumont family name.[56] Guillaume engaged in sustained patronage of both Beaumont and Plantagenet religious sites, while Raoul dutifully served

55 On the internecine battles between John and his nephew Arthur following the death of Richard the Lionheart (1199), and John's escalating conflicts with Philip Augustus leading up to the desertion of Count Robert d'Alençon, Juhel de Mayenne and Viscount Raoul de Beaumont in 1202–1203, see Power, *Norman Frontier*, 432–40; Power, 'End of Angevin Normandy'.
56 Angot, *Généalogies féodales mayennaises*, 41, 91. Angot twice quotes Guillaume's 1209 exhortation to Raoul to honour Richard's bequest, 'si vestram vultis nobilitatem et honorem ab infamia evitare'.

in the military campaigns of Philip Augustus and those of his son, the future Louis VIII.[57] Guillaume proved an impassioned proponent of his episcopal diocese, enhancing his cathedral's collection of relics, financing the rebuilding and decoration of its transept and choir, largely out of his own resources, and advocating for reparations to his cathedral for damages inflicted by the Capetian monarchy during the revolts that plagued the early years of Louis IX's reign.[58]

Postcolonialism and Frontier Studies

Postcolonial theory and frontier studies offer tools beyond historical contextualisation that facilitate interrogation both of the Angers window's equivocal narrative and the ambivalent saintly triumvirate (Thomas, George and Blaise) who grace the lancets of Coutances Cathedral's north transept [Figs 9.1–9.5]. Long employed in the fields of anthropology, literature and modern history,

57 Raoul pledged fealty to Philip in 1210 and led a contingent of men on the side of Philip Augustus in the battle of Bouvines (1214). He swore homage to Philip again in 1216 and exhorted the *chatelains* of his castles to do the same. In 1216, Raoul participated in Louis of France's invasion of England. Philip, for his part, appears to have rewarded Raoul for his loyalty by allowing him to retain control of Bourg-le-Roi, which his father, Richard, held from Henry II and Richard I. The French king subsequently made Raoul lord of La Flèche, which Power notes had been 'a comital castle since the end of the eleventh century': Angot, *Généalogies féodales mayennaises*, 89, 91–3; Power, *Norman Frontier*, 443.

58 Beginning in 1209, Bishop Guillaume funded the building and glazing of Anger Cathedral's transept and choir in addition to providing for the refurbishment of church ornaments, tapestries and liturgical books. In 1230, a substantial quantity of building materials amassed to complete the choir were confiscated by the French crown for the building of a new castle and fortification wall, executed between 1232 and 1240. Following the revolt of several western barons in 1227, Louis IX had turned control of Angers over to Pierre de Dreux, duke of Brittany. Pierre, along with several Poitevin barons, supported Henry III's invasion of France in 1231, at which point Louis IX's forces occupied the city. Louis and his mother, Blanche, thus had excellent reasons for wanting to strengthen the fortifications of Angers, a highly convenient vantage point from which to observe, or intervene in, the machinations of the Poitevin nobility, the English king and the duplicitous Pierre de Dreux. The wall and castle – both fabulously large structures – were demolished under orders of Napoleon between 1809 and 1815. The castle's construction necessitated the destruction of numerous churches, chaplaincies and vineyards, as well as lay and ecclesiastical residences belonging to the cathedral of St-Maurice and other diocesan churches. Guillaume undertook demands for reparations for the buildings destroyed and materials confiscated. His 1232 letter to the French court states that Louis' officers confiscated 'lapides et calcem et multam aliam materiam ad opus fabrice nostre ecclesie preparatem', and estimated the value of these in excess of fifteen hundred pounds: *Layettes du trésor des chartes*, ed. A. Teulet *et al.*, 5 vols (Paris, 1863–1909), ii, 238–9 (no. 2200). Thanks to Guillaume's efforts, the affected individuals and churches received at least a dozen indemnities from the crown, 'pro damnis et deperditis, quae ob clausuram fortalitiae Andegavensis passus est', although at least two of these recipients (the church of St-Aubin and Angers Cathedral) stated that the monies received 'longe insufficiens esset ad predicta dampna congrue restauranda': *Layettes du trésor des chartes*, ii, 238–9 (nos. 2200–2204), 242–3 (nos. 2215–20); *Layettes du trésors des chartes*, iv, 34 (no. 4741), 47 (no. 4792).

postcolonial theory has more recently been engaged by medieval scholars such as Jeffrey Jerome Cohen, Ananya Jahanara Kabir and Deanne Williams, who have demonstrated the applicability of such seminal postcolonial concepts as hybridity, disparate temporality and the existence of heterogeneous, localised discourses to medieval studies. Applications of postcolonial theory in art history have focused on the nineteenth century, although some postcolonial explorations of medieval art have begun to appear.[59] More fully integrated into the theoretical toolbox of medievalists, frontier studies have sought to deconstruct traditional monolithic understandings of the Christian medieval west through exploration of specific geographic areas in which divergent political, military, social and cultural institutions interacted. As Nora Berend has observed, a frontier in the Middle Ages comprised not a linear demarcation in the modern sense of a border, but rather a region or zone – a fluid spatial entity containing comparably fluid institutions and structures which, in turn, enabled and encouraged the construction of multiple loyalties and multivalent identities.[60] Meanwhile, the work of Daniel Power has done much to articulate the complex, often contradictory, dynamics animating the Angevin marches of Normandy. His excavation of religious and charitable donations, marital records and dowries, and traditions of standing surety has illuminated the extent to which the families inhabiting these regions operated according to complex patterns of local loyalties and historical customs within the larger contingencies of Capetian and Plantagenet agency.[61]

The Beaumonts of Maine are a prime example of the dense, often conflicting tapestry of identities and allegiances realised by the aristocratic inhabitants of the Angevin territories in the period encompassing the coalescence and dissolution of the Plantagenet empire in western France.[62] In the span of scarcely

59 J. J. Cohen (ed.), *The Postcolonial Middle Ages* (New York, 2000); A. J. Kabir and D. Williams (eds), *Postcolonial Approaches to the European Middle Ages: Translating Cultures* (Cambridge, 2005). For an informative analysis of postcolonial theory as applied to medieval art, see K. E. Overbey, 'Postcolonial', in *Special Issue: Medieval Art History Today – Critical Terms*, ed. N. Rowe, *Studies in Iconography*, 33 (2012), 145–56. Eva Frojmovic and Catherine Karkov have signalled the centrality of postcolonial interrogations of medieval art in a series of conference sessions, and in their founding of a research network, 'Postcolonising the Medieval Image', at the University of Leeds [http://post-col-med.leeds.ac.uk, accessed 15 January 2015].

60 N. Berend, 'Medievalists and the Notion of the Frontier', *The Medieval History Journal*, 2/1 (1999), 55–72, with extensive bibliography. Seminal early applications of frontier studies to medieval history appear in R. Bartlett and A. Mackay (eds), *Medieval Frontier Societies* (Oxford, 1989).

61 See above at n. 29. Power, 'What did the Frontier of Angevin Normandy Comprise?', 186–91, describes the south and south-west borders between Normandy and Maine as especially fluid.

62 The conundrum of conflicted loyalties that faced the noble families of the Angevin empire during and after John's loss of Normandy and the western territories emerges as a recurrent theme in Daniel Power's studies of this period. See, for example, Power, 'King John and the Norman Aristocracy', 127–33.

three generations, the Beaumonts were transformed from a *Manceau* family of moderate import to intimate, loyal relations of the Plantagenet dynasty. Richard de Beaumont, his brother, Bishop Raoul, and his sons, Raoul and Bishop Guillaume, enjoyed close contact with Henry II, Richard I and John, and could claim the king of Scotland as a brother-in-law.[63] The Beaumont lands expanded from one castle along the Normandy-Maine border to a cluster of castles that protected the primary north-south route between Normandy and the southern Plantagenet domains of Maine and Anjou, together with holdings in Normandy and, via marriage, northern England and Scotland.[64] The family became the viscounts of Maine and boasted two generations of bishops in the diocese that had been a comital holding of Henry II. In far less time than it took for the Beaumonts to rise to prominence, the family endured a dramatic diminution in status concomitant with that of the Angevin territories themselves. The prolonged Plantagenet-Capetian wars decimated the region. Raoul de Beaumont's desertion of King John severed the royal connections upon which the family's prestige rested. Maine and Anjou themselves shifted from central territories of the Plantagenet empire to subjugated colonies at the periphery of Capetian France.[65]

Jeffrey Cohen has observed that geographies transformed by war, occupation and conquest give rise to contiguous cultures which 'in their difference and overlap struggle not simply over space as *patria* and colony, but over time'.[66] The Plantagenet-turned-Capetian territories of western France comprised just such topographically and temporally contested sites. Their conquest by Philip Augustus engendered a cataclysmic reconfiguration, fracturing families, properties, identities and histories. Bishop Guillaume de Beaumont embodied what Cohen has called the 'impossible simultaneity' such political upheaval engenders.[67] An ardent supporter of the Plantagenet monarchy, Guillaume de Beaumont's identity was predicated on a dense matrix of genealogical, cultural, political and spiritual ties. Forced to disavow the very king to whom he owed his episcopal appointment, Guillaume dedicated the rest of his long tenure as

---

63 Angot, *Généalogies féodales mayennaises*, 83–8, records numerous instances of Viscount Richard, his brother, Bishop Raoul, and his son, Raoul, the future viscount, witnessing acts of Henry II, Richard I and John. In one such document Henry II describes Bishop Raoul as 'dilectum cognatum nostrum'.

64 Angot, *Généalogies féodales mayennaises*, 47, describes the string of Beaumont castles, running in a longitudinal orientation north-east to south-west over a distance of seventy kilometres, as 'the most complete system of defence' between Maine and Normandy.

65 For a concise and cogent history of the rise and fall of the Plantagenet continental territories, see J. Gillingham, *The Angevin Empire*, 2nd edn (London and New York, 2001).

66 J. J. Cohen, 'Introduction', in *The Postcolonial Middle Ages*, ed. *idem* (New York, 2000), 1–17, at 2.

67 J. J. Cohen, 'Hybrids, Monsters, Borderlands: The Bodies of Gerald of Wales', in *The Postcolonial Middle Ages*, ed. *idem* (New York, 2000), 85–104, at 85.

bishop to the cathedral and city that had once stood at the epicentre of the Angevin dynasty's hereditary domains but which, by the 1230s, had become a marginalised French backwater.

On the other side of the Channel, however, Guillaume's sister, Ermengarde, and her descendants continued to thrive within the orbit of Plantagenet life. In 1212, Ermengarde took part in a meeting at Durham between her aged husband and King John, during which the two monarchs renewed their mutual allegiance to the other, swore that each would do whatever necessary to secure the inheritance of the other's son to his respective throne, and agreed upon a timetable for the marriage of William and Ermengarde's son, Alexander, to John's daughter, Joan. John knighted Alexander in London later that year. Between 1212 and 1214, Ermengarde and Alexander assumed heightened profiles in Scottish royal administration and, upon William's death in 1214, Alexander assumed the Scottish throne as Alexander II.[68] The genealogical and political bonds between the Beaumonts of Maine and the Plantagenet monarchy endured – via the progeny engendered by Bishop Guillaume's sister and brother-in-law – into the fourteenth century. The vehicle by which Bishop Guillaume might reify the illustrious linkage of the Beaumont and Plantagenet families, and articulate its present and future (if politically and geographically disjointed) continuation, lay in the life of Thomas Becket.

The Practice of Theory

Like most visual narratives, the Angers Thomas Becket window encourages interpretation on multiple levels. As Karine Boulanger has shown, it functions as part of a larger programme devoted to the celebration of bishops, which emerges as an overriding theme throughout the choir glass ensemble. It operates more specifically as part of a visual dialectic on positive and negative episcopal-royal relationships, situated as it is across the choir from the window devoted to St Eloi, who, in contrast to St Thomas, enjoyed the support of his monarch, Clotaire.[69] On a personal level, Guillaume's inclusion of Thomas Becket among the saints of his cathedral choir served to visually link the

---

68 R. D. Oram, *Domination and Lordship: Scotland 1070–1230* (Edinburgh, 2011), 174–5, describes Ermengarde as having 'mediated' the 1212 meeting between William and John. A similar description of Ermengarde's role appears in A. A. M. Duncan, 'John King of England and the Kings of Scots', in *King John: New Interpretations*, ed. S. D. Church (Woodbridge, 1999), 247–71, at 263–5, though with the caveat that Ermengarde's role might have been limited to that of translating between French and Early Scots. In May 1212, Ermengarde presided over a special court comprising the *curia regis* and numerous Scottish bishops: *Acts of William I King of Scots*, 58.

69 Boulanger, 'Les Vitraux du chœur', 200–202; Boulanger, *Les Vitraux de la cathédrale d'Angers*, 390.

bishop with his sister Ermengarde, queen of Scots, and her royal family, whose veneration of St Thomas Ermengarde's husband, William, had established with his foundation of Arbroath Abbey. William's son and heir, Alexander II, continued his father's tradition of benefactions to Arbroath, albeit on a lesser scale, a pattern sustained by Scottish monarchs even after their specific dynastic linkage to William the Lion had come to an end.[70] St Thomas, for his part, repaid the family's devotion by bestowing miraculous cures on numerous Scots, including Robert, a servant of King William's brother, David, earl of Huntingdon.[71]

The Angers window's eccentric collection of scenes, prominent display of Beaumont heraldry and emphasis on Becket's assassins, proffers still another vector in its reconfiguration of the narrative. The window could have served, in part, as an expiatory offering for the role played by Beaumont relations and associates in the saint's death. In addition to Hugh de Moreville, the brother of William the Lion's constable, it is possible that another of Becket's murderers, Reginald Fitz Urse, was, like the Beaumonts of Maine, descended from Henry I and thus a blood relation. A third assassin, William de Tracy, held a baronage in England as well as extensive lands in Maine. Nicholas Vincent has described William as perhaps 'the most remorseful' of St Thomas's assassins, making penitential gifts of his English holdings to Canterbury and founding a leper hospital in Maine at Couesmes-en-Froulay, near Ambrières, the site of his family's estates. William de Tracy and the Beaumonts made donations to some of the same Maine religious establishments and, given their shared status as *Manceau* nobility, would surely have known each other.[72] Hugh, the most 'socially exalted' of the four knights, had been raised in the Scottish court and was intimately associated with the court of Henry II. He witnessed the Constitutions of Clarendon in 1164, as well as many of Henry II's charters in England, Normandy and Anjou. Thus, in addition to his connection to William the Lion, Hugh de Moreville, like William de Tracy, could have had direct contact with the Beaumonts of Maine. Hugh may also have had close ties with Thomas Becket, who addressed him by name during the altercation at Canterbury. Having positioned himself at the door to the cathedral to deny

---

70 Penman, 'Bruce Dynasty, Becket and Scottish Pilgrimage to Canterbury', 354–7. Robert I (Robert Bruce, king of Scots 1306–29) lavishly patronised Arbroath during his reign and was most likely responsible for the impressive early fourteenth-century tomb sculpture of William the Lion excavated from the abbey ruins in 1816: G. S. Gimson, 'Lion Hunt: A Royal Tomb-Effigy at Arbroath Abbey', *Proceedings of the Society of Antiquaries of Scotland*, 125 (1995), 901–16.

71 Stringer, 'Arbroath Abbey in Context', 117; Penman, 'Bruce Dynasty, Becket and Scottish Pilgrimage to Canterbury', 349–50. Penman cites thirteen Scots cured through St Thomas's intervention.

72 Vincent, 'Murderers', 232–8, 242; Angot, *Généalogies féodales mayennaises*, 94. The abbey of St-Pierre de la Couture in Le Mans is among the institutions patronised by both William de Tracy and the Beaumonts.

entrance to the crowd of people attempting to get inside, Hugh was the only knight not to strike the archbishop, although one of his men, Hugh of Horsea, brutally distinguished himself by stamping on the slain archbishop's neck and scattering his brains across the cathedral's paving stones.[73]

While all of these connections exist at some remove from the Angevin bishop and his family, in the Middle Ages, guilt by association, like family honour and memory, could exert a long reach. Although all the archbishop's killers appear to have died c.1173 on pilgrimage to the Holy Land, Nicholas Vincent has traced the penitential foundations dedicated to St Thomas by Hugh de Moreville's brother, Richard, and Reginald Fitz Urse's grandson, William de Courtenay, both of which were patronised by descendants of Richard Brito (the fourth assassin) and Hugh of Horsea.[74] Barlow observed that 'Many of [Henry's] knights … must have felt that they were in some way involved in the tragedy for which four of their members were responsible', and Vincent found that several knights who participated in Henry's 1171–72 Irish campaign subsequently made pilgrimages to Canterbury, perhaps out of a sense of 'shared guilt' that fellow members of the king's military retinue could have committed so heinous an act.[75] If, as Daniel Power has said, 'a nobleman's war was the concern of his whole lineage to the seventh degree', how far might a nobleman's murder of a sainted archbishop reverberate in the consciousness – and conscience – of even distant relatives and associates?[76] This reading posits the Angers window, with its repetition of Beaumont heraldry and emphasis on St Thomas's murderers [Fig. 9.4], as a penitential gesture for the Beaumont family's myriad connections to those responsible for the archbishop's death, an interpretation supported by the survival of several *ampullae* in which Becket's murderers appear comparably foregrounded [Fig. 9.7].[77] At the same time, a window honouring a saint favoured by Angers' new French rulers, whose own patronage of Becket amplified the collective sanctity

73 Vincent, 'Murderers', 226; Knowles, *Thomas Becket*, 148; Barlow, 247; *Lives of Thomas Becket*, 203; Duggan, *Thomas Becket*, 212. Hugh of Horsea's actions are also noted at the beginning of Anne J. Duggan's essay in this volume (chapter 2).
74 Vincent, 'Murderers', 262–3.
75 Barlow, 257; Vincent, 'Murderers', 257.
76 Power, *Norman Frontier*, 226. A telling demonstration of the longevity of guilt by association appears in the Lanercost Chronicle's account of the defeat by Edward I (in 1296) of John Balliol, who had claimed the crown of Scotland following Margaret of Norway's death (in 1290). The chronicler observed that Balliol's July 1296 surrender, 'by divine ordinance … [was] accomplished on the morrow of the translation of St Thomas the Martyr, in retribution for the crime of Hugh de Moreville, from whom that witless creature [Balliol] was descended': *Chronicon de Lanercost MCII–MCCCXLVI*, ed. J. Stevenson, Bannatyne Club, 65, and Maitland Club, 46 (Edinburgh, 1839), 179; quoted in translation in Penman, 'Bruce Dynasty, Becket and Scottish Pilgrimage to Canterbury', 353.
77 Spencer, *Pilgrim Souvenirs*, 37–133; Spencer, *Salisbury and South Wiltshire Museum. Medieval Catalogue, Part 2*, 16–24; Jordan, 'Water of Thomas Becket', 489–95.

Figure 9.7. St Thomas Becket ampulla, c.1200–50, obverse, St Thomas flanked by knights. British Museum, #1921,0216.62.

of the Capetian monarchy by memorialising Louis VII's efforts to defend the archbishop – a point foregrounded in the Sens and Chartres Becket windows – could be construed as a gesture of support on the part of Bishop Guillaume for his region's French conqueror and king.[78]

Such an expiatory and honorific reading, however, appears at odds with the visual evidence of the stained-glass panels themselves [Figs 9.3–9.4]. Nothing ignoble defines these images, quite the opposite. These knights are visually arresting. They impress by their scale, their compositional sophistication

---

78 Louis VII's role in protecting the archbishop is recounted in the third lesson of the rhymed office *Studens livor*, which was widely adopted throughout the Continent to celebrate St Thomas's feast day: 'Louis, the most Christian king of the French, received him [Archbishop Thomas] with the greatest honour when he was driven from Pontigny, and he sustained him most kindly until peace was restored': Slocum, *Liturgies*, 215. St Thomas Becket appears among the martyrs decorating the dado of Louis IX's famous Parisian palace chapel, the Sainte-Chapelle: R. Branner, 'The Painted Medallions in the Sainte-Chapelle', *Transactions of the American Philosophical Society*, ns 58 (1968), 5–41; and E. D. Guerry, 'The Wall Paintings of the Sainte-Chapelle' (unpublished Ph.D. dissertation, University of Cambridge, 2013).

Figure 9.8. Seal of Richard de Beaumont, viscount of Maine, c.1240.

– evident in the frontal, foreshortened rendering of the equestrian knight and his mount – and the attention lavished upon their aristocratic trappings, in particular the minute articulation of their chain mail. The artistic engagement with such noble signifiers resonates with the recurrent inclusion of Beaumont heraldry in the lancet's borders. This pictorial articulation of knightly status extends beyond the Becket lancet to the viscounts of Maine themselves, who, in the second quarter of the thirteenth century, adopted a seal bearing with, on its reverse side, the Beaumont arms and, on the obverse, an equestrian, chain-mailed knight brandishing an outstretched sword [Fig. 9.8].[79] The renderings of Becket's murderers, in other words, evince a visual valorising of aristocratic accoutrements comparable to and contemporary with that of the Beaumont family itself.

A postcolonial reading of the Becket lancet in light of these details proffers something more complex, ambivalent and provocative than a penitential offering: a life of Thomas Becket that engages, manipulates and subverts prevalent Becket iconography in ways that reify – even celebrate – the fierce loyalty of Henry II's knights, the nexus of immediate and extended

79 Hucher, 'Monuments funéraires et sigillographiques des vicomtes de Beaumont au Maine', 357–8, with images.

genealogical and historical ties that bound the Beaumonts of Maine to the Plantagenet dynasty, and the links of family and patronage that, as late as the 1240s, sustained those auspicious connections. All four of Becket's assassins were 'knights conspicuous for their birth' and 'familiar companions to the King'.[80] If, by the 1230s, the Beaumonts of Maine could no longer claim a comparable stature in the eyes of their former or current monarchs, the foregrounding of Henry's knights in the Angers Becket window might at least establish for posterity the family's historic prominence within the constellation of Plantagenet court life.

A modern observer might well question the likelihood, not to mention the efficacy and decorum, of such a shame-turned-fame-by-association strategy to exalt a family's import. However, as Nicholas Vincent observed, 'Links to a king, even to a King who countenanced the murder of an archbishop, were to be prized and cultivated'.[81] That Henry's knights undertook their heinous odyssey as an act of loyalty to their Plantagenet monarch appears clear in their repeated shouts of 'king's men, king's men' before and after Thomas's murder, something Henry himself acknowledged when he said that 'it was certainly "for" him, if not "by" him … that the murder was committed'.[82] Bishop Guillaume's invocation of Becket's murderers could have served to realise his own connections to the king in whose name that murder was committed. Guillaume's invocation of a saint venerated by his French rulers for the purpose of articulating a linkage and loyalty to their English rivals suggests the sort of understated, subversive mimicry that Homi Bhabha has dubbed 'sly civility'. The interpretive lens of postcolonialism thus illuminates the Becket lancet as a subtly transgressive response to the French conquest of Plantagenet territories and its concomitant erasure of Beaumont prominence.[83]

The life of Thomas Becket proffered a narrative scaffold upon which Bishop Guillaume could construct his own family's story of Plantagenet allegiance. Reference to the archbishop's murderers visualised the long shared history of the Beaumonts of Maine with the Plantagenets. Guillaume's inclusion of a St Thomas Becket lancet in his cathedral choir, personalised through the display of Beaumont heraldry, comprised a devotional act paralleling those of his royal Scottish relations. In this sense the Thomas Becket window spoke simultaneously to the past, present and future of Beaumont-Plantagenet

---

80 Vincent, 'Murderers', 214, quoting the descriptions of Gervase of Canterbury and Edward Grim.

81 Vincent, 'Murderers', 215. Vincent emphasises this point in his description of Henry II's arrival in Canterbury to do penance at Becket's tomb in July 1174, where the king 'had forcefully to remind [the Canterbury prior and monks who met him] that he had come as a penitent pilgrim to be scourged; not as an honoured guest to be received in procession'.

82 Vincent, 'Murderers', 243–5, quoting Herbert of Bosham.

83 Cohen, 'Hybrids, Monsters, Borderlands', 86–7; H. K. Bhabha, *The Location of Culture* (London, 1994; repr. 2008), 132–44.

history. By the 1230s, when the Angers choir glazing was underway, both Guillaume's brother-in-law, William the Lion, and his sister, Ermengarde, were long dead. However, Guillaume's nephew, Alexander II, ruled Scotland and had established himself as a close ally of Henry III of England. Alexander II's marriage to Henry's sister, Joan, and Alexander III's marriage to Henry III's daughter, Margaret, established a complex range of family ties. Alexander II honoured his father's memory in his continued patronage of Thomas Becket and Arbroath Abbey, perhaps securing some of the saint's relics for the abbey during his reign.[84] Other Scottish relations sustained the family's veneration of St Thomas. In one of many devotional acts performed by this branch of the Beaumont clan, Alexander II's cousin (a niece of William and Ermengarde) attended the saint's spectacular translation ceremony at Canterbury in July 1220 and, with her husband Lord Robert Bruce, made a grant 'of one Scottish mark per annum in perpetuity for themselves and their heirs to "St Thomas, Martyr"'.[85] Though he didn't attend the translation, Alexander II undertook his own pilgrimage to Canterbury in 1223. His wife, Queen Joan, visited Canterbury in 1237. A third generation of Scottish royal devotion is attested by a letter from the abbot of Arbroath to Canterbury Cathedral documenting the abbey's annual payment of monies to Canterbury 'to enable the latter to feed thirteen poor people every Tuesday on behalf of King Alexander III in honour of St Thomas'.[86]

Coutances Revisited

The Thomas Becket lancet at Coutances, with its equivocal depiction of Henry II conversing with his archbishop and its deployment within a larger ensemble of saints favoured in England and the former Angevin empire, also encourages a postcolonial reading [Figs 9.1–9.2]. I have already discussed the dense tapestry of contextual connections that might account for the inclusion of a Becket window in this Norman cathedral, but I do not think that is necessarily the end of the story.[87] Coutances Cathedral embodied an illustrious

84 Stringer, 'Arbroath Abbey in Context', 125; Penman, 'Bruce Dynasty, Becket and Scottish Pilgrimage to Canterbury', 356 n. 54.
85 Penman, 'Bruce Dynasty, Becket and Scottish Pilgrimage to Canterbury', 351. Might this event be referenced in the scene traditionally identified as the archbishop's entombment [Fig. 9.5], but which is anachronistically depicted at Angers being presided over by a bishop (Stephen Langton)?
86 Stringer, 'Arbroath Abbey in Context', 121; G. W. S. Barrow, 'A Scottish Collection at Canterbury', *Scottish Historical Review*, 31 (1952), 16–28. Barrow traces a continuous connection between Canterbury and the Scottish royal line from the early twelfth century until the reign of Alexander III.
87 The Coutances Becket window is discussed above beginning at n. 11.

history. The Romanesque cathedral was consecrated in 1056 by Archbishop Maurilius of Rouen in the presence of William, duke of Normandy, the future William the Conqueror, and survived intact into the early thirteenth century, despite having been set ablaze by Philip Augustus in 1194. Its reconstruction as a gothic edifice – described as the finest in Normandy – occurred primarily under the auspices of its bishop, Hugh de Morville (1208–38), with substantial financing from the same king responsible for its earlier vandalism. Thus, soon after Philip's conquest of Normandy, he sought to ameliorate ecclesiastical–monarchic relations in this Cotentin diocese through a lavish monetary gift to rebuild its cathedral. Bishop Hugh de Morville oversaw construction of the nave, choir and transepts.[88]

Scholars have long debated the potential familial connections between Hugh de Morville, bishop of Coutances, and the infamous Hugh de Moreville, who numbered among Archbishop Thomas's assassins. Nicholas Vincent, whose assiduous research on Becket's murderers comprises by far the most thorough genealogical analysis, has traced two Moreville lines deriving from a common Norman ancestry. Vincent characterised the two branches as 'closely related', noting that, prior to Henry II's 1174 confiscation of Hugh-the-murderer's properties, the Morville/Moreville clans held the adjacent Cumberland baronies of Burgh by Sands and Appleby.[89] Bishop Hugh de Morville's connection to Hugh, Becket's assassin, is sometimes cited in the Coutances literature to account for the inclusion of a Becket lancet in the cathedral's north transept.[90] And, as I have argued for Angers, Becket's vitreous presence at Coutances could certainly be explained as an expiatory gesture on the part of Bishop Hugh for the sins of his distant ancestor. Three of the Becket window's six surviving panels at Coutances include scenes related to the saint's death [Fig. 9.1]. And while these commonplace episodes of the

---

88   L. Grant, *Architecture and Society in Normandy, 1120–1270* (New Haven, CT, and London, 2005), 168–79.

89   Vincent, 'Murderers', 224–5. Many sources (although not Vincent) distinguish the Scottish/English Morevilles from the Norman Morvilles by including an 'e' in the middle of the former's names. While far from consistent in the scholarship, I have adopted that practice here to help distinguish discussions of Hugh de Moreville, Becket's murderer, from Hugh de Morville, bishop of Coutances.

90   The genealogy of Bishop Hugh de Morville established by René Toustain de Billy in his *Histoire ecclésiastique du diocèse de Coutances*, 3 vols (Rouen, 1874–86), i, 311, identified him as a descendent of Hugh de Moreville, Becket's assassin, providing an expiatory motive for Bishop Hugh's inclusion of a window and altar dedicated to the archbishop in his new transept, as Pigeon, *Histoire de la cathédrale de Coutances*, 184–5, suggested. Lafond, 'Les Vitraux', 46, who follows Pigeon in mistakenly identifying Becket's murderer as 'Simon de Morville', described the purported genealogical connection between the archbishop's assassin and Bishop Hugh as 'aujourd'hui abandonnée'. Fournée, 'Les Vitraux de la cathédrale', 93, considered the genealogical connection 'contestée'. Grant, *Architecture and Society in Normandy*, 171, described the bishop of Coutances as 'probably distantly related' to Hugh, Becket's murderer.

archbishop's murder, entombment and apotheosis do not share the Angers window's peculiar emphasis on Thomas's murderers, their general emphasis on Thomas's death is consistent with a penitential donation.

A postcolonial reading might look more broadly to Bishop Hugh's Anglo-Norman heritage and to the larger iconographic context in which the Coutances Becket lancet appears. Archbishop Thomas shares company with St George and St Blaise. Veneration of George in regions of what became the Angevin empire dated to the sixth century. Gregory of Tours records the presence of George's relics in Limoges and Le Mans (the birthplace of Henry II) and notes the especial powers manifested by the saint's relics at this latter site, where 'the blind, the lame, those with chills, and other ill people are often … rewarded with the favour of health'.[91] Nineteenth- and twentieth-century historians attribute the Cotentin cult of St George to the miraculous arrival of his relics in 747 on the coast of Portbail (near Cherbourg) and their equally miraculous journey to the town of Brix, where a church was built in his honour.[92] St Blaise's particular identification with Plantagenet England derived from the tortures he endured, one of which involved the tearing of his flesh from his body with iron combs. The perceived similarity of the iron combs to those used by wool-makers made Blaise a subject of veneration among those who worked in that trade. A primary source of the nation's wealth, the medieval English wool industry also occasioned the augmentation of Blaise's cult, as evidenced in the 1222 declaration of his feast day as a public holiday.[93] Thomas Becket's significance for England requires no elaboration. Beyond their common import, in current and former regions of Plantagenet rule, this saintly triumvirate shared other similarities: Blaise and Thomas were both episcopal martyrs; all three saints were ultimately beheaded; and all three were credited with miracles and (or) miraculous healings involving water.

I have found no pattern of sustained Plantagenet loyalty on the part of Bishop Hugh comparable to that of Bishop Guillaume. It is, however, not implausible that Bishop Hugh, a member of a Norman family of high rank, elected as bishop of a Norman see whose cathedral had sustained damage at

91 Gregory of Tours, *Glory of the Martyrs*, trans. R. Van Dam (Liverpool, 1988), 123–4.
92 *Gesta Abbatum Fontanellensium*, ed. S. Loewenfeld, MGH SS rerum Germanicarum 28 (Hannover, 1886), 40–42; A. Lecanu, *Histoire des évêques de Coutances depuis la fondation de l'évêché jusqu'à nos jours* (Coutances, 1839), 75–7; Fournée, 'Les Vitraux de la cathédrale', 94. On the cult of St George in England, see H. Summerson, 'George (d. c. 303?)', *ODNB* (Oxford, 2004; online edn, 2010) [http://www.oxforddnb.com/view/article/60304, accessed 19 December 2015]. Summerson persuasively critiques the association of Richard I with the cult of St George. I am grateful to Paul Webster for bringing this source to my attention.
93 B. Williams, 'St Blaise's Well, Bromley, Kent', *Source: The Holy Wells Journal*, 6 (1998) [http://people.bath.ac.uk/liskmj/living-spring/sourcearchive/ns6/ns6bw1.htm, accessed 16 January 2015]; J. P. Kirsch, 'St Blaise', in *The Catholic Encyclopaedia* [http://www.newadvent.org/cathen/02592a.htm, accessed 16 January 2015].

the hands of the French king in a territory that king subsequently conquered, might have entertained some lingering fealty to his former Plantagenet monarchs.[94] In his important study of Anglo-Norman history between 1204 and 1240, Daniel Power persuasively demonstrates that, if modern scholars have accepted 1204 as the clear temporal demarcation of Normandy's fall to France, its significance as a definitive marker in the minds of the Plantagenet kings and the region's inhabitants is far less apparent. Decades following the loss of Normandy, John and his son Henry III can be found offering their English subjects gifts of Norman lands and the restitution of hereditary properties confiscated by Philip Augustus, in exchange for their support.[95] And, despite the fact that both Philip and John ordered the confiscation of English or continental holdings depending upon which monarch a family's titular head had decided to pledge their allegiance to, in actuality, many families sought, and found, ways to retain control of lands on both sides of the Channel in the hope that the former Angevin territories would one day be reunited. Henry III urged the inhabitants of Normandy to renew their fealty to England following Philip's death in 1223. The untimely death of Philip's heir, Louis VIII, in 1226, which left France under the rule of a child-king and a female, foreign-born regent (Blanche of Castile), offered another promising opportunity for Plantagenet reconquest. Indeed, numerous western rebellions transpired between 1224 and 1227, culminating in Henry III's expedition to the Continent in 1230. Henry III hoped particularly for the secession of the dioceses of Coutances and Avranches so as to provide a corridor by which he could penetrate the southern domains of Maine, Anjou, Poitou and Touraine, a hope at least partially realised by a 1230 Cotentin uprising orchestrated by Henry himself.[96]

Though clear in light of history, the futility of these events to effect the reunification of former Plantagenet domains with England could not have been evident to those Angevin supporters living through them. In such times, might a bishop descended from an old Norman family long loyal to the kings of England perhaps take the opportunity to erect a visual paean to his former monarchs in the guise of a luminous glazing campaign showcasing three holy figures of particular Angevin import? George and Blaise, like Thomas, were, of course, popular saints on both sides of the Channel. As at Angers,

94 D. Power, 'The Norman Church and the Angevin and Capetian Kings', *JEH*, 56 (2005), 205–34, effectively challenges the 'historiographical tradition', due in part to the murder of Thomas Becket, 'that not only depicts the Plantagenet dukes as oppressors of the Norman Church, but also suggests that they alienated the higher clergy to the point where they preferred to be ruled by Philip Augustus'. Power argues that most Norman Church support was, in fact, local, and that there is minimal evidence that the Norman Church would have found Capetian rule preferable to that of the Plantagenets.

95 Power, '"Terra regis Anglie et terra Normannorum"', 193–4.

96 Power, '"Terra regis Anglie et terra Normannorum"', 189–99.

Becket's inclusion at Coutances could be seen as a nod toward the central role Louis VII played in securing the archbishop's protection, a gesture certainly appropriate for a Norman bishop looking to secure the continued favour of his French overlord. And, as at Angers, a postcolonial lens can illuminate these windows as a manifestation of 'sly civility', a subtly subversive act of mimicry, in which Bishop Hugh invoked a saint favoured by his French conquerors for the express purpose of destabilising their conquest.[97] Like Bishop Guillaume, Bishop Hugh was obliged to renounce his Plantagenet allegiance and swear fealty to his new French monarch. That Hugh employed Capetian largesse to construct a splendid new transept celebrating three saintly icons of Anglo-Norman devotion expands the interpretive field of both the bishop's motivations and allegiances and the role of Thomas Becket in their articulation.[98]

Conclusion

The myriad conditions and events that sustained hopes of reunification would surely not have been lost on Guillaume de Beaumont. Indeed, Guillaume seemed to articulate just such aspirations following Philip's death, when he swore allegiance to Louis VIII 'sous la réserve que si le comté d'Anjou était séparé de la couronne, il ne serait pas tenu de faire ce serment au comte'.[99] Bishop Guillaume numbered among those who had managed to retain possession of lands on both sides of the Channel long after 1204, selling his English properties to the bishop of Winchester, Peter des Roches, only in 1233.[100] Daniel Power has employed the extended Beaumont family as a case study of the myriad connections that fuelled such aspirations on both sides of the Channel. In 1175, Bishop Guillaume's sister, Constance, wed the powerful lord Roger de Tosny, whose extensive properties included four castles

97 See above, n. 83. The subtlety of Hugh and Guillaume's gestures is attested by the number of scholars who have interpreted Thomas Becket windows donated by these bishops as comparable to those of Sens and Chartres in their condemnation of Henry II: Brisac, 'Thomas Becket dans le vitrail français', 230–31; Boulanger, 'Les Vitraux du chœur', 200; Boulanger, Les Vitraux de la cathédrale d'Angers, 119, 122–3, 160, 401–2; Chaussé, Les Verrières de la cathédrale Notre-Dame de Coutances, 18.
98 Overbey, 'Postcolonial', 153, underscores the ability of postcolonial analyses to reveal 'more possibilities, more heterogeneity, and a medieval viewer whose subjectivity is not solely or wholly determined by his religious identity'.
99 Angot, Généalogies féodales mayennaises, 95. I have wondered if Viscount Raoul's renewal, the same year, of a gift to La Flèche by Richard I might have stemmed from a like motivation: Angot, Généalogies féodales mayennaises, 95.
100 Power, '"Terra regis Anglie et terra Normannorum"', 202 n. 65. I suspect Guillaume's long-delayed sale of his English properties at this time was prompted by the need for additional revenue to continue construction of Angers Cathedral and to replace the building materials confiscated by Louis IX. See above, n. 58.

in Normandy and vast territories in England, to which the Tosnys relocated after Philip Augustus confiscated the family's Norman holdings. Constance, however, remained in contact with her brothers, Raoul and Guillaume, and, after the death of her husband in 1208/1209, returned to Maine, where she lived until her own death in 1234. Again resident in her birthplace, Constance sustained communication with her English and Scottish relations on the other side of the Channel. Power observes that until her death Constance styled herself 'dame de Conches', despite Philip's confiscation of her husband's ancestral lands thirty years earlier.[101]

The contacts between the Beaumonts of Maine and their English and Scottish relations continued into the next generation. Roger and Constance de Tosny's daughter, Marguerite, married Malcolm I, earl of Fife, a venerable Scottish family long numbered among the closest allies of the Scottish kings, a match surely enhanced by Marguerite's status as queen Ermengarde's niece.[102] In 1235, Raoul, viscount of Maine, gifted Marguerite a parcel of land near the Beaumont ancestral chateau of Ste-Suzanne where, the following year, Marguerite established a Carthusian priory in memory of her mother, Constance, the sister of Raoul and Bishop Guillaume.[103] Throughout her life, Marguerite also made donations to Angers Cathedral, whilst her brother, Richard, served as treasurer there during his uncle Guillaume's tenure as bishop. Yet another thread, this one visual, can be added to Daniel Power's meticulous tracking of this dense web of cross-Channel familial connections. The lancet adjacent to that of Thomas Becket in the Angers Cathedral choir contains a life of John the Baptist, its borders embellished with the Tosny arms (*argent, à maunch, gules*). Karine Boulanger's conclusion that the appearance of the Tosny heraldry, repeated multiple times in the lancet's borders, signalled a donation by Anger's treasurer and Guillaume's nephew, Richard, is logical.[104] Angers Cathedral's possession of a relic of John the Baptist provides a straight-forward explanation for the saint's inclusion in the glazing programme.

The placement of these lancets side-by-side and their shared heraldic proclamation of Beaumont-Tosny ancestry, however, suggests a further associa-tional register. Like Becket, John the Baptist was linked with acts of healing

101 Power, '"Terra regis Anglie et terra Normannorum"', 200.
102 Power, '"Terra regis Anglie et terra Normannorum"', 200–202; B. A. McAndrew, *Scotland's Historic Heraldry* (Woodbridge, 2006), 37–8. The centrality of the Fife dynasty in Scottish royal politics is evinced by the inclusion of the family arms adjacent to those of the Scottish king on a seal believed to have been used during the reign of Alexander III. The earl of Fife is one of two figures flanking the seated king at his coronation: Gimson, 'Lion Hunt', 913.
103 As Constance had done with her own donations, Marguerite's gift in memory of her mother, and related acts witnessing Marguerite's donation, consistently identify Constance as 'dame de Conches': Angot, *Généalogies féodales mayennaises*, 97–9.
104 Boulanger, 'Les Vitraux du chœur', 199; Boulanger, *Les Vitraux de la cathédrale d'Angers*, 36–7, 122.

involving water. Simon de Tosny, a former monk at the Scottish monastery of Melrose and later bishop of Moray, had effected a miraculous cure employing the water of St Thomas. Arbroath Abbey was built on the site of a local chapel dedicated to St John the Baptist, and the abbey's foundation charter established four annual fairs, two of which occurred on the feast days of Thomas Becket and John the Baptist respectively. John the Baptist was the patron saint of a hospital added to Arbroath Abbey, in addition to being the patron saint of the nearby town of Perth (known during the Middle Ages as St John's Town), which was given the status of a royal burgh by William I because of its proximity to Scone Castle, site of the Scottish kings' coronation.[105] The aligned lancets devoted to St Thomas and St John the Baptist, then, proffered a visual compendium of interconnected histories, a tribute to two powerful families related by blood, one of which had severed its ties to the Plantagenet monarchy to retain its ancestral properties, the other of which had sustained its ancestral allegiance at the cost of its ancestral lands. Thirty-five years after each had fallen victim to the vagaries of King John and the tactical acumen of King Philip, the bonds of family, history and memory resonated in a resounding hagiographic and heraldic display from Bishop Guillaume's choir windows.[106]

Prior scholarship has described the four French Becket windows as uniformly emphasising Thomas's sojourn in France and commemorating Louis VII's role as the protector of the exiled prelate. Scrutiny of the narrative crafting specific to each window, however, reveals a phenomenon less clear-cut. A martyred defender of Church rights, Thomas Becket was also a figure of recent history, a Norman who, in life, had enjoyed the favour of his Plantagenet king and, in death, was credited with securing that king's victory over his enemies. The saint's import to the monarchies of both England and France facilitated his invocation in both countries, even for the purpose of garnering his help in one to advance the aspirations of the other. Evidence exists that St Thomas's intervention was sought on at least one occasion in support of a political uprising.[107] In those parts of the former Plantagenet empire that Capetians viewed as

105 Perry, 'A New Look at Old Arbroath', 269–70; Penman, 'Bruce Dynasty, Becket and Scottish Pilgrimage to Canterbury', 356, 360.
106 Power, *Norman Frontier*, 226–7, observes that: 'Memories within a lineage could be long, particularly where claims to land were concerned … and … could be perpetuated and proclaimed publicly through heraldry'. While the Beaumont arms appear four times in the Becket window, the Tosny arms appear no fewer than nine times in that of John the Baptist. Boulanger, *Les Vitraux de la cathédrale d'Angers*, 40, figs 269–70, identifies and accounts for the addition of Chaumont family heraldry (repeated five times) in the John the Baptist window as evidence that the Chaumonts financed an early fourteenth-century restoration of the lancet. Might the Chaumonts, a Norman family with hereditary connections to both the Beaumonts and the Tosnys, have perceived the particular import of these windows to their Anglo-Norman ancestors?
107 Duggan, 'Cult', 32, details the 'surprising' association of Becket patronage with baronial conspiracy evinced in a hymn to the saint '[invoking] his aid for the earl of Leicester and the Young King in his 1173–74 rebellion against Henry II'.

conquered French territories but which many of their inhabitants perceived as estranged Angevin lands awaiting reunification, the martyred archbishop of Canterbury may himself have comprised what postcolonialism calls a 'resistant site'.[108] Between Church and State, and between the realms of England and France, the life of Thomas Becket composed a capacious discursive field, across which many stories might be told.

108 Cohen, 'Introduction', 12; bell hooks (G. Watkins), 'Marginality as a Site of Resistance', in *Out There: Marginalization and Contemporary Cultures*, ed. R. Ferguson *et al.* (Cambridge, MA, 1990), 341–3. A resistant site can find its origin in a subject, object or place, but in postcolonial discourse is more accurately understood as a concept or space 'where authority is deformed and subverted'. In his own inherent hybridity – chancellor and archbishop, worldly warrior, shrewd politician, saintly martyr, Norman and English, or English and French, depending on one's perspective – Thomas Becket offers a space, or site, within which heterogeneous, even contradictory, identities and loyalties might find articulation. A possible early manifestation of Thomas Becket's invocation as resistant site – and a source of connection between the inhabitants of Angers and their Angevin monarch – may be found in the many donations made to the *Hôpital St-Jean* in Angers (founded and enlarged by Henry II) in the years immediately following the fall of Anjou and Maine in 1204: Angot, *Généalogies féodales mayennaises*, 82, 89–90, 94. The concept of Thomas Becket as a resistant site is the topic of my current research, provisionally entitled 'Remembering Thomas Becket in Normandy'.

Bibliography

Manuscript Sources

Baltimore	The Walters Art Museum	MS W. 10
Budapest	Biblioteca nazionale Széchényi	MS Nyelvemlékek 1
Cambridge	Fitzwilliam Museum	MS 369
Cambridge	Trinity College	MS R.17.1
Canterbury	Cathedral Library	Addit. MS 6 Chartae Antiquae B337 Chartae Antiquae F132 MS Lit. E. 42 MS Lit. E. 42A
Clermont-Ferrand	Bibliothèque Municipale	MS 148
Dijon	Bibliothèque Municipale	MS 574 MS 646
Douai	Bibliothèque Municipale	MS 838
Edinburgh	University Library	MS 123
Évreux	Bibliothèque de la Ville	MS Lat. 10
Heiligenkreuz	Stiftsbibliothek	Cod. 209
Laon	Bibliothèque municipale	MS 471
León	Colegiata de San Isidoro	Inventario de Bienes Muebles, Object nos: 11C-3-089-002-0024; 11C-3-089-002-0025
London	British Library	MS Addit. 37517 MS Addit. 38112 MS Addit. 39759 MS Addit. 40146 MS Addit. 42130 MS Addit. 46203

London (cont.)	British Library (cont.)	MS Addit. 57531
		MS Arundel 155
		MS Cotton Claudius A. iii
		MS Cotton Galba E. iv
		MS Cotton Nero C. vii
		MS Cotton Tiberius A. ii
		MS Cotton Tiberius A. iii
		MS Cotton Tiberius B. iii
		MS Egerton 2818 (formerly Phillipps 10227)
		MS Harley 315
		MS Harley 624
		MS Lansdowne 381
		MS Royal 2 B vii
		MS Royal 10 A. xiii
	The National Archives	E. 329/428
Maidstone	Kent County Archives Office	S/Rm Fae. 2
Nürnberg	Stadtbibliothek	MS Solgr 4.4°
Oxford	Bodleian Library	MS Bodl. 509
		MS Add. C 260
Paris	Archives Nationales (AN)	*K23 15 22
		S4889B
	Bibliothèque de l'Arsenal	MS 938
	Bibliothèque Nationale	MS Lat. 2098
		MS Lat. 5347
	Bibliothèque Sainte-Geneviève	MS cc.1 in quarto 19 (cat. 1370)
Montpellier	Bibliothèque interuniversitaire, section médicine (formerly École de Médicine)	cod. 2
Reims	Bibliothèque Municipale	MS 502
Rouen	Archives départementales de Seine-Maritime (ADSM)	9H1275
		25HP (archive of Mont-aux-Malades)
	Bibliothèque Municipale	MS U. 24 (cat. 1042)
Toledo	Cathedral Archives of Toledo	AC Toledo, A-2-G-1–5

Vatican City	Biblioteca Apostolica Vaticana	Cod. Sancti Petri in Vaticano, A 7
		Cod. Sancti Petri in Vaticano, C 107
		Cod. Vat. Lat. 1276
Wolfenbüttel	Herzog August Bibliothek	Cod. Guelf. 105, noviss. 2

Printed Primary Sources

Acta Stephani Langton, Cantuariensis Archiepiscopi, A.D. 1207–1228, ed. K. Major, Canterbury and York Society, 50 (Oxford, 1950)

Analecta Hymnica medii aevi, ed. C. Blume, G. Dreves, and H. M. Bannister, 55 vols (Leipzig, 1886–1922)

Los Anales Toledanos I y II, ed. J. Porres Martin-Cleto (Toledo, 1993)

Ancient Charters, Royal and Private, Prior to A.D. 1200, ed. J. H. Round, PRS 10 (London, 1888)

Anglia Sacra, ed. H. Wharton, 2 vols (London, 1691)

Annales de Burton (A.D. 1004–1263), in *Annales Monastici*, ed. H. R. Luard, RS 36, 5 vols (London, 1864–69), vol. I, 181–500

Annales Monasterii de Waverleia (A.D. 1–1291), in *Annales Monastici*, ed. H. R. Luard, RS 36, 5 vols (London, 1864–69), vol. II, 127–411

Annales Prioratus de Dunstaplia (A.D. 1–1297), in *Annales Monastici*, ed. H. R. Luard, RS 36, 5 vols (London, 1864–69), vol. III, 1–420

Annales Stederburgenses, MGH SS, xvi (Hannover, 1859)

Annals of Stanley, in *Chronicles of the Reigns of Stephen, Henry II and Richard I*, ed. R. Howlett, RS 82, 4 vols (London, 1884–89), vol. II, 501–83

Antiphonarium Nidrosiensis ecclesiae, ed. L. Gjerløw, Libri liturgici provinciae Nidrosiensis mediae aevi, 3 (Oslo, 1979)

Arnold of Lübeck, *Chronica Slavorum*, MGH SS, xiv (Hannover, 1868)

Bede, *The Ecclesiastical History of the English People*, ed. and trans. by B. Colgrave and R. A. B. Mynors, OMT (Oxford, 1969)

Breviarium ad usum insignis ecclesie Eboracensis, ed. S. W. Lawley, Surtees Society, 71 and 75, 2 vols (London, 1880–82)

Breviarium ad usum insignis ecclesiae Sarum, ed. F. Proctor and C. Wordsworth, 3 vols (Cambridge, 1879–86)

Breviarium Eberhardi Cantoris, ed. E. K. Farrenkopf, Liturgie-Wissenschaftliche Quellen und Forschungen, 50–51 (Münster, 1969)

Breviarium Lincopense, ed. K. Peters, Laurentius Peti Sällskapets Urkundsserie (Lund, 1951)

Calendar of the Liberate Rolls Preserved in the Public Record Office: Henry III. Vol. I. A.D. 1226–1240, ed. W. H. Stevenson, HMSO (London, 1916)

Calendar of the Liberate Rolls Preserved in the Public Record Office: Henry III. Vol. II. A.D. 1240–1245, ed. J. B. W. Chapman, HMSO (London, 1930)

The Canterbury Psalter, with an introduction by M. R. James (London, 1935)

The Canterbury Tales: Fifteenth-Century Continuations and Additions, ed. J. M. Bowers (Kalamazoo, MI, 1992)

Los Cartularios de Toledo: Catálogo documental, ed. F. J. Hernández (Madrid, 1985)

Chartae, Privilegia et Immunitates, Being Transcripts of Charters and Privileges to Cities, Towns, Abbeys, and Other Bodies Corporate: 18 Henry II to 18 Richard II (1171 to 1395), Irish Record Commission (Dublin, 1829–30) [available online at the website of *Circle: A Calendar of Irish Chancery Letters, c. 1244–1509*: http://chancery.tcd.ie/images/cpi/0?page=1, accessed 28 June 2012]

Charters and Custumals of the Abbey of Holy Trinity Caen. Part 2: The French Estates, ed. J. Walmsley (Oxford, 1994)

Chronica de Mailros, e codice unico in bibliotheca Cottoniana servato, ed. J. Stevenson, Bannatyne Club, 49 (Edinburgh, 1835)

Chronica Magistri Rogeri de Hovedene, ed. W. Stubbs, RS 51, 4 vols (London, 1868–71)

The Chronicle of Battle Abbey, ed. and trans. E. Searle, OMT (Oxford, 1980)

The Chronicle of Bury St Edmunds, ed. and trans. A. Gransden, NMT (London, 1964)

The Chronicle of Richard of Devizes of the Time of King Richard I, ed. and trans. J. T. Appleby, NMT (Oxford, 1963)

The Chronicles of Ralph Niger, ed. R. Anstruther, Caxton Society (London, 1851)

Chronicles of the Reigns of Stephen, Henry II, and Richard I, ed. R. Howlett, RS 82, 4 vols (London, 1884–89)

Chronicon de Lanercost MCII–MCCCXLVI, ed. J. Stevenson, Bannatyne Club, 65, and Maitland Club, 46 (Edinburgh, 1839)

Chronicon Magni Presbiteri, ed. W. Wattenbach, MGH SS, xvii

Chronique de la Guerre entre les Anglois et les Ecossais en 1173 et 1174, in *Chronicles of the Reigns of Stephen, Henry II, and Richard I*, ed. R. Howlett, RS 82, 4 vols (London, 1886), vol. III, 202–377

Close Rolls of the Reign of Henry III Preserved in the Public Record Office: A.D. 1237–1242, HMSO (London, 1911)

Continuation of Sigebert of Gembloux, MGH SS, vi

The Correspondence of Sir Thomas More, ed. E. F. Rogers (Princeton, NJ, 1947)

The Correspondence of Thomas Becket, Archbishop of Canterbury 1162–1170, ed. and trans. A. J. Duggan, OMT, 2 vols (Oxford, 2000)

Curia Regis Rolls of the Reign of Henry III Preserved in the Public Record Office: A.D. 1237–1242, HMSO (London, 1979)

Decrees of the Ecumenical Councils, trans. and ed. N. P. Tanner, 2 vols (London, 1990)

Decretales ineditae saeculi XII, ed. and revised S. Chodorow and C. Duggan, Monumenta Iuris Canonici Series B: Corpus Collectionum, 4 (Città del Vaticano, 1982)

The Deeds of Pope Innocent III, by an Anonymous Author, trans. J. M. Powell (Washington D.C., 2004)

Documentación de la Catedral de Burgos (1184–1222), ed. J. M. Garrido (Burgos, 1983)

Documentos de los Archivos Catedralicio y Diocesano de Salamanca (siglos XII y XIII), ed. J. L. Martín *et al.* (Salamanca, 1977)

Dugdale, W., *Monasticon Anglicanum*, rev. edn by J. Caley, H. Ellis and B. Bandinel, 6 vols in 8 (London, 1817–30; repr. 1846)

Eadmer of Canterbury: Lives and Miracles of Sts Oda, Dunstan and Oswald, ed. and trans. A. J. Turner and B. J. Muir, OMT (Oxford, 2006)

Eadmer, *De reliquiis S. Audoenis et quorumdam aliorum sanctorum quae Cantuariae in aecclesia Domini Sancti Saluatoris habentur*, ed. A. Wilmart, *Revue des sciences religieuses* 15 (1935), 184–219, 354–79

Eadmer, *Vita Sancti Anselmi*, ed. R. W. Southern, NMT (London, 1962)

The Early Charters of the Augustinian Canons of Waltham Abbey, Essex, 1062–1230, ed. R. Ransford (Woodbridge, 1989)

The Early South-English Legendary; or, Lives of saints. I. Ms. Laud, 108, in the Bodleian library, ed. C. Horstmann, Early English Text Society, Original Series, 87 (London, 1887)

The Ecclesiastical History of Orderic Vitalis, ed. and trans. M. Chibnall, OMT, 6 vols (Oxford, 1969–80)

Enamels of Limoges, 1100–1350, ed. J. P. O'Neill *et al.*, The Metropolitan Museum of Art (New York, 1996)

English Benedictine Calendars After AD 1100, ed. F. Wormald, Henry Bradshaw Society 77 (London, 1939)

English Episcopal Acta 26: London 1189–1228, ed. D. P. Johnson (Oxford, 2003)

English Episcopal Acta 34: Worcester 1186–1218, ed. M. Cheney, D. Smith, C. Brooke and P. M. Hoskin (Oxford, 2008)

English Kalendars Before 1100, ed. F. Wormald, Henry Bradshaw Society lxxii (London, 1934)

Epistolae Cantuarienses, the Letters of the Prior and Convent of Christ Church, Canterbury, ed. W. Stubbs, *Chronicles and Memorials of the Reign of Richard I*, RS 38, 2 vols (London, 1864–65), vol. II

Das Evangeliar Heinrichs des Löwen. Kommentar zum Faksimile, ed. D. Kötzsche (Frankfurt-am-Main, 1989)

Expugnatio Hibernica. The Conquest of Ireland, ed. A. B. Scott and F. X. Martin (Dublin, 1978)

Fragmenta codicum in bibliothecis Hungariae, i/1: Fragmenta latina codicum in bibliotheca universitatis Budapestensis, i/2: Fragmenta latina codicum in bibliotheca seminarii cleri Hungariae Centralis, ed. L. Mesey (Budapest and Wiesbaden, 1983; repr. Budapest, 1988)

Garnier's Becket, trans. J. Shirley (Felinfach, 1975)

Gerald of Wales, *De Invectionibus*, ed. W. S. Davies, *Y Cymmrodor*, 30 (1920), 1–248

Gervase of Canterbury, *Opera Historica*, ed. W. Stubbs, RS 73, 2 vols (London, 1879–80)

Gesta Abbatum Fontanellensium, ed. S. Loewenfeld, MGH SS rerum Germanicarum 28 (Hannover, 1886)

Giraldi Cambrensis opera, ed. J. S. Brewer *et al.*, RS 21, 8 vols (London, 1861–91)

The Great Roll of the Pipe for the Thirtieth Year of the Reign of King Henry the Second, A.D. 1183–1184, PRS 33 (London, 1912)

The Great Roll of the Pipe for the First Year of the Reign of King John, Michaelmas 1199 (Pipe Roll 45), ed. D. M. Stenton, PRS 48, ns 10 (London, 1933)

Gregory of Tours, *Glory of the Martyrs*, trans. R. Van Dam (Liverpool, 1988)

Guernes de Pont-Sainte-Maxence, *La Vie de S. Thomas le Martyr*, ed. E. Walberg (Paris, 1922)

Herbert of Bosham, *Liber Melorum*, in *Patrologiae cursus completes: series Latina*, ed. J.-P. Migne, 221 vols (Paris, 1841–64), vol. CXC

The Hereford Breviary, ed. W. H. Frere and L. E. G. Brown, 2 vols (London, 1904)

Les Heures de Nuremberg, ed. E. Simmons (Paris, 1994)

Historia Selebiensis Monasterii: The History of the Monastery of Selby, ed. and trans. J. Burton with L. Lockyer, OMT (Oxford, 2013)

History of William Marshal, ed. A Holden, trans. S. Gregory, with historical notes by D. Crouch, Anglo-Norman Text Society, Occasional Publications Series, 4–6, 3 vols (London, 2002–2004)

The Inventories of Christ Church, Canterbury, ed. J. Wickham-Legg and W. H. St John Hope (London, 1902)

Itinerarium Peregrinorum et Gesta Regis Ricardi, ed. W. Stubbs, *Chronicles and Memorials of the Reign of Richard I*, RS 38, 2 vols (London, 1864–65), vol. I, 3–450

Jacobus de Voragine, *The Golden Legend*, trans. W. G. Ryan, 2 vols (Princeton, NJ, 1993)

Jordan Fantosme's Chonicle, ed. and trans. R. C. Johnston (Oxford, 1981)

Lamberti Ardensis historia comitum Ghisensium, ed. J. Heller, in MGH SS, xxiv

'The Lament of Simon de Montfort', ed. T. Wright, *The Political Songs of England, From the Reign of John to that of Edward II*, Camden Society, Old Series, 6 (London, 1839), 125–7

Layettes du trésor des chartes, ed. A. Teulet *et al.*, 5 vols (Paris, 1863–1909)

The Letters and Charters of Gilbert Foliot, Abbot of Gloucester (1139–48), Bishop of Hereford (1148–63) and London (1163–87), ed. A. Morey and C. N. L. Brooke (Cambridge, 1967)

Letters and Papers, Foreign and Domestic, on the Reign of Henry VIII, ed. J. S. Brewer, J. Gairdner, and R. H. Brodie (London, 1862–1910)

The Letters of Arnulf of Lisieux, ed. F. Barlow, Camden Third Series, 61 (London, 1939)

The Letters of John of Salisbury, Volume I: The Early Letters (1153–1161), ed. and trans. W. J. Millor and H. E. Butler, NMT (London, 1955), reissued OMT (Oxford, 1986)

The Letters of John of Salisbury, Volume II: The Later Letters (1163–1180), ed. and trans. W. J. Millor and C. N. L. Brooke, OMT (Oxford, 1979)

The Letters of Peter of Celle, ed. and trans. J. Haseldine, OMT (Oxford, 2001)

The Letters of Pope Innocent III (1198–1216) Concerning England and Wales: A Calendar with an Appendix of Texts, ed. C. R. Cheney and M. G. Cheney (Oxford, 1967)

Liber Albus: The White Book of the City of London, trans. H. T. Riley (London, 1861)

Liber Eliensis, ed. E. O. Blake, Camden Third Series, 92 (London, 1962)

Liber Eliensis: A History of the Isle of Ely from the Seventh Century to the Twelfth, trans. J. Fairweather (Woodbridge, 2005)

Liber Gaufridi Sacristae de Coldingham de statu Ecclesiae Dunhelmensis, ed. J. Raine,

Historiae Dunelmensis Scriptores Tres, Gaufridus de Coldingham, Robertus de Graystanes, et Willelmus de Chambre, Surtees Society, 9 (London, 1839), 3–31

Liber Memoriam Sancti Blasii, MGH SS, xxiv (Hannover, 1879)

Liber S. Thome de Aberbrothoc. Registrum abbacie de Aberbrothoc, ed. C. Innes and P. Chalmers, Bannatyne Club, 86, 2 vols (Edinburgh, 1848–56)

The Lives of Thomas Becket, ed. and trans. M. Staunton (Manchester, 2001)

Magna Vita Sancti Hugonis: The Life of St Hugh of Lincoln, ed. D. L. Douie and H. Farmer, NMT, 2 vols (London, 1961–62)

M. P. Marchegay, 'Chartes de Fontevraud concernant l'Aunis et la Rochelle', *Bibliothèque de l'École des Chartes*, 19 (1857–58), 132–70 and 321–47

Materials for the History of Thomas Becket, Archbishop of Canterbury, ed. J. C. Robertson and J. B. Sheppard, RS 67, 7 vols (London, 1875–85)

'Matthaei Parisiensis, Vita sancti Stephani archiepiscopi Cantuariensis', in *Ungedruckte Anglo-Normannische Geschichtsquellen*, ed. F. Liebermann (Strasbourg, 1879)

Matthew Paris, *Chronica Majora*, ed. H. R. Luard, RS 57, 7 vols (London, 1872–83)

Memorials of St Dunstan, ed. W. Stubbs, RS 63 (London, 1874)

MGH *Diplomata Frederici I*, 5 vols (Hannover, 1975–1990)

The Monastic Breviary of Hyde Abbey, Winchester (Oxford Bodl. Library, MSS Rawlinson liturg. E.1 and Gough liturg. 8), ed. J. B. L. Tolhurst, Henry Bradshaw Society, 69–71 and 76, 4 vols (London, 1932–33 and 1938)

The Monastic Constitutions of Lanfranc, ed. and trans. D. Knowles, 2nd edn, rev. by C. N. L. Brooke, OMT (Oxford, 2002)

Nigellus Wireker, The Passion of St Lawrence. Epigrams and Marginal Poems, ed. and trans. J. M. Ziolkowski (Leiden, 1994)

Norman Charters from English Sources: Antiquaries, Archives and the Rediscovery of the Anglo-Norman Past, ed. N. Vincent, PRS 97, ns 59 (London, 2013)

L'obituaire de la cathédrale d'Angers, ed. C. Urseau, Mémoires de la Société nationale d'agriculture, sciences, et arts d'Angers, 7 (1930)

'The Office of St Thomas of Lancaster', ed. T. Wright, *The Political Songs of England, From the Reign of John to that of Edward II*, Camden Society, Old Series, 6 (London, 1839), 268–72

The Ordinal of the Papal Court from Innocent III to Boniface VIII and Related Documents, ed. S. J. P. Van Dijk, completed by J. H. Walker, Spicilegium Friburgense, 22 (Fribourg, 1975)

Ordo Nidrosiensis ecclesiae, ed. L. Gjerløw, Libri liturgici provinciae Nidrosiensis mediae aevi, 2 (Oslo, 1968)

Papsturkunden für Kirchen im Heiligen Lande, ed. R. Hiestand, Vorarbeiten zum oriens pontificius, 3, Abhandlungen … Göttingen, phil.-hist. Klasse, 3rd Ser., 136 (Göttingen, 1985)

Patrologiae cursus completes: series Latina, ed. J.-P. Migne, 221 vols (Paris, 1841–64)

Petri Blesensis Opera Omnia, ed. J. A. Giles, 4 vols (Oxford, 1846–47)

The Poems of the Troubadour Bertran de Born, ed. W. Paden, T. Sankovitch and P. Stäblein (Berkeley and Los Angeles, CA, and London, 1986)

The Political Songs of England, from the Reign of John to that of Edward II, ed. T. Wright, Camden Society, Old Series, 6 (London, 1839)

Radulfi de Diceto decani Lundoniensis opera historica, ed. W. Stubbs, RS 68, 2 vols (London, 1876)

Radulphi de Coggeshall Chronicon Anglicanum, ed. J. Stevenson, RS 66 (London, 1875)

Recueil des actes des ducs de Normandie (911–1066), ed. M. Fauroux (Caen, 1961)

Recueil des historiens des Gaules et de la France, ed. M. Bouquet *et al.*, new edn, directed by L. Delisle, 19 vols (Paris, 1869–80)

Regesta Regum Scottorum I: The Acts of Malcolm IV King of Scots 1153–1165, ed. G. W. S. Barrow (Edinburgh, 1960)

Regesta Regum Scottorum II: The Acts of William I King of Scots 1165–1214, ed. G. W. S. Barrow (Edinburgh, 1971)

Register of the Abbey of St Thomas, Dublin, ed. J. T. Gilbert, RS 94 (London, 1889)

The Riverside Chaucer, ed. L. D. Benson (based on the edition of F. N. Robinson), 3rd edn (Oxford, 2008)

Robert of Torigni, *Chronica*, in *Chronicles of the Reigns of Stephen, Henry II, and Richard I*, ed. R. Howlett, RS 82, 4 vols (London, 1886) vol. IV, 3–315

Robert of Torigni, *Chronique de Robert de Torigni*, ed. L. Delisle, 2 vols (Rouen, 1872–73)

Roger of Howden, *Chronica Magistri Rogeri de Houedene*, ed. W. Stubbs, RS 51, 4 vols (London, 1868–71)

[Roger of Howden], *Gesta Regis Henrici Secundi Benedicti Abbatis: The Chronicle of the Reigns of Henry II and Richard I, 1169–1192, known commonly under the name of Benedict of Peterborough*, ed. W. Stubbs, RS 49, 2 vols (London, 1867)

Rogeri de Wendover liber qui dicitur Flores Historiarum ab anno domini MCLIV annoque Henrici Anglorum Regis Secundi Primo, ed. H. G. Hewlett, RS 84, 3 vols (London, 1886–89)

Das Rolandslied des Pfaffen Konrad, ed. C. Wesle (Tübingen, 1967)

Rotuli Chartarum in Turri Londinensi asservati, Vol. 1, pt. 1, 1199–1216, ed. T. D. Hardy, Record Commission (London, 1837)

Rotuli de Liberate ac de Misis et Praestitis regnante Johanne, ed. T. D. Hardy, Record Commission (London, 1844)

Rotuli Litterarum Clausarum In Turri Londinensi asservati, Vol. 1, 1204–1224, ed. T. D. Hardy, Record Commission (London, 1833)

Rotuli Normanniae in Turri Londinensi asservati: Johanne et Henrico Quinto, Angliae Regibus. Vol. I. 1200–1205, necnon de anno 1417, ed. T. D. Hardy, Record Commission (London, 1835)

The Sarum Missal, ed. J. Wickham Legg (Oxford, 1916)

Select Charters and Other Illustrations of English Constitutional History, ed. W. Stubbs, 9th edn, rev. by H. W. C. Davis (Oxford, 1921)

Selected Letters of Pope Innocent III Concerning England (1198–1216), ed. and trans. C. R. Cheney and W. H. Semple, NMT (London, 1953)

The Sermons of Thomas Brinton (1373–1389), ed. Sr M. Aquinas Devlin, Camden Third Series, 85–6, 2 vols (London, 1954)

Statuta capitulorum generalium ordinis Cisterciensis ab anno 1116 ad annum 1786. Tomus I. Ab anno 1116 ad annum 1220, ed, J.-M. Canivez (Louvain, 1933)

The Statutes of the United Kingdom of Great Britain and Ireland, 7 & 8 George IV, 1827, ed. G. K. Richards (London, 1827)

Stephen of Rouen, *Draco Normannicus*, in *Chronicles of the Reigns of Stephen, Henry II and Richard I*, ed. R. Howlett, RS 82, 4 vols (London, 1884–89), vol. II, 589–781

Thómas Saga Erkibyskups. A Life of Archbishop Thomas Becket in Icelandic, with English translation, notes and glossary, ed. and trans. E. Magnússon, RS 65, 2 vols (London, 1875–84)

Thomas Wright's Political Songs of England: From the Reign of John to that of Edward II, ed. P. Coss (Cambridge, 1996)

Twelfth-Century Statutes from the Cistercian General Chapter. Latin Text with English Notes and Commentary, ed. C. Waddell, Citeaux, Studia et Documenta, 12 (Brecht, 2002)

Die Urkunden Heinrichs des Löwen, Herzogs von Sachsen und Bayern, ed. K. Jordan, Monumenta Germaniae Historica, Diplomata, 5, Laienfürsten- und Dynastenurkunden der Kaiserzeit, 1 (Leipzig, 1941–49, reprinted 1957–60)

'La Vie de S. Edouard le Confesseur par Osbert de Clare', ed. M. Bloch, *Analecta Bollandiana*, 41 (1923), 5–131

Vita Alberti episcopi Leodiensis, ed. I. Heller, MGH SS, xxv (Berlin, 1880)

Vita S. Elphegi authore Osberno, ed. H. Wharton, *Anglia Sacra*, 2 vols (London, 1691)

Walter of Coventry, *Memoriale*, ed. W. Stubbs, RS 58, 2 vols (London, 1872–73)

Willelmus Tyrensis, *Chronicon*, ed. R. B. C. Huygens, *Corpus Christianorum Continuatio Mediaevalis*, 63A (Turnhout, 1986)

William of Newburgh, *Historia Rerum Anglicanum* in *Chronicles of the Reigns of Stephen, Henry II, and Richard I*, ed. R. Howlett, RS 82, 4 vols (London, 1886), vol. I, 1–408

Secondary Works

Age of Chivalry: Art in Plantagenet England 1200–1400, Royal Academy of Arts Exhibition Catalogue, ed. J. Alexander and P. Binski (London, 1987)

Angot, Abbé A., *Généalogies féodales mayennaises du XIe au XIIIe siècle* (Laval, 1942)

Arnoux M. (ed.), *Des clercs au service de la réforme: études et documents sur les chanoines réguliers de la province de Rouen*, Bibliotheca Victorina, 11 (Turnhout, 2000)

Backhouse, J. and C. de Hamel, *The Becket Leaves* (London, 1988)

Bailey, R., 'St Oswald's Heads', in *Oswald: Northumbrian King to European Saint*, ed. C. Stancliffe and E. Cambridge (Stamford, 1995), 195–209

Baldwin, J. W., *Masters, Princes and Merchants: The Social Views of Peter the Chanter and His Circle*, 2 vols (Princeton, NJ, 1970)

Balfour, D., 'William Longchamp: Upward Mobility and Character Assassination in Twelfth-Century England' (unpublished Ph.D. thesis, University of Connecticut, 1996)

Barber, R., 'Edward, Prince of Wales and of Aquitaine (1330–1376)', *ODNB*

(Oxford, 2004; online edn, 2008) [http://www.oxforddnb.com/view/article/8523, accessed 24 October 2010]

Barlow, F., 'Becket, Thomas (1120?–1170)', *ODNB* (Oxford, 2004) [http://www.oxforddnb.com/view/article/27201, accessed 22 July 2015]

Barlow, F., *Thomas Becket* (London, 1986; repr. London, 2000)

Barrow, G. W. S., *The Anglo-Norman Era in Scottish History* (Oxford, 1980)

Barrow, G. (ed.), *The Declaration of Arbroath: History, Significance, Setting* (Edinburgh, 2003)

Barrow, G. W. S., 'A Scottish Collection at Canterbury', *Scottish Historical Review*, 31 (1952), 16–28

Barth, M., 'Zum Kult des hl. Thomas Becket in deutschen Sprachgebiet, in Skandinavien und Italien', *Freiburger Diözesan-Archiv*, 80 (1960), 97–166

Bartlett, R., *Gerald of Wales: A Voice of the Middle Ages*, 2nd edn (Stroud, 2006)

Bartlett, R. and A. Mackay (eds), *Medieval Frontier Societies* (Oxford, 1989)

Bartlett, R., *Why Can the Dead Do Such Great Things? Saints and Worshippers from the Martyrs to the Reformation* (Princeton, NJ, and Oxford, 2013)

Barton, S., *The Aristocracy in Twelfth-Century León and Castile* (Cambridge, 1997)

Becquet, J., 'Les sanctuaires dédiés à saint Thomas de Cantorbéry en Limousin', in *Sédières*, 159–61

Berend, N., 'Medievalists and the Notion of the Frontier', *The Medieval History Journal*, 2/1 (1999), 55–72

Bertau, K., *Deutsche Literatur im europäischen Mittelalter*, 2 vols (Munich, 1972–73)

Bhabha, H. K., *The Location of Culture* (London, 1994; repr. 2008)

Biggs, S. J., 'Erasing Becket', *British Library Medieval Manuscripts Blog* [http://britishlibrary.typepad.co.uk/digitisedmanuscripts/2011/09/erasing-becket.html, accessed 31 December 2015]

Binski, P., *Becket's Crown: Art and Imagination in Gothic England, 1170–1300* (New Haven, CT, and London, 2004)

Binski, P., *Westminster Abbey and the Plantagenets: Kingship and the Representation of Power, 1200–1400* (New Haven, CT, and London, 1995)

Black's Medical Dictionary, ed. H. Marcovitch, 41st edn (London, 2005)

Blick, S., 'Comparing Pilgrim Souvenirs and Trinity Chapel Windows at Canterbury Cathedral: An Exploration of Context, Copying and the Recovery of Lost Stained Glass', *Mirator* (September, 2001) [http://www.glossa.fi/mirator/index_en.html, accessed 16 July 2016], 1–27

Blick, S., 'Reconstructing the Shrine of St Thomas Becket, Canterbury Cathedral', in *Art and Architecture of Late Medieval English Pilgrimage in Northern Europe and the British Isles*, ed. S. Blick and R. Tekippe, 2 vols (Leiden, 2005)

Bollermann, K. and C. J. Nederman, 'John of Salisbury and Thomas Becket', in *A Companion to John of Salisbury*, ed. C. Grellard and F. Lachaud, Brill's Companions to the Christian Tradition, 57 (Leiden, 2015), 63–104

Borenius, T., 'Addenda to the Iconography of St Thomas of Canterbury', *Archaeologia*, 81 (1931), 19–32

Borenius, T., 'The Iconography of St Thomas of Canterbury', *Archaeologia*, 79 (1929), 29–54

Borenius, T., *St Thomas Becket in Art* (London, 1932, repr. Port Washington, NY, 1970)

Borenius, T., 'Some Further Aspects of the Iconography of St Thomas of Canterbury', *Archaeologia*, 83 (1933), 171–86

Botineau, P., 'Chronique de G. de Breuil, prieur de Vigeois' (unpublished Ph.D. thesis, École des Chartes, 1964)

Boulanger, K., *Les Vitraux de la cathédrale d'Angers*, Corpus Vitrearum: France, Recensement III (Paris, 2010)

Boulanger, K., 'Les Vitraux du chœur de la cathédrale d'Angers: commanditaires et iconographie', in *Anjou: Medieval Art, Architecture, and Archaeology*, ed. J. McNeill and D. Prigent, *British Archaeological Association Conference Transactions*, 26 (2003), 196–209

Boulanger, K., 'Les Vitraux du XIIIe siècle', in *La Cathédrale de Coutances: art et histoire. Actes du colloque organisé au Centre culturel international de Cerisy du 8 au 11 octobre 2009*, ed. F. Laty, P. Bouet and G. Désiré dit Gosset, with photographs by A. Poirier (Bayeux, 2012), 99–105

Bowie, C., *The Daughters of Henry II and Eleanor of Aquitaine* (Turnhout, 2014)

Boyer, J.-F. *et al.*, 'Catalogue des œuvres exposées', in *Valérie et Thomas Becket: De l'influence des princes Plantagenêt dans l'Œuvre de Limoges*, ed. V. Notin *et al.* (Limoges, 1999), 69–131

Branner, R., 'The Painted Medallions in the Sainte-Chapelle', *Transactions of the American Philosophical Society*, ns 58 (1968), 5–41

Brenner, E., 'Charity in Rouen in the Twelfth and Thirteenth Centuries (with special reference to Mont-aux-Malades)' (unpublished Ph.D. thesis, University of Cambridge, 2008)

Brenner, E. and L. V. Hicks, 'The Jews of Rouen in the Eleventh to the Thirteenth Centuries', in *Society and Culture in Medieval Rouen, 911–1300*, ed. L. V. Hicks and E. Brenner, Studies in the Early Middle Ages, 39 (Turnhout, 2013), 369–82

Brenner, E., *Leprosy and Charity in Medieval Rouen* (Woodbridge, 2015)

Brisac, C., 'Thomas Becket dans le vitrail français au début du XIIIe siècle', in *Sédières*, 221–31

Brooks, N., 'The Anglo-Saxon Cathedral Community, 597–1070', in *A History of Canterbury Cathedral*, ed. P. Collinson, N. Ramsay and M. Sparks (Oxford, 1995), 1–37

Buc, P., *L'ambiguïté du livre: Prince, pouvoir et peuple dans les commentaires de la bible au moyen âge* (Paris, 1995)

Buc, P., 'Pouvoir royal et commentaires de la bible (1150–1350)', *Annales: Économies, Sociétés, Civilisations*, 44 (1989), 691–713

Buc, P., '*Principes Gentium Dominantur Eorum*: Princely Power Between Legitimacy and Illegitimacy in Twelfth-Century Exegesis', in *Cultures of Power: Lordship, Status and Process in Twelfth-Century Europe*, ed. T. N. Bisson (Philadelphia, PA, 1995) 310–28

Budny, M. and T. Graham, 'Les cycles des saints Dunstan et Alphège dans les vitraux romans de la cathédrale de Canterbury', *CCM*, 38 (1995), 55–78

Burton, J., 'Selby Abbey and its Twelfth-Century Historian', in *Learning and Literacy in Medieval England and Abroad*, ed. S. Rees-Jones (Turnhout, 2003), 49–68

Butler, J., *The Quest for Becket's Bones: The Mystery of the Relics of St Thomas of Canterbury* (New Haven, CT, and London, 1995)

Callias Bey, M. and V. David, *Les Vitraux de Basse-Normandie*, Corpus Vitrearum: France-Recensement VIII (Rennes, 2006)

Canel, A., *Essai historique, archéologique et statistique sur l'arrondissement de Pont-Audemer (Eure)*, 2 vols (Paris, 1834)

Caudron, S., 'Les châsses de Thomas Becket en émail de Limoges', in *Sédières*, 233–41

Caudron, S., 'La diffusion des chasses de saint Thomas Becket dans l'Europe médiévale', in *L'Œuvre de Limoges et sa diffusion: Trésors, objets, collections*, ed. D. Gaborit-Chopin and F. Sandron (Rennes, 2011), 23–41

Caudron, S., 'Thomas Becket et l'Œuvre de Limoges', in *Valérie et Thomas Becket: De l'influence des princes Plantagenêt dans l'Œuvre de Limoges*, ed. Véronique Notin *et al.* (Limoges, 1999), 56–68

Cavero Domínguez, G. (coord), *Tomás Becket y la Península Ibérica (1170–1230)* (León, 2013)

Caviness, M. H., *The Early Stained Glass of Canterbury Cathedral circa 1175–1220* (Princeton, NJ, 1977)

Caviness, M. H., 'The Feminist Project: Pressuring the Medieval Object', *Frauen Kunst Wissenschaft*, 24 (1997), 13–21

Caviness, M. H., 'A Lost Cycle of Canterbury Paintings of 1200', *Antiquaries Journal*, 54 (1974), 66–74

Caviness, M. H., *Reframing Medieval Art: Difference, Margins, and Boundaries* (Tufts University, 2001) [http://dca.lib.tufts.edu/caviness/abstract.html, accessed 14 January 2015]

Caviness, M. H., *Visualizing Women in the Middle Ages: Sight, Spectacle and Scopic Economy* (Philadelphia, PA, 2001)

Caviness, M. H., *The Windows of Christ Church Cathedral, Canterbury*, Corpus Vitrearum Medii Aevi: Great Britain, 2 (Oxford, 1981)

Cazel Jr, F. A., 'Langton, Simon (d. 1248)', *ODNB* (Oxford, 2004) [http://www.oxforddnb.com/view/article/16043, accessed 26 June 2012]

Cerda, J. M., 'The Marriage of Alfonso VIII of Castile and Leonor Plantagenet: The First Bond between Spain and England in the Middle Ages', in *Les Stratégies Matrimoniales (IXe–XIIIe siècles)*, ed. M. Aurell (Turnhout, 2013), 143–153

Chaney, W. A., *The Cult of Kingship in Anglo-Saxon England* (Manchester, 1970)

Chaussé, V., *Les Verrières de la cathédrale Notre-Dame de Coutances*, Itinéraires du patrimoine, 210 (Caen, 1999)

Cheney, C. R., 'The Alleged Deposition of King John', in *Studies in Medieval History Presented to Frederick Maurice Powicke*, ed. R. W. Hunt, W. A. Pantin, and R. W. Southern (Oxford, 1948), 100–16

Cheney, C. R., *Hubert Walter* (London, 1967)

Cheney, C. R., 'Magna carta beati Thome: Another Canterbury Forgery', in *Medieval Texts and Studies*, by C. R. Cheney (Oxford, 1973), 78–110

Cheney, C. R., *Pope Innocent III and England* (Stuttgart, 1976)

Chibnall, M., *The Empress Matilda: Queen Consort, Queen Mother and Lady of the English* (Oxford, 1991)

Choisselet, D. and P. Vernet, *Les ecclesiastica officia cisterciens du XIIème siècle*, La Documentation Cistercienne, 22 (Reiningue, 1989)

Church, M., 'The Shocking Death of Thomas Becket is Brought to Life in Opera',

The Independent, Tuesday 28 February 2006 [http://www.independent.co.uk/arts-entertainment/music/features/the-shocking-death-of-thomas-becket-is-brought-to-life-in-an-opera-6108168.html, accessed 4 August 2015]

Clarke, P. D., *The Interdict in the Thirteenth Century: A Question of Collective Guilt* (Oxford, 2007)

Clarke, P. D., 'Introduction', in *Pope Alexander III (1150–81): The Art of Survival*, ed. P. D. Clarke and A. J. Duggan (Farnham, 2012), 1–12

Cohen, J. J., 'Introduction', in *The Postcolonial Middle Ages*, ed. *idem* (New York, 2000), 1–17

Cohen, J. J., 'Hybrids, Monsters, Borderlands: The Bodies of Gerald of Wales', in *The Postcolonial Middle Ages*, ed. *idem* (New York, 2000), 85–104

Cohen, J. J. (ed.), *The Postcolonial Middle Ages* (New York, 2000)

Collet, C., P. Leroux and J.-Y. Marin, *Caen, cité médiévale: bilan d'archéologie et d'histoire* (Caen, 1996)

Combalbert, G., 'Archbishops and the City: Powers, Conflicts, and Jurisdiction in the Parishes of Rouen (Eleventh–Thirteenth Centuries)', in *Society and Culture in Medieval Rouen, 911–1300*, ed. L. V. Hicks and E. Brenner, Studies in the Early Middle Ages, 39 (Turnhout, 2013), 185–223

Conklin, G., 'Ingeborg of Denmark, Queen of France, 1193–1223', in *Queens and Queenship in Medieval Europe*, ed. A. J. Duggan (Woodbridge, 1997), 37–52

Cowdrey, H. E. J., 'An Early Record at Dijon of the Export of Becket's Relics', *Bulletin of the Institute of Historical Research*, 54 (1981), 251–3

Creamer, J., 'St Edmund of Abingdon and Henry III in the Shadow of Thomas Becket', in *Thirteenth Century England XIV: Proceedings of the Aberystwyth and Lampeter Conference, 2011*, ed. J. Burton, P. Schofield and B. Weiler (Woodbridge, 2013), 129–39

Crook, J., *English Medieval Shrines* (Woodbridge, 2011)

Crouch, D., *William Marshal*, 3rd edn (London and New York, 2016)

Davidson Cragoe, C., 'Reading and Rereading Gervase of Canterbury', *Journal of the British Archaeological Society*, 154 (2001), 40–53

Davis, J. F., 'Lollards, Reformers and St Thomas of Canterbury', *University of Birmingham Historical Journal*, 9 (1963), 1–15

D'Avray, D. L., '"Magna Carta": Its Background in Stephen Langton's Academic Biblical Exegesis and its Episcopal Reception', *Studi Medievali*, 38 (1997), 423–38

Dearmer, P., *Fifty Pictures of Gothic Altars* (London, 1910)

de la Cruz, F. V., *Berenguela la Grande. Enrique I el chico (1179–1246)* (Gijón, 2006)

Denton, J. H., 'Winchelsey, Robert (c. 1240–1313)', *ODNB* (Oxford, 2004; online edn, 2008) [http://www.oxforddnb.com/view/article/29713, accessed 11 August 2015]

Deremble, C. and J.-P. Deremble, *Les Vitraux de Chartres* (Paris, 2003)

Deremble, C. M. with J.-P. Deremble, *Les Vitraux narratifs de la cathédrale de Chartres: étude iconographique* (Paris, 1993)

Dickinson, J. C., 'Some Medieval English Representations of St Thomas Becket in France', in *Sédières*, 265–71

Dodgson, S. E., 'Thomas Á Becket and the Cathedral Church of Sigüenza', *Notes and Queries* (1902), s9-IX (227)

Du Boulay, F. R. H., 'The Fifteenth Century', in *The English Church and the Papacy in the Middle Ages*, ed. C. H. Lawrence (London, 1965; revised 1999), 185–242

Draper, P., 'Interpretations of the Rebuilding of Canterbury Cathedral, 1174–1186. Archaeological and Historical Evidence', *Journal of the Society of Architectural Historians*, 56 (1997), 184–203

Draper, P., 'King John and St Wulfstan', *Journal of Medieval History*, 10 (1984), 41–50

Draper, P., 'William of Sens and the Original Design of the Choir Termination of Canterbury Cathedral, 1175–9', *Journal of the Society of Architectural Historians*, 42 (1983), 238–48

Duffy, E., *The Stripping of the Altars: Traditional Religion in England c. 1400–c. 1580* (New Haven, CT, and London, 1992)

Duggan, A. J., '*Alexander ille meus*: The Papacy of Alexander III', in *Pope Alexander III (1150–81): The Art of Survival*, ed. P. D. Clarke and A. J. Duggan (Farnham, 2012), 13–49

Duggan, A. J., 'A Becket Office at Stavelot: London, BL, MS Addit. 16964', in *Omnia disce: Medieval Studies in Memory of Leonard Boyle, O.P.*, ed. *eadem*, J. Greatrex, and B. Bolton (Aldershot, 2005), 161–82; repr. with the same pagination in Duggan, *Friends, Networks*, no. XI

Duggan, A. J., 'Canterbury: the Becket Effect', in *Canterbury, A Medieval City*, ed. C. Royer-Hemet (Newcastle-upon-Tyne, 2010), 67–91

Duggan, A. J., 'The Cult of St Thomas Becket in the Thirteenth Century', in *St Thomas Cantilupe Bishop of Hereford: Essays in his Honour*, ed. M. Jancey (Hereford, 1982), 21–44

Duggan, A. J., 'Diplomacy, Status, and Conscience: Henry II's Penance for Becket's Murder', in *Forschungen zur Reichs-, Papst- und Landesgeschichte: Peter Herde zum 65. Geburtstag von Freunden, Schülern und Kollegen dargebracht*, ed. K. Borchardt and E. Bünz, 2 vols (Stuttgart, 1998), vol. I, 265–90.

Duggan, A. J., 'Eystein, Thomas Becket, and the Wider Christian World', in *Eystein Erlendsson – erkebiskop, politiker og kirkebygger*, ed. K. Bjørlykke, Øystein Ekroll, *et al.* (Trondheim, 2012), 24–41

Duggan, A. J., 'Henry II, the English Church and the Papacy, 1154–76', in *Henry II: New Interpretations*, ed. C. Harper-Bill and N. Vincent (Woodbridge, 2007), 154–83

Duggan, A. J., '"The hooly blisful martir for to seke"', in *Chaucer In Context: A Golden Age of English Poetry*, ed. G. Morgan (Oxford, Berlin, *et alibi*., 2012), 15–41

Duggan, A. J., 'John of Salisbury and Thomas Becket', *The World of John of Salisbury*, ed. M. Wilks, SCH Subsidia, 3 (Oxford, 1984), 427–38

Duggan, A. J., 'The Lorvão Transcription of Benedict of Peterborough's *Liber miraculorum beati Thome*: Lisbon, cod. Alcobaça CCXC/143', *Scriptorium*, 51 (1997), 51–68

Duggan, A. J., 'The Making of a Myth. Giraldus Cambrensis, *Laudabiliter*, and Henry II's Lordship of Ireland', *Studies in Medieval and Renaissance History*, Third Series, 4 (2007), 107–68

Duggan, A. J., '*Ne in dubium*: The Official Record of Henry II's Reconciliation at Avranches, 21 May, 1172', *EHR*, 115 (2000) 643–58

Duggan, A. J., 'Religious Networks in Action: the European Expansion of the Cult of St Thomas of Canterbury', in *International Religious Networks*, ed. J. Gregory and H. McLeod, SCH Subsidia, 14 (Woodbridge, 2012), 20–43

Duggan, A. J., 'The Santa Cruz Transcription of Benedict of Peterborough's *Liber miraculorum beati Thome*: Porto, BPM, cod. Santa Cruz 143', *Mediaevalia. Textos e estudos*, 20 (Porto, 2001), 27–55

Duggan, A. [J.], *Thomas Becket* (London, 2004)

Duggan, A. [J.], *Thomas Becket: A Textual History of his Letters* (Oxford, 1980)

Duggan, A. J., *Thomas Becket: Friends, Networks, Texts, and Cult* (Aldershot, 2007)

Duggan, C. and A. Duggan, 'Ralph de Diceto, Henry II and Becket, with an Appendix on Decretal Letters', in *Authority and Power: Studies on Medieval Law and Government Presented to Walter Ullmann on his Seventieth Birthday*, ed. B. Tierney and P. Linehan (Cambridge, 1980), 59–81

Duncan, A. A. M., 'John King of England and the Kings of Scots', in *King John: New Interpretations*, ed. S. D. Church (Woodbridge, 1999), 247–71

Duncan, A. A. M., *The Kingship of the Scots, 842–1292* (Edinburgh, 2002)

Eales, R., 'The Political Setting of the Becket Translation of 1220', in *Martyrs and Martyrologies*, ed. D. Wood, SCH, 30 (Oxford, 1993), 127–39

Elkins, S. K., *Holy Women of Twelfth-Century England* (Chapel Hill, NC, and London, 1988)

Encina, F. A., *Historia de Chile desde la prehistoria hasta 1891*, 20 vols (Santiago de Chile, 1948–53)

Evans, M., *The Death of Kings: Royal Deaths in Medieval England* (London, 2003)

Eyton, R. W., *Court, Household, and Itinerary of King Henry II* (Dorchester, 1878)

de Farcy, L., *Monographie de la cathédrale d'Angers*, 4 vols (Angers, 1901–26)

Favreau, R., 'Aliénor d'Aquitaine et Fontevraud', *303 Arts, Recherches et Créations*, 81 (2004), 41–4

Fawcett, R., 'Arbroath Abbey: A Note on its Architecture and Early Conservation History', in *The Declaration of Arbroath: History, Significance, Setting*, ed. G. Barrow (Edinburgh, 2003), 50–85

Fawcett, R., *The Architecture of the Scottish Medieval Church* (New Haven, CT, and London, 2011)

Fernández Conde, F. J., *La religiosidad medieval en España: Plena Edad Media (ss. XI–XII)* (Gijón, 2005)

Fernie, E., 'The Litigation of an Exempt House, St Augustine's Canterbury, 1182–1237', *Bulletin of the John Rylands Library*, 39 (1957), 390–415

Finucane, R. C., *Miracles and Pilgrims: Popular Beliefs in Medieval England* (London, Melbourne and Toronto, 1977)

Flahiff, G. B., 'Ralph Niger: an Introduction to his Life and Works', *Mediaeval Studies*, 2 (1940), 104–26

Flanagan, M. T., 'Henry II, the Council of Cashel and the Irish Bishops', *Peritia. Journal of the Medieval Academy of Ireland*, 10 (1996), 184–211

Fletcher, C., *Richard II: Manhood, Youth and Politics, 1377–99* (Oxford, 2008)

Foreville, R., 'Alexandre III et la canonisation des Saints', in *Miscellanea Rolando Bandinelli: Papa Alessandro III*, ed. F. Liotta (Siena, 1986), 217–36

Foreville, R., 'Le culte de saint Thomas Becket en France: Bilan provisoire des recherches', in *Sédières*, 163–87

Foreville, R., 'Le culte de saint Thomas Becket en Normandie: Enquête sur les sanctuaires anciennement placés sous le vocable du martyr de Canterbury', in *Sédières*, 135–52

Foreville, R., 'La diffusion du culte de Thomas Becket dans la France de l'Ouest avant la fin du XIIe siècle', CCM, 19 (1976), 347–69

Foreville, R., *Le jubilé de saint Thomas Becket: Du XIIIe au XVe siècle (1220–1470). Étude et documents*, Bibliothèque générale de l'École pratique des hautes-études, VIe section (Paris, 1958)

Foreville, R., 'Les "Miracula S. Thomae Cantuariensis"', in *Actes du 97e Congrès National des Sociétés Savants, Nantes 1972, Section de Philologie et d'histoire jusqua'à 1610* (Paris, 1979), 443–68

Foreville, R., 'Mort et survie de saint Thomas Becket', CCM, 14 (1971), 21–38

Foreville, R., 'Les origines normandes de la famille Becket et le culte de saint Thomas en Normandie', in *Mélanges offerts à Pierre Andrieu-Guitrancourt, L'année Canonique*, 17 (1973), 433–80

Foreville, R., 'Regard neuf sur le culte de saint Anselme à Canterbury au XIIe siècle (à la mémoire de William G. Urry)', in *Les Mutations socio-culturelles au tournant des XIe–XIIe siècles, Spicilegium Beccense II* (Paris, 1984), 299–316

Foreville, R. (ed.), *Thomas Becket: Actes du Colloque International de Sédières* (Paris, 1975)

Foreville, R., *Thomas Becket dans la tradition historique et hagiographique* (London, 1981)

Forey, A. J., 'The Military Order of St Thomas of Acre', EHR, 92 (1977), 481–503

Fournée, J., 'Contribution à l'histoire de la lèpre en Normandie. Les maladreries et les vocables de leurs chapelles', *Lèpre et lépreux en Normandie, Cahiers Léopold Delisle*, 46 (1997), 49–142

Fournée, J., 'Les lieux de culte de Saint Thomas Becket en Normandie', *Annales de Normandie*, 45 (1995), 377–92

Fournée, J., 'Les Vitraux de la cathédrale', in *Coutances, ville d'art et d'histoire, Art de Basse Normandie*, 95 (1987), 93–6

Galván Freile, F., 'Culto e Iconografía de Tomás de Canterbury en la Peninsula Ibérica (1173–1300)', in *Hagiografía peninsular en els segles medievals*, ed. F. Español and F. Fité (Lleida, 2008), 197–216

Gameson, R., *The Earliest Books of Canterbury Cathedral: Manuscripts and Fragments to c. 1200* (London, 2008)

Gameson, R., 'The Early Imagery of Thomas Becket', in *Pilgrimage: The English Experience from Becket to Bunyan*, ed. C. Morris and P. Roberts (Cambridge, 2002), 46–89

Gauthier, M.-M., 'Le meurtre dans la cathédrale, thème iconographique médiéval', in *Sédières*, 248–53

Gelin, M.-P., 'The Citizens of Canterbury and the Cult of St Thomas Becket', in *Canterbury: A Medieval City*, ed. C. Royer-Hemet (Newcastle-upon-Tyne, 2010), 93–118

Gelin, M.-P., 'Gervase of Canterbury, Christ Church and the Archbishops', JEH, 60 (2009), 449–463

Gelin, M.-P., 'Heroes and Traitors: The Life of Thomas Becket in French

Stained-Glass Windows', *Vidimus*, 14 (2008) [http://vidimus.org/issues/issue-14/feature/, accessed 17 December 2015]

Gelin, M.-P., *Lumen ad revelationem gentium: Iconographie et liturgie à Christ Church, Canterbury, 1175–1220* (Turnhout, 2006)

Gillingham, J., *The Angevin Empire*, 2nd edn (London and New York, 2001)

Gimson, G. S., 'Lion Hunt: A Royal Tomb-Effigy at Arbroath Abbey', *Proceedings of the Society of Antiquaries of Scotland*, 125 (1995), 901–16

Given-Wilson, C., *Chronicles: The Writing of History in Medieval England* (London and New York, 2004)

Golding, B., *Gilbert of Sempringham and the Gilbertine Order, c. 1130–c. 1300* (Oxford, 1995)

González, J., 'Un arquitecto de las Huelgas de Burgos', *Revista de Archivos, Bibliotecas y Museos*, 53 (1947), 47–50

González, J., *El Reino de Castilla durante el reinado de Alfonso VIII*, 3 vols (Madrid, 1960)

Gransden, A., *Historical Writing in England, c. 500 to c. 1307* (Ithaca, NY, New York and London, 1974)

Grant, L., *Architecture and Society in Normandy, 1120–1270* (New Haven, CT, and London, 2005)

Grant, L. (trans. B. Duchet-Filhol), 'Le patronage architectural de Henri II et de son entourage', CCM, 37, no. 145–6 (1994), 73–84

Grassin, J.-M., 'Le mythe littéraire de Thomas Becket a l'époque moderne', in *Sédières*, 285–97

Grodecki, L., *Les Vitraux du centre et des pays de la Loire*, Corpus Vitrearum: France, Recensement II (Paris, 1981)

Guerry, E. D., 'The Wall Paintings of the Sainte-Chapelle' (unpublished Ph.D. thesis, University of Cambridge, 2013)

Győrffy, G., *Az Árpad-Kori Magyarorszag Tőténeti Főldrajsa* (Budapest, 1987)

Győrffy, G., 'Thomas à Becket and Hungary', *Angol Filológiai Tanulmányok [Hungarian Studies in English]*, iv (1969), 45–52

Hallam, E. M., 'Henry II as a Founder of Monasteries', *JEH*, 28 (1977), 113–32

Hamilton, S., 'A New Model for Royal Penance? Helgaud of Fleury's *Life of Robert the Pious*', *Early Medieval Europe*, 6 (1997), 189–200

Hansen, N. A., 'Making the Martyr: The Liturgical Persona of Saint Thomas Becket in Visual Imagery' (unpublished M.A. Thesis, University of Illinois at Urbana-Champaign, 2011)

Hardy, T. D., 'Itinerary of King John, &c.', in *Rotuli Litterarum Patentium in Turri Londinensi asservati. Vol. 1, Pt. 1, 1199–1216*, ed. T. D. Hardy, Record Commission (London, 1835), unpaginated

Harris, A. F., 'Pilgrimage, Performance, and Stained Glass at Canterbury Cathedral', in *Art and Architecture of Late Medieval English Pilgrimage in Northern Europe and the British Isles*, ed. S. Blick and R. Tekippe (Leiden, 2005), 243–81

Harthan, J., *Books of Hours and their Owners* (London, 1977; repr. 1982)

Harvey, K., *Episcopal Appointments in England, c. 1214–1344: From Episcopal Election to Papal Provision* (Farnham, 2014)

Hassall, A. (ed.), *Historical Introductions to the Rolls Series: By William Stubbs, D.D., formerly Bishop of Oxford and Regius Professor of Modern History in the University* (New York, 1902)

Hayward, J. and L. Grodecki, 'Les Vitraux de la cathédrale d'Angers', *Bulletin Monumental*, 124 (1966), 29–53

Hearn, M. F., 'Canterbury Cathedral and the Cult of Becket', *Art Bulletin*, 76 (1994), 19–54

Heffernan, T. J., '"God hathe schewed ffor him many grete miracules": Political Canonization and the *Miracula* of Simon de Montfort', in *Art and Context in Late Medieval English Narrative: Essays in Honour of Robert Worth Frank, Jr.*, ed. R. R. Edwards (Cambridge, 1994), 177–91

Herrera Casado, A., *Heráldica Seguntina* (Guadalajara, 1990)

Herrero Sanz, M. J., *Guide to Santa María la Real de las Huelgas, Burgos* (Madrid, 2002)

Heslop, T. A., 'The Canterbury Calendars and the Norman Conquest', in *Canterbury and the Norman Conquest: Churches, Saints and Scholars*, ed. R. Eales and R. Sharpe (London,1995), 53–85

Heslop, T. A., '"Dunstanus archiepiscopus" and painting in Kent around 1120', *Burlington Magazine*, 126 (1984), 195–204

Holdsworth, C., 'Langton, Stephen (*c.* 1150–1228)', *ODNB* (Oxford, 2004) [http://www.oxforddnb.com/view/article/16044, accessed 21 December 2015]

Holt, J. C., *Magna Carta*, 2nd edn (Cambridge, 1992)

Houliston, V., 'St Thomas Becket in the Propaganda of the English Counter-Reformation', *Renaissance Studies*, 7 (1993), 43–70

Hucher, E., 'Monuments funéraires et sigillographiques des Vicomtes de Beaumont au Maine', *Revue historique et archéologique du Maine*, 11 (1882), 319–408

Hughes, A., 'British Rhymed Offices: A catalogue and commentary', in *Music in the Medieval English Liturgy*, ed. S. Rankin and D. Hiley (Oxford, 1993), 239–84

Hughes, A., 'Chants in the Rhymed Office of St Thomas of Canterbury', *Early Music*, 16 (1988), 185–201

Hughes, A., 'Rhymed Offices', *Dictionary of the Middle Ages*, x (New York, 1989), 367, 370–71

Huling, R. W., 'English Historical Writing under the Early Angevin Kings, 1170–1210' (unpublished Ph.D. thesis, State University of New York, Binghamton, 1981)

Jamison, E., 'The Alliance of England and Sicily in the Second Half of the 12th Century', *Journal of the Warburg and Courtauld Institutes*, 6 (1943), 20–32

Janauschek, L., *Origines Cisterciensium* (Vienna, 1877)

Jansen, S., *Wo ist Thomas Becket? Der ermordete Heilige zwischen Erinnerung und Erzählung* (Husum, 2002)

Jeater, M., 'Animating Thomas Becket', *Museum of London Blog* [http://blog.museumoflondon.org.uk/animating-thomas-becket/, accessed 3 October 2015]

Johnson, P., 'Speaight, Robert William (1904–1976)', *ODNB* (Oxford, 2004; online edn, 2011) [http://www.oxforddnb.com/view/article/31704, accessed 24 July 2015]

Johrendt, J., 'The Empire and the Schism', in *Pope Alexander III (1159–81): The Art of Survival*, ed. P. D. Clarke and A. J. Duggan (Farnham, 2012), 99–126

Jonsson, R., *Historia. Études sur la genèse des offices versifiés*, Studia Latina Stockholmiensis, 15 (Stockholm, 1968)

Jordan, A. A., 'Rhetoric and Reform: The St Thomas Becket Window of Sens Cathedral,' in *The Four Modes of Seeing: Approaches to Medieval Imagery in Honor of Madeline Harrison Caviness*, ed. E. Staudinger Lane, E. Carson Pastan and E. M. Shortell (Farnham, 2009), 547–64

Jordan, A. A., 'The "Water of Thomas Becket": Water as Medium, Metaphor and Relic', in *The Nature and Function of Water, Baths, Bathing and Hygiene from Antiquity through the Renaissance*, ed. C. Kosso and A. Scott (Leiden, 2009), 479–500

Jordan, K. (trans. P. S. Falla), *Henry the Lion: A Biography* (Oxford, 1986)

Kabir, A. J. and D. Williams (eds), *Postcolonial Approaches to the European Middle Ages: Translating Cultures* (Cambridge, 2005)

Kealey, E. J., *Medieval Medicus: A Social History of Anglo-Norman Medicine* (Baltimore, MD, 1981)

Keefe, T. K., 'Shrine Time: King Henry II's Visits to Thomas Becket's Tomb', *Haskins Society Journal*, 11 (2003), 115–22

Kellett, A., 'King John in Knaresborough: The First Known Royal Maundy', *Yorkshire Archaeological Journal*, 62 (1990), 69–90

Ker, N. R. *Medieval Manuscripts in British Libraries, Vol. II, Abbotsford-Keele* (Oxford, 1977)

Kerr, B. M., *Religious Life for Women, c. 1100–c. 1350: Fontevraud in England* (Oxford, 1999)

Kidson, P., 'Gervase, Becket, and William of Sens', *Speculum*, 68 (1993), 969–91

King, E., 'Benedict (*c.* 1135–1193)', *ODNB* (Oxford, 2004) [http://www.oxforddnb.com/view/article/2081, accessed 4 November 2015]

Kirsch, J. P., 'St Blaise', in *The Catholic Encyclopedia* [http://www.newadvent.org/cathen/02592a.htm, accessed 16 January 2015]

Knowles, M. D., 'The Canterbury Election of 1205–6', *EHR*, 53 (1938), 211–20

Knowles, D., 'The Early Community at Christ Church, Canterbury', *Journal of Theological Studies*, 39 (1938), 126–31

Knowles, D., C. N. L. Brooke and V. C. M. London, *The Heads of Religious Houses: England and Wales 940–1216* (Cambridge, 1972; repr. 2001)

Knowles, M. D., A. J. Duggan and C. N. L. Brooke, 'Henry II's Supplement to the Constitutions of Clarendon', *EHR*, 87 (1972), 757–71

Knowles, D. and R. N. Hadcock, *Medieval Religious Houses in England and Wales* (London, 1971)

Knowles, D., *Thomas Becket* (London, 1970; repr. London, 1971)

Koopmans, R., 'Early Sixteenth-Century Stained Glass at St Michael-le-Belfrey and the Commemoration of Thomas Becket in Late Medieval York', *Speculum*, 80 (2014), 1040–1100

Koopmans, R., 'Visions, Reliquaries, and the Image of "Becket's Shrine" in the Miracle Windows of Canterbury Cathedral', *Gesta*, 54 (2015), 37–57

Koopmans, R., *Wonderful to Relate: Miracle Stories and Miracle Collecting in High Medieval England* (Philadelphia, PA, 2011)

Kosztolnyik, Z. J., 'The Church and Béla III of Hungary (1172–92): The Role of Archbishop Lukács of Esztergom', *Church History*, 49 (1980), 375–86

Kosztolnyik, Z. J., *From Coloman the Learned to Béla III (1095–1196): Hungarian Domestic Policies and Their Impact upon Foreign Affairs* (Boulder, CO, 1987)

Lafond, J., 'Les Vitraux', in *La Cathédrale de Coutances*, ed. P. Colmet-Daage (Paris, 1967), 44–7

Lamia, S., 'The Cross and the Crown: Decoration and Accommodation for England's Premier Saints', in *Decorations for the Holy Dead: Visual Embellishments on Tombs and Shrines of Saints*, ed. S. Lamia and E. Valdez del Álamo (Turnhout, 2002), 39–56

Landon, L., *The Itinerary of King Richard I with Studies on Certain Matters of Interest Connected with his Reign*, PRS 51, ns 13 (London, 1955)

Langenbahn, S. K., '"de cerebro Thomae Cantuariensis". Zur Geschichte und Hagiologie der Himmeroder Thomas Becket-Reliquie von 1178', in *875 Jahre Findung des Klosterortes Himmerod*, ed. B. Fromme (Mainz, 2010), 55–91

Langlois, P., *Histoire du prieuré du Mont-aux-Malades-lès-Rouen, et correspondance du prieur de ce monastère avec saint Thomas de Cantorbéry, 1120–1820* (Rouen, 1851)

Lapidge, M. et al., *The Cult of St Swithun*, Winchester Studies 4.ii (Oxford, 2003)

Lapidge, M., 'Dunstan [St Dunstan] (*d*. 988)', *ODNB* (Oxford, 2004) [http://www.oxforddnb.com/view/article/8288, accessed 20 September 2015]

Larue, A., 'Enquête sur l'iconographie et le mobilier de Thomas Becket en Normandie', in *Sédières*, 211–19

Lawrence, C. H., *St Edmund of Abingdon: A Study of Hagiography and History* (Oxford, 1960)

Lawson, M. K., *Cnut: The Danes in England in the Early Eleventh Century* (London and New York, 1993)

Lecanu, A., *Histoire des évêques de Coutances depuis la fondation de l'évêché jusqu'à nos jours* (Coutances, 1839)

Leclercq, J., 'Épitres d'Alexandre III sur les Cisterciens', *Revue Bénédictine*, 64 (1954), 68–82

Lelégard, M., 'L'Hôtel-Dieu de Coutances', in *Coutances, ville d'art et d'histoire*, Art de Basse Normandie, 95 (1987), 42–9

Lemoine, F. and J. Tanguy, *Rouen aux 100 clochers: dictionnaire des églises et chapelles de Rouen (avant 1789)* (Rouen, 2004)

Lenz, P., 'Construire un recueil de miracles: les *Miracula sancti Thomae Cantuariensis* de Benoît de Peterborough' (unpublished Ph.D. thesis, University of Geneva, 2003)

Leroquais, V., *Les Bréviares manuscrits des bibliothèques publiques de France*, 6 vols (Paris, 1934)

Leroquais, V., *Le Bréviaire-Missel du prieuré clunisien de Lewes* (Paris, 1935)

Leroquais, V., *Les Psautiers manuscrits latins des bibliothèques publiques de France*, 3 vols (Mâcon, 1940–41)

Leroquais, V., *Les Sacramentaires et les missels manuscrits des bibliothèques publiques de France* (Paris, 1924)

Lett, D., 'Deux hagiographes, un saint et un roi: conformisme et créativité dans les deux recueils de *miracula* de Thomas Becket', in *Auctor & Auctoritas: Invention et conformisme dans l'écriture médiévale. Actes du colloque de Saint-Quentin-en-Yvelines (14–16 juin 1999)*, ed. M. Zimmermann (Paris, 2001), 200–16

Lewis, A. W., 'The Birth and Childhood of King John: Some Revisions', in *Eleanor of Aquitaine: Lord and Lady*, ed. B. Wheeler and J. C. Parsons (New York and Basingstoke, 2002), 159–75

Leyser, H., 'Ælfheah (*d*. 1012)', *ODNB* (Oxford, 2004; online edn, 2006) [http://www.oxforddnb.com/view/article/181, accessed 20 December 2015]

Lindblom, A., *Björsätersmålningarna: The Legends of St. Thomas Becket and of the Holy Cross painted in a Swedish Church*, Arkeologiska monografier, 38 (Stockholm, 1953)

Little, C. T., 'The Road to Glory: New Early Images of Thomas Becket's Life', in *Reading Medieval Images: The Art Historian and the Object*, ed. E. Sears and T. K. Thomas (Ann Arbor, MI, 2002), 201–211

Lizoaín Garrido, J. M. and J. José García, *El Monasterio de las Huelgas: Historia de un Señorío Cisterciense Burgalés (siglos XII–XIII)* (Burgos, 1988)

Lovatt, M., 'Geoffrey (1151?–1212)', *ODNB* (Oxford, 2004; online edn, 2007) [http://www.oxforddnb.com/view/article/10535, accessed 29 June 2012]

Loxton, H., *Pilgrimage to Canterbury* (Newton Abbot, 1978)

Lunt, W. E., *Papal Revenues in the Middle Ages*, 2 vols (New York, 1965)

Luscombe, D., 'Salisbury, John of (late 1110s–1180)', *ODNB* (Oxford, 2004; online edn, 2011) [http://www.oxforddnb.com/view/article/14849, accessed 17 December 2015]

Lutan-Hassner, S., *Thomas Becket and the Plantagenets: Atonement Through Art* (Leiden, 2015)

MacCulloch, D., *Thomas Cranmer* (New Haven, CT, and London, 1996)

Mackie, R. L. *et al.*, *Arbroath Abbey* (Edinburgh, 1982)

Maddicott, J. R., 'Follower, Leader, Pilgrim, Saint: Robert de Vere, Earl of Oxford, at the Shrine of Simon de Montfort, 1273', *EHR*, 99 (1994), 641–53

Maddicott, J. R., 'The Oath of Marlborough, 1209: Fear, Government and Popular Allegiance in the Reign of King John', *EHR*, 126 (2011), 281–318

Marcombe, D., *Leper Knights: The Order of St Lazarus of Jerusalem in England, 1150–1544* (Woodbridge, 2003)

Marosszéki, S. R., 'Les origines du Chant Cistercien. Recherches sur les réformes du plain-chant cistercien au XIIe siècle', *Analecta Sacri Ordinis Cisterciensis*, 8 (1952), 1–179

Martin, H., 'Le culte de saint Thomas Becket dans les diocèses de la province de Tours', in *Sédières*, 153–8

Martinic, Z., 'Relaciones Iglesia-Estado en Chile, desde 1820 hasta la muerte del arzobispo Rafael Valentín Valdivieso en 1878', *Archivum*, 4 (2002), 21–8

Mason, A. J., *What Became of the Bones of St Thomas? A Contribution to his Fifteenth Jubilee* (Cambridge, 1920)

Matthew, D., *Britain and the Continent, 1000–1300: The Impact of the Norman Conquest* (London, 2005)

Matthew, D., *The Norman Kingdom of Sicily* (Cambridge, 1992)

Mayer, H. E., 'Henry II of England and the Holy Land', *EHR*, 97 (1982), 721–39

Mayer, T. F., 'Becket's Bones Burnt! Cardinal Pole and the Invention and Dissemination of an Atrocity', in *Martyrs and Martyrdom in England, c. 1400–1700*, ed. T. S. Freeman and T. F. Mayer (Woodbridge, 2007), 126–43

Mayr-Harting, H., *Religion, Politics and Society in Britain 1066–1272* (Harlow, 2011)

McAndrew, B. A., *Scotland's Historic Heraldry* (Woodbridge, 2006)

McKenna, J. W., 'Popular Canonisation as Political Propaganda: The Cult of Archbishop Scrope', *Speculum*, 45 (1970), 608–23

McKiernan, E., 'Monastery and Monarchy: The Foundation and Patronage of Santa María la Real de Las Huelgas and Santa María la Real de Sigena' (unpublished Ph.D. thesis, University of Texas at Austin, 2005)

McNiven, P., 'Scrope, Richard (*c.* 1350–1405)', *ODNB* (Oxford, 2004; online edn, 2008) [http://www.oxforddnb.com/view/article/24964, accessed 5 November 2015]

Mesley, M., 'The Construction of Episcopal Identity: The Meaning and Function of Episcopal Depictions within Latin Saints' Lives of the Long Twelfth Century' (unpublished Ph.D. thesis, University of Exeter, 2009)

Michael, M. A., *Stained Glass of Canterbury Cathedral* (London, 2004)

Moon, J. O., 'The European Connection – Aspects of Canterbury Cathedral Priory's Temporalities Overseas', in *Canterbury, A Medieval City*, ed. C. Royer-Hemet (Newcastle-upon-Tyne, 2010), 177–93

Moore, J. C., *Pope Innocent III (1160/61–1216): To Root Up and to Plant* (Leiden and Boston, MA, 2003)

Morey, A. and C. N. L. Brooke, *Gilbert Foliot and his Letters* (Cambridge, 1965)

Napran, L., 'Marriage and Excommunication: The Comital House of Flanders', in *Exile in the Middle Ages: Selected Proceedings from the International Medieval Congress, University of Leeds 8–11 July 2002*, ed. L. Napran and E. van Houts (Turnhout, 2004), 69–79

le Neve, J., *Fasti Ecclesiae Anglicanae, 1066–1300: Vol. 1: St Paul's, London*, rev. edn. by D. E. Greenway (London, 1968)

Neveux, F., 'Hugues de Morville et l'épiscopat normand des XIIe–XIIIe siècles', in *La Cathédrale de Coutances: art et histoire. Actes du colloque organisé au Centre culturel international de Cerisy du 8 au 11 octobre 2009*, ed. F. Laty, P. Bouet and G. Désiré dit Gosset, with photographs by A. Poirier (Bayeux, 2012), 47–56

Newton, P. A., 'Some New Material for the Study of the Iconography of St Thomas Becket', in *Sédières*, 255–63

Niel, C. and M.-C. Truc (with B. Penna), 'La chapelle Saint-Thomas d'Aizier (Eure): premiers résultats de six années de fouille programmée', in *Étude des lépreux et des léproseries au Moyen Âge dans le nord de la France: histoire – archéologie – patrimoine*, ed. B. Tabuteau, *Histoire Médiévale et Archéologie*, 20 (2007), 47–107

Niel, C. and M.-C. Truc, 'Fouille d'une léproserie médiévale' [http://w3.unicaen.fr/ufr/histoire/craham/spip.php?article120&lang=fr, accessed 24 June 2013]

Nilgen, U., 'The Manipulated Memory: Thomas Becket in Legend and Art', in *Memory and Oblivion: Proceedings of the XXIXth International Congress of the History of Art held in Amsterdam, 1–7 September 1996*, ed. W. Reinink and J. Stumpel (Dordrecht, 1999), 765–72

Nilgen, U., 'Thomas Becket en Normandie', in *Les saints dans la Normandie médiévale*, ed. P. Bouet and F. Neveux (Caen, 2000), 189–204

Nilson, B., *Cathedral Shrines of Medieval England* (Woodbridge, 1998)

Nordahl, H. and J. W. Dietrichson, *Menneske, Myte, Motiv: Erkebiskop Thomas Becket i histoirie og diktning* (Oslo, 1980)

Norgate, K., 'Matilda, Duchess of Saxony (1156–1189)', rev. by T. Reuter, *ODNB* (Oxford, 2004) [http://www.oxforddnb.com/view/article/18339, accessed 9 January 2015]

Ó Clabaigh, C. and M. Staunton, 'Thomas Becket and Ireland', in '*Listen, O Isles, Unto Me': Studies in Medieval Word and Image in Honour of Jennifer O'Reilly*, ed. E. Mullins and D. Scully (Cork, 2011), 87–101, 340–43

Ocón, D., 'Alfonso VIII, la llegada de las corrientes artísticas de la corte inglesa y el bizantinismo de la escultura hispánica a fines del siglo XII', in *Alfonso VIII y su época* (Aguilar de Campoo, 1990), 307–20

Oexle, O. G., 'Lignage et parenté, politique et religion dans la noblesse du XIIe siècle: l'évangélaire de Henri le Lion', *CCM*, 36 (1993), 339–58 and Plates 1–4

Oppitz-Trotman, G., 'Penance, Mercy and Saintly Authority in the Miracles of St Thomas Becket', in *Saints and Sanctity*, ed. P. D. Clarke and T. Claydon, SCH, 47 (Woodbridge, 2011), 136–47

Ó Riain-Raedel, D., 'Edith, Judith, Matilda: The Role of Royal Ladies in the Propagation of the Continental Cult', in *Oswald: Northumbrian King to European Saint*, ed. C. Stancliffe and E. Cambridge (Stamford, 1995), 210–29

Ormrod, M., 'The Personal Religion of Edward III', *Speculum*, 64 (1989), 849–77

Ortenberg, V., 'Aspects of Monastic Devotions to the Saints in England, c.950 to c.1100: The Liturgical and Iconographical Evidence' (unpublished Ph.D. thesis, University of Cambridge, 1987)

Overbey, K. E., 'Postcolonial', in *Special Issue: Medieval Art History Today – Critical Terms*, ed. N. Rowe, *Studies in Iconography*, 33 (2012) 145–56

Owen, D. D. R., *William the Lion, 1143–1214: Kingship and Culture* (East Linton, 1997)

Peces Rata, F.-G., *La Fortis Seguntina: La Catedral de Sigüenza* (Barcelona, 1997)

Peces Rata, F.-G., *Paleografía y epigrafía en la Catedral de Sigüenza* (Sigüenza, 1988)

Peltzer, J., *Canon Law, Careers and Conquest: Episcopal Elections in Normandy and Greater Anjou, c. 1140–c. 1230* (Cambridge, 2008)

Penman, M., 'The Bruce Dynasty, Becket and Scottish Pilgrimage to Canterbury, c. 1178–c. 1404', *Journal of Medieval History*, 32 (2006), 346–70

Pérez Rodríguez, E., *Vita Didaci, Poema sobre el Fundador de Benevívere* (León, 2008)

Perry, D., 'A New Look at Old Arbroath', *Tayside and Fife Archaeological Journal*, 4 (1998), 260–78

Petersohn, J., *Der südliche Ostseeraum im kirchlich-politischen Kräftespiel des Reichs, Polens und Dänemarks vom 10. bis 13. Jahrhundert. Mission–Kirchenorganisation–Kultpolitik* (Cologne, 1979)

Pfaff, R., 'The Calendar', in *The Eadwine Psalter: Text, Image and Monastic Culture in Twelfth-Century Canterbury*, ed. M. Gibson, T. A. Heslop and R. W. Pfaff (London and University Park, PA, 1992), 62–87

Pfaff, R., 'Lanfranc's Supposed Purge of the Anglo-Saxon Calendar', in *Warriors and Churchmen in the High Middle Ages: Essays presented to Karl Leyser*, ed. T. Reuter (London, 1992), 95–108; repr. with same pagination in *Liturgical Calendars, Saints and Services in Medieval England* (Aldershot, 1998)

Pigeon, Abbé E.-A., *Histoire de la cathédrale de Coutances* (Coutances, 1876)

Piroyansky, D., 'Bloody Miracles of a Political Martyr: The Case of Thomas Earl of Lancaster', in *Signs, Wonders, Miracles: Representations of Divine Power in the*

Life of the Church, ed. K. Cooper and J. Gregory, SCH, 41 (Woodbridge, 2005), 228–38

Piroyansky, D., *Martyrs in the Making: Political Martyrdom in Late Medieval England* (Basingstoke, 2008)

Power, D., 'The End of Angevin Normandy: The Revolt at Alençon (1203)', *Historical Research*, 74 (2001), 444–64

Power, D., 'King John and the Norman Aristocracy', in *King John: New Interpretations*, ed. S. D. Church (Woodbridge, 1999), 117–36

Power, D., 'The Norman Church and the Angevin and Capetian Kings', *JEH*, 56 (2005), 205–34

Power, D., *The Norman Frontier in the Twelfth and Early Thirteenth Centuries* (Cambridge, 2004)

Power, D., '"Terra regis Anglie et terra Normannorum sibi invicem adversantur": les héritages anglo-normands entre 1204 et 1244', in *La Normandie et l'Angleterre au Moyen Âge*, ed. P. Bouet and V. Gazeau (Caen, 2003), 189–209

Power, D., 'What did the Frontier of Angevin Normandy Comprise?', *Anglo-Norman Studies*, 17 (1995), 181–201

Powicke, F. M., *Stephen Langton* (Oxford, 1928)

Poza Yagüe, M., 'Santo Tomás Becket', *Revista Digital de Iconografía Medieval*, 5, no. 9 (2013), 53–62

Prestwich, M., *Edward I* (Berkeley, CA, 1988)

Radó, P., revised L. Mezey, *Libri liturgici manuscripti bibliothecarum Hungariae et limitropharum regionum* (Budapest, 1973)

Ramsay, N. and M. Sparks, 'The Cult of St Dunstan at Christ Church, Canterbury', in *Saint Dunstan: His Life, Times and Cult*, ed. N. Ramsay, M. Sparks and T. Tatton-Brown (Woodbridge, 1992), 311–23

Ramsay N., M. Sparks and T. Tatton-Brown (eds), *Saint Dunstan: His Life, Times and Cult* (Woodbridge, 1992)

Rawcliffe, C., 'Learning to Love the Leper: Aspects of Institutional Charity in Anglo-Norman England', *Anglo-Norman Studies*, 23 (2000), 231–50

Rawcliffe, C., *Leprosy in Medieval England* (Woodbridge, 2006)

Real, U., 'Die Merseburger Neumarktkirche St. Thomas. Überlegungen zur Funktion der Kirche und zum Patrozinium des Thomas von Canterbury', in *Pfarrkirchen in Städten des Hanseraumes. Beiträge eines Kolloquiums vom 10. bis 13. Dezember 2003 in der Hansestadt Stralsund*, ed. F. Biermann, M. Schneider, T. Terberger, *Archäologie und Geschichte im Ostseeraum*, 1 (Rahden, 2006), 275–90

Reames, S., 'Liturgical Offices for the Cult of St Thomas Becket', in *Medieval Hagiography: An Anthology*, ed. T. [F.] Head (New York, 2000), 561–93

Reames, S., 'Reconstructing and Interpreting a Thirteenth-Century Office for the Translation of Thomas Becket', *Speculum*, 80 (2005), 118–70

Reames, S. L., 'The Remaking of a Saint: Stephen Langton and the Liturgical Office for Becket's Translation', *Hagiographica*, 7 (2000), 17–34

Renardy, C., 'Notes concernant le culte de saint Thomas Becket dans le diocèse de Liège aux XIIe et XIIIe siècles', *Revue belge de philologie et d'histoire*, 55 (1977), 381–9

Reuter, T., 'John of Salisbury and the Germans', in *The World of John of Salisbury*, ed. M. Wilks, SCH Subsidia, 3 (Oxford, 1984), 415–25

Richards, P., *The Medieval Leper and his Northern Heirs* (Cambridge, 1977)

Richardson, C. M., 'Durante Alberti, the Martyrs' Picture and the Venerable English College, Rome', *Papers of the British School at Rome*, 73 (2005), 223–63

Richardson, H. G. and G. O. Sayles, *The Governance of Medieval England from the Conquest to Magna Carta* (Edinburgh, 1963)

Roberts, P[eter], 'Politics, Drama, and the Cult of Thomas Becket in the Sixteenth Century', in *Pilgrimage: The English Experience from Becket to Bunyan*, ed. C. Morris and P. Roberts (Cambridge, 2002), 199–237

Roberts, P[hyllis] B., 'Archbishop Stephen Langton and his Preaching on Thomas Becket in 1220', in *De Ore Domini: Preacher and Word in the Middle Ages*, ed. T. L. Amos, E. A. Green and B. M. Kienzle (Kalmazoo, MI, 1989), 75–92

Roberts, P. B., *Thomas Becket in the Medieval Latin Preaching Tradition: An Inventory of Sermons about Thomas Becket, c. 1170–c. 1400* (The Hague, 1992)

Roberts, P. B., 'Thomas Becket: The Construction and Deconstruction of a Saint from the Middle Ages to the Reformation', in *Models of Holiness in Medieval Sermons*, ed. B. C. M. Kienzle (Louvain-la-Neuve, 1996), 1–22

Roberts, P. B., 'The Unmaking of a Saint: The Suppression of the Cult of St Thomas of Canterbury', *Hagiographica*, 7 (2000), 35–46

Robertson, S., 'Burial-Places of the Archbishops of Canterbury', *Archaeologia Cantiana*, 20 (1893), 276–94

Robertson Hamer, E., 'Christ Church, Canterbury: The Spiritual Landscape of Pilgrimage', *Essays in Medieval Studies*, 7 (1990), 59–69

Robinson, J. A., 'The Early Community at Christ Church, Canterbury', *Journal of Theological Studies*, 27 (1926), 225–40

Rollason, D., *Saints and Relics in Anglo-Saxon England* (Oxford, 1989)

Die romanische Neumarktkirche zu Merseburg und ihr Patron Thomas Becket von Canterbury, publ. by the Förderkreis Museum, Schloss Merseburg (Merseburg, 2014)

Romera, L., 'Iglesia de San Nicolás en Soria: las pinturas sobre el asesinato de Tomás Becket', *Revista de Arqueología*, 329 (2008), 40–43

Rubenstein, J., 'The Life and Writings of Osbern of Canterbury', in *Canterbury and the Norman Conquest: Churches, Saints and Scholars, 1066–1109*, ed. R. Eales and R. Sharpe (London, 1995), 27–40

Rucquoi, A., *Rex, Sapientia, Nobilitas. Estudios sobre la Península Ibérica Medieval* (Granada, 2006)

Rumble, A. R., *The Reign of Cnut, King of England, Denmark and Norway* (London and New York, 1994)

Russell, J. C., 'The Canonisation of Opposition to the King in Angevin England', in *Anniversary Essays in Medieval History by Students of Charles Homer Haskins*, ed. C. H. Taylor (Boston, MA, 1929), 279–90

Russell, J. C., 'The Development of the Legend of Peter of Pontefract', *Medievalia et Humanistica*, 13 (1960), 21–31

Sayers, J., *Innocent III: Leader of Europe* (London and New York, 1994)

Sayers, J., 'Peter's Throne and Augustine's Chair: Rome and Canterbury from

Baldwin (1184–90) to Robert Winchelsey (1297–1313)', *JEH*, 51 (2000), 249–66

Scarisbrick, J. J., 'Warham, William (1450?–1532)', *ODNB* (Oxford, 2004; online edn, 2008) [http://www.oxforddnb.com/view/article/28741, accessed 22 October 2010]

Schleif, C., 'Introduction/Conclusion: Are We Still Being Historical? Exposing the Ehenheim Epitaph Using History and Theory', *Different Visions: A Journal of New Perspectives on Medieval Art*, 1 (2008) [http://differentvisions.org/issue-one/, accessed 14 January 2015]

Schmandt, R. H., 'The Election and Assassination of Albert of Louvain, Bishop of Liege, 1191–2', *Speculum*, 42 (1967), 653–60

Schnith, K., 'Betrachtungen zum Spätwerk des Giraldus Cambrensis: "De principis instructione"', in *Festiva Lanx: Studien zum mittelalterlichen Geistesleben Johannes Sporl dargebracht* (Munich, 1966), 54–63

Scott Robertson, W. A., *The Crypt of Canterbury Cathedral: Its Architecture, its History and its Frescoes* (London, 1880)

Scully, R. E., 'The Unmaking of a Saint: Thomas Becket and the English Reformation', *Catholic Historical Review*, 84 (2000), 579–602

Shadis, M., *Berenguela of Castile (1180–1246) and Political Women in the High Middle Ages* (New York, 2009)

Shadis, M., 'Piety, Politics, and Power: The Patronage of Leonor of England and Her Daughters Berenguela of León and Blanche of Castile', in *The Cultural Patronage of Medieval Women*, ed. J. H. McCash (Athens, GA, and London, 1996), 202–27

Shadis, M. and C. H. Berman, 'A Taste of the Feast: Reconsidering Eleanor of Aquitaine's Female Descendants', in *Eleanor of Aquitaine: Lord and Lady*, ed. B. Wheeler and J. C. Parsons (London, 2002), 177–211

Shahan, T., 'Arnulf of Lisieux', in *The Catholic Encyclopedia*, I [http://www.newadvent.org/cathen/01752a.htm, accessed 29 June 2013]

Sheppard, J. B., 'A Notice on Some Manuscripts Selected from the Archives of the Dean and Chapter of Canterbury', *Archaeological Journal*, 33 (1876), 151–67

Sigal, P. A., 'Naissance et premier développement d'un vinage exceptionnel: l'eau de saint Thomas', *CCM*, 44 (2001), 35–44

Slocum, K. B., 'Angevin Marriage Diplomacy and the Early Dissemination of the Cult of Thomas Becket', *Medieval Perspectives*, 14 (1999), 214–28

Slocum, K. B., *Liturgies in Honour of Thomas Becket* (Toronto, 2004)

Slocum, K. B., 'The Making, Remaking and Unmaking of the Cult of Thomas Becket', *Hagiographica*, 7 (2000), 3–16

Slocum, K. B., '*Martir quod Stillat Primatis ab Ore Sigillat*: Sealed with the Blood of Becket', *Journal of the British Archaeological Association*, 165 (2012), 61–88

Slocum, K. B., '*Optimus Egrorum Medicus Fit Thomas Bonorum*: Images of Saint Thomas Becket as Healer', in *Death, Sickness and Health in Medieval Society and Culture*, ed. S. Ridyard, Sewanee Mediaeval Studies, 10 (Sewanee, TN, 2000), 173–80

Smalley, B., *The Becket Conflict and the Schools: A Study of Intellectuals in Politics* (Oxford, 1973)

Smalley, B., *Historians in the Middle Ages* (London, 1974)

Solymosi, L., 'Magyar főpapok angliai zarándoklata 1220-ban (The pilgrimage of Hungarian prelates to England in 1220)', *Történelmi Szemle* (Historical Miscellany), 55, no 4 (2013), 527–40

Southern, R. W., *The Monks of Canterbury and the Murder of Archbishop Becket* (Canterbury, 1985)

Sparks, M., 'The Liturgical Use of the Nave, 1077–1540', in *Canterbury Cathedral Nave: Archaeology, History and Architecture*, ed. K. Blockley, M. Sparks and T. Tatton-Brown (Canterbury, 1997), 121–8

Speaight, R., *Thomas Becket*, 2nd edn (London, 1949)

Spencer, B., *Pilgrim Souvenirs and Secular Badges*, Medieval Finds from Excavations in London, 7, new edn (Woodbridge, 2010, first published London, 1998)

Spencer, B., *Salisbury and South Wiltshire Museum. Medieval Catalogue, Part 2: Pilgrim Souvenirs and Secular Badges* (Salisbury, 1990)

Stancliffe, C. and E. Cambridge (eds), *Oswald: Northumbrian King to European Saint* (Stamford, 1995)

Stanton, A. R., *The Queen Mary Psalter: A Study of Affect and Audience*, Transactions of the American Philosophical Society, 91 Pt. 6 (Philadelphia, PA, 2001)

Staunton, M., 'The Lives of Thomas Becket and the Church of Canterbury', in *Cathedrals, Communities and Conflict in the Anglo-Norman World*, ed. P. Dalton, C. Insley and L. J. Wilkinson (Woodbridge, 2011), 169–86

Staunton, M. W. J., 'Politics and Sanctity in the Lives of Anselm and Becket' (unpublished Ph.D. thesis, University of Cambridge, 1994)

Staunton, M., *Thomas Becket and his Biographers* (Woodbridge, 2006)

Stevens, D., 'Music in Honour of St Thomas of Canterbury', *The Musical Quarterly*, 56 (1970), 311–38

Stevens, D., 'Thomas Becket et la musique médiévale', in *Sédières*, 277–84

Strickland, M., 'Fantosme, Jordan (*fl.* 1170–1180)', *ODNB* (Oxford, 2004) [http://www.oxforddnb.com/view/article/48310, accessed 20 November 2010]

Stringer, K., 'Arbroath Abbey in Context, 1178–1320', in *The Declaration of Arbroath: History, Significance, Setting*, ed. G. Barrow (Edinburgh, 2003), 116–41

Stringer, K. J., *Earl David of Huntingdon, 1152–1219* (Edinburgh, 1985)

Summerson, H., 'George (*d. c.* 303?)', *ODNB* (Oxford, 2004; online edn, 2010) [http://www.oxforddnb.com/view/article/60304, accessed 19 December 2015]

Sweetinburgh, S., 'Caught in the Cross-Fire: Patronage and Institutional Politics in Late Twelfth-Century Canterbury', in *Cathedrals, Communities and Conflict in the Anglo-Norman World*, ed. P. Dalton, C. Insley and L. J. Wilkinson (Woodbridge, 2011), 187–202

Symons, T., 'The Introduction of Monks at Christ Church, Canterbury', *Journal of Theological Studies*, 27 (1926), 409–11

Tabuteau, B., 'Le grand saint Nicolas, patron de léproseries: une histoire d'influences', *Lèpre et lépreux en Normandie, Cahiers Léopold Delisle*, 46 (1997), 1–18

Tatton-Brown, T., 'Canterbury and the Architecture of Pilgrimage Shrines in England', in *Pilgrimage: The English Experience from Becket to Bunyan*, ed. C. Morris and P. Roberts (Cambridge, 2002), 90–107

Taylor, A. J., 'Edward I and the Shrine of St Thomas of Canterbury', *Journal of the British Archaeological Association*, 132 (1979), 22–8

Thacker, A., 'Cults at Canterbury: Relics and Reform under Dunstan and his Successors', in *Saint Dunstan: His Life, Times and Cult*, ed. N. Ramsay, M. Sparks and T. Tatton-Brown (Woodbridge, 1992), 221–45

Theilmann, J. M., 'Political Canonization and Political Symbolism in Medieval England', *Journal of British Studies*, 29 (1990), 241–66

Theiner, A., *Vetera Monumenta historica Hungariam sacram illustrantia*, i (Rome, 1859)

Tolley, T., 'Eleanor of Castile and the "Spanish" Style in England', in *England in the Thirteenth Century: Proceedings of the 1989 Harlaxton Symposium*, ed. W. M. Ormrod (Stamford, 1991), 167–92

Touati, F.-O., 'Les léproseries aux XIIème et XIIIème siècles, lieux de conversion?', in *Voluntate dei leprosus: les lépreux entre conversion et exclusion aux XIIème et XIIIème siècles*, ed. N. Bériou and F.-O. Touati, Testi, Studi, Strumenti, 4 (Spoleto, 1991), 1–32

Toustain de Billy, R., *Histoire ecclésiastique du diocèse de Coutances*, 3 vols (Rouen, 1874–86)

Turner, D. H., 'The Customary of the Shrine of St Thomas of Canterbury', *Canterbury Cathedral Chronicle*, 70 (1976), 16–22

Turner, R. V., 'Longchamp, William de (d. 1197)', *ODNB* (Oxford, 2004; online edn, 2007) [http://www.oxforddnb.com/view/article/16980, accessed 12 June 2012]

Turner, R. V., *Men Raised from the Dust: Administrative Service and Upward Mobility in Angevin England* (Philadelphia, PA, 1988)

Turner, R. V., 'Richard Lionheart and English Episcopal Elections', *Albion: A Quarterly Journal Concerned with British Studies*, 29 (1997), 1–13

Urry, W., *Canterbury under the Angevin Kings* (London, 1967)

Urry, W., 'The Resting Places of St Thomas', in *Sédières*, 195–209

Urry, W., *Thomas Becket: His Last Days*, ed. P. A. Rowe (Stroud, 1999)

Urry, W., 'Two Notes on Guernes de Pont-Sainte-Maxence: Vie de St Thomas', *Archaeologia Cantiana*, 66 (1953), 92–7

Valente, C., 'Simon de Montfort, Earl of Leicester, and the Utility of Sanctity in Thirteenth-Century England', *Journal of Medieval History*, 21 (1995), 27–49

Valente, C., *The Theory and Practice of Revolt in Medieval England* (Aldershot, 2003)

van Houts, E., *Memory and Gender in Medieval Europe, 900–1200* (London, 1999)

van Houts, E., 'Women and the Writing of History in the Early Middle Ages: The Case of Abbess Matilda of Essen and Aethelweard', in *eadem, History and Family Traditions in England and the Continent, 1000–1200* (Aldershot, 1999), 53–68

Vann, T. M., 'The Theory and Practice of Medieval Castilian Queenship', in *Queens, Regents, and Potentates*, ed. T. M. Vann (Sawston, 1993), 125–48

Vincent, N., 'Beyond Becket: King Henry II and the Papacy (1154–1189)', in *Pope Alexander III (1150–81): The Art of Survival*, ed. P. D. Clarke and A. J. Duggan (Farnham, 2012), 257–99

Vincent, N., 'Master Simon Langton, King John and the Court of France', unpublished

Vincent, N., 'The Murderers of Thomas Becket', in *Bischofsmord im Mittelalter: Murder of Bishops*, ed. N. Fryde and D. Reitz (Göttingen, 2003), 211–72

Vincent, N., *Peter des Roches: An Alien in English Politics, 1205–1238* (Cambridge, 1996)

Vincent, N., 'The Pilgrimages of the Angevin Kings, 1154–1272', in *Pilgrimage: The English Experience from Becket to Bunyan*, ed. C. Morris and P. Roberts (Cambridge, 2002), 12–45

Vincent, N., 'Stephen Langton, Archbishop of Canterbury', in *Étienne Langton: Prédicateur, Bibliste, Théologien*, ed. L.-J. Bataillon, N. Bériou, G. Dahan and R. Quinto (Turnhout, 2010), 51–123

Vincent, N., 'The Strange Case of the Missing Biographies: The Lives of the Plantagenet Kings of England 1154–1272', in *Writing Medieval Biography, 750–1250: Essays in Honour of Professor Frank Barlow*, ed. D. Bates, J. Crick and S. Hamilton (Woodbridge, 2006), 237–57

Vincent, N., 'William of Canterbury and Benedict of Peterborough: The Manuscripts, Date and Context of the Becket Miracle Collections', in *Hagiographie, idéologie et politique au Moyen Âge en Occident: Actes du colloque international du Centre d'Études supérieures de Civilisation médiévale de Poitiers, 11–14 septembre 2008*, ed. E. Bozóky (Turnhout, 2012), 347–87

Vogt, C., 'Episcopal Self-Fashioning: The Thomas Becket Mitres', in *Iconography of Liturgical Textiles in the Middle Ages*, ed. E. Wetter (Riggisberg, 2010), 117–28

Walker, D., 'Crown and Episcopacy under the Normans and Angevins', *Anglo-Norman Studies*, 5 (1983), 220–33

Walker, R., 'Leonor of England and Eleanor of Castile: Anglo-Iberian Marriage and Cultural Exchange in the Twelfth and Thirteenth Centuries', in *England and Iberia in the Middle Ages, 12th–15th Century: Cultural, Literary and Political Exchanges*, ed. M. Bullón-Fernández (New York, 2007), 67–87

Walker, S., 'Political Saints in Later Medieval England', in *The McFarlane Legacy: Studies in Late Medieval Politics and Society*, ed. R. H. Britnell and A. J. Pollard (Stroud, 1995), 77–106

Warren, W. L., *Henry II* (London, 1973)

Warren, W. L., *King John* (London, 1974)

(Watkins, G.) bell hooks, 'Marginality as a Site of Resistance', in *Out There: Marginalization and Contemporary Cultures*, eds. R. Ferguson *et al.* (Cambridge, MA, 1990), 341–43

Watt, J. A., *The Church and the Two Nations in Medieval Ireland* (Cambridge, 1970)

Webb, D., *Pilgrimage in Medieval England* (London and New York, 2000)

Webster, P., 'Crown, Cathedral and Conflict: King John and Canterbury', in *Cathedrals, Communities and Conflict in the Anglo-Norman World*, ed. P. Dalton, C. Insley and L. J. Wilkinson (Woodbridge, 2011), 203–19

Weiler, B., 'Bishops and Kings in England, *c.* 1066–*c.* 1215', in *Religion and Politics in the Middle Ages: Germany and England by Comparison*, ed. L. Körntgen and D. Wassenhoven (Berlin and Boston, MA, 2013), 87–134

Williams, B., 'St Blaise's Well, Bromley, Kent', *Source: The Holy Wells Journal*, 6 (1998) [http://people.bath.ac.uk/liskmj/living-spring/sourcearchive/ns6/ns6bw1.htm, accessed 16 January 2015]

Willis, R., *The Architectural History of Canterbury Cathedral* (London, 1845)

236

Woodman, F., *The Architectural History of Canterbury Cathedral* (London, 1981)

Woodruff, C. E., 'The Financial Aspect of the Cult of St Thomas of Canterbury', *Archaeologia Cantiana*, 44 (1932), 13–32

Yvernault, M., 'Reading History in Enamel: The Journey of Thomas Becket's Experience from Canterbury to Limoges', in *Canterbury: A Medieval City*, ed. C. Royer-Hemet (Newcastle-upon-Tyne, 2010), 137–59

Additional online resources

'Becket (1964)', *Internet Movie Database* [http://www.imdb.com/title/tt0057877/, accessed 24 July 2015]

The British Museum Collection Online [http://www.britishmuseum.org/research/collection_online/search.aspx, accessed 3 October 2015]

Chartres windows [http://www.medievalart.org.uk/Chartres/18_pages/Chartres_Bay18_key.htm, accessed 13 January 2015]

Coutances windows [http://cathedralecoutances.free.fr/vitraux1.htm, accessed 14 January 2015]

Mould for the production of a pilgrim's badge [https://sketchfab.com/models/707ca a9c575c4c7cb981e305dac61bdb, accessed 3 October 2015]

Museum of London pilgrim badges [http://collections.museumoflondon.org.uk/online/search/#!/results?terms=pilgrim%20badge%20Thomas%20Becket, accessed 3 October 2015]

Portable Antiquities Scheme pilgrim badges [https://finds.org.uk/database/search/results/objecttype/PILGRIM+BADGE/description/thomas+becket, accessed 3 October 2015]

'Postcolonising the Medieval Image', at University of Leeds [http://post-col-med.leeds.ac.uk, accessed 15 January 2015]

Sens windows [http://www.medievalart.org.uk/Sens/23_Pages/Sens_Bay23_key.htm, accessed 14 January 2015]

Index

Abel 30, 31
Abelard, Peter 31
Acre, military order of St Thomas of 41
Adelard of Bath 53 n.3
Aelfric, archbishop of Canterbury
  (995–1005) 60 n.27
Aethelhard, archbishop of Canterbury
  (790–805) 58 n.20
Agincourt, battle of 44
Aizier, leper hospital 81, 82, 89–93
  archaeological excavation 91
Albert, papal chancellor 134
Alberti, Durante 49
Alcabón 136, 138, 142
Alençon, Count Robert d' 190 n.55
Alexander II, king of Scots 194, 195, 200
Alexander III, king of Scots 200
Alexander III, pope (1159–81) 26, 28,
  40, 41 n.88, 85, 114, 155, 157, 159, 160,
  167–8, 174–5
Alfonso VIII, king of Castile 16, 44, 133,
  135–6
Almazán, church of S. Miguel de 140
Alphege, archbishop of Canterbury. See
  St Alphege
Amesbury nunnery 149
Amiens, Hugh of, archbishop of Rouen
  (1130–64) 90
ampullae. See pilgrim badges and ampullae
Anagni Cathedral 16, 98, 160
Andres, William monk of 32 n.33
Andreu, Richard 90
Angers 185
  bishops of. See Beaumont, Guillaume
    de; Beaumont, Raoul de
  Cathedral 14, 74 n.79, 205
    stained glass 74 n.79, 171–3,
      178–9, 181 (Fig. 9.4), 182, 183
      (Fig. 9.5), 187–9, 191, 194, 196,
      200, 201–6
    treasurer. See Tosny, Richard
  Hôpital St-Jean-l'Évangeliste 179
    n.25, 207 n.108

Anglo-Saxon royal saints 122
Angot, Abbé Alphonse-Victor 190
Anjou, Geoffrey of 87
Annales Toledanos 136
Anonymous I 35 n.51, 97
Anouilh, Jean 23
Anselm, archbishop of Canterbury. See
  St Anselm
Appleby, Cumberland 201
Aquitaine, clergy 137 n.14
Aquitaine, Eleanor of. See Eleanor of
  Aquitaine
Arbroath Abbey 41 n.84, 46, 186, 187,
  195, 200, 206
Arden, Robert of 25 n.3
Ardres 97
Argentan 114
  hospital 88
Arthies, leper hospital 83
Arundel, Thomas, archbishop of
  Canterbury (1397–1414) 5
Athelstan, king of England 124 n.45
Avilés (Asturias) 142
Avranches, settlement of 2, 39–40, 105,
  134 n.4, 155, 168, 178. See also Henry
  II, Avranches penance

Bailey, Richard 125 n.49
Baldwin, archbishop of Canterbury
  (1184–90) 41, 65 n.44, 66, 78–9, 103,
  104, 106–8, 151, 186
Baldwin, count of Boulogne 36
Baldwin II of Guines 97
Bale, John 21
Balliol, John, king of Scots 196 n.76
Barcelona Cathedral 142
Barfleur 84
Barlow, Frank 2, 39, 40, 196
Barre, Richard, royal clerk 25 n.3
Bartlett, Robert 19, 20
Bath, Reginald of 45
Battle Abbey chronicle 97
Bayeux Cathedral 89

238

Beaumont, Constance   204–5

Beaumont, Ermengarde de, wife of William
   I, king of Scots   184, 186, 194–5

Beaumont family   179, 181 (Fig. 9.4), 182,
   187, 189, 190, 192–6, 198, 200, 204,
   206

Beaumont, Guillaume de, bishop of Angers
   (1202–40)   179, 182, 190, 191, 193–4,
   197–8, 202, 204–6

Beaumont-le-Roger, Rotrou de, archbishop
   of Rouen (1165–84)   26, 83–4, 85

Beaumont, Raoul de, bishop of Angers
   (1177–97)   179 n.27

Beaumont, Raoul de, viscount of Maine
   182, 190 n.55, 191 n.57, 193, 205

Beaumont, Richard de, viscount of Maine
   (1175–1200/1)   182 n.30, 184, 198
   (Fig. 9.8), 204 n.99

Beaumont, Roscelin de, viscount of Maine
   (1145–75)   182 n.30

Becket, Thomas
   altars dedicated to   20, 90, 93, 134,
      136–8, 140, 143, 201 n.90
   Anglican attitudes to   23
   anti-Royal saint   169 n.125
   as archbishop of Canterbury (1162–70)
      1, 5–7, 11, 12, 24–6, 40, 53–4, 65,
      68, 72, 79, 82, 85–7, 97–100, 103–5,
      144, 147, 149, 155, 165–8, 171–3,
      175, 178–9, 189, 194, 199, 200, 202,
      204, 206–7
   appointment as archbishop   158
   arguments put forward by   165
   austere habits   54
   censure of those crowning Henry the
      Young King   98
   consecration as archbishop   159
   Council of Tours (1163)   97
   defends freedoms of the church   96,
      98, 103, 108, 133, 145, 154, 157
   defends monastic community of
      Christ Church Canterbury   151
   dispute with Henry II   40, 41, 54,
      72, 85, 97 n.10, 98–9, 101, 103,
      105–6, 114, 118, 135, 147, 154,
      165, 167–8, 172
   doubts that his life entitled him to
      sanctity   67
   exile   10, 26, 41, 53, 74, 85, 87, 96,
      102, 103, 106, 109, 147, 160, 172,
      175, 179, 189, 198

   intransigence   156
   negotiations with Henry II   97
   nominal abbot of Christ Church
      Canterbury   54
   opposition to the Constitutions of
      Clarendon   150
   reconciliation with Henry II (1170)
      105, 160
   relations with Canterbury monks
      54
   return from exile (1170)   53, 97–8,
      109, 160, 174 (Fig. 9.2), 179, 189
   royal servant   54
   seeks canonisation of Anselm   54
   sermons preached by   53, 69 (Fig.
      3.1)
   sufferings   166 n.106
   threats faced by   160
   trial at Northampton   97, 99
   arrest, attempts before murder   110
   art. See Becket, Thomas, iconography
   biographers
      medieval   1, 2, 53, 54 n.8, 68, 114,
         154
      modern   1, 118
   birth in London   6, 8, 43, 50, 189
   blood of   7–8, 13, 18, 30, 40, 45, 54,
      106, 157, 175, 188
      See also Becket, Thomas, head of;
         Becket, Thomas, water of
   body of   54, 56 n.14, 107
   bones   21, 49
   breviaries   140
   burial   54, 174, 178, 182 (Fig. 9.5),
      187, 200 n.85, 202
   canonisation   1–2, 12, 27–8, 40, 45,
      55, 56 n.14, 67, 81, 84, 98, 113, 120,
      134, 141, 160, 185, 188
   Chancellor of England (1154–62)   1,
      12, 96–8, 100
   clerks of   26, 179 n.25, 185
   codex related to   143
   cult of   1–6, 8–11, 13, 15, 17–21,
      24, 44, 54–7, 66, 78–9, 81–3, 85,
      89, 92–3, 96, 106 n.56, 111, 116,
      118–20, 122 n.39, 124–5, 129–31,
      134–5, 137, 139–42, 144–5, 147,
      169, 172, 174, 188
   criticism of   20
   in Castile   135 n.11, 139, 141, 144
   in Europe   134 n.7

in France   10
in German Empire   45 n.110
in Hungary   45, 141 n.33
in Iberia   11, 45–6, 49
   in Iberian poetry   142
in Latin America   135
in Normandy   10, 11 n.39, 81, 89, 174
in Sicily   141
in Spain   135–7, 141
political significance of   17, 20
propaganda against   21, 22
royal involvement   19
spread   3, 9, 10, 11
suppression   41, 67 n.59
death of   1–7, 9–11, 15, 18, 21, 23–31, 34, 36–7, 40, 44, 47–9, 53–6, 61, 68, 70–4, 77–9, 81, 83, 85, 88–9, 95–100, 102–5, 109–11, 113–18, 128, 133–4, 138–42, 145, 147, 150, 153, 155, 157–9, 163, 168, 171–2, 174–5, 178, 179 n.25, 185, 187–9, 195–6, 199, 201–2, 203 n.94, 206–7
dedication of chapels to   83–5, 89, 90, 93, 136–7, 142
dedication of churches and hospitals to   8, 13, 45 n.110, 46, 49–51, 78, 81, 83–5, 88, 93, 106, 134, 137, 142, 149, 186, 196
defacing of name   22 n.86
defender of church freedoms   11, 206
depictions   67, 110, 134 n.7
   alabaster   13
   altarpieces   49, 119
   apparition   76 (Fig. 3.5)
   books of hours   34, 35, 43
   brasses   13
   breviaries   35
   chronicles   24
   defender of the church   68, 72
   diptychs   17
   effigies   7
   enamel   142, 171
   good shepherd (bonus pastor)   11, 12, 30, 32–3, 68, 72
   Gospel books   119, 120, 122, 130, 131, 141
   Helmarshausen Gospels   44
   horseback   189
   ideal prelate   72
   liturgical combs   17

manuscript illuminations   13, 24, 120, 171, 179, 189
martyr   68, 72
medallions   22, 101
miracle worker   68
modelled on Dunstan and Alphege, 78
mosaic   45, 141
painting   13, 18, 22 n.86, 128, 139, 140, 142, 197 n.78
plaques   17
psalters   35, 43
religious equipment   16, 17
reliquaries (Limoges enamel)   15, 16, 42 n.95, 45
sculpture   13, 20, 24, 89, 140
seals   47, 50
stained glass   7, 8, 13–15, 20, 21, 24, 42 n.95, 43–4, 48, 49 n.136, 50, 58, 65–72, 74, 76 (Fig. 3.5), 77, 79, 89, 171–5, 176 (Fig. 9.1), 178, 179, 180 (Fig. 9.3), 184 n.33, 187–9, 191, 194–204, 206
standing on a peacock   7
travelling by ship   189
vestments   16
wall painting. See Becket, Thomas, depictions, painting
woodcuts   13
wood panels   13
devotion to   113–16, 119, 129, 130–1, 135, 138, 141, 143–4, 179, 187, 195, 200
in Saxony   129
education   87
estates   26
as an exemplar   11, 20
father (Gilbert)   11, 81
feast days   6, 11, 12, 28, 31–2, 47, 53, 57, 64, 129, 197 n.78, 206
   Feast of martyrdom (29 December) 11, 12, 28–9, 32, 35, 48, 64, 103, 129, 142 n.38
      text and music for   28–36, 48
   Feast of return from exile (Regressio) 6, 12, 41, 64, 189
   Feast of translation (7 July, from 1220)   11–13, 29 n.22, 42, 48, 64, 196 n.76
   sermons for Feast   31

friends and followers 3, 10, 15, 27, 87, 137 n.14, 179 n.25, 185
garments 54
    Archiepiscopal vestments 54, 74, 77
    blood-stained 45
    cowl 45
    hair shirt 45, 54, 88
    rochet 88
    shirt 45
    shoes 45
    stole 88
guardian of realm or dynasty 118, 122, 125, 130, 131
hagiography 68. *See also* Becket, Thomas, Lives of
head of 106–7
healer 82, 83, 175, 188, 195, 202, 205
historical writing on, medieval 95–111
hospitals. *See* Becket, Thomas, dedication of churches and hospitals to
iconography 2 n.5, 4–5, 13–15, 17, 21–2, 55, 68, 72, 79, 89, 171, 175, 188–9, 198
    in Iberia/Spain 135–6 n.11, 140
identification with 159, 160 n.73
illness 86, 89
influence 48, 49
    people's saint 49
intercession of 88, 101, 105, 117, 134, 136, 144, 178, 185–6, 206
interpretation of life and fate of 155
invocation of 160
Jubilees 5, 42, 43, 57 n.16, 66 n.53, 169
    Indulgences for 43
largesse to the poor 11
lectionaries
    Cîteaux 27
    Clairvaux 27
    Clermond-Ferrand 27
    Jumièges 27
    Heilingenkreuz 27
    Hereford 33
    Hyde Abbey 33
    Lyre (Normandy) 27
    Marchiennes 27
    Moissac 27
    Paris 27
    Pontigny 27
    Reims 27

    St-Martial-de-Limoges 27
legacy 96, 104, 106, 110, 111, 147, 172–3, 189
leper hospitals. *See* Becket, Thomas, dedication of churches and hospitals to
lepers, patron of 81–3
letters about 27
letters of 2, 26, 54 n.3, 87, 95, 97, 111, 155, 163, 166–7
letters to 87, 167
literature, theatre and film representations 2 n.5, 23, 24
liturgy relating to 2 n.5, 12, 21, 27–36, 53, 55, 67, 68, 110, 172, 188, 189, 197 n.78
    Canterbury liturgy 29 n.22, 34–5, 67 n.59
    Cistercian 35
    Hereford liturgy 33
    Salisbury liturgy 29 n.22, 34, 35, 48 n.130, 67 n.59
    Spain 135 n.11
    translation liturgy 29 n.22, 42
    York liturgy 32, 33, 34 n.44
Lives of 2, 10, 12, 13, 22 n.86, 29, 32–3, 43 n.102, 46, 55 n.9, 67–8, 95, 97, 104–5, 108–9, 111, 115 n.11, 117 n.18, 118, 134–5, 140. *See also* Anonymous I; Becket Leaves; Benedict; Bosham; Canterbury, William of; Fitz Stephen; Grim; Lansdowne Anonymous; Pont-Sainte-Maxence; *Quadrilogus*; Salisbury, John of; Tewkesbury
London, protector of 6, 8–10, 50
martyrdom of. *See* Becket, Thomas, death of
Mass of 33, 36
memory of 147, 149, 151, 154, 157–8, 165
military order of. *See* Acre
miracles associated with 1–3, 5, 8–12, 14, 24, 26–8, 51, 55 n.9, 67, 79, 82, 95–6, 102, 105, 110, 111, 115, 133, 171, 174, 188, 195, 202
    involving water 174, 188, 189, 202, 205
mitres (Becket Mitres) 6, 16–17
mother (Matilda) 81
murder of. *See* Becket, Thomas, death of

murderers of 2, 6, 15, 25–6, 35, 102,
107, 115, 140, 159, 179, 181 (Fig.
9.4), 185, 187–9, 195–6, 197 (Fig.
9.7), 198–9, 201–2
excommunicated 26
See also Horsea; Moreville, Hugh de;
Tracy; Urse
nephews 107
offerings 79. *See also under* Becket,
Thomas, shrines
opponents 84–5, 99, 106, 155
parallels with Christ 12, 15, 68, 72
parents 11, 20, 30 n.23, 43, 81, 85,
174
patron saint
Brunswick Cathedral 129
Saxony 129
persecution of 1–7, 108
portrayal of 2
posthumous image 2
posthumous reputation
as a doctor/healer 8, 12
personal protector of Angevins 148
presentation in heaven 43
prophecies 102
recusant works defending 22
Regressio (return from exile) 44. *See
also* Becket, Thomas, feast days;
Becket, Thomas, liturgy
relics of 3, 4, 8, 10, 42, 45, 48, 49
n.131, 51, 55, 57, 66, 74, 88–9, 142,
169, 171–2, 179, 200
goblet 88
See also Becket, Thomas, garments;
Becket, Thomas, translation of
relics
reliquaries 15, 143
reputation
place in spiritual hierarchy 67
relationship with predecessors 68
royal devotions 169
Saga of, *Thómas Saga Erkibyskups* 30
Saviour
from drowning 13
from peril on the sea 13
of the sick 83, 86, 93
seal 84, 85
sermon model 11
shrines 1, 4, 6, 7, 56, 66, 82, 134, 171,
188
candles 42

Corona 51
Crypt tomb 4, 7
Customary of 5
destruction 2, 8, 21, 22, 29 n.22,
43, 47–9, 50
Head Shrine 4, 6, 7, 35
income from 4, 5, 20, 50 n.138
offerings at 57 n.16
principal shrine 1, 4, 5, 6, 7, 14,
21, 22
shrine keepers/custodians 7, 16, 50
n.138, 188
shrine site candle 1
See also Becket, Thomas, tomb
Society of (Chile) 135
soul of 6
student 10
supporters 87
symbol
of church resistance to temporal
authority 12, 15, 17, 18, 38,
48, 50
for Counter Reformation 22–3
for English Catholics 22
tomb 26–8, 37, 40–2, 47–8, 56, 65–7,
79, 88, 93, 100, 101, 105, 109,
115–18, 120, 131, 133, 148, 153,
160, 178, 185–6, 199 n.81. *See also*
Becket, Thomas, shrines
translation of relics (7 July 1220) 1, 4,
5, 9, 12, 14, 15, 24, 42, 48, 56 n.14,
57 n.16, 63–4, 66, 88, 169, 171–2,
182 (Fig. 9.5), 187, 188, 200
planned (1186) 3
Tuesdays (Thomas Tuesdays) 160, 189
veneration. *See* Becket, Thomas,
devotion to
visions of 18, 97, 104, 107, 151
water of 7, 8, 13, 79, 135, 175, 188–9,
206
Welfs, patron of 44
Wine of St Thomas (gift of Louis VII)
47 n.127
'winner of battles' 136, 137, 145
Becket Leaves, illustrated verse life 179
n.24, 189 n.53
Becket Mitres 16
Bela III, king of Hungary 19, 45, 141
Benedict, monk of Canterbury, Prior
(1175–77), Abbot of Peterborough
(1177–93) 1, 2, 8, 9 n.33, 16, 25 n.1,

28, 29, 32–3, 36, 67, 82 n.6, 95, 188
  n.46
Benefit of Clergy   40
Berend, Nora   192
Berenguela, queen of León   137, 145
Bertau, Karl   121
Berwick   41
Béziers   100
Bhabba, Homi   199
Binski, Paul   22
Blanchemains, William aux, archbishop of
  Sens (1168–76)   25–6
Blick, Sarah   7
Blois, Henry of, bishop of Winchester
  (1129–71)   102
Blois, Mary of   47 n.125
Blois, Peter of   39 n.70, 134
Blois, Theobald of   26 n.7
Boissy-Lamberville, leper hospital   83
Borenius, Tancred   13, 22, 24, 141 n.35
Borszörcsök, church of St Thomas the
  Martyr   46
Bosham, Herbert of   15, 97, 104–5, 108–9,
  114 n.6
Boulanger, Karine   194, 205
Boulogne, Matthew, count of   46, 47
  n.125
Bourg-l'Abbesse. See Caen, leper hospital
Bourg-le-Roi   191 n.57
Bowie, Colette   19
Braga Cathedral   16
Bregwine, archbishop of Canterbury
  (760–64)   58 n.20
Bremen   45
Brewood (Staffs), leper house   91
Brinton, Thomas, bishop of Rochester
  (1373–89)   31
Brisac, Catherine   15
British Museum   7
Brito, Richard   196
Brix   202
Brotonne, forest   89
Bruce, Robert, king of Scots (1306–29)
  195 n.70
Brunswick   45, 126
  Agidienkloster   120
  annals of   114 n.4
  Basilica of SS John and Blaise   44, 113,
    120, 128, 130
Brunswick, Henry of, son of Henry the Lion
  113, 114, 128, 131

Buc, Philippe   154 n.41
Budny, Mildred   66
Burgh by Sands, Cumberland   201
Burgos Cathedral   142, 143
  tomb of Leonor Plantagenet   139
  tomb of one of Leonor's children   140
Burton Annals   158
Burton Lazars (Leics)   92
Burton, Richard   23
Bury St Edmunds   116 n.13

Caen   81, 88
  Avranches settlement confirmed   2,
    115 n.9
  leper hospital   83, 85, 86
Calix, William of   85–6
Canterbury   16, 36–7, 195
  Archbishops of. See Aelfric; Aethelhard;
    Baldwin; Becket; Bregwine;
    Courtenay; Cranmer; Cuthbert;
    Deane; Dover, Richard of; Lanfranc;
    Langton, Stephen; Morton; Oda;
    Plegmund; Pole; St Alphege;
    St Anselm; St Dunstan; St Edmund
    of Abingdon; Walter; Warham;
    Winchelsey
  Cathedral (Christ Church)   21, 28
    n.19, 56–7, 60, 105–8, 169
    annuity of wine from Louis of France
      106
    archiepiscopal election disputed
      under John   153
    Calendars   64
    Corona Chapel   4, 56
    fire of 1174   56
    income from shrine and relics   4, 5,
      50 n.138, 57 n.18
    letter collection   104
    Prior Conrad's choir   59 n.24, 63
    reconstruction after fire   56, 59,
      66, 79
    relic collection   57 n.17, 58
    scriptorium   62
    stained glass   58–9, 65, 67–8, 73
      (Fig. 3.3), 75 (Fig. 3.4), 76 (Fig.
      3.5), 77–9, 171, 188
    Trinity Chapel   1, 8, 14, 21, 56,
      66–8, 72, 77, 79, 169
  Gervase, monk of. See Gervase
  John, Andrew, monk of   107
  John of. See Poitiers

leper hospital, later alms houses. *See*
  Harbledown
  quitclaim of (1189)   41, 186
  St Augustine's Abbey   57, 104, 105
  St Dunstan, Chapel   37, 48
  St John's church   57
  William of   1, 2, 3, 8, 28 n.19, 37, 67,
    82 n.6, 95, 104, 115 n.11, 188 n.46
Cantilupe, Thomas, bishop of Hereford
  (1275–82)   18
Canville-les-Deux-Églises, leper hospital
  83
Castello, Hugh de   38
Castile, Blanche of   203
Catalonia, church of S. Maria de Terrasa
  140
Catherine, daughter of Charles VII, king of
  France, wife of Henry V, king of England
  34 n.47
Caudron, Simone   16
Caviness, Madeline   14, 65, 66–7, 172,
  173 n.9
Caxton, William   35 n.52
Celestine III, pope (1191–98)   140, 145
Celle, Peter abbot of   27
Chantry records   20
Charlemagne   126
Charles V, Holy Roman Emperor   21, 44
Chartres Cathedral   14, 15, 68, 70–1 (Fig.
  3.2), 72, 171, 172 n.7
  stained glass   70, 71 (Fig. 3.2), 72, 74,
    175, 189, 197, 204 n.97
Chaucer, *Canterbury Tales*   5, 49–50
Chaumont family   206 n.106
Cherbourg, leper hospital   83, 84
Chester   16
  Earl of   36, 38
Chronicles   95–111
Cistercians   35
Clarendon
  Assize of   105
  Constitutions of (1164)   85, 105, 150,
    195
Clarke, Peter   167
Clotaire II, king of the Franks   194
Cnut, king of England, Denmark and
  Norway   60
Coggeshall, Ralph of   96, 100
Cohen, Jeffrey Jerome   192, 193
Coldingham, Geoffrey of   164 n.96
Combe (Warks)   33

Constance, illegitimate daughter of
  Henry I, king of England   182 n.30
Couesmes-en-Froulay (Maine), leper
  hospital   195
Courtenay, William, archbishop of
  Canterbury (1381–96)   5
Courtenay, William de   196
Coutances Cathedral   14, 74, 79, 174,
  200, 201
  stained glass   74, 79, 171–5, 176 (Fig.
    9.1), 177 (Fig. 9.2), 178, 182, 184,
    189, 191, 200, 201–4
Cranmer, Thomas, archbishop of
  Canterbury (1533–56)   22 n.86
  seal   5–6
Criel, leper hospital   83
Cromwell, Thomas   2
Crook, John   9
Csanád, bishop of   42 n.93
Cuenca   136, 137, 138
Cuthbert, archbishop of Canterbury
  (740–60)   57, 58 n.20

Dassel, Rainald of   100
David, earl of Huntingdon, brother of
  William I (the Lion)   185
Davidson Cragoe, Carol   65 n.47
Deane, Henry, archbishop of Canterbury
  (1501–1503)   5
Denmark, Ingeborg of, queen of France
  165 n.100
Devizes, Richard of   109, 110, 153 n.10
Diceto, Ralph de, dean of St Paul's London
  38, 41, 99, 100, 101
  *Series causae inter Henricum regem et
    Thomam archiepiscopum*   99
  Ymagines Historiarum   99
Dijon, Abbey of St-Bénigne   10
Dover
  Richard of, archbishop of Canterbury
    (1174–84)   103–4
  St Martin's Priory   109, 110
Draco Normannicus   97
Dreux, Pierre de, duke of Brittany   191
  n.58
Dublin, Augustinian priory   88, 149
Duffy, Eamon   22
Duggan, Anne   2, 10, 54 n.6, 55 n.9, 100,
  115 n.7, 116, 119, 130, 141 n.31
Duggan, Charles   100

Dunstan, archbishop of Canterbury. *See* St Dunstan
Dunwich (Suffolk), leper house   91
Durand, papal envoy   158
Durham   16, 38 n.66, 150 n.19, 194

Eadmer   62, 66, 77, 108
Eadwig, king of England   60, 66, 74, 75 (Fig. 3.4), 77
Eadwine Psalter   64 n.44
Eastry, Henry of, prior of Christchurch Canterbury (1285–1331)   57 n.17
Edith, wife of Otto the Great of Saxony   123–4
Edward I, king of England   34 n.47, 43, 44, 196 n.76
Edward II, king of England   19, 43
Edward III, king of England   43
Edward, the Black Prince   44
Edward, the Confessor, king of England and saint   4 n.12, 19, 49, 148, 158, 169
Egidio, chancellor of Leonor of Castile   138
Egres (Igriş, Romania), Cistercian monastery   46
Eleanor, daughter of King Henry II of England. *See* Leonor
Eleanor of Aquitaine   36, 41, 88, 121
Eliot, T. S.   23
Elizabethan Settlement   22
Ely, Eustace, bishop of (1198–1215)   150, 156
Ely, William, bishop of. *See* Longchamp
Ephraim   107
Erdő, Cardinal Professor Peter   46 n.118
Esztergom
    Archbishop Lukás   46
    Church of Szent Tamás   46
    John, bishop of   42 n.93
Eu, Henry, count of (1170–91)   83
Eugenius, archbishop of Armagh (1206–16)   151
Évreux, dean of. *See* Neufbourg, Robert of
Évreux, Giles, bishop of (1170–79)   25 n.3
Exeter, Bartholomew, bishop of (1161–84)   40 n.76, 102
Eynsham, Adam of   98

Falaise, Treaty of   185–6
Faversham,   104
Fécamp, Abbey   82, 86, 89

Fernández, Teresa, wife of Nuño Pérez de Lara   136, 137
Fernando II, king of León   137
Ferrers, William Earl   38 n.66
Fife, earl of   205
Finchale, Godric of, hermit   97
Finland   32
Finucane, Ronald C.   4 n.11
Fitz Nigel, William   107
Fitz Stephen, William   95, 99
Flanders, Philip, count of. *See* Philip I
Foliot, Gilbert, bishop of London (1163–87)   84, 99, 106, 179 n.24
Fontevraud Abbey   147
    grant by Alfonso and Leonor of Castile   144
Ford, Baldwin of. *See* Baldwin, archbishop of Canterbury
Forest   106
Foreville, Raymonde   10, 81, 91, 134 n.7, 179
Fournée, Jean   81, 83, 84
Foxe, John   21, 22
Frascati. *See* Tusculum
Frederick I, Emperor   155, 160
French rulers, patronage of Becket   196
Fréteval, Peace of (1170)   155 n.26
Frojmovic, Eva, 192 n.59

Galván Freile, Fernando   140
Gameson, Richard   16 n.59, 119 n.25, 131
Gandersheim, Hrotsvita of   123 n.45
Geoffrey, son of Henry II, Chancellor (1181/2–89), archbishop of York (1189–1212)   36, 109, 110, 153
Gerald of Wales. *See* Wales, Gerald of
Gerberga, abbess of Gandersheim   123 n.45
Gervase, monk of Canterbury   56–9, 63, 65–6, 79, 104–9, 111, 148, 157 n.56, 199 n.81
    Actus Pontificum   58 n.19
Gesta Ottonis   123 n.45
Gilbert, bishop of London. *See* Foliot
Gmunden Gospels   33, 44, 114, 119, 123, 126, 130–1, 141
Golden Legend   175
González, Julio   137 n.15
Gorron   115 n.9
Graham, Timothy   66
Gravelines   38

Gray, John de, bishop of Norwich
(1200–14)   153
Gray, Walter de, Chancellor (1205–14),
later archbishop of York (1215–55)
151
Great Rebellion (1173–74)   36, 40, 88,
100, 101, 105, 116–18, 121, 134 n.6,
157, 178, 185–6, 206
Gregory I. *See* St Gregory the Great
Grim, Edward   35 n.51, 95, 101, 104, 115
n.11, 117 n.18, 134, 182, 199 n.81
Grosseteste, Robert, bishop of Lincoln
(1235–53)   18

Hackington   78, 98 n.14, 106–8, 151
Halberstadt (Saxony)   45
Hamburg   45
Cathedral   119
Hamo, bishop of León   100
Hansa   45
Hansen, Natalie A   172 n.7
Harbledown, St Nicholas leper house   37,
38, 89, 92
Harcourt, leper hospital   83
Harcourt, Robert II, lord of   83
Helmarshausen   44, 119, 126
Henry I, king of England   87, 162, 182
Henry II, Emperor, reliquary   126
Henry II, king of England   1, 10, 19, 25,
38, 49, 72, 81–2, 86–8, 100, 102–3,
105–8, 110, 120, 130, 147, 150, 167,
169, 174–5, 182, 183 (Fig. 9.5), 184–5,
195, 202, 206
aristocracy of   84
Avranches penance (May 1172)   36,
102, 115–16, 118, 148, 178
Canterbury pilgrimages   2, 39, 115–17,
134, 136, 148–9, 178, 185
daughters   19, 44, 114 n.5, 118, 135,
141, 142 n.36, 182 n.30
embassy to pope   25–6
failure to go on crusade   102
family connections   184
grant to Canterbury   37
Interdicts threatened and imposed   26,
39 n.69, 115, 155, 157
king *dei gratia*   118
knights   196, 198–9
marriage   100, 102
papal absolution   85

penance   1, 8, 36–40, 48, 78, 85, 88,
100, 101, 134
reconciliation with pope   115
Windsor Council (1170)   185
Henry III, king of England   42, 49, 157,
169, 200, 203
Henry IV, king of England   44
Henry V, Count Palatine   44–5
Henry V, king of England   44
Henry VI, Emperor   110 n.74
Henry VI, king of England   18, 117 n.17
Henry VII, king of England   20
Henry VIII, king of England   5, 21, 44,
47–8
Henry, bishop of Winchester. *See* Blois,
Henry of
Henry the Lion, Duke of Saxony and
Bavaria   44, 106, 113, 119, 120–3,
126–30, 141
pilgrimage to Canterbury   120
relations depicted   120, 121
See also Gmunden Gospels
Henry, the Young King   36, 40, 41, 88, 98,
100, 105–6, 116, 166 n.108, 178–9, 183
(Fig. 9.5), 185
Hereford   16
Hermann the Lame of Reichenau   124
Hertzburg   113
Hildersheim   123, 124, 125
reliquary   122, 125 n.49
Historia Selebiensis Monasterii   9
Horsea, Hugh of (alias Mauclerc)   25, 195
Houts, Elizabeth van   121, 124 n.47
Howden, Roger of   97, 101
Howsham, Lincs   149
Hugh, archbishop of Tarragona   100
Hugh, bishop of Durham. *See* Puiset
Hugh, bishop of Lincoln. *See* St Hugh
Hugh, earl of Norfolk   38 n.66
Hugucio, Cardinal-Legate   106
Hungary   32

Igriş. *See* Egres
Ilchester, Richard of, later bishop of
Winchester (1173–88)   99, 103
indulgences   43
Innocent III, Pope (1198–1216)   32 n.33,
145, 151, 153, 157, 160–1, 165, 167–8
Deeds of Innocent III   156–7
England and Ireland as a papal fief   168

excommunicates King John (1209–13)
    154, 156
use of biblical examples in letters
    159–67
Interdict (1208–14)   147, 154, 156
Ireland   102, 105
Isabella of France, queen of England, wife
    of Edward II   43
Israel   31

James II, king of England   23
Jamison, Evelyn   141
Jehoash (Joas) of Judah   30
Jeremiah   31
Jerusalem, church of the Holy Sepulchre
    113
Joan, daughter of King John, wife of
    Alexander II, king of Scots   200
Joanna (Joan), daughter of Henry II, wife of
    William II, king of Sicily   19, 45, 141
John, king of England   41–2, 116 n.12,
    147–69, 182, 190 n.55, 194, 203
Jordan Fantosme   37 n.64, 39, 100, 101,
    117, 118, 134 n.6, 185
Jordan, Karl   121 n.38, 123 n.42, 126, 127,
    129 n.80
Jordan, river   92
Joscius, bishop of Acre   106
Jumièges, Abbey archives   90

Kabir, Ananya Jahanara   192
Karkov, Catherine   192 n.59
Knaresborough   159
Knowles, David   178
Koopmans, Rachel   11, 20, 21, 42 n.95,
    67 n.58

Lacy, Hugh de   103
Lambert, chaplain of Ardres   97
Lambeth   98 n.14, 106, 151
Lambeth Palace   20
Lancaster, Thomas earl of (d.1322)   18,
    117
Landshut. See Seligenthal
Lanercost Chronicle   196 n.76
Lanfranc, archbishop of Canterbury
    (1070–89)   53, 62, 63, 77
Langton, Simon   163
Langton, Stephen, archbishop of
    Canterbury (1207–28)   4, 5, 17, 48, 66,
    153, 155–6, 159, 160, 169, 200 n.85

contested election of   66, 153–4, 157–8
    seal   159
Lansdowne Anonymous   114 n.6, 115
Lara, Count Nuño Pérez de   136–8, 140–1
Las Huelgas   140, 142–4
Lateran Council
    Third (1179)   81, 150
    Fourth (1215)   11
Leicester, Robert, third earl of   38
Le Liget (Touraine)   149
Le Mans   202
    Hôpital-Dieu   179 n.25
Leonor (Eleanor, daughter of Henry II),
    wife of Alfonso VIII, king of Castile
    16, 45, 133–45
leper hospitals. See Aizier; Arthies;
    Boissy-Lamberville; Brewood; Caen;
    Canville-les-Deux-Églises; Cherbourg;
    Couesmes-en-Froulay; Criel; Dunwich;
    Harbledown; Harcourt; Mont-aux-
    Malades; Oxford; Vesley; Vittefleur
Le Valasse, Richard Abbot of   25 n.3
Lewes, Cluniacs of   32
Liber Eliensis   96
Limoges   202
    enamels   15, 16
Lincoln, bishops of. See Grosseteste;
    St Hugh
Linkoping (Sweden)   32, 34 n.44
Lisieux
    Arnulf, bishop of (1141–81)   25 n.3,
        84–5
    bishop, election of (1200)   151
    Cathedral   14
    hospital   83, 84, 89
    Robert, archdeacon of   25 n.3
liturgical combs   17
liturgy, Becket inspired   12, 189. See also
    Becket, Thomas, liturgy
Llewelyn, Alexander   103
Lollards   20
London   41 n.88
    bishops of. See Foliot; Ste-Mère-Église
    Chapel of St Thomas (London Bridge)
        50
    hospital of St Thomas   51
    martyrdom of St Alphege   61
    Museum of   6 n.20
Longchamp, William de, Chancellor and
    bishop of Ely (1189–97)   109, 110
    n.74, 150

Loquet, Richard   90
Louis VII, king of France   19, 26, 36, 47, 72, 88, 105–6, 115–16, 175, 197, 204, 206
Louis VIII, king of France   191, 203–4
Louis IX, king of France   191, 203, 204 n.100
Louvain, Albert, bishop of (1166–92)   110 n.74
Lübeck   45
Lucca Cathedral   16 n.59
Luttrell Psalter   35 n.52
Lydgate, John   50 n.137

Maclou-de-Folville   84
Maddicott, John R.   155 n.48, 156 n.49, 157 nn.55–7
Magán, near Toledo   144
Magdeburg   124
Magna Carta   48, 152, 157
Magus, Simon   97
Mandeville, William de   105
Mantes   87
Marcombe, David   92
Margaret, daughter of King Henry III, wife of Alexander III, king of Scots   200
Margaret of Navarre, queen of Sicily   45
Margaret, sister of King Philip IV of France, wife of Edward I, king of England   34 n.47, 43
Margaret, wife of Henry the Young King and King Bela III of Hungary   19, 45–6, 141
Marlborough, Oath of (1209)   155 n.48, 157
Marsay, Etienne de   179 n.25
Marshal, William   162, 185
Martínez, García   144 n.45
Matilda, abbess of Essen   124 n.47
Matilda, abbess of Quedlinburg   124 n.47
Matilda, eldest daughter of Henry II, king of England, Duchess of Saxony   113–31, 141
Matilda, Empress   87, 88, 90, 120, 166
Matilda, wife of Henry I, king of England   184
Mauger, bishop of Worcester (1200–12)   150, 156, 160
Maundy Thursday commemoration   159
Mayenne, Juhel de   190 n.55
Mélinais, Abbey   190

Melrose, chronicle of   98
Merseburg (Saxony)   45
Merton, Augustinian priory   87
Milford Haven   102
Monreale   45, 141
Mont-aux-Malades (outside Rouen), leper hospital   81–2, 84, 86–90, 93, 149. See also Nicholas
Montfort, Simon de, eighth earl of Leicester   17, 116
More, Thomas   22, 48
Moreville family   187
Moreville, Hugh de, Becket assassin   195–6, 201
Moreville, Richard de   185, 187, 196
Morimondo   36 n.56
Morton, John, archbishop of Canterbury (1486–1500)   5
Morville, Hugh de, bishop of Coutances (1208–38)   174, 201–2, 204
Morville, Simon de   201 n.90
Mowbray, Roger de   38 n.66

Naaman the Syrian   92
Namur, Nôtre-Dame   16
Neufbourg, Robert of, dean of Évreux   25 n.3
Newburgh, William of   98, 99, 100, 101
Newstead, Lincs   149
New York, Metropolitan Museum of Art   45
Nicholas, prior of Mont-aux-Malades   82, 86–7
Nidaros   32
Niel, Cécile   91
Niger, Ralph   100
Nilgen, Ursula   81, 85
Nilson, Ben   4, 50 n.138, 57 n.16
Nordhausen   124
Norham   38 n.66
Northallerton   38 n.66
Northampton   158
   Assize of (1176)   157
   Council (1164)   108
   trial of Becket   97
Northampton, Henry of, royal clerk   25 n.3
Northeim, monastery   113
Nuño, Count. See Lara
Nuremburg Hours   34, 43

Oda, archbishop of Canterbury (942–58)
58 n.20
Odo, prior of Canterbury   105
Oexle, Otto Gerhard   120 n.27, 121
Oldenburg   119
Olivalla, Bernat d', archbishop of Tarragona
16
Oppitz-Trotman, Gesine   3
opponents of the crown as heirs of Becket
159
Orderic Vitalis   87, 162
Ordo Nidrosiensis   32
Ó'Riain-Raedel, Dagmar   123, 124 n.46
Osbern, monk of Canterbury   62, 66, 77
Oswald, king of Northumbria. *See*
St Oswald
Oxford
Oriel College   89
St Bartholomew's leper house   89

Palencia, Cathedral   16
Becket reliquary   142
Palermo, Walter, archbishop of (1168–91)
39 n.70, 134
Pandulf, papal envoy   158
Paris   101
Sainte-Chapelle   197 n.78
Paris, Matthew   9
Peltzer, Jörg   150
Penman, Michael   195 n.70
Pereira, Dom Gonçalo, archbishop of Braga
(1326–48)   16
Pérez Rodríguez, Estrella   142 n.39
Pest, church of St Thomas   46
Peterborough. *See* Benedict
Petersohn, Jürgen   45
Peter the Chanter   154
Philip I, count of Flanders   36, 105, 116
Philip II (Augustus), king of France   165
n.100, 178, 190 n.55, 191, 193, 197,
201, 203–4
Pierleone, Cardinal Hugh   40
pilgrim badges and ampullae   6, 7, 18, 41,
49 n.136, 189, 190 (Fig. 9.6), 196, 197
(Fig. 9.7)
pilgrims and pilgrimage   1–8, 10, 14, 15,
20, 32 n.32, 37, 40, 47, 49, 50 n.137,
55–7, 65, 115–16, 133–5, 147–9, 160,
169, 178, 186, 187 n.44, 188–9, 196,
199 n.81, 200

Pipe Rolls   143, 149
Piroyansky, Danna   20
Pizzetti, Ildebrando   23 n.97
Plegmund, archbishop of Canterbury
(890–923)   57 n.17
poetry, Castilian   142
Poitiers, John (of Canterbury), bishop of
Poitiers (1162–82), later archbishop of
Lyons   27, 137 n.14
Pole, Reginald, Cardinal Archbishop of
Canterbury (1555–58)   22
seal   5
political saints   116
Pontigny, Abbey   10, 46, 160
Pontigny, Roger of. *See* Anonymous I
Pont l'Évêque, Roger of, archbishop of York
(1154–81)   106, 178 n.20, 179 n.24
Pont-Sainte-Maxence, Guernes of   95,
136
Portable Antiquities Scheme   6
Portbail (near Cherbourg)   202
Power, Daniel   182 n.29, 190 n.55, 192,
196, 203–5
Pray Codex   45
Provence, Eleanor of, queen of England
169
Psalter, Arundel, 61 n.35
Psalter, Queen Mary   13, 43
Puiset, Hugh du, bishop of Durham
(1153–95)   38 n.66

Quadrilogus II   30 n.23

Rachel   31
Radó, Fr Polycarp   46
Ralph the Jew, burgess of Rouen   88
Ratzeburg   45, 129
Reading Abbey, hand of St James   9
Reames, Sherry   68
Regensburg   125 n.49
Conrad of   126
Diet   121 n.37
Regimina sanitatis   92
Reginald, sub-prior of Canterbury   153
Regressio. See Becket, Thomas, *Regressio*
Reichersberg   96
Reims, Henry of   47 n.125
Rich, Edmund. *See* St Edmund of Abingdon
Richard I, king of England   36, 41, 108,
109, 116 n.12, 148, 150–1, 153, 190
Richard II, duke of Normandy   90

Rievaulx 36 n.56

Ringelheim, Matilda of, wife of Emperor
    Henry I 124

Roberts, Peter 21

Roberts, Phyllis B. 11

Roches, Peter des, bishop of Winchester
    (1205–38) 150–1, 204

Rochester 31

Roland, Chanson de (or *Rolandslied*) 126–7

Rome
    Church of S. Costanza 51
    English hospice 10
    Jesuit College 49
    Porta Flaminia 49
    St Giovanni in Laterano 16 n.59

Roper, Margaret (daughter of Thomas
    More) 48

Roscelin, chamberlain of Henry II 84

Rouen 81, 83, 86, 88
    archbishops of. *See* Amiens;
        Beaumont-le-Roger
    burgesses 90
    Cathedral 89
    hospitals 88 n.38
    St-Ouen 89
    Stephen of 97
    See also Mont-aux-Malades; St-Gervais

Roxburgh 41

Russell, Josiah Cox 17

St Albans 9

St Alphege, archbishop of Canterbury
    (1006–12) 53, 55, 57–61, 63–6, 68,
    72, 73 (Fig. 3.3), 74, 77–9
    as bishop of Winchester (984–1006)
        61
    Lives of 62, 66, 68

St Anselm, archbishop of Canterbury
    (1093–1109) 53–4, 58 n.20, 63, 74
    n.76, 77, 106, 155 n.48

Ste-Barbe-en Auge, Augustinian Priory
    89

St Bartholomew 82, 89

St Benedict 96

St Blaise 122, 173–4, 175 n.15, 178 n.22,
    202–3
    relics 126

St Catherine 107

St Cuthbert 9

St David's, bishopric 151

St Dunstan, archbishop of Canterbury
    (959–88) 53, 55, 57–60, 63–6, 68, 72,
    74, 75 (Fig. 3.4), 77–9
    Lives of 59 n.26, 60, 62, 66, 68, 77

St Edmund, king of the East Angles and
    martyr 49, 89, 116 n.13, 148

St Edmund of Abingdon, archbishop of
    Canterbury (1234–40) 17, 169

St Edward (the Confessor). *See* Edward, the
    Confessor

St Eloi 194

St Frideswide 9

St George 173–5, 178 n.22, 202–3
    relics 202

St-Gervais, Benedictine priory 86, 87,
    89, 90

St Giles 81

St Godric. *See* Finchale

St Gregory the Great 32–3, 44

St Hugh, bishop of Lincoln (1186–1200)
    98, 110, 153

St James 81

St John, gospel 32

St John of Beverley 9

St John the Baptist 205, 206

St Julian 81

St Julian of Le Mans 179

St Ladislas

St Lawrence 16, 45, 82

St Lazarus 81, 92

St Magnus the Martyr, church 50 n.143

St Margaret of Hungary 46

St Mary Magdalene 81

St Matthew 31

Ste-Mère-Église, William de, bishop of
    London (1199–1221) 150, 156

St Michael-le-Belfrey 20 n.80

St Nicholas 81

St Oswald, king of Northumbria 122,
    124–5, 131
    cult 123
    relics 123–4

St Paul 98

St Peter 89, 98, 107

St-Pierre-des-Ifs 83

St Richard of Wyche, bishop of Chichester
    (1245–53) 18

St Silvester 45

St Stephen 16, 46, 106

Ste-Suzanne, chateau and priory 205

St Thomas Cantilupe. *See* Cantilupe

St Thomas' Water. *See* Becket, Thomas, water of
St William of York, archbishop of York (1143–54)   9
St Wulfstan, bishop of Worcester (1062–95)   158
Salamanca, San Tomás Cantuariense   45, 137, 142
Salisbury, John of, bishop of Chartres (1176–80)   15, 27, 29, 33, 35 n.53, 68, 87, 95, 97, 106, 155, 166, 167, 179 n.25
Salisbury, Reginald, archdeacon of   25 n.3
Salisbury Breviary   67 n.59
Sandwich   41
San Lorenzo in Lucina, Albert, Cardinal priest of   28 nn.17 and 19
Santiago, Chile. *See* Becket, Society of
San Vitale, Theodwin, Cardinal priest of   28 nn.17 and 19
Sausseusse, Augustinian priory   89
Savigny   115 n.9
Scone   206
Scotland, royal crown of   43
Scrope, Richard, archbishop of York (1398–1405)   18, 117
Sédières   10
Sées, Sylvester, bishop of (1203?-20)   151
Selby   9
Seligenthal, Cistercian monastery   16
Sens
    Cathedral   14, 68, 69 (Fig. 3.1), 171, 172 n.7
        stained glass   68, 69 (Fig. 3.1), 72, 175, 189, 197, 204 n.97
    Council of   25
    William, archbishop of. *See* Blanchemains
Shadis, Miriam   138
Sigüenza   140
    Jocelin, bishop of   137 n.14, 140
    Rodrigo, bishop of, breviary   140
Silva   97
Slocum, Kay Brainerd   8, 19, 68, 135, 142 n.36
Smalley, Beryl   100 n.24
Soria, Castile   139, 140
Southern, Robert   54 n.5
Speaight, Robert   23
Spencer, Brian   8
stained glass. *See under* Becket, Thomas, depictions; Angers Cathedral;

Canterbury Cathedral; Chartres; Coutances; Sens
Staunton, Michael   2, 68
Stavelot-Malmedy   32 n.34
Stralsund, St Nicholas   119
Strängnäs (Sweden)   32, 34 n.44
Stubbs, William   56 n.12
Sully, Henry de, abbot of Fécamp (1139–88)   90
Summerson, Henry   202 n.92

Talbot family   84
Tarragona, Cathedral   16
Tennyson, Alfred Lord   23
Terrasa (Catalonia)   142
Tewkesbury, Alan of   95
Thames boatman   20
Thames mudlarks   6
Theobald, archbishop of Canterbury (1139–61)   1, 27
Theodinus, bishop of San Vitale   134
Thérouanne, bishop of   47 n.125
Toledo Cathedral   136–8
Torigni, Robert of, chronicler, abbot of Mont St Michel   133, 145
Toro (León)   142
Tosny
    family   205, 206 n.106
    Marguerite, wife of Malcolm I of Fife   205
    Richard, treasurer of Angers Cathedral   205
    Roger de   204, 205
    Simon de, monk of Melrose, bishop of Moray   206
Tours
    Council of (1163)   97, 189
    Gregory of   202
Tracy, William de   102, 195
triangulation   172
Trincavel, William   100
Tristan und Isolde   126
Trondheim   32
Truc, Marie-Cécile   91
Tusculum (Frascati)
    Nicholas of, papal legate   168
    papal court   26
Tyndale, William   21
Tyre, William of   96

Uppsala   32

Urse, Reginald fitz   35 n.51, 195

Vác   45
Vange (Essex)   84
Vann, Theresa M.   138
Várad, Alexander, bishop of   42 n.93
Vauclair   35
Vegas di Matute (Segovia)   142
Vesley, leper hospital   83
Vézelay, censures   99, 105
Vieux-Port (near Aizier)   90
Vigeois, Geoffrey of, Limoges chronicler
    95
Vincent, Nicholas   3, 44, 118, 159, 162
    n.88, 168, 195–6, 198, 201
Viterbo   153
Vitry, Jacques de, Cardinal Bishop   16
Vittefleur, leper hospital   83
Vladislav I, duke of Bohemia   121 n.37
Vogt, Caroline   16

Wakefield, Peter of   163
Wales, Alexander of, clerk of Becket   26
Wales, Gerald of   101, 102, 103, 104, 109,
    153 n.10
    De Principis Instructione   101
    De Vita Galfridi   109
    Expugnatio Hibernica   101
    Vita S. Remigii   102–3
Walter, Hubert, archbishop of Canterbury
    (1193–1205)   104, 106–7, 148, 150–1,
    153
    seal   5, 159
Waltham Holy Cross, Augustinian priory
    148
Warham, William, archbishop of
    Canterbury (1503–32)   5, 48
    seal   5
Warren, W. Lewis,   39
Welf
    mausoleum   44
    power   123
    Treasury   126 n.56, 128 n.80
Wells, cathedral   51
Wendover, Roger of   164 n.95

Westminster   108
    Council of (1176)   106
William, bishop of London. See
    Ste-Mère-Église
William, chaplain to Count Nuño Pérez de
    Lara   136, 137
William, chaplain to Ralph de Diceto   41
William, monk of Canterbury. See
    Canterbury, William of
William I, the Conqueror, king of England
    87, 158, 201
William I, the Lion, king of Scots   36, 38,
    41, 46, 101, 116–17, 134, 148, 184–8,
    194–5, 206
William II, Rufus, king of England   162
William II, king of Sicily   44, 141
William the Englishman   14
Williams, Deanne   192
wills   20
Winchelsey, Robert, archbishop of
    Canterbury (1294–1313)   17
Winchester
    annals   110 n.74
    bishops of. See Blois, Henry of; Ilchester;
        Roches; St Alphege
    Gunther of, clerk of Becket   26
    Newminster Abbey   120 n.28
Windsor, Council (1170)   185
Wiseman, Cardinal Nicholas   49 n.134
Wismar, St Jürgen   119
Worcester, bishops of
    Roger (1164–79)   25 n.3, 102
    See also Mauger; St Wulfstan
Worksop   16
Wyche, Richard of. See St Richard
Wyclif, John   20

York
    archbishops of. See Geoffrey; Gray,
        Walter de; Pont l'Évêque;
        St William; Scrope
    Minster   14, 20 n.80

Zachariah   30